Teacher Resources
Meeting Individual Needs Toolkit
to accompany

World of Chemistry

Steven S. Zumdahl

Susan L. Zumdahl

Donald J. DeCoste

McDougal Littell
A Houghton Mifflin Company
Evanston, Illinois • Boston • Dallas

ISBN-13: 978-0-618-85749-4   ISBN-10: 0-618-85749-4

3456789 – CRS – 11 10 09 08 07

To the Teacher

The Meeting Individual Needs Toolkit, or "MINT," is a new collection of materials to help support students who are achieving at levels either above or below their grade level. The toolkit provides multiple teaching and learning support tools in a single ancillary. Materials are appropriate as teacher resources or as handouts if desired.

Section 1: Math Concepts

This section provides additional support for eight critical basic math topics that are essential to success in high-school chemistry. For each topic, there is a teaching lesson that includes worked examples and practice problems, followed by a worksheet. Materials can be used by teachers as the basis for classroom lessons, or as blackline masters for student handouts. Answer keys for all exercises are provided.

Section 2: Reading Concepts

This section supports foundational reading and study skills that students need in order to use their chemistry text effectively. Using examples taken directly from the Student Edition, this section covers topics such as active reading, making and using graphic organizers and outlines, and reading chemical symbols and math notation.

Section 3: Leveled Chapter Review Worksheets

This section offers three levels of review worksheets for chapters in the student text: Basic, Standard, and Challenge. Worksheets are designed for individual students to use for review after studying a chapter. Answer keys are provided.

Section 4: Chapter Summaries

This section offers easy-to-read chapter summaries and additional active reading questions to help students who are having difficulty comprehending a chapter or section of the text.

Section 5: Challenge Projects

This section offers challenge projects and activities for students who will benefit from the opportunity to stretch their understanding and skills by applying their chemistry knowledge to real-world situations. The projects are appropriate for either group work or individual use. Answer keys are provided.

We hope you enjoy using the Meeting Individual Needs Toolkit!

S.S.Z.
S.L.Z.
D.J.D.

Table of Contents

Section 1: Math Concepts

Algebraic Equations MC–1

Dimensional Analysis MC–16

Exponents and Square Roots...MC–27

Estimation MC–38

Graphing MC–46

Percent MC–61

Scientific Notation...MC–74

Significant Figures...MC–81

Section 2: Reading Concepts

Introduction RC–1

Actively Reading Section 2.1: Teaching Notes RC–3

Actively Reading Section 2.1...RC–4

Active Reading Tips RC–16

Making Outlines RC–18

Making and Using Graphic Organizers RC–20

Reading Chemical Symbols RC–24

Making and Using Flashcards RC–25

Reading Math RC–27

Taking Notes RC–28

Reading Chemical Equations RC–30

Section 3: Leveled Chapter Review Worksheets

Chapter 2..RW–1

Chapter 3..RW–4

Chapter 4..RW–9

Chapter 5..RW–12

Chapter 6..RW–15

Chapter 7 .... RW–18

Chapter 8 .... RW–21

Chapter 9 .... RW–24

Chapter 10 .... RW–27

Chapter 11 .... RW–32

Chapter 12 .... RW–37

Chapter 13 .... RW–42

Chapter 14 .... RW–47

Chapter 15 .... RW–50

Chapter 16 .... RW–54

Chapter 17 .... RW–59

Chapter 18 .... RW–63

Chapter 19 .... RW–66

Chapter 20 .... RW–69

Chapter 21 .... RW–72

Answer Keys RW–74

Section 4: Chapter Summaries

Chapter 1 .... CS–1

Chapter 2 .... CS–4

Chapter 3 .... CS–7

Chapter 4 .... CS–10

Chapter 5 .... CS–13

Chapter 6 .... CS–16

Chapter 7 .... CS–19

Chapter 8 .... CS–21

Chapter 9 .... CS–23

Chapter 10 .... CS–25

Chapter 11 .... CS–28

Chapter 12 .... CS–32

Chapter 13 .... CS–35

Chapter 14 .... CS–38

Chapter 15 .... CS–41

Chapter 16 .... CS–44

Chapter 17 .... CS–47

Chapter 18 .... CS–50

Chapter 19 .... CS–53

Chapter 20 .... CS–56

Chapter 21 .... CS–60

Section 5: Challenge Projects

Chapter 2 Project: Elements in the News CP–1

Chapter 4 Project: Investigating Polyatomic Ions CP–2

Chapter 6 Project: Using Analogies to Explain Molecular and Empirical Formulas CP–3

Chapter 9 Project: Limiting Reactants in a Combustion Reaction CP–4

Chapter 14 Project: Surface Tension and Capillary Action CP–5

Chapter 15 Project: Investigating Solubility and Immiscibility CP–6

Chapter 16 Project: Titration Procedure CP–7

Chapter 17 Project: Determining Ksp CP–8

Chapter 19 Project: Medical Treatment by Radioisotopes CP–9

Chapter 21 Project: Investigating Biological Topics CP–10

Answer Keys CP–11

Section 1: Math Concepts

This section provides additional support for eight critical basic math topics that are essential to success in high-school chemistry. For each topic, there is a teaching lesson that includes worked examples and practice problems, followed by a worksheet. Materials can be used by teachers as the basis for classroom lessons, or as blackline masters for student handouts. Answer keys for all exercises are provided.

Contents

Algebraic Equations MC–1

Dimensional Analysis..MC–16

Exponents and Square Roots MC–27

Estimation MC–38

Graphing MC–46

Percent MC–61

Scientific Notation..MC–74

Significant Figures MC–81

Algebraic Equations

One mathematical concept that we must understand in chemistry is how to solve algebraic equations. Without knowing how to do this, we cannot mathematically determine variables such as the pressure of a gas in a system or the temperature of a room in degrees Celsius. Solving algebraic equations is also useful in our daily lives.

> Joe wants to buy a new sound system for his car. The sound system costs $500. His neighbor, Fran, pays Joe $25 every time he mows her lawn. How many times does Joe have to mow Fran's lawn before he can purchase the sound system?

This problem can be solved by setting up an algebraic equation. The key points for setting up and solving equations are

- An algebraic equation contains an equal (=) sign.

  Left side = right side

- The expressions on either side of the equation are *always* equal.

- Algebraic equations contain at least one variable. A variable is an unknown value that is related to other variables or values in an algebraic equation.

- To determine the value of a variable in an equation, we must isolate the variable on the left or right side so that it stands alone. To make this happen, we must perform the same operation(s) on *both sides* of the equal sign so that we do not change the equality.

Let's return to our example and write an equation to determine how many times Joe must mow Fran's lawn before purchasing his new sound system.

The total cost of the sound system is $500.

$$= \$500$$

Joe gets paid $25 per mow. Our variable is the number of times Joe must mow the lawn until he makes $500. The letter x will represent this variable.

$$\frac{\$25}{\text{mow}} \times (\text{number of mows}) = \$500$$

$$25x = 500$$

To isolate x on a side by itself (in this case, the left side), we must divide *both* sides of the equation by 25. This is so because 25 is multiplied by x, so we perform the "opposite" operation to isolate the variable (division is the "opposite" of multiplication, and subtraction is the "opposite" of addition).

$$\frac{25x}{25} = \frac{500}{25}$$

$$x = 20$$

Example 1

Kelly and Matt are bowling. Kelly is a much better bowler than Matt and currently has a score of 130 points. Matt's current score is only 104 points. How many more points must Matt gain in order to catch up to Kelly?

Solution

The total number of points Matt must have to catch up to Kelly is 130.

$$= 130$$

Matt currently has 104 points. Our variable x is the number of points that must be added to Matt's current score to equal 130.

$$x + 104 = 130$$

Since 104 is added to x, we must subtract 104 from both sides to get x on a side by itself.

$$x + 104 - 104 = 130 - 104$$
$$x = 26$$

Matt must get 26 more points to catch up to Kelly.

Example 2

The temperature on a warm, sunny day in Sydney, Australia, is 83°F. What is this temperature in °C? Use the equation $T_{^\circ F} = 1.80\left(T_{^\circ C}\right) + 32$ to help solve the problem.

Solution

This equation (as written) contains two variables. We can use the equation two different ways to convert the temperature to °C.

1. Substitute the value for °F into $T_{^\circ F}$ in the equation and then solve for $T_{^\circ C}$.

$$T_{^\circ F} = 1.80\left(T_{^\circ C}\right) + 32$$
$$83 = 1.80\left(T_{^\circ C}\right) + 32$$

To isolate $T_{^\circ C}$ on the right side, the first step is to remove the 32 by subtracting it from both sides of the equation.

$$83 - 32 = 1.80\left(T_{^\circ C}\right) + 32 - 32$$
$$51 = 1.80\left(T_{^\circ C}\right)$$

The next step is to divide both sides by 1.80.

$$\frac{51}{1.80} = \frac{1.80\left(T_{^\circ C}\right)}{1.80}$$

$$28^\circ C = T_{^\circ C}$$

2. The second way to solve the problem is to leave all the variables in the equation, and isolate $T_{^\circ C}$ on a side by itself before substituting the value in for $T_{^\circ F}$.

$$T_{^\circ F} - 32 = 1.80\left(T_{^\circ C}\right) + 32 - 32$$

$$T_{^\circ F} - 32 = 1.80\left(T_{^\circ C}\right)$$

$$\frac{\left(T_{^\circ F} - 32\right)}{1.80} = \frac{1.80\left(T_{^\circ C}\right)}{1.80}$$

$$\frac{\left(T_{^\circ F} - 32\right)}{1.80} = T_{^\circ C}$$

Now substitute 83°F in for $T_{^\circ F}$.

$$\frac{\left(83 - 32\right)}{1.80} = T_{^\circ C}$$

$$28^\circ C = T_{^\circ C}$$

Practice Problem Set 1

1. Solve for the variable in each of the following expressions:
   a. $8x = 112$

   b. $2y - 14 = 2846$

   c. $10z + 3z = 104$

   d. $6x = 52 - 7x$

2. Melinda worked 36 hours at the fast-food restaurant over a two-week period. Her paycheck amounted to $243 before any deductions. How much does Melinda get paid per hour (not including any deductions)?

3. The temperature in your room is a comfortable 72°F. What is the temperature in °C? What is the temperature in kelvins? Use the following equations to help solve the problems:

$$T_{^\circ F} = 1.80\left(T_{^\circ C}\right) + 32 \qquad T_{^\circ C} = T_K - 273$$

4. An ideal gas is in a 1.3-L container at 2.00 atm of pressure and 298 K. How many moles of gas are in the container? Use the following information:

$PV = nRT$, where

P = pressure (in atmospheres)
V = volume (in liters)
n = moles of gas
$R = 0.08206 \dfrac{L \cdot atm}{mol \cdot K}$
T = temperature (in kelvins)

5. Oxygen gas in a 2.0-L container at 1.50 atm of pressure is moved into a new container at 3.00 atm of pressure. Assuming constant temperature, what is the new volume of the container (in liters)? Use the following equation:

$$P_1V_1 = P_2V_2 \quad \text{(1 and 2 represent different values for pressure and volume)}$$

Let's take the concept of algebraic equations one step further and discuss how to solve for a variable that is part of a fraction. Consider the following equation:

$$292 = \frac{x}{4}$$

To get x on a side by itself, we must move the 4 out of the denominator. Multiply both sides of the equation by the reciprocal of $\frac{1}{4}$. The reciprocal of $\frac{1}{4}$ is $\frac{4}{1}$.

$$\frac{4}{1} \times 292 = \frac{x}{4} \times \frac{4}{1}$$

$$\frac{(4 \times 292)}{1} = \frac{x}{4} \times \frac{4}{1} = \frac{x}{1} = x$$

$$4 \times 292 = x$$

$$1168 = x$$

Example 3

A driver traveling an average speed of $65 \frac{mi}{hr}$ makes it from his college dorm room to his family's home in 3.5 hours. How far did he travel (in miles)? Use the equation $s = \frac{d}{t}$, where s = speed, d = distance, and t = time, to help solve the problem.

Solution

If we substitute in the values for all possible variables, the equation looks like this:

$$s = \frac{d}{t}$$

$$65 \frac{mi}{hr} = \frac{d}{3.5 \, hr}$$

Multiplying both sides by 3.5 hr we get:

$$65 \frac{mi}{hr} \times 3.5 \, hr = \frac{d}{3.5 \, hr} \times 3.5 \, hr$$

$$227.5 \, mi = d$$

$$d = 230 \, mi \text{ or } 2.3 \times 10^2 \, mi \text{ (rounded to 2 significant figures)}$$

Example 4

Using the distance we calculated in Example 3, determine how long it takes the driver to travel back to his dorm room if his average speed is $72 \frac{mi}{hr}$ on the way back.

Solution

Substitute in the values for all possible variables.

$$s = \frac{d}{t}$$

$$72 \frac{mi}{hr} = \frac{227.5 \, mi}{t} \quad \text{(Note that we use the unrounded result from the previous example here.)}$$

Multiplying both sides by t, we get

$$72\ \frac{mi}{hr} \times t = \frac{227.5\ mi}{\cancel{t}} \times \cancel{t}$$

$$\frac{\left(72\ \cancel{\frac{mi}{hr}}\right)t}{72\ \cancel{\frac{mi}{hr}}} = \frac{227.5\ \cancel{mi}}{72\ \cancel{\frac{mi}{hr}}}$$

$$t = 3.2\ hr$$

Practice Problem Set 2

1. Solve for the variable in each of the following expressions:

    a. $1040 = \dfrac{x}{11}$

    b. $\dfrac{185}{y} = 25$

    c. $961 = \dfrac{z}{4} - 24$

    d. $\dfrac{1}{4}x + 3x = 26$

2. For each expression below, solve for the specified variable:

    a. $s = \dfrac{d}{t}$, solve for t

    b. $\dfrac{V_1}{T_1} = \dfrac{V_2}{T_2}$, solve for V_1

    c. $\dfrac{n_1}{P_1} = \dfrac{n_2}{P_2}$, solve for P_1

    d. $\dfrac{P_1V_1}{T_1} = \dfrac{P_2V_2}{T_2}$, solve for V_2

3. A race car accelerates at 7.0 $\dfrac{m}{s^2}$ for 12 seconds in one direction. What top speed does the driver attain? Use the following equation:

$$\bar{a} = \frac{v_f - v_i}{t_f - t_i}$$

    where $\bar{a}$ = average acceleration
            v_f = final velocity (or speed)
            v_i = initial velocity (or speed)
            t_f = final time
            t_i = initial time

4. An ideal gas is placed in a 3.0-L container with a movable piston at 273 K. The temperature is changed to 298 K, which causes the piston to move, essentially keeping the pressure of the gas constant but changing the volume. What is the new volume of the gas? Use the following equation to solve the problem:

$$\frac{V_1}{T_1} = \frac{V_2}{T_2}$$

where
V_1 = initial volume
T_1 = initial temperature
V_2 = final volume
T_2 = final temperature

Practice Problem Set Solutions

Set 1

1. a.
$$\frac{8x}{8} = \frac{112}{8}$$
$$x = 14$$

   b.
$$2y - 14 + 14 = 2846 + 14$$
$$2y = 2860$$
$$\frac{2y}{2} = \frac{2860}{2}$$
$$y = 1430$$

   c.
$$10z + 3z = 104$$
$$13z = 104$$
$$\frac{13z}{13} = \frac{104}{13}$$
$$z = 8$$

   d.
$$6x + 7x = 52 - 7x + 7x$$
$$13x = 52$$
$$\frac{13x}{13} = \frac{52}{13}$$
$$x = 4$$

2. The total amount of money earned was $243.

$$= \$243$$

Melinda worked 36 hours. The variable x is the amount of money paid per hour.

$$\text{Amount per hour} \times 36 \text{ hours} = \$243$$
$$x \times 36 = 243$$
$$36x = 243$$
$$\frac{36x}{36} = \frac{243}{36}$$
$$x = 6.75 \Rightarrow \$6.75/\text{hour}$$

3. Substitute in the value for $T_{°F}$ using the equation

$$T_{°F} = 1.80(T_{°C}) + 32$$
$$72 - 32 = 1.80(T_{°C}) + 32 - 32$$
$$40. = 1.80(T_{°C})$$
$$\frac{40.}{1.80} = \frac{1.80(T_{°C})}{1.80}$$
$$22°C = T_{°C}$$

Substitute in the value for $T_{°C}$ using the equation

$$T_{°C} = T_K - 273$$
$$22 + 273 = T_K - 273 + 273$$
$$295\ K = T_K$$

4. Substitute in the values for as many variables as possible using the equation

$$PV = nRT$$
$$(2.00\ \text{atm})(1.3\ \text{L}) = n\left(0.08206\frac{\text{L}\cdot\text{atm}}{\text{mol}\cdot K}\right)(298\ K)$$
$$(2.6\ \text{atm}\cdot\text{L}) = \left(24.5\frac{\text{L}\cdot\text{atm}}{\text{mol}}\right)n$$
$$\frac{(2.6\ \text{atm}\cdot\text{L})}{\left(24.5\frac{\text{L}\cdot\text{atm}}{\text{mol}}\right)} = \frac{\left(24.5\frac{\text{L}\cdot\text{atm}}{\text{mol}}\right)}{\left(24.5\frac{\text{L}\cdot\text{atm}}{\text{mol}}\right)}n$$
$$0.11\ \text{mol} = n$$

5. Substitute in the values for as many variables as possible using the equation

$$P_1V_1 = P_2V_2$$
$$(1.50\ \text{atm})(2.0\ \text{L}) = (3.00\ \text{atm})V_2$$
$$(3.00\ \text{atm}\cdot\text{L}) = (3.00\ \text{atm})V_2$$
$$\frac{(3.00\ \text{atm}\cdot\text{L})}{(3.00\ \text{atm})} = \frac{(3.00\ \text{atm})V_2}{(3.00\ \text{atm})}$$
$$1.0\ \text{L} = V_2$$

Set 2

1. a. $1040 = \dfrac{x}{11}$; multiply both sides by 11.

$$1040 \times 11 = \dfrac{x}{11} \times 11$$

$$11440 = x$$

b. $\dfrac{185}{y} = 25$; multiply both sides by y.

$$\dfrac{185}{y} \times y = 25 \times y$$

$$\dfrac{185}{25} = \dfrac{25y}{25}$$

$$7.4 = y$$

c.

$$961 + 24 = \dfrac{z}{4} - 24 + 24$$

$$985 = \dfrac{z}{4} ;\; \text{Multiply both sides by 4.}$$

$$985 \times 4 = \dfrac{z}{4} \times 4$$

$$3940 = z$$

d. $\dfrac{1}{4}x + 3x = 26$

Add the two fractions together, but first find a common denominator.

$$\dfrac{1}{4}x + \dfrac{3(4)}{1(4)}x = 26$$

$$\dfrac{1}{4}x + \dfrac{12}{4}x = 26$$

$$\dfrac{13}{4}x = 26$$

Multiply by the reciprocal of $\frac{13}{4}$ to isolate x on the left side.

$$\frac{4}{13} \times \frac{13}{4}x = 26 \times \frac{4}{13}$$
$$x = 8$$

2.　a.

$$s = \frac{d}{t}, \text{ multiply both sides by } t.$$

$$s \times t = \frac{d}{\cancel{t}} \times \cancel{t}, \text{ isolate } t \text{ by dividing both sides by } s.$$

$$\frac{\cancel{s}t}{\cancel{s}} = \frac{d}{s}$$

$$t = \frac{d}{s}$$

b.

$$\frac{V_1}{T_1} = \frac{V_2}{T_2}, \text{ multiply both sides by } T_1.$$

$$\frac{V_1}{\cancel{T_1}} \times \cancel{T_1} = \frac{V_2}{T_2} \times T_1$$

$$V_1 = \frac{V_2 T_1}{T_2}$$

c.

$$\frac{n_1}{P_1} = \frac{n_2}{P_2}, \text{ multiply both sides by } P_1.$$

$$\frac{n_1}{\cancel{P_1}} \times \cancel{P_1} = \frac{n_2}{P_2} \times P_1; \text{ isolate } P_1 \text{ by multiplying both sides by } \frac{P_2}{n_2}.$$

$$\frac{P_2}{n_2} \times n_1 = \frac{\cancel{n_2}}{\cancel{P_2}} \times \frac{\cancel{P_2}}{\cancel{n_2}} \times P_1$$

$$\frac{n_1 P_2}{n_2} = P_1$$

d.

$$\frac{P_1V_1}{T_1} = \frac{P_2V_2}{T_2}, \text{ multiply both sides by } \frac{T_2}{P_2}.$$

$$\frac{P_1V_1}{T_1} \times \frac{T_2}{P_2} = \frac{\cancel{P_2}V_2}{\cancel{T_2}} \times \frac{\cancel{T_2}}{\cancel{P_2}}$$

$$\frac{P_1V_1T_2}{T_1P_2} = V_2$$

3. $\bar{a} = \dfrac{v_f - v_i}{t_f - t_i}$; substitute in values for all possible variables.

$$7.0 \ \frac{m}{s^2} = \frac{v_f - 0}{12s - 0}$$

$$7.0 \ \frac{m}{s^2} = \frac{v_f}{12 \ s}; \text{ multiply both sides by 12 s.}$$

$$7.0 \ \frac{m}{s^{\cancel{2}}} \times 12 \ \cancel{s} = \frac{v_f}{\cancel{12 \ s}} \times \cancel{12 \ s}$$

$$84 \ \frac{m}{s} = v_f$$

4.

$$\frac{V_1}{T_1} = \frac{V_2}{T_2}; \text{ substitute in values for all possible variables.}$$

$$\frac{3.0 \ L}{273 \ K} = \frac{V_2}{298 \ K}; \text{ multiply both sides by 298 K.}$$

$$298 \ \cancel{K} \times \frac{3.0 \ L}{273 \ \cancel{K}} = \frac{V_2}{\cancel{298 \ K}} \times \cancel{298 \ K}$$

$$3.3 \ L = V_2$$

Algebraic Equations Worksheet

Solve for the variable in each of the following expressions:

1. $16 + x = 229$

2. $54y = 27$

3. $4z + 9 = 57$

4. $12y + 22 = 88 + y$

5. $\dfrac{x}{16} = 15$

6. $6 + \dfrac{b}{2} = 37$

7. $\dfrac{28}{w} = 7$

8. $19 + \dfrac{834}{z} = 21$

9. $\dfrac{85}{q} - 3 = 14$

10. $7 + \dfrac{1}{2x} = 57 - 2x$

11. A jogger ran around a block 12 times for a total distance of 3.0 miles. What distance is the jogger traveling to run around the block once?

12. The temperature on a nice spring day in the Midwest is 65°F. What is this temperature in °C? What is this temperature in kelvins? Use the following equations:

$$T_{°F} = 1.80\left(T_{°C}\right) + 32 \qquad T_{°C} = T_K - 273$$

13. The temperature on a cold winter day in the Midwest is 12°F. What is this temperature in °C? What is this temperature in kelvins? Use the following equations:

$$T_{°F} = 1.80\left(T_{°C}\right) + 32 \qquad T_{°C} = T_K - 273$$

14. The temperature in a freezer is –7°C. What is this temperature in kelvins? What is this temperature in °F? Use the same equations that are in Exercises 12 and 13 to help solve the problems.

15. The temperature of a substance is 108 K. What is this temperature in °C? What is this temperature in °F? Use the same equations that are in Exercises 12 and 13 to help solve the problems.

16. Solve for g: $\qquad M = \dfrac{g}{n}$

17. Solve for V: $\qquad M = \dfrac{n}{V}$

18. Solve for T: $\qquad PV = nRT$

19. Solve for $\dfrac{n}{V}$: $\qquad PV = nRT$

20. Solve for M_2: $\qquad M_1V_1 = M_2V_2$

21. 1.66 mol of an ideal gas is in a 3.5-L container at 208 K. What is the pressure of the gas? Use the following equation:

$$PV = nRT \text{ (where } R = 0.08206 \text{ L} \cdot \text{atm/mol} \cdot \text{K)}$$

22. a. A car travels 228 miles in 4.00 hours. What is the car's average speed (in miles per hour)?

   b. Using the average speed from part a, determine how far (in miles) the car would travel in 9.50 hours.

23. What must the volume of a solution be (in liters) if 1.25 mol of table salt is dissolved in water to make a 2.50 M solution? Use the following equation to help solve the problem:

$$M = \dfrac{n}{V}, \text{ where } M = \text{molarity of soln, } n = \text{moles of solute, and } V = \text{volume of soln}$$

24. Hydrogen gas is in a steel container at 1.00 atm of pressure and 298 K. The temperature of the gas is raised to 335 K. What is the new pressure of the gas? Use the following equation to help solve the problem:

$$\dfrac{P_1}{T_1} = \dfrac{P_2}{T_2}$$

$\qquad\qquad$ where $\qquad P_1$ = initial pressure
$\qquad\qquad\qquad\qquad\qquad T_1$ = initial temperature
$\qquad\qquad\qquad\qquad\qquad P_2$ = final pressure
$\qquad\qquad\qquad\qquad\qquad T_2$ = final temperature

25. Ammonia gas is in 2.0-L container at 1.50 atm of pressure and 273 K is transferred to a 1.5-L container at 301 K. What is the new pressure of the gas? Use the following equation to help solve the problem:

$$\dfrac{P_1V_1}{T_1} = \dfrac{P_2V_2}{T_2}$$

Answers to Algebraic Equations Worksheet

1. $x = 213$

2. $y = 0.50$ or $\frac{1}{2}$

3. $z = 12$

4. $y = 6$

5. $x = 240$

6. $b = 62$

7. $w = 4$

8. $z = 417$

9. $q = 5$

10. $x = 20$

11. 0.25 mi or $\frac{1}{4}$ mi

12. $18°C$, 291 K

13. $-11°C$, 262 K

14. 266 K, $19°F$

15. $-165°C$, $-265°F$

16. $g = Mn$

17. $V = \dfrac{n}{M}$

18. $T = \dfrac{PV}{nR}$

19. $\dfrac{n}{V} = \dfrac{P}{RT}$

20. $\dfrac{M_1 V_1}{V_2} = M_2$

21. $P = 8.1$ atm

22.   a. 57.0 mi/hr

       b. 542 mi

23. $V = 0.500$ L of soln

24. $P_2 = 1.12$ atm

25. $P_2 = 2.2$ atm

Dimensional Analysis

Solving chemistry problems that involve dimensional analysis can seem complex and confusing. But, when broken down into smaller parts, these problems make more sense. Dimensional analysis is important to understand for many reasons other than chemistry. Many of the products we buy are made in countries that use the metric system. For example, suppose that we buy an entertainment center online. The entertainment center arrives from England and requires assembly. The instructions specify inserting screws at certain distances from the edges. All of the measurements are in centimeters or meters. But we are used to making measurements in inches or yards. How would we make these conversions? Dimensional analysis is the key.

Multiplying Fractions

When multiplying fractions, multiply all of the numbers in the numerators first, followed by multiplying all of the numbers in the denominators. The last step is to divide the numerator product by the denominator product.

Example 1   What is the product of $\dfrac{1}{3}$ and $\dfrac{2}{5}$?

Solution

The expression could be written in one of two ways:

$$\frac{1}{3} \times \frac{2}{5} \quad or \quad \left(\frac{1}{3}\right)\left(\frac{2}{5}\right)$$

We then obtain the result as follows:

$$\left(\frac{1}{3}\right)\left(\frac{2}{5}\right) = \frac{(1\times 2)}{(3\times 5)} = \frac{2}{15} = 0.133$$

Whenever the same number occurs in both the numerator and denominator, they cancel.

$$\left(\frac{1}{\cancel{3}}\right)\left(\frac{\cancel{3}}{5}\right) = \frac{1}{5} = 0.20$$

If the number we are analyzing is a whole number, remember that this really means that the number is over 1 (the whole number in the numerator and the number 1 in the denominator). For example, the number 4 really means $\dfrac{4}{1}$. We do not actually write these numbers as fractions, but it is important to remember that the whole number acts like it is a numerator in the product.

Example 2   What is $\frac{1}{4}$ of 5?

Solution

Remember, the number 5 really means $\frac{5}{1}$.

$$\frac{1}{4} \times 5 = \frac{(1 \times 5)}{(4 \times 1)} = \frac{5}{4} = 1.25$$

We also can multiply several fractions together at once using the same guidelines. We can cancel out numbers to simplify the expression (but it is not necessary).

$$2 \times \frac{1}{3} \times \frac{4}{5} \times \frac{6}{7} \times \frac{5}{8} = \frac{(2 \times 1 \times 4 \times 6 \times 5)}{(1 \times 3 \times 5 \times 7 \times 8)} = \frac{240}{840} = 0.29$$

Practice Problem Set 1

1. What is the product of $\frac{4}{7}$ and $\frac{2}{3}$?

2. What is $\frac{4}{10}$ of 60?

3. Evaluate the following expressions:
   a. $\left(\frac{1}{3}\right)\left(\frac{2}{5}\right)\left(\frac{1}{2}\right) =$

   b. $\left(\frac{1}{4}\right)\left(\frac{9}{10}\right)\left(\frac{3}{5}\right)(7) =$

   c. $\left(\frac{1}{2}\right)^3 =$

Multiplying Units

When multiplying units, use the same principle that you use for multiplying fractions. If one unit is in the numerator, and the identical unit is in the denominator, they cancel each other out. Any remaining units are used in the answer.

$$\left(\cancel{\text{centimeter}}\right)\left(\frac{\text{meter}}{\cancel{\text{centimeter}}}\right) = \frac{\text{meter}}{1} = \text{meter}$$

You also can multiply several units together at once using the same principle as for fractions containing numbers.

$$\left(\frac{\cancel{\text{centimeter}}}{\text{second}}\right)\left(\frac{\cancel{\text{meter}}}{\cancel{\text{centimeter}}}\right)\left(\frac{\cancel{\text{kilometer}}}{\cancel{\text{meter}}}\right)\left(\frac{\text{megameter}}{\cancel{\text{kilometer}}}\right) = \frac{\text{megameter}}{\text{second}}$$

It is very important to note that if a unit appears once in the numerator but more than once in the denominator, we can only cancel one of the unit expressions in the denominator. Think of this concept in terms of fractions. If the number 4 is in the numerator, and two 4s are in the denominator of different fractions, we only cancel out one of the 4s on the bottom, not both.

$$\left(\frac{\cancel{4}}{5}\right)\left(\frac{3}{\cancel{4}}\right)\left(\frac{1}{4}\right) = \frac{(3\times1)}{(5\times4)} = \frac{3}{20} = 0.15$$

Example 3   Evaluate the unit expression below:

$$\left(\frac{\text{kilogram}}{\text{second}}\right)^2\left(\frac{\text{meter}}{\text{kilogram}}\right)^2\left(\frac{\text{second}}{\text{meter}}\right) =$$

Solution

The squared factor is equivalent to multiplying the fraction by itself.

$$\left(\frac{\text{kilogram}}{\text{second}}\right)\left(\frac{\text{kilogram}}{\text{second}}\right)\left(\frac{\text{meter}}{\text{kilogram}}\right)\left(\frac{\text{meter}}{\text{kilogram}}\right)\left(\frac{\text{second}}{\text{meter}}\right) =$$

Now we can evaluate the expression by canceling out units.

$$\left(\frac{\cancel{\text{kilogram}}}{\text{second}}\right)\left(\frac{\cancel{\text{kilogram}}}{\cancel{\text{second}}}\right)\left(\frac{\text{meter}}{\cancel{\text{kilogram}}}\right)\left(\frac{\cancel{\text{meter}}}{\cancel{\text{kilogram}}}\right)\left(\frac{\cancel{\text{second}}}{\cancel{\text{meter}}}\right) = \frac{\text{meter}}{\text{second}}$$

Practice Problem Set 2

1. Evaluate the following unit expressions:

a. $(\text{kilogram})\left(\dfrac{\text{grams}}{\text{kilogram}}\right)\left(\dfrac{\text{milligrams}}{\text{gram}}\right) =$

b. $(\text{mole})\left(\dfrac{\text{grams}}{\text{mole}}\right)\left(\dfrac{\text{liter}}{\text{gram}}\right) =$

c. $(\text{mL})\left(\dfrac{\text{cm}^3}{\text{mL}}\right)\left(\dfrac{\text{mg}}{\text{cm}}\right) =$

d. $\left(\dfrac{\text{kg}}{\text{m}}\right)^2\left(\dfrac{\text{g}}{\text{kg}}\right)\left(\dfrac{\text{m}^2}{\text{g}}\right) =$

e. $\left(\dfrac{g}{ft^2}\right)\left(\dfrac{ft}{mL}\right)\left(\dfrac{mL}{g}\right) =$

2. Fill in the missing unit expression in each problem below:

a. $(\text{cup})\left(\dfrac{\text{pint}}{\text{cups}}\right)\left(\dfrac{?}{?}\right)\left(\dfrac{\text{liter}}{\text{gallon}}\right) = \text{liter}$

b. $\left(\dfrac{\text{moles}}{\text{liter}}\right)\left(\dfrac{\text{liter}}{\text{gram}}\right)\left(\dfrac{?}{?}\right) = \dfrac{\text{moles}}{\text{second}}$

Performing Conversions—Dimensional Analysis

Now that we know how to evaluate number and unit expressions separately, we just combine the two steps to do conversions! We use the same principles as in the previous sections, just make sure that the final answer contains *both* a number and a unit.

Example 4   One side of a backyard fence measures 312 inches in length. How many feet does this represent?   (1 ft = 12 in.)

Solution

To convert from inches to feet, we are going to have to use the conversion factor given in the problem. We have to understand one key point about conversion factors. When the factors are given to us, we can write them as a ratio to help us solve our problem. The equivalence statement 1 ft = 12 in. can be written two different ways:

$$\dfrac{1\ \text{ft}}{12\ \text{in.}} \quad \text{or} \quad \dfrac{12\ \text{in.}}{1\ \text{ft}}$$

This does not change the meaning of the conversion factor. There are always 12 inches in 1 foot, which is expressed in both ratios above. We set up our expression so that our units cancel, and we are left with feet (since this is what the problem is asking for).

$$\left(312\ \cancel{\text{in.}}\right)\left(\dfrac{1\ \text{ft}}{12\ \cancel{\text{in.}}}\right) = \dfrac{(312 \times 1)\text{ft}}{(12)} = 26.0\ \text{ft}$$

Example 5   A golfer putted a golf ball 7.8 ft across a green. How many inches does this represent?

Solution

We use the equivalence statement as we did in Example 4, except we use the ratio that causes our units to cancel so that we are left with inches.

$$(7.8 \text{ ft})\left(\frac{12 \text{ in.}}{1 \text{ ft}}\right) = \frac{(7.8 \times 12) \text{in.}}{1} = 94 \text{ in.}$$

Opposite ratio than in Example 4

Example 6   How many centimeters are in 15.0 inches? (2.54 cm = 1 in.)

Solution

Again, to convert from inches to centimeters, we are going to have to use the conversion factor given to us in the problem. The equivalence statement 2.54 cm = 1 in. can be written two different ways:

$$\frac{2.54 \text{ cm}}{1 \text{ in.}} \quad \text{or} \quad \frac{1 \text{ in.}}{2.54 \text{ cm}}$$

We set up our expression so that our units cancel, and we are left with centimeters.

$$(15.0 \text{ in})\left(\frac{2.54 \text{ cm}}{1 \text{ in}}\right) = \frac{(15.0 \times 2.54) \text{cm}}{1} = 38.1 \text{ cm}$$

Sometimes performing conversions requires us to use more than one conversion factor. We can solve these problems as separate steps or all in one step.

Example 7   An iron sample has a mass of 3.50 lb. What is the mass of this sample in grams?

$$(2.2046 \text{ lb} = 1 \text{ kg})$$
$$(1 \text{ kg} = 1000 \text{ g})$$

Solution

The conversion factors can be written in the following ways:

$$\frac{2.2046 \text{ lb}}{1 \text{ kg}} \quad \text{or} \quad \frac{1 \text{ kg}}{2.2046 \text{ lb}}$$

$$\frac{1000 \text{ g}}{1 \text{ kg}} \quad \text{or} \quad \frac{1 \text{ kg}}{1000 \text{ g}}$$

We can first convert our mass sample from pounds to kilograms and then perform a second step to convert from kilograms to grams.

Step 1: $(3.50 \text{ lb})\left(\dfrac{1 \text{ kg}}{2.2046 \text{ lb}}\right) = \dfrac{(3.50 \times 1) \text{kg}}{(2.2046)} = 1.58 \text{ kg}$

Step 2: $$\left(1.58 \ \cancel{kg}\right)\left(\frac{1000 \ g}{1 \ \cancel{kg}}\right) = \frac{(1.58 \times 1000)g}{1} = 1580 \ g$$

We also could solve this problem in one step by setting up an expression such that all of the units cancel except for grams.

$$\left(3.50 \ \cancel{lb}\right)\left(\frac{1 \ \cancel{kg}}{2.2046 \ \cancel{lb}}\right)\left(\frac{1000 \ g}{1 \ \cancel{kg}}\right) = \frac{(3.50 \times 1 \times 1000)g}{(2.2046 \times 1)} = 1580 \ g$$

Practice Problem Set 3

1. A dining room table measures 6.0 ft in length. How many inches does this represent? (1 ft = 12 in.)

2. How many cups are in a 64-oz. pitcher of lemonade? (8 fluid ounces = 1 cup)

3. Perform the following conversions:

     Useful conversion factors: 1 kg = 1000 g
                                    1 g = 1000 mg
                                    1 ft = 12 in.
                                    1 in = 2.54 cm
                                    1 km = 1000 m
                                    1 hr = 3600 s
                                    1 mi = 1.6093 km

   a. 0.128 kg = _____ g = _____ mg

   b. 1.15 ft = _____ in. = _____ cm

   c. 6.00 m/s = _____ km/hr = _____ mi/hr

4. Baking soda and vinegar are mixed in a balloon. A gas is produced and the balloon expands to a volume of 2.00 L. What is the volume of the balloon in cm^3? (1 L = 1 dm^3; 1 dm = 10 cm)

Practice Problem Set Solutions

Set 1

1. $\left(\dfrac{4}{7}\right)\left(\dfrac{2}{3}\right) = \dfrac{(4\times2)}{(7\times3)} = \dfrac{8}{21} = 0.38$

2. $(60)\left(\dfrac{4}{10}\right) = \dfrac{(60\times4)}{(1\times10)} = \dfrac{240}{10} = 24$

3. a. $\dfrac{(1\times2\times1)}{(3\times5\times2)} = \dfrac{2}{30} = 0.07$

    b. $\dfrac{(1\times9\times3\times7)}{(4\times10\times5\times1)} = \dfrac{189}{200} = 0.95$

    c. $\left(\dfrac{1}{2}\right)\left(\dfrac{1}{2}\right)\left(\dfrac{1}{2}\right) = \dfrac{(1\times1\times1)}{(2\times2\times2)} = \dfrac{1}{8} = 0.13$

Set 2

1. a. $\left(\text{kilogram}\right)\left(\dfrac{\text{grams}}{\text{kilogram}}\right)\left(\dfrac{\text{milligrams}}{\text{gram}}\right) = \text{milligrams}$

    Note: The difference between "grams" and "gram" within the expression does not matter. The units still cancel.

    b. $\left(\text{mole}\right)\left(\dfrac{\text{grams}}{\text{mole}}\right)\left(\dfrac{\text{liter}}{\text{gram}}\right) = \text{liter}$

    c. $(\text{mL})\left(\dfrac{\text{cm}^3}{\text{mL}}\right)\left(\dfrac{\text{mg}}{\text{cm}}\right) = \left(\text{mL}\right)\left(\dfrac{\text{cm}\times\text{cm}\times\text{cm}}{\text{mL}}\right)\left(\dfrac{\text{mg}}{\text{cm}}\right) = \text{cm}^2\cdot\text{mg}$

    d. $\left(\dfrac{\text{kg}}{\text{m}}\right)^2\left(\dfrac{\text{g}}{\text{kg}}\right)\left(\dfrac{\text{m}^2}{\text{g}}\right) = \left(\dfrac{\text{kg}}{\text{m}}\right)\left(\dfrac{\text{kg}}{\text{m}}\right)\left(\dfrac{\text{g}}{\text{kg}}\right)\left(\dfrac{\text{m}\times\text{m}}{\text{g}}\right) = \text{kg}$

    e. $\left(\dfrac{\text{g}}{\text{ft}^2}\right)\left(\dfrac{\text{ft}}{\text{mL}}\right)\left(\dfrac{\text{mL}}{\text{g}}\right) = \left(\dfrac{\text{g}}{\text{ft}\times\text{ft}}\right)\left(\dfrac{\text{ft}}{\text{mL}}\right)\left(\dfrac{\text{mL}}{\text{g}}\right) = \dfrac{1}{\text{ft}}$

2. a. Cancel the appropriate units so that you are left with "liter" as your end result. Determine what units must go into the unit expression so that all units cancel except for "liter."

    $\left(\text{cup}\right)\left(\dfrac{\text{pint}}{\text{cups}}\right)\left(\dfrac{\text{gallon}}{\text{pint}}\right)\left(\dfrac{\text{liter}}{\text{gallon}}\right) = \text{liter}$; therefore, the answer is $\dfrac{\text{gallon}}{\text{pint}}$.

b. Cancel the appropriate units so that you are left with $\dfrac{\text{moles}}{\text{second}}$ as your end result.

Determine what units must go into the unit expression so that all units cancel except for " $\dfrac{\text{moles}}{\text{second}}$."

$$\left(\dfrac{\text{moles}}{\text{liter}}\right)\left(\dfrac{\text{liter}}{\text{gram}}\right)\left(\dfrac{\text{gram}}{\text{second}}\right) = \dfrac{\text{moles}}{\text{second}} \; ; \text{ therefore, the answer is } \dfrac{\text{gram}}{\text{second}} .$$

Set 3

1. $(6.0 \text{ ft})\left(\dfrac{12 \text{ in.}}{1 \text{ ft}}\right) = 72 \text{ in.}$

2. $(64 \text{ oz})\left(\dfrac{1 \text{ cup}}{8 \text{ oz}}\right) = 8.0 \text{ cups}$

3. a. $(0.128 \text{ kg})\left(\dfrac{1000 \text{ g}}{1 \text{ kg}}\right) = 128 \text{ g}$

   $(128 \text{ g})\left(\dfrac{1000 \text{ mg}}{1 \text{ g}}\right) = 128,000 \text{ mg}$

   b. $(1.15 \text{ ft})\left(\dfrac{12 \text{ in.}}{1 \text{ ft}}\right) = 13.8 \text{ in.}$

   $(13.8 \text{ in.})\left(\dfrac{2.54 \text{ cm}}{1 \text{ in.}}\right) = 35.1 \text{ cm}$

   c. $\left(\dfrac{6.00 \text{ m}}{\text{s}}\right)\left(\dfrac{1 \text{ km}}{1000 \text{ m}}\right)\left(\dfrac{3600 \text{ s}}{1 \text{ hr}}\right) = 21.6 \text{ km/hr}$

   $\left(\dfrac{21.6 \text{ km}}{\text{hr}}\right)\left(\dfrac{1 \text{ mi}}{1.6093 \text{ km}}\right) = 13.4 \text{ mi/hr}$

4. $(2.00 \text{ L})\left(\dfrac{1 \text{ dm}^3}{1 \text{ L}}\right)\left(\dfrac{10 \text{ cm}}{1 \text{ dm}}\right)\left(\dfrac{10 \text{ cm}}{1 \text{ dm}}\right)\left(\dfrac{10 \text{ cm}}{1 \text{ dm}}\right) = 2.00 \times 10^3 \text{ cm}^3$

Dimensional Analysis Worksheet

1. What is the product of $\frac{5}{7}$ and $\frac{1}{4}$?

2. What is the product of $\frac{6}{5}$ and $\frac{3}{4}$?

3. The product of $\frac{1}{3}$ and some unknown number is $\frac{2}{15}$. What is the unknown number (in its reduced form)?

4. The product of $\frac{4}{5}$ and some unknown number is 0.20. What is the unknown number (in its reduced form)?

For Problems 5–10, evaluate the expressions.

5. $\left(\frac{6}{9}\right)\left(\frac{1}{4}\right)(2) =$

6. $\left(\frac{1}{2}\right)\left(\frac{10}{7}\right)\left(\frac{2}{3}\right) =$

7. $\left(\frac{2}{3}\right)^4 =$

8. $\left(\frac{4}{5}\right)^2\left(\frac{1}{6}\right)\left(\frac{7}{3}\right) =$

9. $(cm)\left(\dfrac{m}{cm}\right)\left(\dfrac{km}{m}\right) =$

10. $\left(\dfrac{m}{s}\right)\left(\dfrac{s}{km}\right)\left(\dfrac{km}{min}\right) =$

11. What is the resulting unit in the following expression?

$$\left(cm^3\right)\left(\dfrac{mL}{cm^3}\right)\left(\dfrac{dm}{mL}\right)^3 =$$

12. Fill in the missing unit expression in the problem below.

$$\left(\dfrac{?}{?}\right)\left(\dfrac{mol}{grams}\right)\left(\dfrac{liter}{mol}\right) = liter$$

13. What unit expression is needed to complete the following problem?

$$\left(\frac{mi}{hr}\right)\left(\frac{km}{mi}\right)\left(\frac{?}{?}\right)\left(\frac{hr}{min}\right)\left(\frac{min}{s}\right) = m/s$$

Use the conversion factors in Appendix F of your text to assist you in Problems 14–25.

14. An object is 155 inches in height. Express this height in centimeters.

15. An object is 155 inches in height. Express this height in feet.

16. A toy measures 38 cm in length. How many inches does this represent?

17. A runner jogs 3.5 miles every morning. How many kilometers does this represent?

18. How many quarts are in a 10.0-gallon cooler of fruit punch?

19. A car tire has a pressure of 32 psi (pounds per square inch). What is the pressure of the tire in atmospheres?

20. How many liters are in a 20.-oz bottle of pop?

21. Your friend is 5.0 feet, 9.0 inches tall. What is your friend's height in meters?

22. A cat weighs 9.4 lb. What is the mass of the cat in kilograms?

23. A person walks a distance of 1.3 miles. How many inches did the person walk?

24. A person has a mass of 9.48×10^4 g. What is this person's mass in pounds?

25. The volume of a helium balloon is 2.8 L. What is this volume in cm^3?

$(1 \ dm^3 = 1 \ L; \ 1 \ dm = 10 \ cm)$

Answers to Dimensional Analysis Worksheet

1. $\dfrac{5}{28} = 0.18$

2. $\dfrac{18}{20} = 0.90$

3. $\dfrac{2}{5}$

4. $\dfrac{1}{4}$

5. $\dfrac{12}{36} = \dfrac{1}{3} = 0.3\bar{3}$

6. $\dfrac{10}{21} = 0.48$

7. $\dfrac{16}{81} = 0.20$

8. $\dfrac{112}{450}$ 0.25

9. km

10. m/min

11. dm^3/mL^2

12. $\left(\dfrac{grams}{1}\right)$

13. $\left(\dfrac{m}{km}\right)$

14. 394 cm

15. 12.9 ft

16. 15 in.

17. 5.6 km

18. 40.0 quarts

19. 2.2 atm

20. 0.59 L

21. 1.8 m

22. 4.3 kg

23. 8.2×10^4 in.

24. 209 lbs

25. 2800 cm^3

Exponents and Square Roots

In addition to scientific notation, exponents are a great way of expressing very large or small numbers in shorthand form. Exponential growth is prevalent in our lives everyday. Dandelions spreading in a field, mold forming on a piece of bread, and compound interest accumulating on a sum of money are just a few examples. In chemistry, we use exponents to express very large or small measurements and to perform calculations faster.

Numbers with exponents consist of a *base* and an *exponent* (also called *power*). Exponents are used to express a series of multiplications. The exponent tells us how many times the base is multiplied by itself. For example, the number 3 multiplied by itself five times can be expressed as

$$3 \times 3 \times 3 \times 3 \times 3 = 243$$

Or it can be expressed using an exponent:

$$3^5 = 243$$

Here, 3 is the base, and 5 is the exponent.

One exception is that any base (except 0) that has an exponent of 0 is equal to 1.

$$2^0 = 1, \quad 3^0 = 1, \quad 4^0 = 1, \quad \text{etc.}$$

Base numbers with negative exponents are the reciprocals of their positive-exponent counterparts.

$$3^{-2} = \frac{1}{3^2} = \frac{1}{(3 \times 3)} = \frac{1}{9}$$

or

$$\frac{1}{3^2} = 3^{-2} = \frac{1}{9}$$

We simply change the sign on the exponent when moving the base number from numerator to denominator or from denominator to numerator.

Every time we move the decimal point in a number to the left or right by one place, we are multiplying or dividing by 10. For this reason, one of the most common base numbers that we use with an exponent is 10. For example, Avogadro's number is 6.022×10^{23}. This means that 6.022 is multiplied by 10 twenty-three times!

$$6.022 \times 10 \times 10 \times 10 \times 10 \times 10 \times 10 \times \uparrow \times 10 \ (23 \text{ times})$$

A number such as 1.04×10^{-11} is equivalent to 1.04 multiplied by $\frac{1}{10^{11}}$ or $\frac{1}{10}$ eleven times.

$$1.04 \times \frac{1}{10} \times \frac{1}{10} \times \frac{1}{10} \times \frac{1}{10} \times \frac{1}{10} \times \frac{1}{10} \times \uparrow \times \frac{1}{10} \ (11 \text{ times})$$

A base number also can be an expression. For example, $(x+1)^2$ is equivalent to $(x+1) \times (x+1)$.

Example 1   Write the expression $2 \times 2 \times 2 \times 2 \times 2 \times 2 \times 2$ in exponential form.

Solution

The exponent indicates how many times the base number is multiplied by itself. The base number is 2 and is multiplied by itself seven times. Therefore, the expression is written as 2^7.

Example 2   Write the expression $\frac{1}{10} \times \frac{1}{10} \times \frac{1}{10} \times \frac{1}{10}$ in exponential form.

Solution

This expression can be written two different ways—either with a positive exponent in the denominator or with one with a negative exponent in the numerator.

$$\frac{1}{10} \times \frac{1}{10} \times \frac{1}{10} \times \frac{1}{10} = \frac{1}{(10 \times 10 \times 10 \times 10)} = \frac{1}{10^4} \text{ or } 10^{-4}$$

Example 3   Solve for the following expression: $4^6 = ?$

Solution

The base number 4 is multiplied by itself six times.

$$4^6 = 4 \times 4 \times 4 \times 4 \times 4 \times 4 = 4096$$

Practice Problem Set 1

1. Write the following expressions in exponential form.

    a. $5 \times 5 \times 5 \times 5 \times 5 \times 5 \times 5 \times 5 \times 5$

    b. $4.97 \times 10 \times 10 \times 10 \times 10 \times 10$

    c. $3 \times 3 \times 3 \times 3 \times 3 \times 3 \times 3 \times 3 \times 3 \times 3$

2. Write the following expressions in exponential form.

   a. $\dfrac{1}{6} \times \dfrac{1}{6}$

   b. $\dfrac{1}{4} \times \dfrac{1}{4} \times \dfrac{1}{4} \times \dfrac{1}{4}$

   c. $\dfrac{1}{10}$

3. Solve the following expressions.

   a. $13^3 = ?$

   b. $K = \dfrac{[0.10][0.25]^3}{[0.080]^2}$

   c. $(x + 1)^2 = ?$

Mathematical Operations with Exponential Numbers

It is often necessary to add, subtract, multiply, or divide exponential numbers. Here are the general rules:

- To add or subtract exponential numbers with the same base, evaluate the exponential numbers separately before performing the addition or subtraction. *Do not* add the exponents.

$$y^a + y^b = y^a + y^b$$

$$2^4 + 2^2 = 16 + 4 = 20$$

- To multiply exponential numbers with the same base, add the exponents.

$$y^a \times y^b = y^{a+b}$$

$$2^3 \times 2^4 = 2^{3+4} = 2^7$$

- To divide exponential numbers with the same base, subtract the exponent in the denominator from the exponent in the numerator.

$$\dfrac{y^a}{y^b} = y^{a-b}$$

$$\dfrac{2^5}{2^3} = 2^{5-3} = 2^2 = 4$$

- To add, subtract, multiply, or divide exponential numbers with different bases, evaluate the exponential numbers separately before performing the mathematical operation.

$$y^a \times z^b = y^a \times z^b$$

$$2^3 \times 4^1 = 8 \times 4 = 32$$

- The expression $(y^a)^b$ can be re-written as $y^{a \times b}$, and $\dfrac{y^a}{z^a}$ can be rewritten as $\left(\dfrac{y}{z}\right)^a$.

$$(3^2)^3 = 3^{2 \times 3} = 3^6 = 729$$

$$\frac{2^3}{4^3} = \left(\frac{2}{4}\right)^3 = \left(\frac{1}{2}\right)^3 = \frac{1}{8}$$

Practice Problem Set 2

1. Solve the following expressions.

   a. $3^2 + 3^4 = ?$

   b. $6^3 - 6^2 = ?$

   c. $2^4 + 3^3 = ?$

2. Solve the following expressions.

   a. $4^2 \times 4^5 = ?$

   b. $3^3 \times 2^3 = ?$

   c. $10^{-3} \times 10^2 = ?$

3. Solve the following expressions.

   a. $\dfrac{10^6}{10^2} = ?$

   b. $\dfrac{3^2}{4^2} = ?$

   c. $\dfrac{4^3}{2^4} = ?$

4. Solve the following expressions.

   a. $\dfrac{2^3 \times 5^2}{5^3} = ?$

   b. $\dfrac{10^3 - 6^3}{4^1} = ?$

   c. $(2^2 + 2^4) \times 2^2 = ?$

Square Roots

One common misconception about exponents is that they can only be integers (whole numbers). An exponent can be any number, including fractions (and hence decimals). Fractional exponents represent roots. Consider the base number 16 with an exponent of ½.

$$16^{\frac{1}{2}} = 4$$

The exponent ½ means to take the second root of 16 (also called the *square root of 16*). Another way of writing this expression is to use the radical symbol $\sqrt{}$.

$$\sqrt{16} = 4$$

Consider the following general expressions when dealing with roots (fractional exponents):

$$y^{\frac{1}{a}} = \sqrt[a]{y}$$

$$y^{\frac{b}{a}} = \sqrt[a]{y^b} = \left(\sqrt[a]{y}\right)^b$$

Therefore, $16^{\frac{1}{2}}$ can be expressed as

$$16^{\frac{1}{2}} = \sqrt[2]{16^1} = \left(\sqrt[2]{16}\right)^1 = \sqrt[2]{4 \times 4} = 4$$

Practice Problem Set 3

Solve the following expressions.

1. $121^{\frac{1}{2}} = ?$

2. $225^{\frac{1}{2}} = ?$

3. $\sqrt{400} = ?$

4. $\sqrt{1296} = ?$

5. $49^{\frac{1}{2}} = ?$

Practice Problem Set Solutions

Set 1

1. a. The base number 5 is multiplied by itself nine times.

    $$5 \times 5 \times 5 \times 5 \times 5 \times 5 \times 5 \times 5 \times 5 = 5^9$$

    b. The base number 10 is multiplied by itself five times.

    $$4.97 \times 10 \times 10 \times 10 \times 10 \times 10 = 4.97 \times 10^5$$

    c. The base number 3 is multiplied by itself ten times.

    $$3 \times 3 \times 3 \times 3 \times 3 \times 3 \times 3 \times 3 \times 3 \times 3 = 3^{10}$$

2. a. The base number 6 is multiplied by itself two times.

    $$\frac{1}{6} \times \frac{1}{6} = \frac{1}{6^2} \quad or \quad 6^{-2}$$

    b. The base number 4 is multiplied by itself four times.

    $$\frac{1}{4} \times \frac{1}{4} \times \frac{1}{4} \times \frac{1}{4} = \frac{1}{4^4} \quad or \quad 4^{-4}$$

    c. We can leave the expression as is because it means $\frac{1}{10^1}$, or we can rewrite it as 10^{-1}.

3. a. The base number 13 is multiplied by itself three times.

    $$13^3 = 13 \times 13 \times 13 = 2197$$

    b. $K = \dfrac{(0.10)(0.25)(0.25)(0.25)}{(0.080)(0.080)} = 0.24$

    c. $(x + 1)^2 = (x + 1) \times (x + 1) = x^2 + 2x + 1$

Set 2

1. Evaluate each exponential number separately.

    a. $3^2 + 3^4 = 9 + 81 = 90$

    b. $6^3 - 6^2 = 216 - 36 = 180$

    c. $2^4 + 3^3 = 16 + 27 = 43$

2. a. $4^2 \times 4^5 = 4^{2+5} = 4^7 = 16,384$

   b. $3^3 \times 2^3 = 27 \times 8 = 216$ (evaluate each exponential number separately)

   c. $10^{-3} \times 10^2 = 10^{-3+2} = 10^{-1} = 0.10$

3. a. $\dfrac{10^6}{10^2} = 10^{6-2} = 10^4 = 10,000$

   b. $\dfrac{3^2}{4^2} = \left(\dfrac{3}{4}\right)^2 = \dfrac{9}{16}$

   c. $\dfrac{4^3}{2^4} = \dfrac{64}{16} = 4$ (evaluate each exponential number separately)

4. a. $\dfrac{2^3 \times 5^2}{5^3} = \dfrac{8 \times 25}{125} = \dfrac{200}{125} = \dfrac{8}{5} = 1.6$ (evaluate each exponential number separately)

   b. $\dfrac{10^3 - 6^3}{4^1} = \dfrac{1000 - 216}{4} = \dfrac{784}{4} = 196$ (evaluate each exponential number separately)

   c. $(2^2 + 2^4) \times 2^2 = (4 + 16) \times 4 = 20 \times 4 = 80$ (evaluate each exponential number separately)

Set 3

1. $121^{\frac{1}{2}} = \sqrt[2]{121} = \sqrt{121} = 11$

2. $225^{\frac{1}{2}} = \sqrt[2]{225} = \sqrt{225} = 15$

3. $\sqrt{400} = 20$

4. $\sqrt{1296} = 36$

5. $49^{\frac{1}{2}} = \sqrt[2]{49} = \sqrt{49} = 7$

Exponents and Square Roots Worksheet

Write the following expressions in exponential form.

1. $10 \times 10 \times 10 \times 10 \times 10$

2. $5 \times 5 \times 5$

3. $\dfrac{1}{9} \times \dfrac{1}{9} \times \dfrac{1}{9} \times \dfrac{1}{9}$

4. Write the following expression in exponential form using only a positive exponent.

$$\dfrac{1}{4} \times \dfrac{3}{4} \times \dfrac{2}{4}$$

5. Write the following expression in exponential form using only a negative exponent.

$$\dfrac{1}{15} \times \dfrac{1}{15}$$

6. Write the following expression in exponential form using only a negative exponent.

$$\dfrac{1}{8} \times \dfrac{1}{8} \times \dfrac{1}{8}$$

Solve the following expressions.

7. $8^4 = ?$

8. $\dfrac{1}{5^4} = ?$

9. $\dfrac{1}{2^4} = ?$

10. $K = \dfrac{[0.20][0.11]}{[0.10]^2}$

11. $K = \dfrac{[0.35]^2[0.14]^4}{[2.00]}$

12. $(x + 2)^2$

13. $(2x - 3)^2$

14. $2^3 \times 2^7 = ?$

World of Chemistry

15. $1^3 \times 3^1 = ?$

16. $\dfrac{10^{-2}}{10^4} = ?$

17. $\dfrac{3^2}{2^3} = ?$

18. $\dfrac{9^2 - 3^2}{2^2} = ?$

19. $\dfrac{4^2}{2^2} - 3^0 = ?$

20. $169^{\frac{1}{2}} = ?$

21. $324^{\frac{1}{2}} = ?$

22. $\sqrt{144} = ?$

23. $\sqrt{2500} = ?$

24. Solve for x in the following expression: $1.8 \times 10^{-5} = \dfrac{x^2}{(0.90)}$

25. Solve for x in the following expression: $0.090 = \dfrac{(0.20)(x)}{(0.85)}$

Answers to Exponents and Square Roots Worksheet

1. 10^5

2. 5^3

3. $\dfrac{1}{9^4}$

4. $\dfrac{6}{4^3}$

5. 15^{-2}

6. 8^{-3}

7. 4096

8. $\dfrac{1}{625} = 0.0016$

9. $\dfrac{1}{16} = 0.0625$

10. $K = 2.2$

11. $K = 2.4 \times 10^{-5}$

12. $x^2 + 4x + 4$

13. $4x^2 - 12x + 9$

14. 1024

15. 3

16. $10^{-6} = 1 \times 10^{-6}$

17. 1.125

18. 18

19. 3

20. 13

21. 18

22. 12

23. 50

24. 0.0040

25. 0.38

Estimation

Once we understand how to solve problems, it is useful to make estimates so that we can solve problems faster or determine if our final calculated answers make sense. For example, at a sit-down restaurant, our total bill is $24.89. Our waiter is very good and deserves a 20% tip. What is the amount of the waiter's tip?

Instead of getting out a calculator or working out the problem on paper, we can figure this out in our heads by using estimation. Estimate (or round) the total amount of the bill at $25.00. Ten percent of $25.00 is $2.50; therefore, 20% of $25.00 is $5.00 (twice the amount of $2.50). The estimated amount of the tip is $5.00. By estimating the amount of the bill, we determined the amount of the tip much faster than by trying to determine 20% of $24.89 (and we are only giving the waiter just a little more than 20% of the total bill).

The key to making good estimations is to round the values up or down so that they are easier to add, subtract, multiply, or divide. Recall the rules for rounding:

- If the digit to be removed is less than 5, the preceding digit stays the same.

- If the digit to be removed is greater than 5, the preceding digit is increased by 1.

Estimation can be done with any type of problem, although the more mathematical steps that are required by a problem, the more difficult it is to determine an estimated final answer. Estimating takes practice. The more we use it in our everyday lives, the easier it is to estimate answers to chemistry problems.

Example 1   Beth walks 3 miles every morning for her daily exercise. Her friend, Kelly, calculates this distance at 45,840 feet. Using estimation and no calculator, is Kelly's answer reasonable?

Solution

To simplify the multiplication, round 5280 ft (the number of feet in a mile) down to 5000 ft (the digit to be rounded is 2, which is less than 5). If we estimate that 1 mile ≈ 5000 ft, then 3 miles is approximately 15,000 ft.

$$3 \text{ mi} \times \frac{5000 \text{ ft}}{1 \text{ mi}} = 15,000 \text{ ft}$$

Kelly's calculated answer of 45,000 feet is not reasonable (way too high).

Practice Problem Set 1

1. A recipe states that for every scoop of powdered Kool-Aid, 8.1 cups of water should be added. If 4 scoops of powdered Kool-Aid are added to a large dispenser, approximately how much water should be added?

2. A new pair of jeans is on sale for 50% off the regular price of $59.95. Excluding tax, approximately how much should the jeans cost at the sale price? What is the exact cost of the jeans at the sale price?

3. Helium gas is in a 4-L balloon. If half the gas is let out of the balloon, estimate the new volume of the gas without using a calculator (assuming constant temperature and pressure).

4. Oxygen gas is in a 1-L steel container at 3.0 atm of pressure. If the gas is moved into a 2-L steel container at constant temperature, estimate the new pressure of the gas without using a calculator.

Estimation is also useful when performing multiplication or division calculations that include scientific notation. It helps us to quickly determine if the calculated answer is to the correct order of magnitude. Recall the rules for multiplication and division with exponential numbers:

$$10^a \times 10^b = 10^{a+b}$$
$$\frac{10^a}{10^b} = 10^{a-b}$$

Example 2 a. Using estimation, determine the order of magnitude of the equilibrium constant (K) if $[H^+] = 3.00 \times 10^{-3}\ M$; $[F^-] = 3.00 \times 10^{-3}\ M$, and $[HF] = 1.25 \times 10^{-2}\ M$ using the equation

$$K = \frac{[H^+][F^-]}{[HF]}$$

b. Using a calculator, determine the actual value of K, and compare the order of magnitude to the estimated order of magnitude.

Solution

a. Using the equation, substitute in the order of magnitude values and simplify.

$$K = \frac{(10^{-3})(10^{-3})}{(10^{-2})}$$

$$K = \frac{10^{-3+(-3)}}{10^{-2}} = \frac{10^{-6}}{10^{-2}} = 10^{-6-(-2)} = 10^{-6+2}$$

$$K = 10^{-4}$$

b. Use a calculator to determine the actual value of K.

$$K = \frac{(3.00 \times 10^{-3})(3.00 \times 10^{-3})}{(1.25 \times 10^{-2})}$$

$$K = 7.2 \times 10^{-4}$$

The estimated and calculated values of K both have the same orders of magnitude.

Practice Problem Set 2

1. Determine the estimated order of magnitude for the following expression, and compare this value with the calculated order of magnitude.

$$(1.79 \times 10^{-3}) \times (5.50 \times 10^{5})$$

2. Determine the estimated order of magnitude for the following expression, and compare this value with the calculated order of magnitude.

$$\frac{1.59 \times 10^{-2} \text{ molecules N}_2}{6.022 \times 10^{23} \text{ molecules N}_2/\text{mol N}_2}$$

3. A chemistry student calculated the equilibrium constant for the reaction of NH_4^+ with water and got 5.6×10^{-6}. Using estimation, determine the order of magnitude of the equilibrium constant if $[NH_4^+] = 5.50 \times 10^{-2}$ M, $[NH_3] = 5.55 \times 10^{-6}$ M, and $[H^+] = 5.55 \times 10^{-6}$ M.

$$K = \frac{[NH_3][H^+]}{[NH_4^+]}$$

Is the calculated equilibrium constant a reasonable answer?

Practice Problem Set Solutions

Set 1

1. To simplify the multiplication, round 8.1 cups down to 8 cups (the digit to be rounded is 1, which is less than 5). If we estimate that 1 scoop of Kool-Aid ≈ 8 cups of water, then 4 scoops requires approximately 32 cups of water.

$$4 \text{ scoops} \times \frac{8 \text{ cups}}{1 \text{ scoop}} = 32 \text{ cups}$$

2. Round the regular price of the jeans up to $60 (the digit to be rounded is 9, which is greater than 5). Fifty percent (or ½) of $60 is $30. The approximate sale price of the pair of jeans is $60 – $30 = $30.

   Determine the exact sale price of the jeans by performing the calculation on a calculator, and do not round any values until the last calculation.

$$0.50 \times \$59.95 = \$29.975$$

$$\$59.95 - \$29.975 = \$29.98$$

   The estimated sale price and calculated sale price are very close to each other.

3. Volume and moles of gas are directly related; therefore, the volume of the helium in the balloon will decrease by one-half because the moles of helium decreased by one-half. The final volume of the gas is ½ × 4 L = 2 L. This answer makes sense because a smaller number of gas particles require less space to keep the pressure the same.

4. 1.5 atm. Volume and pressure are inversely related; therefore, the new pressure of the oxygen gas will decrease by one-half because the volume of the gas doubled.

$$½ \times 3.0 \text{ atm} = 1.5 \text{ atm}$$

   This answer makes sense because there is more room for the gas to move around in, and the gas particles will hit the walls of the container less frequently.

Set 2

1. To determine an estimated order of magnitude, only multiply the exponential numbers.

$$10^{-3} \times 10^5 = 10^{-3+5} = 10^2$$

   The calculated answer is 9.845×10^2. The estimated and calculated orders of magnitude are the same.

2. To determine an estimated order of magnitude, only divide the exponential numbers.

$$\frac{10^{-2}}{10^{23}} = 10^{-2-23} = 10^{-25}$$

The calculated answer is 2.64×10^{-26} mol N_2. The estimated and calculated answers have different orders of magnitude, but they are only off by 10. This means that the base numbers must divide in a way that affects the order of magnitude by a factor of 10. If we estimate the base numbers and divide, we get $\frac{2}{6} = 0.3\overline{3}$. Since the answer is less than 1, this causes the estimated order of magnitude to change from 10^{-25} to 10^{-26}.

3. Using the equation, substitute in the order of magnitude values and simplify.

$$K = \frac{\left(10^{-6}\right)\left(10^{-6}\right)}{\left(10^{-2}\right)}$$

$$K = \frac{10^{-6+(-6)}}{10^{-2}} = \frac{10^{-12}}{10^{-2}} = 10^{-12-(-2)} = 10^{-12+2}$$

$$K = 10^{-10}$$

No, the calculated equilibrium constant is not a reasonable answer (10^{-10} is very different from 10^{-6}). The actual answer is $K = 5.6 \times 10^{-10}$.

Estimation Worksheet

Round the following measurements to the nearest whole number.

1. 25.91 cm

2. 8.2 in

3. 53.789 mm

Round the following measurements to the nearest tens place.

4. 551 mi

5. 77 km

6. 933 s

For the following expressions, use estimation to determine if the calculated answers are reasonable.

7. $6 \times 405 = 5430$

8. $1010 \div 5.20 = 194$

9. $207.1 + 31.8 + 10.2 = 249.1$

10. $1004 - 198 = 806$

11. $\dfrac{52.1 \times 3.1}{4.8} = 3.6$

12. $(4.32 \times 10^5) \times (1.09 \times 10^3) = 4.71 \times 10^{15}$

13. $\dfrac{4.73 \times 10^{23}}{2.32 \times 10^{-4}} = 4.90 \times 10^{-28}$

14. $\dfrac{(1.66 \times 10^2) \times (1.66 \times 10^2)}{(1.03 \times 10^4)} = 2.66$

15. $\dfrac{(9.44 \times 10^6)}{(2.11 \times 10^2)(3.21 \times 10^{-4})} = 1.39 \times 10^{-11}$

16. Joe runs 9 miles every day in preparation for an upcoming cross-country race. His coach calculates this distance to be 47,520 ft. Using estimation (do not use a calculator), is his coach's answer reasonable? (1 mi = 5280 ft.)

17. A jacket is on sale for 50% off the regular price of $178.99. Excluding tax, approximately how much should the jacket cost at the sale price? What is the exact cost of the jacket at the sale price?

18. A pair of shoes is on sale for 40% off the regular price of $79.90. Excluding tax, approximately how much should the shoes cost at the sale price? What is the exact cost of the shoes at the sale price?

19. The total bill at a restaurant is $19.26. What is the approximate cost of the waitress's tip if she deserves 20% of the total bill?

20. Nitrogen gas is in a 5-L balloon. If half the gas is let out of the balloon, estimate the new volume of the gas without using a calculator (assuming constant temperature and pressure).

21. A total of 1.0 mol of argon gas is in a 10-L steel container at 6.0 atm of pressure. If an additional 1.0 mol of argon gas is added to the container, estimate the new pressure of the gas without using a calculator (assuming constant temperature and volume)?

22. Chlorine gas is in a 9.1-L steel container at 12.0 atm of pressure. If the gas is moved into a container one-third the size of the original container at constant temperature, estimate the new pressure of the gas without using a calculator.

23. Determine the estimated order of magnitude for the following expression, and compare this value with the calculated order of magnitude.

$$E = mc^2$$

$$E = (1.1 \times 10^{-2}\ kg)(2.998 \times 10^8\ m/s)^2$$

24. Determine the estimated order of magnitude for the following expression, and compare this value with the calculated order of magnitude.

$$\frac{8.49 \times 10^3\ \text{molecules } H_2O}{6.022 \times 10^{23}\ \text{molecules } H_2O/\text{mol } H_2O}$$

25. a. Using estimation, determine the order of magnitude of the equilibrium constant (K) if $[H^+] = 1.34 \times 10^{-3}\ M$, $[C_2H_3O_2^-] = 1.34 \times 10^{-3}\ M$, and $[HC_2H_3O_2] = 1.0 \times 10^{-1}\ M$ using the equation

$$K = \frac{[H^+][C_2H_3O_2^-]}{[HC_2H_3O_2]}$$

b. Using a calculator, determine the actual value of K, and compare the order of magnitude with the estimated value.

Answers to Estimation Worksheet

1.   26 cm   2.   8 in.
3.   54 mm   4.   550 mi
5.   80 km   6.   930 s

7. Not reasonable; $6 \times 405 \approx 6 \times 400 \approx 2400$

8. Reasonable; $1010 \div 5.20 \approx 1000 \div 5 \approx 200$

9. Reasonable; $207.1 + 31.8 + 10.2 \approx 207 + 32 + 10 \approx 249$

10. Reasonable; $1004 - 198 \approx 1000 - 200 \approx 800$

11. Not reasonable; $\dfrac{52.1 \times 3.1}{4.8} \approx \dfrac{50 \times 3}{5} \approx 30$

12. Not reasonable; $(4.32 \times 10^5) \times (1.09 \times 10^3) \approx 10^5 \times 10^3 \approx 10^{5+3} \approx 10^8$

13. Not reasonable; $\dfrac{4.73 \times 10^{23}}{2.32 \times 10^{-4}} \approx \dfrac{10^{23}}{10^{-4}} \approx 10^{23-(-4)} \approx 10^{27}$

14. Reasonable; $\dfrac{\left(1.66 \times 10^2\right) \times \left(1.66 \times 10^2\right)}{\left(1.03 \times 10^4\right)} \approx \dfrac{\left(10^2\right) \times \left(10^2\right)}{\left(10^4\right)} \approx \dfrac{10^{2+2}}{10^4} \approx \dfrac{10^4}{10^4} \approx 1$

15. Not reasonable;

$$\dfrac{\left(9.44 \times 10^6\right)}{\left(2.11 \times 10^2\right)\left(3.21 \times 10^{-4}\right)} \approx \dfrac{\left(10^6\right)}{\left(10^2\right)\left(10^{-4}\right)} \approx \dfrac{10^6}{10^{2+(-4)}} \approx \dfrac{10^6}{10^{-2}} \approx 10^{6-(-2)} \approx 10^8$$

16. Yes, the answer is reasonable. $9 \text{ mi} \times \dfrac{5280 \text{ ft}}{1 \text{ mi}} \approx 9 \text{ mi} \times \dfrac{5000 \text{ ft}}{1 \text{ mi}} \approx 45{,}000 \text{ ft}$

17. Approximate cost: $\$180 \times 0.50 \approx \$90$; exact cost: $\$178.99 \times 0.50 = \$89.50$

18. Approximate cost: $\$80 \times 0.40 \approx \$32$; $\$80. - \$32 = \$48$; exact cost: $\$79.90 \times 0.40 = \$31.96$; $\$79.90 - \$31.96 = \$47.94$

19.   \$4   20.   2.5 L
21.   12 atm   22.   36 atm

23. Estimated: $E \approx (10^{-2})(10^8)^2 \approx (10^{-2})(10^8)(10^8) \approx 10^{-2+8+8} \approx 10^{14}$; calculated: $E = 9.9 \times 10^{14}$ J. The estimated and calculated orders of magnitude are the same.

24. Estimated: $\dfrac{10^3}{10^{23}} \approx 10^{3-23} \approx 10^{-20}$; calculated: 1.41×10^{-20} mol H_2O. The estimated and calculated orders of magnitude are the same.

25. a. $K \approx \dfrac{\left(10^{-3}\right)\left(10^{-3}\right)}{\left(10^{-1}\right)} \approx \dfrac{10^{-3+(-3)}}{10^{-1}} \approx \dfrac{10^{-6}}{10^{-1}} \approx 10^{-6-(-1)} \approx 10^{-5}$

     b. $K = \dfrac{\left(1.34 \times 10^{-3}\right)\left(1.34 \times 10^{-3}\right)}{\left(1.0 \times 10^{-1}\right)} = 1.8 \times 10^{-5}$

The estimated and calculated values both have the same order of magnitude.

Graphing

Graphs, particularly line graphs, are an excellent way of visually representing data from experiments. We can interpret data, verify laws, and draw conclusions about why we are observing certain phenomena. Graphs show mathematical relationships visually. Graphs are used in our everyday lives. If we open a newspaper or watch the news, the media often use graphs to justify or explain their story. Do we know if the graph is accurate? Did they represent the data correctly? Did they make their own conclusions about the data, or could the graph be interpreted another way? Understanding how to draw and interpret line graphs will help us decide about graphs we see every day, in addition to helping us in chemistry.

Drawing a Line Graph

Before we can interpret line graphs, we must understand how to draw them. An experiment might involve finding out how changing one quantity affects the value of another quantity. The quantity that we deliberately change is called the *independent variable*. The quantity that changes due to changing the independent variable is called the *dependent variable*. Once we have this set of data, we can draw a graph to see if any relationship exists between these two variables. Here are the key points to plotting line graphs:

1. Draw x and y axes (preferably on graph paper). Draw the axes as large as possible in order to spread out the data.

2. Identify the independent and dependent variables. The independent variable is plotted on the x axis (horizontal line), and the dependent variable is plotted on the y axis (vertical line).

3. Label each axis with the variable name and the unit.

4. Create a scale on both the x and y axes. The intervals on the x axis must be equally spaced apart but cover the range of values listed for the independent variable. Similarly, the intervals on the y axis also must be equally spaced apart but cover the range of values listed for the dependent variable.

5. Plot the values on the graph using a dark dot for each point.

6. Draw a "best fit" line. Never "connect the dots"! Draw the "best fit" line by having the line go through as many points as possible with approximately the same number of points above the line as below it. This is like drawing the "average" line between the points. The "best fit" line could appear straight, or if the points do not form a straight line, then draw the best smooth curve possible.

Example 1   Judy drove her car down the street, and the following data were recorded. Graph the data, and draw a "best fit" line.

Time (s)	Distance (m)
0	0
1	20.
2	45
3	60.
4	84
5	105

Solution

1. Set up the x and y axes including the scale. Time is the independent variable (x axis), and distance is the dependent variable (y axis). The x-axis interval can be 1 because the values only differ by 1. The y-axis interval can be 20 to make the data fit on the graph and cover the broad distance range. Other intervals can be used if desired. Then plot the data points on the graph.

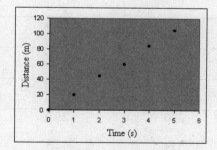

2. Draw the "best fit" line. In this case, the line appears straight (or linear) when we take the "average" between the points.

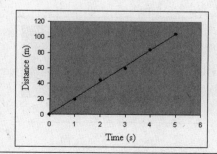

Practice Problem Set 1

1. Graph the following set of data including a "best fit" line.

x	y
4	17
10	39
17	50
25	88
27	112
35	140

2. The following data were collected at various checkpoints for a runner who ran the Boston Marathon. Graph the data including a "best fit" line (the line can be a curve).

Time (min)	Distance (mi)
25	5.0
38	10.0
75	15.0
137	20.0
220	25.0
235	26.2

3. For the following points on the graph, draw a "best fit" line (the line can be a curve).

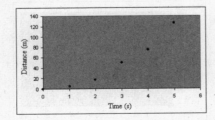

Interpreting Graphs

Now that we understand how to make line graphs, what do these graphs tell us? More specifically, what relationships, if any, exist between the two variables? The two main relationships we will focus on are direct relationships and indirect (inverse) relationships. Many more mathematical relationships exist for line graphs, but for our purposes, we will only focus on these two.

Direct Relationship (Directly Proportional)

A direct relationship exists when the dependent variable varies directly with the independent variable. There is a constant rate of change between the two variables. The graph is a straight line (linear).

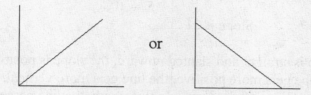

or

The equation for a straight line can be represented in the general form

$$y = mx + b$$

where y is the dependent variable, x is the independent variable, m is the slope, and b is the intercept with the y axis. The slope of a straight line is the change in y to that in x. The slope of a line can be positive or negative.

$$\text{Slope} = m = \frac{\Delta y}{\Delta x} = \frac{y_2 - y_1}{x_2 - x_1}$$

Example 2   For the graphed data from Example 1, what is the slope and y intercept of the "best fit" line?

Time (s)	Distance (m)
0	0
1	20.
2	45
3	60.
4	84
5	105

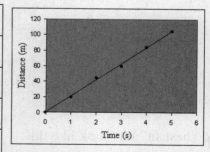

Solution

To determine the slope of our "best fit" line, choose two different coordinates from our data (time versus distance). Remember, time is the independent variable, and distance is the dependent variable.

$$\text{Slope} = m = \frac{\Delta y}{\Delta x} = \frac{y_2 - y_1}{x_2 - x_1}$$

$$\text{Slope} = m = \frac{105 - 0}{5 - 0} = 21$$

$$\text{Slope} = 21$$

Notice that since the line is straight and slanted upward, the slope is positive. Also notice that the slope is *not* 1. As the slope gets more positive, the line gets more vertical. The y intercept is the point where the line passes through the y axis. In this graph, the line passes through the origin (0, 0), so the y intercept is 0. Therefore, the equation for the line is $y = 21x + 0$ or $y = 21x$.

Example 3   Graph the following set of data, draw a "best fit" line, and write an equation for the line using the general form $y = mx + b$.

x	y
0	140
4	120
9	94
12	80
18	50
23	26
26	9

Solution

The graph and "best fit" line look like this:

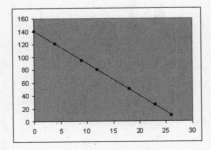

To write an equation for the line, we first determine the slope (m) and y intercept (b).

$$\text{Slope} = m = \frac{\Delta y}{\Delta x} = \frac{y_2 - y_1}{x_2 - x_1}$$

$$\text{Slope} = m = \frac{9 - 140}{26 - 0}$$

$$\text{Slope} = m = -5$$

This is an example of a direct relationship with a negative slope.

The line passes through the y axis at 140; therefore, the y intercept is 140 ($b = 140$).

The equation of the line is $y = -5x + 140$.

Indirect Relationship (Inversely Proportional)

An indirect relationship occurs when the dependent variable does not vary directly with the independent variable. There is not a constant rate of change between the two variables. The graph is the positive part of a hyperbola; therefore, the line is *not* straight.

Notice that the indirect line never touches the x or y axis. It looks very different from a direct relationship, which has a *straight* line with a *positive* or *negative* constant slope.

Correct   Incorrect

Remember, a direct relationship has a constant rate of change between the two variables. For an indirect relationship, the rate of change is not constant (not linear), and we cannot determine the slope the same way that we determine it for a straight line. The general form of the equation is

$$y = \frac{m}{x} \quad or \quad m = xy$$

The data points (independent and dependent variables) can never be zero; therefore, there is no *y* intercept. Determining the rate of change in the curve is beyond the scope of our chemistry course, so we will not discuss it here.

Example 4 Robert Boyle, a scientist, performed an experiment where he varied the volume of a gas and measured the pressure of the gas at each new volume. He kept the amount of gas and temperature constant. Here are some of his results from Table 13.1 in your *World of Chemistry* text. Graph the data and draw a "best fit" line. Is the relationship between the volume and pressure of the gas direct or indirect?

Volume (in^3)	Pressure (in. Hg)
48.0	29.1
40.0	35.3
32.0	44.2
24.0	58.2
20.0	70.7
16.0	87.2
12.0	117.5

Solution

Volume is the independent variable (*x* axis) and pressure is the dependent variable (*y* axis). The *x*-axis scale can be marked in 10.0 in.^{3} spaces. The *y*-axis scale can be marked in 20.0 in. Hg spaces. Plot the data points on the graph and draw a "best fit" line.

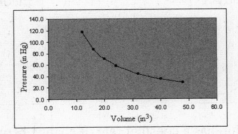

The line is curved and resembles a hyperbola. The relationship between the volume and pressure of the gas is indirect because the rate of change between these two variables is not constant. If we think about this conceptually, Boyle's results make sense. No matter how large the volume of a gas gets, the pressure can never be zero (a gas molecule will always hit the wall of its container and exert pressure). No matter how large the pressure gets, the gas molecules will always take up space and have volume.

Constant Relationship

For some graphs, there is no relationship between the two variables. One variable is not affected in any way by another variable. For example, the number of times a person washes the outside of his or her car in one month will not affect the gas mileage of the car. Consider the following data:

No. of Times Wash Car/Month	Gas Mileage of Car (mi/gal)
1	25
2	25
3	25
4	25
5	25

If we graph these data, we see that the line is straight and exactly horizontal.

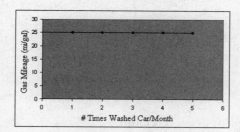

There is no rate of change between the two variables (slope = 0). The gas mileage does not increase or decrease when the number of times the car is washed per month increases.

Practice Problem Set 2

1. For each of the following graphs, indicate whether a direct relationship, indirect relationship, or constant relationship exists between the two variables.

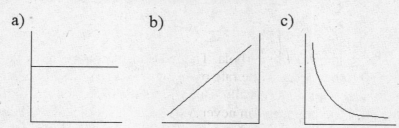

a)   b)   c)

2. Which graph in Problem 1 shows a constant rate of change between the two variables?

3. For the following graph, determine the slope of the line and the y intercept. Write the equation for the line in general form. What type of relationship exists between the two variables?

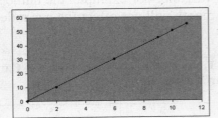

Practice Problem Set Solutions

Set 1

1. The *x* values are the independent variable and the *y* values are the dependent variable. The *x*-axis scale can be in intervals of 5. The *y*-axis scale can be in intervals of 20. Plot the data points on the graph and draw a "best fit" line.

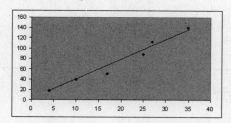

2. Time is the independent variable (*x* axis). Distance is the dependent variable (*y* axis). The *x*-axis scale can be 50-min spaces. The *y*-axis scale can be in 5.0-m spaces. Plot the data points on the graph and draw a "best fit" line.

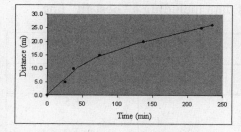

3. Draw the "average" line between the points.

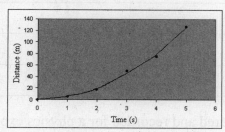

Set 2

1. a. Constant relationship; the *y* variable does not change when the *x* variable changes.

   b. Direct relationship; the line is linear and the slope is constant.

   c. Indirect relationship; as the independent variable increases, the dependent variable decreases nonlinearly.

2. b. The slope is constant.

3. Slope $= \dfrac{\Delta y}{\Delta x} = \dfrac{55 - 10}{11 - 2} = \dfrac{45}{9} = 5$; the line passes through the origin; therefore, the *y* intercept is 0. The general equation therefore is $y = 5x + 0$ or $y = 5x$. A direct relationship exists.

Graphing Worksheet

Use the following graphs to answer Problems 1–3.

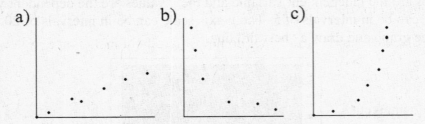

a)   b)   c)

1. For graph a, draw a "best fit" line.

2. For graph b, draw a "best fit" line.

3. For graph c, draw a "best fit" line.

4. Graph the following set of data including a "best fit" line.

Force (N)	Elongation (cm)
0	0.0
1	1.5
2	3.0
3	4.5
4	6.0
5	7.5

The following data were measured and recorded for a physics experiment involving a toy car moving down a track. Use the data to answer Problems 5–10.

Force (N)	Acceleration (m/s^2)
0	0.0
10	6.0
20	12.5
30	19.0
40	25.0

5. Graph the data including a "best fit" line.

6. Describe the relationship between force and acceleration.

7. Write an equation for the "best fit" line.

8. What is the slope of the "best fit" line (do not worry about including units)?

9. Is the slope constant?

10. What is the y intercept?

Use the following set of data to answer Problems 11–14.

x	y
1	80
2	40
3	27
4	20
5	16

11. Graph the data including a "best fit" line.

12. Describe the relationship between x and y.

13. Is the slope of the "best fit" line constant?

14. What is the y intercept of the "best fit" line?

15. Phillip noticed that when he drove down the road at 55 mi/hr, he covered more distance than when he drove 45 mi/hr over the same period of time. What is the relationship between the speed of Phillip's car and the distance he covers (when time is held constant)?

16. Phillip's friend, Kate, noticed that when she drives slower it takes her longer to cover the same distance compared with when she drives faster. What is the relationship between the speed of Kate's car and the time it takes to travel (when the distance is held constant)?

17. Phillip's little sister, Liza, believes that when she wears her seatbelt, the car runs better and more smoothly as compared with when she does not wear her seat belt. What is the relationship between the car's performance and whether or not Liza wears her seat belt?

Use the following graphs to answer Problems 18–25.

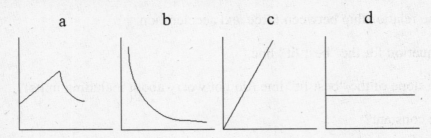

a   b   c   d

18. In which graph(s) is y directly proportional to x?

19. In which graph(s) is y indirectly proportional to x?

20. Which graph does not seem to picture a simple relationship?

21. In which graph(s) is y not related at all to x?

22. In which graph does y decrease as x increases?

23. In which graph does y increase as x increases?

24. In which graph does a constant slope exist?

25. In which graph does a slope of zero exist?

Answers to Graphing Worksheet

1.
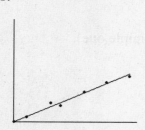

2.

3.

4.
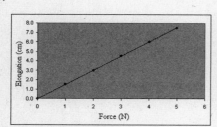

5.
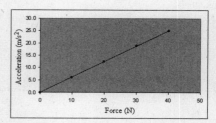

6. There is a direct relationship between force and acceleration.

7. $y = \dfrac{19}{30}x + 0$ or $y = \dfrac{19}{30}x$

8. $\dfrac{19}{30}$

9. Yes, the line is linear.

10. 0

11.
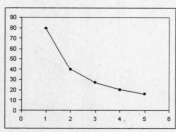

12. There is an indirect (inverse) relationship between x and y.

13. No, the slope is changing.

14. There is no y-intercept. The line will never touch neither the x nor y axes.

15. Speed and distance are directly proportional. When speed increases, the distance also increases.

16. Speed and time are indirectly proportional. When speed decreases, the time increases.

17. There is no relationship between these two factors. Although this might encourage Liza to wear her seat belt, it has no affect on the performance of the car.

18. c

19. b

20. a

21. d (and possibly a) although some relationship could exist, just not a simple one)

22. b

23. c

24. c

25. d

Percent

Why are percents important? Consider the following example:

> There are two key basketball players who play a lot of minutes during games. During practice, we observe that George consistently makes 9 free throws out of 20. Kevin consistently makes 8 free throws out of 10. Whom would we rather have at the free throw line during a basketball game?

> Even though George has made a greater number of free throws (9 versus 8), we would rather have Kevin at the line because he makes a higher *percentage* of his free throws. If we did not understand the concept of percent, we could easily make practical mistakes such as putting George at the line instead of Kevin (during a technical foul, for example).

There is one key concept we need to grasp about percents:

> A percent is a part out of 100. Percents represent a fraction with 100 in the denominator.

For example, look at the drawing of a pepperoni pizza below:

If our friend eats 25% of the pizza, then $\frac{1}{4}$ of the pizza is gone (and we better get some for ourselves before our friend eats it all). Thus 25% is equivalent to $\frac{25}{100}$, which then can be reduced to $\frac{1}{4}$. This means that if you split the pizza into four parts, 1 out of those 4 parts is missing.

Let's consider another example. If you drink $\frac{2}{3}$ of your soda, what percent is missing from the can? If you split the can into 3 parts, 2 of those 3 parts are missing.

missing

Since we want to represent the amount of soda missing as a percent, let's convert our fraction to an equivalent one that has 100 in the denominator. We can do this by writing an equation:

$$\frac{2}{3} = \frac{x}{100}$$

We can now solve for x (by multiplying each side of the equation by 100), and we get

$$\frac{2}{3} \times 100 = x$$

Simplifying the expression (by dividing 2 by 3 and multiplying the answer by 100) leads to

$$\frac{2}{3} \times 100 = 66.6$$

That is $\frac{2}{3} = \frac{66.6}{100}$, so 66.6 parts per hundred of the soda is missing from the can. This represents 66.6%.

Example 1   You earned 15 points on your last chemistry quiz. The maximum number of points you could have earned on the quiz was 20. What percentage of the possible points did you get correct on the quiz?

Solution

The first step is to write our expression as a fraction, with the total (or maximum points possible) in the denominator.

$$\frac{15 \text{ points earned}}{20 \text{ points maximum}} = \frac{15}{20}$$

We can convert $\frac{15}{20}$ to parts per 100 (that is, a fraction with 100 in the denominator) by writing and solving the following equation:

$$\frac{15}{20} = \frac{x}{100}$$

$$x = \frac{(15 \times 100)}{20} = 75$$

So $\frac{15}{20} = \frac{75}{100}$. Therefore, $x = 75\%$

Practice Problem Set 1

1. If 38% of your apple was eaten, what percent still remains?

2. If you pour 65.0% of your 16.0-oz glass of juice down the drain, how many ounces of juice still remain in the glass?

3. You see a great pair of shoes on sale for 40% off the regular price of $69.99. Excluding tax, how much would the shoes cost you?

Percent Error

One practical application of percent that is very important to scientists is percent error. *Percent error* tells us how close our measurements are to the real, or accurate, value. It is calculated using the following equation:

$$\% \text{ Error} = \frac{|\text{measured value} - \text{actual value}|}{\text{actual value}} \times 100\%$$

Example 2	A food scientist tests his equipment, called a *bomb calorimeter,* by measuring the amount of calories in a serving of peanuts and comparing this value with a known standard. Using his instrument, the scientist measures and calculates 172 Calories/serving. The known standard is 185 Calories/serving. What is the percent error?

Solution

The measured value is 172 Calories/serving. The actual value is 185 Calories/serving. Therefore, the percent error is

$$\% \text{ Error} = \frac{|172 - 185|}{185} \times 100\%$$

$$\% \text{ Error} = 7\%$$

Percent Composition

Another important application of percent is percent composition. When we refer to *percent composition,* we are referring to the percent makeup of an object *by mass.*

Example 3   Determine the percent composition of a ham and cheese sandwich using the following information:

Sandwich Item	Mass in Grams
Bread (1 slice)	8.51 g
Ham	18.56 g
Cheese	6.60 g
Mayonnaise	0.95 g

Solution

We first want to determine what percentage of the ham and cheese sandwich is bread. We put the mass of the bread in the numerator (because this represents the "part") and put the mass of the entire sandwich in the denominator (because this represents the "whole"). We then convert this fraction to a percent by multiplying by 100%.

$$\text{Fraction of the whole} \times 100\% = \% \text{ of the "part"}$$

$$\text{Total mass of sandwich} = 2 \text{ slices of bread} + \text{ham} + \text{cheese} + \text{mayonnaise}$$
$$= 2 \text{ slices}(8.51 \text{ g/slice}) + 18.56 \text{ g} + 6.60 \text{ g} + 0.95 \text{ g}$$
$$= 43.13 \text{ g}$$

$$\text{Mass percent of bread} = \frac{\text{mass of bread}}{\text{mass of sandwich}} = \frac{17.02 \text{ g}}{43.13 \text{ g}} \times 100\% = 39.46\% \text{ bread}$$

We use the same procedure to determine the remaining percent composition of the ham and cheese sandwich.

$$\text{Mass percent of ham} = \frac{\text{mass of ham}}{\text{mass of sandwich}} = \frac{18.56 \text{ g}}{43.13 \text{ g}} \times 100\% = 43.03\% \text{ ham}$$

$$\text{Mass percent of cheese} = \frac{\text{mass of cheese}}{\text{mass of sandwich}} = \frac{6.60 \text{ g}}{43.13 \text{ g}} \times 100\% = 15.30\% \text{ cheese}$$

$$\text{Mass percent of mayo} = \frac{\text{mass of mayo}}{\text{mass of sandwich}} = \frac{0.95 \text{ g}}{43.13 \text{ g}} \times 100\% = 2.20\% \text{ mayo}$$

Since we are comparing the mass percents of all the components that make up the sandwich, our answers should add up to 100 (since percents are out of 100). Take note that in some cases, rounding-off effects may produce a small deviation from 100.

$$
\begin{array}{r}
39.46\% \\
43.03\% \\
15.30\% \\
+\ 2.20\% \\
\hline
99.99\%
\end{array}
$$

Now that we understand what percent composition means, let's apply this concept to the percent composition of a compound. Let's determine the mass percent of an element in a compound, as discussed in Chapter 6 of your text. Remember, we put the mass of our element in 1 mol of the compound in our numerator (because this represents the "part"). The mass of 1 mol of the entire compound goes in the denominator (because this represents the "whole").

Example 4   What is the mass percent of oxygen and hydrogen in the compound water (H_2O)?

Solution

$$\text{Mass percent of O} = \frac{\text{mass of O in 1 mol } H_2O}{\text{mass of 1 mol of } H_2O} \times 100\% = \frac{\text{part}}{\text{whole}} \times 100\%$$

$$\text{Mass percent of H} = \frac{\text{mass of H in 1 mol } H_2O}{\text{mass of 1 mol of } H_2O} \times 100\% = \frac{\text{part}}{\text{whole}} \times 100\%$$

Let's first calculate the mass of 1 mol of H_2O, which will go in the denominator because it represents the "whole."

$$2(\text{molar mass of H}) + (\text{molar mass of O}) = 2(1.008 \text{ g/mol}) + 1(16.00 \text{ g/mol}) = 18.016 \text{ g/mol}$$

$$\text{Mass percent of O} = \frac{\text{mass of O in 1 mol } H_2O}{18.016 \text{ g/mol}} \times 100\% = \frac{\text{part}}{18.016 \text{ g/mol}} \times 100\%$$

$$\text{Mass percent of H} = \frac{\text{mass of H in 1 mol } H_2O}{18.016 \text{ g/mol}} \times 100\% = \frac{\text{part}}{18.016 \text{ g/mol}} \times 100\%$$

Now let's calculate the mass of oxygen in 1 mol of H_2O using the molar mass of oxygen.

$$\text{Mass of O in 1 mol of } H_2O = 1 \text{ mol} \times \frac{16.00 \text{ g}}{\text{mol}} = 16.00 \text{ g O}$$

The 16.00 g of oxygen is the "part" that we are comparing with the 1 mol of H_2O (the "whole").

$$\text{Mass percent of O} = \frac{16.00 \text{ g}}{18.016 \text{ g}} \times 100\% = 88.81\% \text{ O}$$

Calculate the mass of hydrogen in 1 mol of H_2O using the molar mass of hydrogen.

$$\text{Mass of H in 1 mol of } H_2O = 2 \text{ mol} \times \frac{1.008 \text{ g}}{\text{mol}} = 2.016 \text{ g H}$$

The 2.016 g of hydrogen is the "part" that we are comparing with the 1 mol of H_2O (the "whole").

$$\text{Mass percent of H} = \frac{2.016 \text{ g}}{18.016 \text{ g}} \times 100\% = 11.19\% \text{ H}$$

Again, our answers should add up to 100.

$$\begin{array}{r} 88.81\% \\ + 11.19\% \\ \hline 100.00\% \end{array}$$

Water is made up of 88.81% oxygen by mass and 11.19% hydrogen by mass. By looking at the formula for water, H_2O, this is not intuitively obvious. In fact, we might think that water has a greater percentage of hydrogen because there are two hydrogen atoms for every one oxygen atom. This is not true when analyzing the molecule by *mass*, so having a thorough understanding of percent composition is essential.

Empirical Formula

Once we understand percent composition, we can apply this concept to determine the empirical formula of a compound. As indicated in Chapter 6 in your text, the *empirical formula* is the simplest whole-number ratio of atoms in a compound. The mass of each element in a compound is an indicator of the number of atoms of that element in the compound, but only if the mass is converted to moles. Often the percent mass of each element in a compound is given. To determine the empirical formula of this compound, these amounts must be converted to moles. Since percents are represented as a fraction out of 100, it is easiest to assume that the total mass of a compound is 100 g; therefore, the mass of each element in the compound is the same as the mass percent given.

Example 5 A hydrocarbon compound is composed of 75% carbon and 25% hydrogen by mass. What is the empirical formula for this compound?

Solution

We need to determine the simplest whole-number ratio between carbon and hydrogen. This comparison can be made only when we know the relative number of each type of atom. If we convert the mass percents of carbon and hydrogen to their corresponding masses in grams, we can easily convert these values to moles. If we assume that we have 100 g of our compound, then we have 75 g of carbon and 25 g of hydrogen, based on the mass percents given.

$$\text{Mass percent of C} = \frac{\text{part}}{\text{whole}} \times 100\% = \frac{75 \text{ g}}{100 \text{ g}} \times 100\% = 75\% \text{ C}$$

$$\text{Mass percent of H} = \frac{\text{part}}{\text{whole}} \times 100\% = \frac{25 \text{ g}}{100 \text{ g}} \times 100\% = 25\% \text{ H}$$

Now that we have the mass of each element, we can convert these values to moles using the molar masses.

$$(75 \text{ g C})\left(\frac{1 \text{ mol C}}{12.01 \text{ g C}}\right) = 6.245 \text{ mol C}$$

$$(25 \text{ g H})\left(\frac{1 \text{ mol H}}{1.008 \text{ g H}}\right) = 24.802 \text{ mol H}$$

To determine the simplest whole-number ratio between carbon and hydrogen, we divide both values by the smallest number of moles, which is 6.245 mol.

$$\frac{6.245 \text{ mol C}}{6.245 \text{ mol}} = 1 \qquad \frac{24.802 \text{ mol H}}{6.245 \text{ mol}} = 4$$

Therefore, the empirical formula of this compound is CH_4.

We could assume that we have a different mass of the compound, such as 200 g instead of 100 g. But then we have to change our masses of carbon and hydrogen to keep the mass percentages at 75% C and 25% H. The empirical formula still would remain the same because the mole ratio would not change.

$$\text{Mass percent of C} = \frac{x \text{ g}}{200 \text{ g}} \times 100\% = 75\% \text{ C}, x = 150 \text{ g C}$$

$$\text{Mass percent of H} = \frac{x \text{ g}}{200 \text{ g}} \times 100\% = 25\% \text{ H}, x = 50 \text{ g C}$$

$$(150 \text{ g C})\left(\frac{1 \text{ mol C}}{12.01 \text{ g C}}\right) = 12.490 \text{ mol C}$$

$$(50 \text{ g H})\left(\frac{1 \text{ mol H}}{1.008 \text{ g H}}\right) = 49.603 \text{ mol H}$$

$$\frac{12.490 \text{ mol C}}{12.490 \text{ mol}} = 1 \qquad \frac{49.603 \text{ mol H}}{12.490 \text{ mol}} = 4$$

The empirical formula is CH_4 as calculated before.

Practice Problem Set 2

1. A chemist performs a chemical reaction and produces 55.4 g of product. According to her calculations, she is supposed to get 63.5 g. What is her percent error?

2. What is the mass percent of each element in ammonia (NH_3)?

3. What is the mass percent of each element in the sugar glucose ($C_6H_{12}O_6$)?

4. A compound consists of 50.00% sulfur and 50.00% oxygen by mass. What is the empirical formula of this compound?

Practice Problem Set Solutions

Set 1

1. Remember, percents are out of 100; therefore, we just subtract the percent that is missing from 100.

$$100\% - 38\% = 62\% \text{ still remains}$$

2. 65.0% means 65 parts per 100 parts or $\frac{65.0}{100}$. You poured $\frac{65.0}{100}$ of your 16.0 oz of juice down the drain:

$$\left(\frac{65.0}{100}\right)(16.0 \text{ oz}) = \frac{(65.0 \times 16.0)\text{oz}}{100} = \frac{1040 \text{ oz}}{100} = 10.4 \text{ oz down drain}$$

Since you started with 16.0 oz and poured out 10.4 oz, the amount of juice remaining in the glass is 16.0 oz − 10.4 oz = 5.6 oz juice remains.

3. 40% also can be written as $\dfrac{40}{100}$. $\dfrac{40}{100} \times \$69.99 = \$28.00$.

This means that you can take $28.00 off the original price of $69.99. The shoes would cost you: $69.99 − $28.00 = $41.99.

Set 2

1. The measured value is 55.4 g of product. The actual value (or theoretical value) is 63.5 g.

$$\% \text{ Error} = \frac{|55.4 - 63.5|}{63.5} \times 100\%$$

$$\% \text{ Error} = 13\ \%$$

2. Mass percent of N $= \dfrac{\text{mass of N in 1 mol NH}_3}{\text{mass of 1 mol of NH}_3} \times 100\%$

   Mass percent of H $= \dfrac{\text{mass of H in 1 mol NH}_3}{\text{mass of 1 mol of NH}_3} \times 100\%$

   Mass of N in 1 mol of $NH_3 = 1\ \text{mol} \times \dfrac{14.01\ \text{g}}{\text{mol}} = 14.01\ \text{g N}$

   Mass of H in 1 mol of $NH_3 = 3\ \text{mol} \times \dfrac{1.008\ \text{g}}{\text{mol}} = 3.024\ \text{g H}$

   Mass of 1 mol $NH_3 = 1(14.01\ \text{g/mol}) + 3(1.008\ \text{g/mol}) = 17.034\ \text{g/mol}$

   Mass percent of N $= \dfrac{14.01\ \text{g}}{17.034\ \text{g}} \times 100\% = 82.25\%\ \text{N}$

   Mass percent of H $= \dfrac{3.024\ \text{g}}{17.034\ \text{g}} \times 100\% = 17.75\%\ \text{H}$

   Check work:
   $$\begin{array}{r} 82.25\% \\ + \ 17.75\% \\ \hline 100.00\% \end{array}$$

3. Mass percent of C $= \dfrac{\text{mass of C in 1 mol C}_6\text{H}_{12}\text{O}_6}{\text{mass of 1 mol of C}_6\text{H}_{12}\text{O}_6} \times 100\%$

   Mass percent of H $= \dfrac{\text{mass of H in 1 mol C}_6\text{H}_{12}\text{O}_6}{\text{mass of 1 mol of C}_6\text{H}_{12}\text{O}_6} \times 100\%$

$$\text{Mass percent of O} = \frac{\text{mass of O in 1 mol } C_6H_{12}O_6}{\text{mass of 1 mol of } C_6H_{12}O_6} \times 100\%$$

$$\text{Mass of C in 1 mol of } C_6H_{12}O_6 = 6 \text{ mol} \times \frac{12.01 \text{ g}}{\text{mol}} = 72.06 \text{ g C}$$

$$\text{Mass of H in 1 mol of } C_6H_{12}O_6 = 12 \text{ mol} \times \frac{1.008 \text{ g}}{\text{mol}} = 12.096 \text{ g H}$$

$$\text{Mass of O in 1 mol of } C_6H_{12}O_6 = 6 \text{ mol} \times \frac{16.00 \text{ g}}{\text{mol}} = 96.00 \text{ g O}$$

$$\text{Mass of 1 mol } C_6H_{12}O_6 = 6(12.01 \text{ g/mol}) + 12(1.008 \text{ g/mol}) + 6(16.00 \text{ g/mol}) = 180.156 \text{ g/mol}$$

$$\text{Mass percent of C} = \frac{72.06 \text{ g C}}{180.156 \text{ g}} \times 100\% = 40.00\% \text{ C}$$

$$\text{Mass percent of H} = \frac{12.096 \text{ g H}}{180.156 \text{ g}} \times 100\% = 6.71\% \text{ H}$$

$$\text{Mass percent of O} = \frac{96.00 \text{ g O}}{180.156 \text{ g}} \times 100\% = 53.29\% \text{ O}$$

4. Assume 100 g of compound; therefore, there are 50.00 g of sulfur and 50.00 g of oxygen present.

$$(50.00 \text{ g S})\left(\frac{1 \text{ mol S}}{32.07 \text{ g S}}\right) = 1.559 \text{ mol S}$$

$$(50.00 \text{ g O})\left(\frac{1 \text{ mol O}}{16.00 \text{ g O}}\right) = 3.125 \text{ mol O}$$

$$\frac{1.559 \text{ mol S}}{1.559 \text{ mol}} = 1 \qquad \frac{3.125 \text{ mol O}}{1.559 \text{ mol}} = 2$$

The empirical formula is SO_2.

Name _____ Section _____ Date _____

Percent Worksheet

1. Which of the following pictures accurately shows 75% of the square shaded?

   a.    b.   c.

   d.   e.

2. Your thirsty friend drinks 33% of a full pitcher of lemonade. Which drawing best represents the amount of lemonade remaining in the pitcher?

3. If you eat $\frac{1}{2}$ of your candy bar, what percent of the candy bar is missing?

4. If $\frac{1}{4}$ of your clothes have been unpacked from your suitcase, what percent has been unpacked?

5. What percent of the clothes in Exercise 4 still needs to be unpacked?

6. If $\frac{3}{7}$ of a room has been painted, what percent of the room still needs to be completed?

7. You earn 45 points on a math quiz that is out of 60 maximum points. What percent of points did you get correct on the quiz?

8. The maximum number of points possible on an exam is 80 points. You got 90% of the problems correct. How many points did you earn on the exam?

9. What is 65% of 200?

10. What is 42% of 75?

11. You use 12.5% of an 8-cup bag of sugar to make cookies. How many cups of sugar still remain in the bag?

12. You take 2 aspirin tablets from an unopened bottle to relieve your headache. Then 95% of the tablets still remain. What was the total number of tablets originally in the bottle?

13. A new backpack costs $42.00 but is on discount for 20% off the original price. How much money would you save with the discount?

14. A new winter coat is on sale for 35% off the original price of $75.00. What is the reduced price of the coat?

15. You make a purchase that totals $22.50, but you used a 10% off coupon first. What was the original price of your purchase?

16. A student measured the height of a book as 10.2 inches. The actual height of the book is 11.0 inches. What is the student's percent error?

17. A chemist performs a reaction between silver nitrate and sodium chloride to produce solid silver chloride. According to her calculations, 25.3 g of silver chloride should be produced, yet she has a percent error of 14% (and she was under the desired amount). How many grams of silver chloride did the chemist actually produce?

18. Chalk is made up of a chemical called calcium carbonate ($CaCO_3$). The percent composition of calcium carbonate consists of 40.04% calcium and 12.00% carbon. What is the percent composition of oxygen in calcium carbonate?

19. What is the mass percent of each element in nitrogen monoxide (NO)?

20. What is the mass percent of each element in carbon dioxide (CO_2)?

21. Determine the percent composition of magnesium sulfate ($MgSO_4$).

22. Determine the percent composition of calcium nitrate [$Ca(NO_3)_2$].

23. What is the mass percent of each element in barium phosphate [$Ba_3(PO_4)_2$]?

24. A compound is composed of 14.8% phosphorus and 85.2% chlorine by mass. What is the empirical formula of this compound?

25. Determine the empirical formula of a compound that contains 66.75% copper and 10.84% phosphorus by mass. The remaining percent composition of the compound consists of oxygen.

Answers to Percent Worksheet

1. e
2. b
3. 50%
4. 25%
5. 75%
6. 57.1%
7. 75%
8. 72 points
9. 130
10. 31.5
11. 7 cups
12. 40 tablets
13. $8.40
14. $48.75
15. $25.00
16. 7%
17. 21.8 g
18. 47.96% O
19. 46.68% N; 53.32% O
20. 27.29% C; 72.71% O
21. 20.19% Mg; 26.64% S; 53.16% O
22. 24.42% Ca; 17.07% N; 58.50% O
23. 68.44% Ba; 10.29% P; 21.27% O
24. PCl_5
25. Cu_3PO_4

Scientific Notation

In chemistry, representing data and results in scientific notation is important because we often work with very large measurements or very small measurements. Using scientific notation is helpful beyond the chemistry classroom. For example, let's imagine that we just won the lottery valued at $252 million ($252,000,000.00)! Now, in order to legally accept our prize, we must pay taxes on this amount, estimated at 32%. We then decide to purchase a house for a price of $350,000 and a car at $81,200. We also travel on a few lavish vacations valued at $43,893. How much money do we have left over? Since we are working with such large numbers, scientific notation would be helpful in our calculations.

Scientific notation represents very large or very small numbers as a product of a number between 1 and 10 and a power of 10. Using scientific notation allows us to make these numbers more compact to write. Scientific notation also shows clearly which numbers are significant, which is very important when making measurements. Another name for scientific notation is *exponential notation*.

The rules for converting a number to scientific notation are

1. Move the decimal point so that the original number is now a number between 1 and 10. If the number does not show a decimal point (because it is a whole number), recall that it is at the far right of the number.

583 is equivalent to 583.

Move the decimal point so that the number is between 1 and 10.

583.

2. For every place that we move the decimal point to the left, we must multiply by 10 to keep the number at its original magnitude. In this example, we moved the decimal point two places; therefore, we must multiply this number by 10^2 to keep the number as 583.

$$5.83 \times 10^2 = 583$$

Whenever we move the decimal point to the left, the power of 10 gets *larger* and more *positive* (left → larger).

3. For every place that we move the decimal point to the right, we must multiply by 10^{-1} (or 0.1) to keep the number at its original magnitude.

0.0583	(convert to a number between 1 and 10)
5.83	(moved two decimal places to the right)

$$5.83 \times 10^{-2}$$

Whenever we move the decimal point to the right, the power of 10 *reduces* and becomes more *negative* (right → reduce).

As long as we follow these three rules carefully, we can convert any number to scientific notation! Let's practice by doing some examples.

Example 1   A fast-food chain has served 436,000,000 customers since its inception. Express this number in scientific notation.

Solution

The first step is to convert this number to a number between 1 and 10.

$$436000000.$$

The decimal point must be moved eight places to the left; therefore, we multiply this new number by 10^8 to keep the original magnitude.

$$436000000 = 4.36 \times 10^8$$

Example 2   On average, a dust mite on a pillow is only 250 microns in size. This is equivalent to 0.000250 m (which is why we cannot see them with our naked eye!). Express this number in scientific notation (in meters).

Solution

Convert this number to a number between 1 and 10.

$$0.000250$$

The decimal point must be moved four places to the right; therefore, we multiply this new number by 10^{-4} to keep the original magnitude.

$$0.000250 = 2.50 \times 10^{-4} \text{ m}$$

Example 3   A car weighs 2.35×10^3 lb. Write this weight as an "ordinary" decimal number.

Solution

This problem requires us to work backwards from our previous examples of converting to scientific notation. When a number is multiplied by a factor of 10 that is positive, this means the number as a whole is large. 10^3 is equivalent to 1000! Therefore, we are multiplying 2.35 × 1000. Instead of doing the multiplication, we can simply move the decimal place three places to the right.

2.35

A zero must go in the missing place at the end to hold the spot because the number is multiplied by 1000, not 100.

$$2.350 = 2350 \text{ lb}$$

Practice Problem Set

1. Represent the following measurements in standard scientific notation.

   a. 961 lb

   b. 63340 ft

   c. 78000000 mm

   d. 602000000000000000000000 atoms

2. Convert the following numbers to standard scientific notation.

   a. 0.0046

   b. 0.00005823

   c. 0.0000009

   d. 0.000000000000165

3. Express the following quantities as an "ordinary" decimal number.

   a. 8.49×10^2 cm

   b. 1.225×10^{-3} kg

   c. 5.0×10^8 ms

   d. 7.1221×10^{-15} mi

4. The mass of the Earth is 5.98×10^{24} kg. Express this mass as an "ordinary" decimal number.

5. The mass of one nitrogen atom is 0.00000000000000000000002326 g. Express this mass in standard scientific notation.

Practice Problem Set Solutions

1. Move the decimal place to the left so that each number is between 1 and 10. Keep track of the number of places moved because that represents the power of 10 each number is multiplied by.

   a. $96\underline{1}. = 9.61 \times 10^2$ lb

   b. $6\underline{3340}. = 6.334 \times 10^4$ ft

   c. $7\underline{8000000}. = 7.8 \times 10^7$ mm

   d. $6\underline{02000000000000000000000}. = 6.02 \times 10^{23}$ atoms

2. Move the decimal point to the right so that each number is between 1 and 10. Keep track of the number of places moved because that represents the power of 10^{-1} (0.1) each number is multiplied by.

   a. $0.\underline{004}6 = 4.6 \times 10^{-3}$

   b. $0.\underline{00005}823 = 5.823 \times 10^{-5}$

   c. $0.\underline{0000009} = 9 \times 10^{-7}$

   d. $0.\underline{000000000000}165 = 1.65 \times 10^{-13}$

3. If the power of 10 is positive (or large), move the decimal place to the right. If the power of 10 is negative, move the decimal place to the left. In both cases, fill in zeros as necessary placeholders.

   a. $8.\underline{49} \times 10^2 = 849$ cm

   b. $\underline{00}1.225 \times 10^{-3} = 0.001225$ kg

   c. $5.\underline{00000000} \times 10^8 = 500000000$ ms

   d. $\underline{000000000000007}.221 \times 10^{-15} = 0.000000000000007221$ mi

4. The power of 10 is positive so move the decimal place to the right 24 places.

$$598000000000000000000000000 \text{ kg}$$

5. Move the decimal point 23 places to the right so that the number is between 1 and 10.

$$2.326 \times 10^{-23} \text{ g}$$

Scientific Notation Worksheet

1. If 2397 is written in scientific notation, will the exponent of 10 be positive or negative?

2. If 1,490,000 is written in scientific notation, will the exponent of 10 be positive or negative?

3. If 0.00391 is written in scientific notation, will the exponent of 10 be positive or negative?

4. If 59.42×10^1 is written in scientific notation, will the exponent of 10 be positive or negative?

5. If 0.0000000596×10^5 is written in scientific notation, will the exponent of 10 be positive or negative?

Write each of the following numbers in scientific notation.

6. 10,400

7. 87

8. 5,908,000,000,000

9. 0.022

10. 0.00006

11. 0.00000000431

12. 0.00592

13. 6,980,000

14. 0.12

15. 49682×10^3

16. 1.66×10^{-5}

17. 0.000341×10^9

18. To sail around the world, a person must sail a distance of at least 21,600 miles. Represent this number in scientific notation.

19. At a given point in time, the distance between the Earth and Mars is 55,000,000 kilometers. What is this value expressed in scientific notation?

20. The size of a human hair is about 200 microns, or 0.0002 m. What is the value of this measurement (in meters) represented in scientific notation?

Express each of the following as an "ordinary" decimal number.

21. 1.0×10^{-8}

22. 2.372×10^{-4}

23. 9.8×10^{5}

24. 908×10^{2}

25. 16.4×10^{-4}

Answers to Scientific Notation Worksheet

1. Positive (10^3)
2. Positive (10^6)
3. Negative (10^{-3})
4. Positive (10^2)
5. Negative (10^{-3})
6. 1.04×10^4
7. 8.7×10^1
8. 5.908×10^{12}
9. 2.2×10^{-2}
10. 6×10^{-5}
11. 4.31×10^{-9}
12. 5.92×10^{-3}
13. 6.98×10^6
14. 1.2×10^{-1}
15. 4.9682×10^7
16. 1.66×10^{-5}
17. 3.41×10^5
18. 2.16×10^4 mi
19. 5.5×10^7 km
20. 2×10^{-4} m
21. 0.00000001
22. 0.0002372
23. 980000
24. 90800
25. 0.00164

Significant Figures

Understanding and using significant figures for measurements and calculations in chemistry can be a source of frustration for many students. Why are significant figures so important in science and the real world? They help us to determine the degree of uncertainty in a measurement. For example, if we plan to build a tree house in an oak tree, it is important to make the most exact measurements possible. We must record our measurements to as many decimal places as the tape measure allows. If we make general estimations with our measurements, these errors could compound as we put the tree house together. We could end up with a very poorly made tree house that is unsafe to play in!

By using significant figures, we can determine the degree of uncertainty, even after several calculations. Significant figures are also referred to as *significant digits*.

The rules for counting significant figures and determining them in calculations are listed in Section 5.2 of your text (and listed below). The purpose of this handout is to elaborate on each rule and do practice problems to further develop our understanding of this concept.

Rule 1:   *Nonzero integers*. Nonzero integers *always* count as significant figures.

Example 1   The distance between San Diego, California, and Charlotte, North Carolina, is 2387 miles. State the number of significant figures for this distance.

Solution

The distance contains four significant figures. All the numbers in the distance measurement are nonzero integers; therefore, they are all counted as significant.

Rule 2:   *Zeros*. There are three classes of zeros:

A. *Leading zeros* are zeros that *precede* all of the nonzero digits. They *never* count as significant figures.

Example 2   A bug weighs only 0.0000046 lb. State the number of significant figures for this measurement.

Solution

The measurement contains two significant figures. The five zeros to the right of the decimal point do not count as significant figures. They only indicate the position of the decimal point. The 4 and the 6 are significant.

B. *Captive zeros* are zeros that fall *between* nonzero digits. They *always* count as significant figures.

Example 3 There are 2.2046 lb in 1 kilogram. State the number of significant figures for the measurement stated in pounds.

Solution

The measurement contains five significant figures. The zero in between the 2 and 4 in 2.2046 is significant and an important place holder in the measurement.

C. *Trailing zeros* are zeros at the *right end* of the number. They are significant only if the number is written with a decimal point.

Example 4 There are 95 tortilla chips in an average bag with a mass of 390. g. State the number of significant figures for the mass measurement.

Solution

The 390. g contain three significant figures because the measurement contains a trailing zero with a decimal point. The 0 is the uncertain digit.

<u>Rule 3</u>: *Exact numbers.* Often calculations involve numbers that were not obtained using measuring devices but were determined by counting. These numbers are called *exact numbers*. They can be assumed to have an unlimited number of significant figures. For example, the 95 tortilla chips stated in Example 4 is an exact number. Exact numbers also can arise from definitions. For example, 1 inch is defined as *exactly* 2.54 centimeters. Thus, in the statement 1 in. = 2.54 cm, neither 2.54 nor 1 limits the number of significant figures when it is used in a calculation.

Example 5 List three examples of numbers that are considered to be exact.

Solution

(Choose examples that require counting, not measuring devices.)

There are 5 pretzels in the bag.

The bowl contained 16 pieces of candy.

The student wrote his name on the chalkboard 25 times.

Scientific Notation. Rules 1–3 also apply to numbers written in scientific notation. Look at the number between 1 and 10 to determine the number of significant figures.

Example 6 A car weighing 2.605×10^3 lb has traveled 1.5×10^5 miles since it was first manufactured. How many significant figures do each of these measurements contain?

Solution

2.605×10^3 lb contains four significant figures because the number between 1 and 10 contains three nonzero integers with one captive zero in between.

1.5×10^5 miles contains two significant figures because the number between 1 and 10 contains two nonzero integers.

Practice Problem Set 1

1. State the number of significant figures for each of the following measurements.

   a. 7.83 m

   b. 150 lb

   c. 0.22198 kg

2. State the number of significant figures for each of the following measurements.

   a. 0.000119 km

   b. 250,000 mL

   c. 0.008006 mol

3. Indicate the number of significant figures in each of the following.

   a. 5.440×10^{10} nm

   b. 3600 s = 1 hr

   c. 0.00320×10^{-4} kg

Counting Significant Figures in Calculations

The next step in working with significant figures is to understand how to determine them in calculations. These rules are listed in Section 5.2 of your text.

For *multiplication* or *division*:   The number of significant figures in the result is the same as that in the measurement with the smallest number of significant figures. The smallest number limits the number of significant figures in the result (it is the measurement with the greatest degree of uncertainty).

Example 7   Calculate the answer to the following expression, and record the result to the correct number of significant figures.

$$\frac{75.3}{4.9} = ?$$

Solution

When we perform the calculation in our calculator, we get 15.36734694 as the result. As written, this result has 10 digits! Unfortunately, neither value in the expression contains this many significant figures. To express the result correctly, we must do the following:

1. Determine how many significant figures the final result must have. The measurement with the smallest number of significant figures dictates the number of significant figures in the result. In this case, the number of significant figures is two.

3 sig figs

↓

$$\frac{75.3}{4.9} = 15.36734694$$

↑

2 sig figs   (Final result needs to be recorded

to 2 sig figs.)

2. Once we determine the number of significant figures for the result, we have to figure out how the result should be rounded off. In this case, the first digit to be removed is 3 (to record the result to two significant figures). If the digit to be removed is less than 5, the preceding digit stays the same. If the digit to be removed is equal to or greater than 5, the preceding digit is increased by 1. Since 3 is less than 5, the 5 in the number 15 will remain the same. Therefore, the final answer is 15:

$$\frac{75.3}{4.9} = 15$$

For *addition* or *subtraction*:   The limiting term is the one with the smallest number of decimal places.

Example 8   Calculate the answer to the following expression, and record the result to the correct number of significant figures.

$$8.96 + 12.4 + 6.03 = ?$$

Solution

When performing addition or subtraction operations, the best way to determine the number of significant figures for the final result is to line up the measurements vertically (like we are going to add the values using the long-hand method instead of using the calculator).

$$\begin{array}{r} 8.96 \\ 12.4 \\ + \ 6.03 \\ \hline 27.39 \end{array}$$

As written now, the number of significant digits in the final answer is four. But the limiting term is the measurement with the smallest number of decimal places. The value of 12.4 is to the tenths place; therefore, the final result *must be* reported to the tenths place.

$$\begin{array}{r} 8.9|6 \\ 12.4| \\ + \ 6.0|3 \\ \hline 27.3|9 \\ \uparrow \end{array}$$

(Final result must be recorded

to the tenths place.)

Since the first digit to be removed is a 9, the preceding digit 3 is increased by 1 (since 9 is greater than 5). The final result contains three significant figures.

$$8.96 + 12.4 + 6.03 = 27.4$$

In summary, for multiplication and division, significant figures are counted. For addition and subtraction, the decimal places are counted.

Practice Problem Set 2

1. Without performing the calculations, tell how many significant figures each answer should contain.

   a. 100.1×3.7

   b. $6.917 - 2.8849$

   c. $2000 \div 4.58$

2. Calculate the answer to each expression, and record each result to the correct number of significant figures.

   a. $2188 - 314.7$

   b. 0.000890×15.75

   c. The total length of 5 cars lined up in a row at 4.35 m per car.

3. Calculate the answer to each expression, and record each result to the correct number of significant figures.

    a. 100×20

    b. $0.00662 + 14.1$

    c. $(6.039 \times 10^3) \div (7.1 \times 10^{-2})$

Counting Significant Figures in Multiple-Step Calculations

The final step to understanding significant figures is determining the number of significant figures in a result that requires more than one mathematical operation. As your text states, in a series of calculations, carry the extra digits through to the final result and *then* round off. Therefore, all of the digits that show on your calculator should be carried over and *not* rounded off until the final answer is obtained. But keep track of significant figures throughout each step of the calculation even though the digits are not rounded until the end.

Example 9   Solve the following mathematical expression, and record the result to the correct number of significant figures.

$$(5.761) \times (8.93 \times 10^{-2}) \div 1.2 = ?$$

Solution

The first mathematical operation to calculate is $(5.761) \times (8.93 \times 10^{-2}) = 0.5144573$. All of the digits in our calculators should remain, although we will determine the number of significant figures for this step.

$$(5.761) \times (8.93 \times 10^{-2})$$

$$\uparrow \qquad\qquad \uparrow$$

4 sig figs   3 sig figs

The least precise measurement in this operation contains three significant figures, so the "intermediate" answer would be to three significant figures as well (but we still must keep all of the digits in the calculator!).

The next mathematical operation is to divide the "intermediate" answer by 1.2.

$$\frac{0.5144573}{1.2} = 0.428714417$$

Since this is the final step, we record this answer to the correct number of significant figures. Remember, the value in the numerator (our "intermediate" answer) technically contains three significant figures. The denominator contains two significant figures. The denominator is the least precise measurement; therefore, the final answer is reported to two significant figures.

"Intermediate" answer reported to 3 sig figs $\Rightarrow$ 0.514.

$\downarrow$

$$\frac{0.5144573}{1.2} = 0.43$$

$\uparrow$ $\uparrow$

2 sig figs   (Final result needs to be recorded to 2 sig figs.)

Example 10   Solve the following mathematical expression, and record the result to the correct number of significant figures.

$$12.94 - (1.62 \times 4.9) = ?$$

Solution

The first mathematical operation to perform is the one containing the parentheses.

$$(1.62 \times 4.9) = 7.938$$

Again, all the digits in our calculator must remain, although the number of significant figures should be determined.

$$(1.62 \times 4.9) = 7.9 \leftarrow \text{"intermediate" answer}$$

$\uparrow$ $\uparrow$

3 sig figs   2 sig figs

The next and final operation is to add 12.94 to the answer calculated above.

$$
\begin{array}{r}
12.94 \\
+ \ 7.938 \\
\hline
20.878
\end{array}
$$

To determine the number of significant figures for the final answer, take into account the number of decimal places for each added number. The number with the fewest number of decimal places determines the number of decimal places for the final answer (and thus the number of significant figures).

$$
\begin{array}{r}
12.9|4 \quad \leftarrow \text{ hundredths place} \\
+ \ 7.9| \quad \leftarrow \text{ tenths place; use "intermediate" answer to determine sig figs.} \\
\hline
20.8|78
\end{array}
$$

Since the least precise measurement is to the tenths place, the final answer is to the tenths place (and the 8 rounds up to 9 because the 7 is greater than 5).

$$20.878 \Rightarrow 20.9$$

Practice Problem Set 3

1. Without performing the calculation, state how many significant figures will be in the answer to the following expression.

$$9.7820 + 2.93 - 4.038$$

2. Carry out the following mathematical operations, and report each answer to the correct number of significant figures.

    a. $(2.07 \times 10^{-19}) \times (0.168 \times 10^{-18}) \div 14$

    b. $(0.0086 + 1.243) \times 1.31$

    c. $\dfrac{\left(3.81 \times 10^{-2}\right)\left(6.02 \times 10^{23}\right)}{\left(1.40 \times 10^{3}\right)}$

3. A student counted 150 cars parked in the high school parking lot. The average weight of each car is 1850 lb. Assuming that each car can hold 4 people, what is the total weight of all the cars (in pounds) when each car is filled to capacity? Assume that the average person weighs 165 lb. Report the answer to the correct number of significant figures.

Practice Problem Set Solutions

Set 1

1. a.   3 (all nonzero integers)

    b.   2 (two nonzero integers; one trailing zero with no decimal point does not count.)

    c.   5 (five nonzero integers)

2. a.   3 (three nonzero integers; leading zeros do not count.)

    b.   2 (two nonzero integers; four trailing zeros with no decimal point do not count.)

    c.   4 (two nonzero integers with two captive zeros; leading zeros do not count.)

3. a.   4 (three nonzero integers with a trailing zero with a decimal point)

    b.   Unlimited (exact numbers)

    c.   3 (two nonzero integers with one trailing zero with a decimal point; two leading zeros do not count.)

Set 2

1.

   a. $100.1 \times 3.7 \Rightarrow 2$ significant figures (second value is limiting)

        ↑   ↑

     4 sig figs   2 sig figs

   b. $6.917|$ ← thousandths place

      $- 2.884|9$ ← ten thousandths place

             $\Rightarrow$ 4 significant figures

              (First measurement limits the result to the thousandths place.)

   c. $2000 \div 4.58 \Rightarrow 1$ significant figure (first value is limiting)

       ↑   ↑

     1 sig fig   3 sig figs

2.

    a.   2188.| ← ones place; whole number

      - 314.|7   ← tenths place

       2502.|7 = 2503 (Least precise measurement is to the ones place;

                            round up to 3 because 7 is greater than 5.)

    b. $0.000890 \times 15.75 = 0.0140$ or 1.40×10^{-2} (3 sig figs; first value is limiting.)

            ↑   ↑

       3 sig figs   4 sig figs

    c. $5 \text{ cars} \times \dfrac{4.35 \text{ m}}{\text{car}} = 21.75 \text{ m} \Rightarrow 21.8 \text{ m}$ (3 sig figs; second value is limiting;

        ↑   ↑   round up to 8 because 5 is equal to 5.)

   exact number   3 sig figs

3.

    a. $100 \times 20 = 2000$ or 2×10^{3} (1 sig fig; both values are limiting;

       ↑   ↑   rounding remains at 2 because 0 is less than 5.)

     1 sig fig 1 sig fig

    b.   0.0|0662   ← one hundred thousandths place

      + 14.1| ← tenths place

       14.1|0662 ⇒ 14.1 (Least precise measurement is to the tenths place;

                         rounding remains at 1 because 0 is less than 5.)

    c. $\left(6.039 \times 10^{3}\right) \div \left(7.1 \times 10^{-2}\right) = 8.5056 \times 10^{4} \Rightarrow 8.5 \times 10^{4}$ (2 significant figures;

       ↑   ↑   second value is limiting;

     4 sig figs   2 sig figs   rounding remains at 5

                                            because 0 is less than 5.)

Set 3

1. For addition and subtraction, it is easiest to set the values up vertically (long-hand style) to determine the number of significant figures. The value with the least number of decimal places dictates the number of decimal places in the final answer.

$$9.78|20 \quad \leftarrow \text{ ten thousandths place}$$
$$2.93| \qquad \leftarrow \text{ hundredths place}$$
$$\underline{4.03|8} \qquad \leftarrow \text{ thousandths place}$$
$$\_ \cdot \_ \_ \qquad \text{(The final answer is to the hundredths place. The second value is limiting.)}$$

Since the final answer is to the hundredths place, there are three significant figures.

2. a. The answer to the first mathematical operation is

$$(2.07 \times 10^{-19}) \times (0.168 \times 10^{-18}) = 3.4776 \times 10^{-38}$$

Keep all the digits in the calculator, but keep track of the number of significant figures, which in this case is *three*.

The answer to the second mathematical operation is

"intermediate" answer reported to 3 sig figs $\Rightarrow 3.48 \times 10^{-38}$

$$\downarrow$$

$$\frac{\left(3.4776 \times 10^{-38}\right)}{14} = 2.484 \times 10^{-39} \Rightarrow 2.5 \times 10^{-39}$$

$$\uparrow \qquad\qquad\qquad\qquad\qquad \uparrow$$

2 sig figs $\qquad\qquad$ (Rounded up to 2 sig figs; denominator is limiting.)

b. The answer to the first mathematical operation is

$$0.008|6$$
$$\underline{+\ 1.243|}$$
$$1.251|6 \quad \text{(Keep all of the digits in calculator, but remember}$$
$$\text{that this answer only contains 4 sig figs.)}$$

The answer to the second mathematical operation is

$$1.2516 \ \times \ 1.31 \ = \ 1.639596 \Rightarrow 1.64$$
$$\uparrow \qquad\quad \uparrow \qquad\qquad\qquad\qquad \uparrow$$

really 4 sig figs $\quad$ 3 sig figs $\qquad\qquad$ (round up to 3 sig figs)

c. The answer to the first mathematical operation is

$$(3.81 \times 10^{-2}) \times (6.02 \times 10^{23}) = 2.29362 \times 10^{22}$$

Keep all the digits in the calculator, but keep track of the number of significant figures, which in this case is *three*.

The answer to the second mathematical operation is

"intermediate" answer reported to 3 sig figs $\Rightarrow 2.29 \times 10^{22}$

↓

$$\frac{\left(2.29362 \times 10^{22}\right)}{1.40 \times 10^3} = 1.6383 \times 10^{19} \Rightarrow 1.64 \times 10^{19}$$

↑   ↑

3 sig figs   (rounded up to 3 sig figs)

3. The total weight of one car filled to capacity is

$$1850 \text{ lb} + \left(4 \text{ persons} \times \frac{165 \text{ lb}}{\text{person}} \right) =$$

↑   ↑   ↑

3 sig figs   exact number   3 sig figs

$$1850 \text{ lb} + 660. \text{ lb}$$

↑   ↑

3 sig figs   3 sig figs

Rewrite:

$$\begin{array}{r} 1850 \\ + \ 660. \\ \hline 2510 \end{array}$$ ← precise to the tens place; least precise
← precise to the ones place
(The "intermediate" answer contains 3 sig figs.)

The total weight of all the cars is

$$150 \text{ cars} \times \frac{2510 \text{ lb}}{\text{car}} = 376500 \text{ lb} \Rightarrow 3.77 \times 10^5 \text{ lb}$$

↑   ↑   ↑

exact number   3 sig figs   (round up to 3 sig figs)

Name _____ Section _____ Date _____

Significant Figure Worksheet 1

1. Indicate the number of significant figures in each of the following.

   a. 11

   b. 0.4672

   c. 54803

2. Indicate the number of significant figures in each of the following.

   a. 9.96×10^{-5}

   b. 340,000

   c. 2.54 cm = 1 inch

3. Indicate the number of significant figures in each of the following.

   a. 800.

   b. 0.000000010001

   c. 8000.003

4. Jack climbed up 8 steps to reach the second floor of the building. State the number of significant figures for the value in the statement.

5. Susan rode her bike to the end of the block in 20.07 seconds. State the number of significant figures for the value in the statement.

6. The walk-a-thon fundraiser requires participants to walk 10 miles around a track. State the number of significant figures for the value in the statement.

7. Which of the following measurements contain two significant figures?

   a. 80.09 m

   b. 20 seconds

   c. 0.00040 cm

   d. 6.02×10^{23} molecules

   e. None of these

8. Which of the following contain three significant figures?

   a. 200

   b. 0.083

   c. 14.224

   d. 0.669×10^3

   e. None of these

9. State the number of significant figures for each of the following.

   a. 14.21×10^{10}

   b. 0.002080

   c. 800,400

10. Using zero as your reference point, how much liquid has left the buret? Use the correct number of significant figures.

   a. 20 mL

   b. 22 mL

   c. 22.0 mL

   d. 38 mL

   e. 38.0 mL

11. Round off each of the following values to three significant figures.

    a. 7.115

    b. 8953000

    c. 2.66832×10^{-14}

12. Round off each of the following values to two significant figures.

    a. 66.412

    b. 0.00809

    c. 300.

13. Round off each of the following values to one significant figure.

    a. 54,629

    b. 0.0037

    c. 25.4×10^{4}

14. Indicate which value has a greater number of significant figures in each of the following.

    a. 0.000392 versus 0.03000

    b. 2.691×10^{-4} versus 6.0200×10^{16}

    c. 8×10^{30} versus 80

15. Indicate which value has a greater number of significant figures in each of the following.

    a. 2910 versus 250,000

    b. 400. versus 330

    c. 25.76×10^{-3} versus 0.26105×10^{-3}

Significant Figure Worksheet 2

1. You take 20.0 mL of water from a graduated cylinder and add it to the beaker of water below. What is the new volume of water in the beaker?

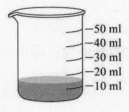

    a. 40 mL

    b. 40. mL

    c. 35 mL

    d. 35.0 mL

    e. 25.0 mL

2. Without doing the calculation, how many significant figures are in the following expression?

$$(2.01 \times 10^{-3}) \times (6.9 \times 10^{-2}) \div (8.930 \times 10^{5})$$

3. Without doing the calculation, how many significant figures are in the following expression?

$$256.09 - 50.8 + 2.768$$

4. Solve the following mathematical expression, and record the result to the correct number of significant figures.

$$5829.2 \div 8.1 \times 3.01 = ?$$

5. Solve the following mathematical expression, and record the result to the correct number of significant figures.

$$(4.861 - 1.22) \div (3.629 \times 10^{-2}) = ?$$

6. Carry out the following mathematical operation, and report the answer to the correct number of significant figures.

$$\frac{(8.223 \times 10^{12})(4.13 \times 10^{-6})}{1 \times 10^{4}} = ?$$

7. What is the answer to the following expression, including the correct number of significant figures?

$$(8.62 + 12.96 + 4.331 + 1.630) \times 1.9 = ?$$

8. Calculate the answer to the following expression, and report the answer to the correct number of significant figures.

$$(12.396 \div 4.61) - (1.72 \times 0.43) = ?$$

9. Calculate the answer to the following expression, and report the answer to the correct number of significant figures.

$$\frac{(5.769 \times 10^{-2})}{(8.3 \times 10^{-3})} + \frac{(4.1 \times 10^{-1})}{(12.8 \times 10^{-2})} = ?$$

10. A coach recorded the following heights (in inches) of each of the following players on the high school basketball team:

65.23

66.49

68.1

69.6

69.94

70.3

70.57

72.1

72.56

82.6

What is the average height (in inches) of a person on the team? Record your answer with the correct number of significant figures.

Answers to Significant Figures Worksheet 1

1. a. 2
   b. 4
   c. 5
2. a. 3
   b. 2
   c. Infinite (exact numbers)
3. a. 3
   b. 5
   c. 7
4. Infinite (exact number)
5. 4
6. 1
7. c
8. d
9. a. 4
   b. 4
   c. 4
10. c
11. a. 7.12
    b. 8950000 or 8.95×10^6
    c. 2.67×10^{-14}
12. a. 66
    b. 0.0081 or 8.1×10^{-3}
    c. 3.0×10^2
13. a. 50,000 or 5×10^4
    b. 0.004 or 4×10^{-3}
    c. 30×10^4 or 3×10^5
14. a. 0.03000
    b. 6.0200×10^{16}
    c. Both values contain the same number of significant figures.
15. a. 2910

b. 400.

c. 0.26105×10^{-3}

Answers to Significant Figures Worksheet 2

1. c
2. 2
3. 4
4. 2200 or 2.2×10^3
5. 100. or 1.00×10^2
6. 3000 or 3×10^3
7. 52
8. 1.95
9. 10.2
10. 70.7 inches

Section 2: Reading Concepts

This section supports foundational reading and study skills that students need in order to use their chemistry text effectively. Using examples taken directly from the Student Edition, this section covers topics such as active reading, making and using graphic organizers and outlines, and reading chemical symbols and math notation.

Contents

Introduction RC–1

Actively Reading Section 2.1: Teaching Notes RC–3

Actively Reading Section 2.1 .... RC–4

Active Reading Tips RC–16

Making Outlines RC–18

Making and Using Graphic Organizers RC–20

Reading Chemical Symbols RC–24

Making and Using Flashcards RC–25

Reading Math RC–27

Taking Notes RC–28

Reading Chemical Equations RC–30

Introduction

One of the most important skills students can learn in high school to prepare them for college and for life is how to read at a deep and critical level. Critically reading a textbook is a skill, and like any other skill, it requires practice and guidance.

We have written this supplement to help students learn how to become more active readers of their chemistry textbook. Most of this supplement consists of handouts for the students, with the exception of *Actively Reading Section 2.1*, which you can use a guide to help students understand what they should be doing as they are reading.

The assumed audience for these materials consists of students who need help getting information from the textbook, who want help in learning this skill, and who also will read the text. That is, these *Reading Concepts* are not meant as a replacement for the text but as a supplement to it.

While students come to school with various levels of science background, their skills in being able to work independently account for a great deal of the differences in their achievement. Knowing how to use the chemistry textbook greatly increases their chances of success in chemistry.

Most students are a bit afraid of their first chemistry course. They may have heard from older students that chemistry is hard. It is true that chemistry can be a challenging subject for many reasons. Chemists generally think about the microscopic world, whereas we live in a macroscopic world. Solving problems in chemistry often requires being adept at algebra. And, of course, chemistry has its own language of vocabulary and symbols. To understand chemistry, our students need to know and understand this vocabulary.

Many students may not be aware that there are different types and levels of reading. We often use the example of different types of novels when explaining this to our students. You may choose to read a particular novel purely for entertainment value, in which you do not really learn anything new about a group of people or a specific time in history. Such a novel is a "quick read" that you often will see people doing on the beach or on an airplane. However, you also may choose to read a novel that not only is pleasurable to read but also teaches you something. Perhaps you need to look up words that you have never seen before. You may stop reading at certain points and ask yourself questions about the novel and look for the answers as you continue to read. You even may find it helpful to seek out others who also have read the book and discuss it with them. You cannot read a book like this well while being distracted.

A textbook is like this second kind of novel. To read a textbook well, our students need to take an active role in the process. This includes asking questions as they read the text and thinking about the significance of what they have read. The students need to learn how to use the graphics to gather further information about the topic and to help them in making comparisons and connections with other material. There are also many example problems given throughout the text. It is important for students to read the explanations and problem-solving techniques that are provided instead of just jumping ahead to the answer.

Learning how to become an active reader takes time, patience, and practice. As with anything important, though, the struggle is worth the effort. We hope that you and your students find this supplement useful. Have a great year!

S.S.Z.
S.L.Z.
D.J.D.

Actively Reading Section 2.1: Teaching Notes

While it is important for our students to actively read the textbook, it is the rare student who understands how to do this. Fortunately, active reading is a skill that can be taught. One of the best ways to do this is to read along with the students and point out what they should be getting out of the reading, along with asking the types of questions we expect the students to be asking themselves as they read.

This section serves as a guide for reading Section 2.1 of *World of Chemistry* along with your students. It is written such that it can be a handout for your students, or it can be for your own use when discussing Section 2.1 with your students.

We suggest that you present this guide after the students have had a chance to read Section 2.1 on their own. Let them know that as they read they should consider two main questions:

"What are the main ideas the authors are getting across?"
"How could I summarize these ideas to someone else in my own words?"

Finally, tell the students not to be discouraged if it seems as though you are pointing out a lot of things that they did not think about as they read the section. Remind them that learning how to read a textbook actively takes time, patience, and practice.

Actively Reading Section 2.1

This section serves as a guide for learning how to read a textbook actively in a way that will bring the greatest understanding of the material. This section uses Section 2.1 of *World of Chemistry* as an example.

We suggest that you use this guide after you have had a chance to read Section 2.1 on your own. As you reread Section 2.1 using this guide, you should consider two main questions:

"What are the main ideas the authors are getting across?"
"How could I summarize these ideas to someone else in my own words?"

SECTION 2.1

A. The Particulate Nature of Matter

Matter, the "stuff" of which the universe is composed, has two characteristics: it has mass and it occupies space. Matter comes in a great variety of forms: the stars, the air that you are breathing, the gasoline that you put in your car, the chair on which you are sitting, the turkey in the sandwich you may have eaten for lunch, the tissues in your brain that allow you to read and understand this sentence, and so on.

This first paragraph from page 24 begins by stating that matter has many different forms. You may even realize that matter can be in a solid state (a chair), a liquid state (gasoline), or a gaseous state (air).

In addition to considering the main ideas, an active reader also will ask questions of the text. The text is like a teacher in that it provides information and explanations. However, when your classroom teacher says something, you have the opportunity to ask questions on points that you do not understand. The teacher then can provide information or a different way of thinking about the ideas. A printed textbook is not interactive in this way. However, you still should ask questions as they come to you, for example, by writing your questions in a notebook as you read.

Why ask questions when the text cannot hear you and respond?

First, by making yourself ask questions, you force yourself to read the text at a deeper level. This will make it more likely that you will get as much out of the text as you can.

Second, asking questions helps you to predict what will be coming next in the textbook. That is, ideas are often introduced in the text and then explained more fully as the text goes on. By developing a list of questions as you read about new ideas, you can look for answers in the paragraphs that come later. This makes you a more active reader and makes it more likely that you will understand the material.

Questions that may come to mind when you read the first part of Section 2.1 include

- If matter can take all these forms, what is not matter?

- Are different types of matter alike in any way?

The first question is not answered in the text, so you may write it in your notes and ask your teacher or classmates about it. Since it is stated that matter must have mass, you also may assume that heat and light are not matter. Is fire matter?

It turns out that the second question will be addressed in the next paragraph on page 24. It may not always be the case that you ask questions that are answered immediately, but it is nice when it happens. It lets you know that you are reading the textbook at a deep level and that you are asking important questions. Here is another selection from page 24 in the text:

> As we look around our world, we are impressed by the great diversity of matter. Given the many forms and types of matter, it seems difficult to believe that all matter is composed of a small number of fundamental particles. It is surprising that the fundamental building blocks in chocolate cake are very similar to the components of air.

We see that although forms of matter appear to be different, they are also very much alike. That is, they are made of the same types of "building blocks." As you read this passage, take a moment to think about how strange that last statement really is:

". . . the fundamental building blocks in chocolate cake are very similar to the components of air."

Did you agree with the authors' idea that this is "surprising"? To most people, it is not at all obvious that a slice of cake would have anything in common with air. This is one of the reasons that learning chemistry can be difficult, and it can be nice to know that you are not alone in finding some of this material strange.

Questions to consider at this point include

- What do we mean by "fundamental particles"?

- How do we know that these fundamental particles are similar?

You should be able to answer the first question from the material in the next selection, "The Atomic Nature of Matter." The second question is of the type you should ask generally. That is, when you are told something new, ask, "How do we know . . . ?" or "Why do we believe . . . ?" As it turns out, this question is addressed in the next paragraphs on page 24.

The Atomic Nature of Matter

How do we know that matter is composed of the tiny particles we call atoms? After all, they are far too small to be seen with the naked eye. It turns out that after literally thousands of years of speculation, we can finally "see" the atoms that are present in matter. In recent years scientists have developed a device called a scanning tunneling microscope (STM) that, although it works quite differently from an optical microscope, can produce images of atoms.

For example, look at the penny shown in **Figure 2.1.** The small objects represent tiny copper atoms. When chemists look at other metals with powerful microscopes, they see atoms in these substances as well. You can see an example of another metal in **Figure 2.2.**

> With ultra-high magnification, objects appear more similar. All objects are made up of small particles called atoms.

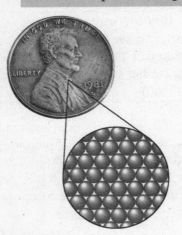

Figure 2.1
The surface of the copper penny is made of copper atoms represented as they would be seen through the lens of a very powerful electronic microscope.

Figure 2.2
A scanning tunneling microscope image of nickel metal. Each peak represents a nickel atom.

Make sure to answer the **Active Reading Question** provided on page 25:

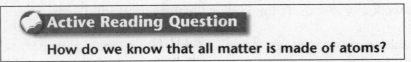

Active Reading Question

How do we know that all matter is made of atoms?

"How do we know that all matter is made of atoms?" It was not unreasonable to predict this question.

Notice the representation of copper atoms in Figure 2.1 and compare this with an actual penny. The atoms are drawn as circles (you can imagine them as spheres in three dimensions), and there are "holes" or spaces between the circles. But a penny feels perfectly solid, without holes. The macroscopic view and the microscopic view appear different. Figure 2.2 provides evidence, though, that the graphic in Figure 2.1 is a reasonable way to think about atoms, even if it appears to contradict how we see matter with our naked eyes.

All matter consists of tiny particles called atoms. But when you look at objects such as nails or pennies, you don't see these particles. Why not? The atoms are very tiny and can be seen only with a powerful magnifying instrument. You may have encountered the same concept in your life when you looked at a beach from a distance. The sand looks uniform—you can't see the separate particles. As you get close, however, the individual grains of sand become apparent. Observe the Impressionist painting by Seurat shown in the photo on the following page. From a distance the scene looks normal. Only when you stand very close to the painting do you see that it is composed of tiny dots of paint.

So, the conclusion is that although objects in the macroscopic world typically look quite continuous and uniform, they are really particulate in nature—they are made of atoms. We can "see" them with powerful electronic microscopes.

These paragraphs from page 24 provide a summary of what you have learned and also provide a way of thinking about how the microscopic can contradict the macroscopic. Are there any other examples besides a beach or Impressionist painting that you can think of to support this idea?

At this point you know that matter takes a variety of forms that look different but are similar at what can be called a "particulate level." As you know more, though, you learn that there are always more questions. Questions that you may be considering at this point include

- Are all atoms the same?

- Why are different forms of matter different?

We should expect to find the answers to these questions as we continue to read the next section, beginning on page 25 of your text.

B. Elements and Compounds

We have just considered the most important idea in chemistry: matter is composed of tiny particles we call **atoms**. If all matter is made up of tiny particles called atoms, are all atoms alike? That is, is copper metal made of the same kind of atoms as gold? The answer is no. Copper atoms and gold atoms are different. Scientists have learned that all matter is composed from about 100 different types of atoms. For example, air is mostly gaseous oxygen and nitrogen. The nitrogen atoms are different from the oxygen atoms, which in turn are different from copper atoms, which differ from gold atoms.

So are all atoms alike? The answer is "No." We do not know how they are different yet, but at least we do know that they are not alike. Can you predict how they could be different?

Note that there are not that many different types of atoms, given all the different types of matter that is made from them. You probably could name 100 different types of matter in the room you are sitting in (just look at the number of types of materials making up your shoes, for example). And yet all the matter of the world is made of only about 100 types of atoms—actually many fewer than 100!

You can think of the matter in the universe like the words in a book. If you break all the words in this book apart into their component letters, you will end up with "large piles" of only 26 letters. The English alphabet allows you to construct thousands of words from just 26 letters. Similarly, all the matter in the universe is constructed by putting approximately 100 types of atoms together in various ways. The different types of matter are like the different words in a book. When we separate all of the universe into its atoms, we find approximately 100 different atoms. We call these 100 types of atoms the *elements* of the universe.

To illustrate this idea, consider the letters A, D, and M. Using these letters you can make many words, such as MAD, DAM, DAD, and MADAM (can you think of others?). Each word represents something very different. Thus, with only three letters, you can represent several unique things or ideas.

The section of text shown above is from page 25 of your text. Note the new term *elements*. You probably are familiar with this term, but you may not know its precise definition in chemistry. What chemical elements can you name?

Earlier, the text used a beach and a painting as analogies to better understand macroscopic versus microscopic perspectives. Here, the text uses words and letters to represent matter and elements. When possible, it is helpful to use something you know to understand something new. Since you are familiar with making words from letters, use your understanding of how this process works if you later become confused about how atoms combine to form matter.

Compounds

In much the same way that we can use a few letters to make thousands of words, we can use a few types of atoms to construct all matter. For example, consider the atoms hydrogen, oxygen, and carbon:

Hydrogen   Oxygen   Carbon

Notice that we represent atoms by using spheres. We get this idea from the highly magnified pictures of metals that show the atoms. Notice in Figure 2.1 that atoms look like spheres.

In the selection above from page 26, note that the atoms have different sizes. While shown in black and white here, atoms in your textbook are represented with different colors. The sizes and colors of different atoms are consistent throughout the text (see the other graphics given in this section, for example). In this way, you can better visualize what is actually too small to visualize in real life.

> We can combine the hydrogen, oxygen, and carbon atoms in a variety of ways. Just as letters combine to form different words, atoms combine to form different compounds. **Compounds** are substances made by bonding atoms together in specific ways. These substances contain two or more different types of atoms bound together in a particular way. A specific compound consists of the same particles throughout. Table 2.1 shows some examples of atoms combined into compounds.

The selection from page 26 introduces the term *compound*. What do you know about compounds? What compounds can you name?

You are told that compounds must contain different types of atoms. What if the same types of atoms are bound together? Would this be called a compound as well?

Next, consider Table 2.1 on p. 26. There are at least two crucial ideas to learn from Table 2.1:

Table 2.1

Some Common Compounds

Atom Combinations	Name	Characteristics
	carbon monoxide	Carbon monoxide is a poisonous gas.
	carbon dioxide	You breathe out carbon dioxide as a waste material, and plants use carbon dioxide to make oxygen.
	water	Water is the most important liquid on Earth.
	hydrogen peroxide	Hydrogen peroxide is used to disinfect cuts and bleach hair.

1. It is possible make more than one compound from the same types of atoms. For example, carbon monoxide and carbon dioxide each consist only of carbon and oxygen atoms.

2. Different compounds made from the same types of atoms have very different characteristics. For example, water and hydrogen peroxide are each made of hydrogen and oxygen. Water is essential for life. Yet a water molecule with one more oxygen atom bonded in a specific way becomes a molecule of hydrogen peroxide, which is poisonous if you drink it.

Consider a glass of water. If you could magically travel inside the water and examine its individual parts, you would see particles consisting of two hydrogen atoms bonded to an oxygen atom:

We call this particle a molecule. A **molecule** is made up of atoms that are "stuck" together. A glass of water, for example, contains a huge number of molecules packed closely together (see **Figure 2.3**).

Figure 2.3
A glass of water contains millions of tiny water molecules packed closely together.

This selection is from page 26–27 of the text. We have a lot of terms introduced in the past few paragraphs: *element*, *atom*, *compound*, and *molecule*. The definitions of these terms are good to know. However, it is also important to have an image in your head of the differences among elements, compounds, atoms, and molecules. Pay attention to the graphics that show the differences among these terms.

Questions that may come to mind at this point include

- Are elements made up of atoms, or can they be made up of molecules too?

- Are compounds made up of atoms? of molecules? of either?

Look at Figure 2.3. Notice how the macroscopic (the water running out of the faucet) is linked to the microscopic (the water molecules). When you read chemistry, try to think in terms of atoms and molecules. When you are asked a question about a particular substance, ask yourself, "What does a really magnified view of this substance look like?" Not only will this help you to understand chemistry better, but it also will help when we get to solving mathematical problems dealing with chemical systems.

Consider this next selection from page 27.

Carbon dioxide is another example of a compound. For example, "dry ice"—solid carbon dioxide—contains molecules of the type ⬭ packed together as shown in **Figure 2.4.**

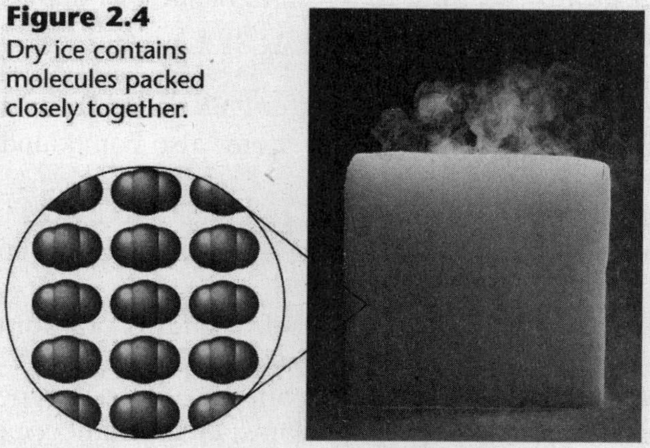

Figure 2.4
Dry ice contains molecules packed closely together.

Notice that the particles (molecules) in water are all the same. Likewise, all the molecules in dry ice are the same. However, the molecules in water differ from the molecules in dry ice. Water and carbon dioxide are different compounds.

Look at the molecules making up carbon dioxide. The text states that the particles in water are different from the particles in dry ice.

- How are they different?
- Are they similar at all?

They are similar because in both cases the molecules are made of different types of atoms, so they are both compounds. They are each made of two types of atoms, and the molecules of each are made of three atoms total.

They are different because a water molecule is made of two hydrogen atoms and one oxygen atom, and a carbon dioxide molecule is made of two carbon atoms, and one oxygen atom. There are two other major differences, which the figures show, but which have not been discussed yet in the text.

First, notice that the shapes of the molecules are different. For example, the carbon dioxide molecules can be called "linear" because the three atoms are in a straight line. The atoms in water are not in a straight line. Later in the text (Chapter 12) we will discuss this in more detail. However, a critical reader of the text should notice this and wonder, "Why is this true?" and "Does this explain any of the differences between water and dry ice?"

Second, dry ice is a solid, and water is a liquid. Notice how the molecules in the different samples are represented. The carbon dioxide molecules are much more orderly that the water molecules. Why would this be true? Is this what you might expect from what you know about the macroscopic difference between solids and liquids?

Elements

Just as hydrogen, oxygen, and carbon can form the compounds carbon dioxide and water, atoms of the same type can also combine with one another to form molecules. For example, hydrogen atoms can pair up ⬤⬤, as can oxygen atoms ⬤⬤. For reasons we will consider later, carbon atoms form much larger groups, leading to substances such as diamond, graphite, and buckminsterfullerene.

Now we can address a question that helps us to better understand the term *compound*. That is, "Are molecules that are made of the same types of atoms also compounds?"

Notice that only one type of atom (in this case, the carbon atom) makes up the three different substances. The arrangement of the atoms alters the characteristics of the substances.

Because pure hydrogen and oxygen each contains only one type of atom, the substances are called elemental substances or, more commonly, **elements**. Elements are substances that contain only one type of atom. For example, pure gold contains only gold atoms, elemental copper contains only copper atoms, and so on. Thus an element contains only one kind of atom; a sample of iron contains many atoms, but they are all iron atoms. Samples of certain pure elements do contain molecules; for example, hydrogen gas contains H—H (usually written H_2) molecules, and oxygen gas contains O—O (O_2) molecules. However, any pure sample of an element contains only atoms of that element, *never* any atoms of any other element. **Figure 2.5** shows examples of elements.

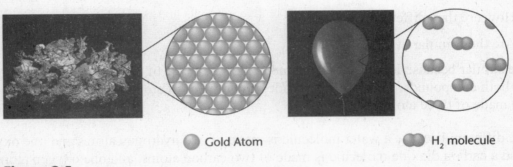

⬤ Gold Atom   ⬤⬤ H_2 molecule

Figure 2.5
Gold and hydrogen are both elements. Gold consists of gold atoms packed together as a solid. Hydrogen is an element that is composed of molecules of hydrogen, not single atoms.

So elements can be made of atoms or of molecules, as long as the molecules contain only the same kind of atoms. Note the use of subscripts. For example, oxygen can be written as O—O or O_2, in which the subscript 2 means there are 2 oxygen atoms bonded together. While learning chemistry, you are expected to learn how graphics, words, and symbols all can mean the same thing. This is why the illustrations in your text are so important.

A compound always contains atoms of different elements.

For example, water contains hydrogen atoms and oxygen atoms, and there are always exactly twice as many hydrogen atoms as oxygen atoms because water consists of H—O—H molecules. A different compound, carbon dioxide, consists of CO_2 molecules and so contains carbon atoms and oxygen atoms (always in the ratio 1:2).

A compound, although it contains more than one type of atom, always has the same composition—that is, the same combination of atoms.

The properties of a compound are typically very different from those of the elements it contains. For example, the properties of water are quite different from the properties of pure hydrogen and pure oxygen.

If water is H—O—H, did you realize that you also can use subscripts to write the formula for water as H_2O?

Make sure to answer the **Active Reading Question** on page 29:

Active Reading Question

Why are hydrogen molecules called "elements," but water molecules are called "compounds"?

Note that the formulas given in the passage from the text do not tell us about the properties of the substances. For example, while we can write water as H_2O, it is not like H_2 or O_2. Also, you have seen that hydrogen peroxide is made of two hydrogen atoms and two oxygen atoms, so we can write the formula H_2O_2. While H_2O and H_2O_2 are almost the same formula, water and hydrogen peroxide are very different chemicals.

C. The States of Matter

Water is one of the most familiar substances in our world. We recognize water in three different states: solid, liquid, and gas. If we lower the temperature of liquid water, it freezes—that is, it changes to ice (solid water). On the other hand, if we heat water to its boiling point, it "disappears" into the air as a gas.

The three states of water have distinctly different properties. If a pond freezes in the winter, you can walk across it. Solid water can support your weight. Conversely, you would never try to walk across the same pond in the summertime!

We can also highlight the differing properties of liquid and solid water with food coloring. A drop of food coloring placed on an ice cube just sits there on top of the ice. In contrast, a drop of food coloring placed in liquid water spreads throughout the liquid. The fact that the food coloring spreads in all directions in the liquid water indicates that the water molecules must be moving, bouncing the "food coloring molecules" around and keeping them suspended. This property is very different from that of ice, where the food coloring does not penetrate the surface. Also, we know that gaseous water is quite different from solid and liquid water because it is invisible to the naked eye, unlike the other states of water.

You already know that if you heat ice, it melts, and that you can boil water by heating it. Here are some questions you could be considering at this point:

- Why do ice, liquid water, and steam appear different from each other if they are all made of water molecules?

- What do you suppose microscopic views of ice, liquid water, and steam look like?

- How are the microscopic views the same, and how are they different?

- How does your knowledge of atoms and molecules help you to explain the differences in solid, liquid, and gaseous water?

> Like water, all substances exist in the *three states of matter:* solid, liquid, and gas. A **solid** is rigid. It has a fixed shape and volume. A **liquid** has a definite volume but takes the shape of its container (see **Figure 2.7**). A **gas** has no fixed volume or shape. It uniformly fills any container.
>
>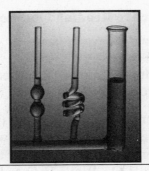
>
> **Figure 2.7**
> Liquid water takes the shape of its container.

It is good to know these definitions, but as you know by now, it is also helpful to visualize the particles. If you have not done so already, draw a microscopic view showing the differences among solids, liquids, and gases (use water as your example). You should expect to see a discussion of these in the text, but it is better if you think about them first, before an answer is given. The more you do this, the better you will understand what you read.

Answer the **Active Reading Question** on page 29:

Active Reading Question

What happens to food coloring when we add it to water? How do our observations support the idea that water is made up of moving molecules?

Not only is water, for example, made of particles that we cannot see, but the particles also are moving, which we also cannot see. This is one reason chemistry is difficult—it cannot always be seen. And this is why taking a molecular view early is so important. Never stop having pictures of atoms and molecules in your head as you read the text or work on questions and problems.

Go back through this discussion and see which questions that have been asked also have been answered. Think about questions that we cannot answer yet, such as

- What holds atoms together in a molecule?

- What holds molecules together in a liquid or solid?

It turns out that the answers to these two questions will come much later in the text. But there is no harm in thinking about them now. The more you are able to develop questions, the better you are reading the text, and the more deeply you will understand the material.

Active Reading Tips

Before You Read

It is a good idea to relate what you already know to what you are going to learn. To help in this, spend some time looking through the chapter before you begin reading each section. Here is a list of what you can do to get the most out of the textbook:

- Begin by reading the chapter title page. Read through the section and subsection titles in the **Looking Ahead** box to see if they sound familiar.

- Read the feature titled, **In Your Life.** This section explains how what you will learn in the chapter relates to your life. Many times (as in Chapter 2, for example) it will contain a few questions that you should consider.

- Read and answer the **Prereading Questions** that are located on the same page as the **In Your Life** feature. Answer these questions to the best of your ability, using what you already know. Learning requires that you start with what you already know and expand it into something new.

- Skim through the chapter and pay attention to the graphs, figures, and photos. Get an idea of what you will be learning about in the chapter.

- Look at the list of **Key Terms** at the end of the chapter (before the exercises at the end of the chapters).

As You Read

Learning how to become an active reader takes time, patience, and practice. Two questions you always should be thinking about as you read are:

- Can I state the main idea in the passage?

- Could I explain what I have read to someone else without looking at the text?

If your answer to either of these questions is "No," you should reread the passage and try again. If you continue to have difficulty understanding the material, talk with your teacher about that particular section.

The following list is a guide to specific activities that you can do that will make sure you are reading your textbook actively:

- Answer the **Active Reading Questions.** Answering these questions should help you understand the material better. These questions are written in a style that models the kind of questions you can ask yourself about the material if you are reading actively.

- Answer the **Critical Thinking Questions** provided throughout the text.

- Think of your own questions while reading. Write your questions in a notebook, and work with your teacher or others in your class to find the answers to these questions.

- Confirm that you can explain what the charts and figures tell you. Make sure that you understand how they are consistent with what is stated in the text.

- Try to work the example problems on your own before you look at the solutions. When you do look at the solutions to example problems, make sure that all the steps make sense to you.

- Take notes as you read and work problems. Use words, pictures, symbols, or other methods that will help you understand and recall what you have read.

After You Read

Once you have read a section in the text, it is important to test your understanding of the section material. Use the following list as a guideline of what to do after reading each section:

- Read through your notes. Add anything that you may have missed that you now realize is important once you have finished the entire section.

- Answer the **Section Review Questions** at the end of the section.

- Answer any **Assessment** exercises that your teacher has assigned for the section. Check your understanding of the exercises by referring to the answer section in the back of the book for the exercises that are numbered in blue.

- Summarize what you have read in your own words. You can write a paragraph, make an outline, or make a concept map.

- Get together with some classmates and discuss the reading.

A Note about Active Learning

Learning chemistry is not a passive event in which you simply absorb facts given by your teacher like a sponge absorbs water. Learning chemistry requires you to take an active role. You are provided with many resources (including your teacher and your textbook), but ultimately, you bear the responsibility for learning chemistry and making it your own. To do this, you must go beyond simple memorization of facts to a deeper understanding of the concepts of chemistry. Two methods that can help include

- Constantly ask questions. This includes while you are reading the textbook, listening to your teacher, performing a laboratory experiment, doing homework problems, reviewing your notes, or studying with classmates. The key is that you consistently ask "Why?" and "What does this mean?"

- It turns out that one of the best ways to find out if you truly understand a concept is whether or not you can explain it clearly to your peers. Take turns "teaching" concepts in your study group, or try to teach someone else what you have learned. Teaching is one of the best ways to learn.

Making Outlines

An outline is a good way to organize the main ideas of what you have read. The outline is not meant to be a complete representation of everything you have read. Instead, it is a summary of the main points. The outline

- Should contain all the main ideas of the material you are outlining

- May contain examples that you find particularly helpful in explaining or illustrating the main ideas

- Should prompt you to remember some of the supporting details of the material

While you do not need to include a discussion of all the supporting details in the chapter, your outline may include a word or phrase that triggers you to recall certain details. The word or phrase may come from the textbook or from your own experience that you can relate to the material. This word or phrase will not mean much to someone who has not read the chapter, but to an active reader of the text, it will be meaningful.

Therefore, an outline will be most helpful in your studying if you make it yourself. If an outline is provided for you, you still will need to read the section to learn the material. Work to add some personal notes to the outline that will trigger your memory of what you have read. Trying to study from an outline made by someone else *instead of* reading the text is not likely to help you learn the material thoroughly. This is so because the purpose of an outline is to organize and remind you of what you have learned rather than to teach you the material.

Here is a sample outline for Section 2.1. How would your outline be the same or different from this one?

Making an Outline for Section 2.1 of *World of Chemistry*

Begin by reviewing the **Key Terms** list for Section 2.1 in the **Chapter Review.** An outline for Section 2.1 will include the terms *matter, atoms, compounds, molecule, elements, solid, liquid,* and *gas*. It also may include examples of these terms.

As you read the section, pay attention to key points that are highlighted in light blue boxes in your textbook. You may wish to add these points to your outline or check what you have written against them.

Can you answer the **Section Review Questions** using your outline? If not, consider revising your outline.

One of Many Possible Outlines for Section 2.1

A. Matter
   1. Matter has mass and occupies space.
   2. Matter has a variety of forms (solids like a chair, liquids like water, and gases like air are all matter).

3. Fundamental building blocks of matter are similar in all types of matter (chocolate cake and air).

B. Particulate Nature of Matter

1. Matter generally appears continuous to the naked eye.

   a. The surface of a tabletop appears smooth.

   b. Sand on a beach looks smooth from a distance

2. At high magnification, matter appears to be made of small particles (atoms).

   a. Think about sand on the beach or a painting made with dots (Impressionist).

   b. Electronic microscopes show individual atoms in a piece of metal.

C. Elements and Compounds

1. Atoms: fundamental units of which matter is made.

2. All atoms are not alike (copper atoms are different from carbon atoms).

3. Word analogy: Matter is like words; atoms are like letters.

4. Compounds are made of two or more different types of atoms bound together in a particular way.

   a. Example: Water is a compound of two types of atoms (hydrogen and oxygen).

   b. A compound always has same particles throughout.

   c. A compound always contains atoms of different elements.

5. A molecule is a collection of atoms bonded together that behaves as a unit.

   a. Example: carbon dioxide (O—C—O or CO_2).

   b. Molecules are the individual particles of compounds.

   c. All compounds are made of molecules. The compound water has molecules H_2O.

6. Elements contain only one type of atom.

   a. Elements can be made of atoms, such as copper or iron.

   b. Elements can be made of molecules, such as hydrogen (H—H or H_2).

D. States of Matter

1. Solids

   a. Rigid; fixed shape and volume.

   b. A rock is an example of a solid.

2. Liquids

   a. Definite volume; takes shape of container.

   b. Water is an example of a liquid.

3. Gases

   a. No fixed volume or shape; uniformly fills any container.

   b. Oxygen is an example of a gas.

Making and Using Graphic Organizers

Material in the textbook often is presented in tables and lists. This is a good way to present information in an orderly way. However, these are not the only ways we can convey information. Graphic organizers can be used as well, and they have advantages over tables and lists. For example, look at the following figures from your *World of Chemistry* text:

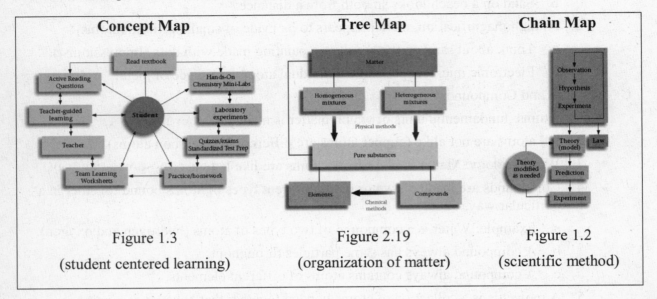

| Concept Map | Tree Map | Chain Map |

Figure 1.3

(student centered learning)

Figure 2.19

(organization of matter)

Figure 1.2

(scientific method)

Concept Maps

Figure 1.3 (see p. 16 of your textbook) is an example of a concept map. A concept map helps to organize facts around a key concept or idea. In Figure 1.3, for example, the student is placed at the center of responsibility for learning and is connected to all the available resources.

Tree Maps

Figure 2.19 (see p. 42 of your textbook) is an example of a tree map. A tree map usually is used to show how items within a system are ordered. This type of graphic organizer is more linear than the concept map, although there can be branches (as on a tree) for a given level. In Figure 2.19, the main concept is *matter*. All the other terms are related at some level to matter. Matter consists of pure substances (note the connector between matter and pure substances on the left of the figure) and both heterogeneous mixtures and homogeneous mixtures. Both types of mixtures can be separated by physical means (as shown) to become pure substances. Pure substances can be either elements or compounds, and compounds can be separated by chemical means (as shown) to become elements.

Generally, the tree map is linear. For example, Figure 2.19 shows that elements make up compounds, which make up pure substances, which make up mixtures, which are a part of matter. This information can be conveyed in an outline as well, but the tree map does so in a more visual way.

Chain Maps

Figure 1.2 (see p. 13 of your textbook) is an example of a chain map. A chain map can be used to describe the steps of a process. It is often linear like a tree map, although topics can "loop back." Figure 1.2 shows that observations are made, a hypothesis is made from these observations, and experiments are performed to test the hypothesis. Depending on the outcome of the experiments, more observations may be necessary (the connector "loops back"), and the process begins again. Theories and laws are developed, and theories are tested with further observations and experimentation. All this is conveyed in the figure, even though there are very few words.

Advantages of Graphic Organizers

- Graphic organizers provide a method of viewing concepts as a whole rather than in parts.

- Graphic organizers present a great deal of information in a visually stimulating way.

- Key ideas are summarized, and this can serve as a good study tool.

- Graphic organizers (especially concept maps) show how key concepts are connected.

- Making graphic organizers requires that you organize key ideas.

Making Graphic Organizers

As mentioned earlier, making a graphic organizer requires you to organize key ideas. The thought processes used in making graphic organizers are important in making sure that you really understand the material.

There are three main questions to answer as you construct a concept map:

- What is the main idea around which to build the map?

- What are the concepts or questions that are connected with the main idea?

- How are the concepts and questions connected?

Let's consider in more detail how to construct a graphic organizer. In this case, we will focus on making a concept map for Section 2.1 in *World of Chemistry*.

The main idea in Section 2.1 is *matter*, so this concept should be central in our map. The concepts connected with this idea are *atoms, molecules, elements, compounds, solids, liquids,* and *gases*. Now we must show how these ideas are all connected.

First, we know that all these ideas are made of matter. Therefore, there should be a link between each of these ideas and matter.

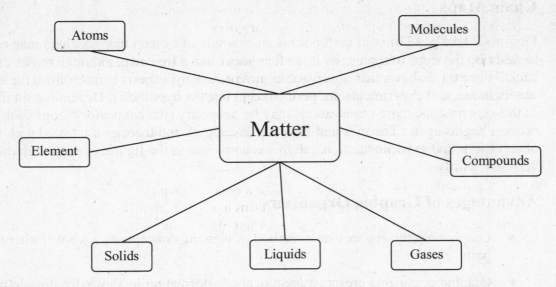

This concept map is helpful in showing us that matter is the central idea and to help us remember the key terms in Section 2.1 (and that they are made of matter). However, we also can show more relationships among these ideas.

For example:

- Elements can be atoms or molecules.
- Compounds are only composed of molecules.
- An element or a compound can exist as a solid, liquid, or gas.
- Because solids, liquids, and gases are collections of atoms or molecules, an atom or a molecule is not considered to be a solid, a liquid, or a gas.

With this new information, we can modify our concept map as follows:

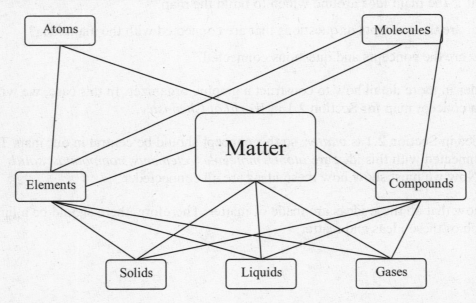

Notice that there is no connection between *compounds* and *atoms* and that neither *atoms* nor *molecules* are connected to *solids, liquids,* or *gases.*

In addition to drawing connections between ideas, you also can draw arrows to show the direction of the link between ideas and even write something on the arrow that explains how the ideas are linked. For example, your concept map may include the following:

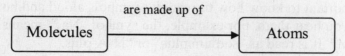

There is more than one correct way to make a concept map (or any graphic organizer). The goal is to make a map that correctly links terms and ideas, that makes sense to you, and that can be used to remind yourself of the important ideas in the text.

Reading Chemical Symbols

The language of chemistry is a combination of words, numbers, and symbols. The symbols are a shorthand notation, and mastering the meaning of the symbols will help you as you read the text. You probably are familiar with abbreviations such as "Dr." for "doctor" and "St." for "street." These abbreviations are used for convenience, much in the same way that the symbols are used in chemistry. In order for a symbol to be convenient, however, you need to know what the symbol means. It is also important to know how to read the symbols aloud and how to recognize these symbols when you hear them. For example, the symbol "Na^+" means "a positively charged ion of sodium." It is read as "sodium plus" or "N-A-plus."

The most important symbols in chemistry are the symbols of the elements. It is helpful if you memorize the chemical symbols that you come across most often. It is also helpful to know how to name compounds (see Chapter 4 in *World of Chemistry* for a discussion of naming compounds).

Superscripts and Subscripts

Numbers often appear as superscripts and subscripts in chemical formulas. The superscript usually indicates the charge on an ion. This is different from a math class, where the superscript is a power. The subscript in a chemical formula tells you how many of a particular kind of atom there are in a given molecule.

In chemistry, if the superscript or subscript is a "1," it is not written. Only the charge is indicated.

Symbol	Meaning	Read as:
Mg^{2+}	A magnesium ion with a positive two charge (the ion has 12 protons and 10 electrons)	Magnesium ion Magnesium two plus M-G-2-plus
Fe^{3+}	An iron ion with a positive three charge (the ion has 26 protons and 23 electrons)	Iron three plus F-E-3-plus
Cl^-	A chloride ion with a negative one charge (the ion has 17 protons and 18 electrons)	Chloride ion C-L-minus
H_2O	A molecule in which two atoms of hydrogen are bonded to one atom of oxygen.	Water H-2-O
CO_2	A molecule in which two oxygen atoms are bonded to one atom of carbon.	C-O-2 Carbon dioxide
$NaCl$	An ionic compound with a 1:1 ratio of sodium ions and chloride ions.	Sodium chloride N-A-C-L

Making and Using Flashcards

Studying chemistry requires both knowledge of facts and understanding of concepts. In order to answer questions and solve problems, it is important to be able to recall information. One way of increasing your skill in recalling information is to make flashcards of key ideas.

Reasons for Making Flashcards

- The act of writing flashcards enhances your ability to recall information.
- A group of flashcards is a compact and convenient study tool.
- Flashcards provide an opportunity to write definitions in your own words.
- Using flashcards can help you to identify strong and weak points in your knowledge so that you can use study time more efficiently.
- You can study flashcards alone or with classmates.

How to Use Flashcards

- Review your flashcards daily. This helps you to avoid the need to cram the night before a quiz or an exam.
- As you are reviewing, separate the cards into two stacks: the cards you have mastered and the cards you need to study more.
- Read the cards aloud when you have the opportunity. This increases your ability to learn the information.
- Trade flashcards with a classmate and study the other person's cards. Let the person know if you find any mistakes in the cards!

Making Flashcards

Flashcards are especially helpful for factual information. Factual information includes

- Vocabulary (definitions of key terms)
- Matching element names with element symbols
- Matching chemical names with chemical formulas
- Learning chemical structures

When making a vocabulary flashcard, consider two definitions—one from the **Glossary** and one in your own words that helps you to remember the concept. For example, consider the following example of a flashcard for the term *compound*:

Compound	← front of flashcard	A substance with constant composition that can be broken down into elements by chemical processes.
	back of flashcard →	Compounds are like words; elements are like letters.
		Water (H_2O) is an example of a compound.

In this case, the second definition is not a scientific one, but you can use it to help recall what is meant by a compound. Including an example is also a good idea.

Reading Math

Solving chemistry problems requires good problem-solving and math skills. It also requires that you know how to read the symbols of mathematics, just as you must learn the symbols of chemistry.

Common Math Symbols

The following table shows some math symbols used in your chemistry course, along with their meanings:

Symbol	Meaning
=	equals, equivalent, is
°	degree
%	percent
÷, /	divided by, per
×	times, multiplied by
≈, ~	approximately
±	plus or minus
Δ	change in (read as "delta")

Superscripts and Subscripts

Numbers often appear as superscripts and subscripts in chemical formulas. The superscript usually indicates the charge on an ion. This is different from a math class, where the superscript is a power. The subscript in a chemical formula tells you the number of a particular atom in a given molecule.

This is different from mathematics, in which a superscript indicates a power, as seen in scientific notation. For example, the number 4.2×10^3 (read as "4 point 2 times 10 to the third") also can be written as 4200.

Taking Notes

Understanding chemistry requires that you recall a great deal of information. You also must understand how the information is related. Making these connections can be difficult, but it will be easier if you take the time to summarize the main points of your reading or of a class period in a notebook. Note taking can be divided into two categories:

1. Taking notes from the textbook

2. Taking notes during class

Reasons for Taking Notes from the Textbook

- The act of taking notes enhances your ability to recall information.

- Taking notes is a good way to organize concepts in a way that makes sense to you.

- Taking notes makes you a more active reader of the textbook and helps you to build connections among concepts.

- Taking notes is a good way to prepare for class. You will have a better sense of what you do understand and what you don't understand if you have tried to write about the material.

- Your notes provide you with a good study tool for exams.

Reasons for Taking Notes during Class

- Taking notes keeps your concentration level high during class.

- Your teacher likely will present information in a differently than the way it is presented in the textbook.

- Your teacher will provide additional examples from those in the textbook. These examples may appear on quizzes or exams.

- Your notes provide you with a good study tool for exams.

How to Take Notes from a Textbook

There is no generally accepted "best" way to take notes from a textbook. You will need to experiment to find the way that works best for you. However, there are some guidelines that can help you in this process.

- Keep all your notes for your chemistry course collected in a single location such as a notebook or binder.

- Notes should be organized in a logical way. One good way to make sure that you do this it to look through the chapter before reading it to see how the chapter is organized.

- The first page of each chapter includes a yellow **Looking Ahead** box that lists the numbered section titles along with subsections. You can use this as a template for your notes. For example, the section titles can serve as main topics in your notes. You should be sure to include at least two important points about each of the section titles.

- Consider referencing in your notes any figures and graphs that you feel convey a great deal of important information. Try your hand at sketching your own version of a figure or diagram directly into your notes.

- You even may find it useful to include a particularly helpful example problem in your notes.

- Chapter notes often are structured in outline form, but generally they are more extensive than an outline.

How toTake Notes on Material Presented in Class

Taking notes on class material is best carried out in two steps: (1) taking notes during class and (2) reviewing and revising the notes after class.

- Make sure that you indicate a date, chapter, or topic reference so that you can remember what the notes cover.

- When taking notes during class, do not write down everything that it said. Focus on the key points. It is a good idea to have your notes from the textbook available so that you do not spend time writing information you already have in your notes.

- Consider developing your own symbols or shorthand in your notes that you can use to mark key points, new examples that aren't in the textbook, material that will be on a test, questions about the material, assignments given, etc.

- After class, review your notes. Include additional material or examples that you did not have time to write during class. Add color coding, sketches, or other information that will help you to remember what was said and make connections with what you know. Make sure that what you have written makes sense to you.

- Make a list of any questions to ask your teacher.

Reading Chemical Equations

Chemical equations are composed of chemical and mathematical symbols to represent chemical reactions. For example, consider the chemical reaction shown by the photograph of the blue flame of a Bunsen burner (see p. 219 in Chapter 7 of *World of Chemistry*). We can represent this reaction using words:

"Methane gas reacts with oxygen gas to produce carbon dioxide and water."

To represent this reaction with chemical symbols, we must know the symbols for methane, oxygen, carbon dioxide, and water. The chemical equation for this reaction is

$$CH_4(g) + O_2(g) \rightarrow CO_2(g) + H_2O(g)$$

The equation also can be read as "C-H-4 plus O-2 reacts to produce C-O-2 plus H-2-O."

Symbol in the Chemical Equation	Meaning of Symbol
$CH_4(g)$	methane (gas)
+	reacts with
$O_2(g)$	oxygen (gas)
$\rightarrow$	to produce (to make, yields)
$CO_2(g)$	carbon dioxide (gas)
+	and
$H_2O(g)$	water (vapor)

Reactants and Products

Reactants are the substances that are present initially in the chemical reaction and appear to the left of the arrow. In the preceding example, methane (CH_4) and oxygen (O_2) are the reactants.

Products are the substances that are produced in the chemical reaction and appear to the right of the arrow. In the preceding example, carbon dioxide (CO_2) and water (H_2O) are the products.

Balanced Chemical Equations

Unbalanced chemical equations tell us the reactants and products, but the equation needs to be balanced in order to indicate the relative amounts of reactants and products. The balanced equation between methane and oxygen is

$$CH_4(g) + 2O_2(g) \rightarrow CO_2(g) + 2H_2O(g)$$

This means that for every 1 molecule (or 1 mol) of methane gas that reacts, 2 molecules (or 2 mol) of oxygen gas are required, and 1 molecule (or 1 mol) of carbon dioxide gas and 2 molecules (or 2 mol) of water vapor are produced.

The balanced equation is read as "C-H-4 plus 2-O-2 reacts to make C-O-2 plus 2-H-2-O."

Section 3: Leveled Chapter Review Worksheets

This section offers three levels of review worksheets for chapters in the student text: Basic, Standard, and Challenge. Worksheets are designed for individual students to use for review after studying a chapter.

Contents

Chapter 2.. RW–1

Chapter 3.. RW–4

Chapter 4.. RW–9

Chapter 5..RW–12

Chapter 6..RW–15

Chapter 7..RW–18

Chapter 8..RW–21

Chapter 9..RW–24

Chapter 10..RW–27

Chapter 11..RW–32

Chapter 12..RW–37

Chapter 13..RW–42

Chapter 14..RW–47

Chapter 15..RW–50

Chapter 16..RW–54

Chapter 17..RW–59

Chapter 18..RW–63

Chapter 19..RW–66

Chapter 20..RW–69

Chapter 21..RW–72

Answer Keys...RW–74

Chapter 2: Basic Review Worksheet

1. What is *matter*? Of what is matter composed?

2. What is an *element*, and what is a *compound*? Give examples of each.

3. Explain the differences among a *gas*, a *liquid*, and a *solid*.

4. What is meant by the term *chemical property*? What is meant by the term *physical property*?

5. What is meant by the term *chemical change*? What is meant by the term *physical change*?

6. What are *alloys*? Provide an example.

7. What is a *mixture*? Provide an example.

8. What is a *solution*? Provide an example.

9. What is meant by the term *pure substance*?

10. What is the difference between a *homogeneous mixture* and a *heterogeneous mixture*?

11. What are some of the techniques by which mixtures can be resolved into their components?

Name _____ Section _____ Date _____

Chapter 2: Standard Review Worksheet

1. What are some of the different types of matter? How do these types of matter differ, and how are they the same?

2. What is the difference between a chemical property and a physical property?

3. What is the difference between a chemical change and a physical change?

4. Classify each of the following as a chemical or physical property or change.

   a. Table salt dissolves in water.
   b. Water boils at 100°C.
   c. You bake a cake.
   d. A tree is struck by lightning.

5. Explain the difference between an *element* and a *compound*.

6. What is the difference between a *mixture* and a *solution*?

7. Are all elements pure substances? Are all compounds pure substances?

8. Are mixtures pure substances? Are solutions pure substances?

9. Explain the processes of *filtration* and *distillation* in your own words.

Name _____   Section _____   Date _____

Chapter 2: Challenge Review Worksheet

1. List three physical properties and three chemical properties that are not in your text.

2. List three physical changes and three chemical changes that are not in your text.

3. Are all physical changes accompanied by chemical changes? Are all chemical changes accompanied by physical changes? Explain.

4. Are all compounds composed of molecules? If so, explain why. If not, provide an example.

5. What does it mean to say that a compound has a *constant composition*?

6. Would samples of a particular compound here and in another part of the world have the same composition and properties?

7. Mixtures do not have constant composition. Give an example of a mixture that you encounter often that has a variable composition.

8. Are all solutions mixtures? Are all mixtures solutions? Explain.

9. Provide an example of each of the following mixtures, and state whether it is a homogeneous or heterogeneous mixture. Support your answer.

   a. A mixture of a solid and a liquid
   b. A mixture of two gases
   c. A mixture of two liquids
   d. A mixture of two solids

10. Are methods used to separate mixtures physical or chemical changes? Explain.

Chapter 3: Basic Review Worksheet

1. What is an *element*? How many elements are presently known? How many of these occur naturally, and how many are human-made? Which elements are most abundant on the earth?

2. What are the three fundamental particles that compose all atoms? Indicate the electrical charge and relative mass of each of these particles. Where is each type of particle found in the atom?

3. What is meant by the term *nuclear atom*?

4. What are *isotopes*?

5. Are most elements found in nature in the elemental or in the combined form? Why? Name several elements that are usually found in the elemental form.

6. Give the names of some of the families of elements in the periodic table.

7. Which general area of the periodic table contains the metallic elements? Which general area contains the nonmetallic elements?

8. What are *ions*? How are ions formed from atoms? To what do the terms *cation* and *anion* refer?

9. What are some general physical properties of ionic compounds such as sodium chloride? How do we know that substances such as sodium chloride consist of positively and negatively charged particles?

10. Write the *symbol* and *atomic number* for each of the following elements: magnesium, tin, lead, sodium, hydrogen, chlorine, and silver.

11. Write the *name* and *atomic number* for each of the following elements:

   a. He   c. Se   e. P
   b. B   d. Ba   f. Sr

12. Write the *name* and *chemical symbol* for each of the following elements:

   a. 19   c. 1   e. 82
   b. 12   d. 6   f. 2

13. Indicate the number of protons, neutrons, and electrons in isolated atoms having the following nuclear symbols:

   a. $_{2}^{4}He$ b. $_{17}^{37}Cl$ c. $_{20}^{40}Ca$

14. What simple ion does each of the following elements most commonly form?

   a. Mg   c. Ba   e. O
   b. F   d. Na   f. Cl

15. For each of the following simple ions, indicate the number of protons and electrons the ion contains.

   a. K^{+} c. Br^{-} e. Na^{+}

Chapter 3: Standard Review Worksheet

1. Why do the symbols for some elements seem to bear no relationship to the name for the element? Give several examples and explain.

2. What is a *compound*? Give examples.

3. Describe the points of Rutherford's model for the nuclear atom and how he tested this model. Based on his experiments, how did Rutherford envision the structure of the atom? How did Rutherford's model for atomic structure differ from Thomson's "plum pudding" model?

4. Which of the subatomic particles is responsible for the chemical behavior of a given type of atom? Why?

5. To what do the *atomic number* and the *mass number* of an isotope refer? How are specific isotopes indicated symbolically? Give an example and explain.

6. Describe the periodic table of the elements. How are the elements arranged in the table? What significance is there in the way the elements are arranged into vertical groups? How can the periodic table be used to predict what ion an element's atoms will form?

7. In terms of subatomic particles, how is a cation related to the atom from which it is formed? An anion? Does the nucleus of an atom change when an atom is converted into an ion?

8. Since ionic compounds are made up of electrically charged particles, why doesn't such a compound have an overall electrical charge?

9. Write the *symbol* and *atomic number* for each of the following elements: potassium, calcium, bromine, neon, aluminum, gold, mercury, and iodine.

10. Write the *name* and *atomic number* for each of the following elements:

    a. Si   c. F   e. O
    b. C   d. Be   f. Cr

11. Write the *name* and *chemical symbol* for each of the following elements:

    a. 36   c. 15   e. 29
    b. 92   d. 79   f. 8

Name _____ Section _____ Date _____

12. Indicate the number of protons, neutrons, and electrons in isolated atoms having the following nuclear symbols:

    a. $^{79}_{35}Br$ b. $^{238}_{92}U$ c. $^{1}_{1}H$

13. What simple ion does each of the following elements most commonly form?

    a. Ag   c. Br   e. S
    b. Al   d. K   f. Ca

14. For each of the following simple ions, indicate the number of protons and electrons the ion contains:

    a. H^+ c. N^{3-} e. F^-

Chapter 3: Challenge Review Worksheet

1. Without consulting any reference, write the name and symbol for as many elements as you can.

2. Without consulting your textbook or notes, state as many points as you can of Dalton's atomic theory. Explain in your own words each point of the theory.

3. What is meant by the *law of constant composition* for compounds, and why is this law so important to our study of chemistry?

4. Do the isotopes of a given element have the same chemical and physical properties? Explain.

5. Do isolated atoms form ions spontaneously? Explain.

6. Can an ionic compound consist only of cations or anions but not both? Explain.

7. Indicate the number of protons, neutrons, and electrons in isolated ions having the following nuclear symbols:

   a. $^{19}_{9}F^-$ b. $^{24}_{12}Mg^{2+}$ c. $^{56}_{26}Fe^{3+}$

8. For each of the following simple ions, indicate the number of protons and electrons the ion contains:

   a. Rb^+ c. H^- e. Cl^-
   b. Fe^{2+} d. Al^{3+} f. O^{2-}

9. Using the ions indicated in question 8, write the formulas and give the names for all possible simple ionic compounds involving these ions.

Chapter 4: Basic Review Worksheet

1. When writing the name of an ionic compound, which is named first, the anion or the cation? Give an example.

2. What ending is added to the root name of an element to show that it is a simple anion in a type I ionic compound? Give an example.

3. What general type of element is involved in type II compounds?

4. What *two* systems are used to show the charge of the cation in a type II ionic compound? Give examples of each system for two compounds.

5. Describe the system used to name type III binary compounds (compounds of nonmetallic elements). Give four examples illustrating the method.

6. What is an *oxyanion*? Give two examples.

7. What is an *acid*? Give two examples (one that contains oxygen and one that does not).

8. Name each of the following binary ionic compounds:

   a. NaCl   c. $MgBr_2$ e. CaS
   b. K_2O d. AlI_3 f. SrO

9. Without consulting the text, name each of the following polyatomic ions:

   a. NH_4^+ c. NO_3^- e. ClO_4^-
   b. SO_3^{2-} d. OH^- f. PO_4^{3-}

10. Name each of the following compounds:

   a. NO_2 b. ICl   c. CO

11. Write the formula for each of the following compounds:

   a. potassium sulfide   c. calcium sulfate
   b. hydrochloric acid   d. copper(II) bromide

Chapter 4: Standard Review Worksheet

1. How does the system used to name type III compounds differ from that used for ionic compounds? How is the system for type III compounds similar to that for ionic compounds?

2. What naming system is used for a series of related oxyanions to indicate the relative number of oxygen atoms in each ion? Give examples.

3. How are acids that do *not* contain oxygen named? Give three examples.

4. Describe the naming system for the oxyacids. Give an example of a series of oxyacids illustrating this system.

5. Name each of the following binary ionic compounds:

   a. $FeCl_3$ c. Al_2O_3 e. $BaCl_2$
   b. NiS d. CuO f. FeO

6. Which of the following formulas are incorrect? Correct each incorrect formula.

   a. NaS c. $NaCl_2$
   b. K_2S d. $CaBr$

7. Without consulting the text, name each of the following polyatomic ions:

   a. NO_2^- c. SO_4^{2-}
   b. ClO^- d. CN^-

8. Name each of the following compounds:

   a. PCl_5 b. N_2O_4 c. SF_6

9. Write the formulas for each of the following compounds:

   a. nitric acid   c. silver sulfite
   b. sodium hydride   d. ammonium acetate

Chapter 4: Challenge Review Worksheet

1. What principle do we use in writing the formula of an ionic compound such as NaCl or MgI_2? How do we know that *two* iodide ions are needed for each magnesium ion, whereas only one chloride ion is needed per sodium ion?

2. What is a *polyatomic* ion? Without consulting a reference, list the formulas and names of at least 10 polyatomic ions. When writing the overall formula of an ionic compound involving polyatomic ions, why are parenthesis used around the formula of a polyatomic ion when more than one such ion is present? Give an example.

3. Name each of the following binary ionic compounds:

   a. Cr_2S_3 c. Fe_2O_3 e. MnO_2
   b. Cu_2S d. AuI_3 f. $CoBr_2$

4. Which of the following formulas are incorrect? Correct each incorrect formula.

   a. Rb_3N c. BaP_2
   b. Cs_3Cl_2 d. AlI_3

5. Name each of the following compounds:

   a. B_2O_3 b. P_4O_{10} c. N_2O_3

6. Write the formulas for each of the following compounds:

   a. hydrosulfuric acid   c. magnesium perchlorate
   b. barium phosphate   d. manganese(II) chloride

Chapter 5: Basic Review Worksheet

1. Explain the scientific meaning of *uncertainty*.

2. Explain how a *unit* is related to a measurement.

3. Explain the terms *conversion factor* and *equivalence statement*.

4. For each of the following, make the indicated conversion:

   a. 122.4×10^5 to standard scientific notation
   b. 5.993×10^{-4} to ordinary decimal notation

5. For each of the following, make the indicated conversion:

   a. 6.0 pt to liters
   b. 6.0 pt to gallons
   c. 5.91 yd to meters
   d. 62.5 mi to kilometers
   e. 88.5 cm to millimeters

6. Evaluate each of the following mathematical expressions, being sure to express the answer to the correct number of significant figures:

   a. $10.20 + 4.1 + 26.0001 + 2.4$
   b. $(1.091 - 0.991) + 1.2$
   c. $(4.06 + 5.1)(2.032 - 1.02)$
   d. $(67.21)(1.003)(2.4)$

7. Make the indicated temperature conversions:

   a. 541 K to Celsius degrees
   b. 221°C to kelvins

8. Given the following mass, volume, and density information, calculate the missing quantity:

   a. Mass = 121.4 g; volume = 42.4 cm^3; density = ? g/cm^3
   b. Mass = 0.721 lb; volume = 241 cm^3; density = ? g/cm^3

Chapter 5: Standard Review Worksheet

1. How does uncertainty enter into measurements? How is uncertainty indicated in scientific measurements?

2. Why must a unit be included with a measurement?

3. Give an everyday example of how you might use dimensional analysis to solve a simple problem.

4. For each of the following, make the indicated conversion:

   a. 0.0004321×10^4 to standard scientific notation
   b. 5.241×10^2 to ordinary decimal notation

5. For each of the following, make the indicated conversion:

   a. 16.0 L to fluid ounces
   b. 5.25 L to gallons
   c. 8.25 m to inches
   d. 4.25 kg to pounds
   e. 4.21 in. to centimeters

6. Evaluate each of the following mathematical expressions, being sure to express the answer to the correct number of significant figures:

   a. $[(7.815 + 2.01)(4.5)]/(1.9001)$
   b. $(1.67 \times 10^{-9})(1.1 \times 10^{-4})$
   c. $(4.02 \times 10^{-4})(2.91 \times 10^3)/(9.102 \times 10^{-1})$
   d. $(1.04 \times 10^2 + 2.1 \times 10^1)/(4.51 \times 10^3)$
   e. $(1.51 \times 10^{-3})^2/(1.074 \times 10^{-7})$
   f. $(1.89 \times 10^2)/[(7.01 \times 10^{-3}) (4.1433 \times 10^4)]$

7. Make the indicated temperature conversions:

   a. $-50.1°C$ to Fahrenheit degrees
   b. $-30.7°F$ to Celsius degrees

8. Given the following mass, volume, and density information, calculate the missing quantity:

   a. Mass = ? g; volume = 124.1 mL; density = 0.821 g/mL
   b. Mass = ? g; volume = 4.51 L; density = 1.15 g/cm^3

Name _____ Section _____ Date _____

Chapter 5: Challenge Review Worksheet

1. Can uncertainty ever be eliminated completely in experiments? Explain.

2. Why is reporting the correct number of significant figures so important in science? Without consulting the text, summarize the rules for deciding whether or not a particular digit in a number used in a calculation is "significant." Summarize the rules for rounding off numbers. Summarize the rules for doing arithmetic with the correct number of significant figures.

3. For each of the following, make the indicated conversion:

   a. 0.0000009814 to standard scientific notation
   b. 14.2×10^0 to ordinary decimal notation

4. Make the indicated temperature conversions:

   a. 351 K to Fahrenheit degrees
   b. 72°F to kelvins

5. At which temperature does the number of Celsius degrees equal the number of Fahrenheit degrees? Prove your answer.

6. Given the following mass, volume, and density information, calculate the missing quantity:

   a. Mass = 142.4 g; volume = ? mL; density = 0.915 g/mL
   b. Mass = 4.2 lb; volume = ? cm^3; density = 3.75 g/cm^3

7. You measure the mass of an object and find it to be 128.1 ± 0.1 g. You measure the volume of this object and report it as 24.3 ± 0.01 mL. Calculate the density and report it as ± ___ g/mL.

Chapter 6: Basic Review Worksheet

1. What does the average *atomic mass* of an element represent? What unit is used for average atomic mass?

2. Define *molar mass*. Using K_2O as an example, calculate the molar mass from the atomic masses of the elements.

3. What is meant by the *percent composition* by mass for a compound? Determine the percent composition by mass for water.

4. For 5.00-g samples of each of the following substances, calculate the number of moles of the substance present, as well as the number of atoms of each type present in the sample:

   a. $Cu(s)$
   b. $NH_3(g)$
   c. $KClO_3(s)$
   d. $Ca(OH)_2(s)$

5. For the compounds in question 4, calculate the percent by mass of each element present in the compounds.

6. Define, compare, and contrast what are meant by the *empirical* and *molecular* formulas for a substance. Give an example of each.

7. A 10.00-g sample of a compound that consists of carbon and hydrogen is found to consist of 7.99 g of carbon and 2.01 g of hydrogen. What is the empirical formula for the compound?

8. The molar mass of the compound in question 7 is 30.07 g/mol. What is the molecular formula of the compound?

Chapter 6: Standard Review Worksheet

1. Express the atomic mass unit in grams. Why is the average atomic mass for an element typically *not* a whole number?

2. What does one mole of a substance represent on a microscopic, atomic basis? What does one mole of a substance represent on a macroscopic, mass basis?

3. Define *molar mass*. Calculate the molar mass of H_3PO_4 from the atomic masses of the elements.

4. Describe in general terms how percent composition by mass is obtained by experiment for new compounds. How can this information be calculated for known compounds?

5. For 5.00-g samples of each of the following substances, calculate the number of moles of the substance present, as well as the number of atoms of each type present in the sample:

   a. $K_2CrO_4(s)$
   b. $AuCl_3(s)$
   c. $SiH_4(g)$
   d. $Ca_3(PO_4)_2(s)$

6. For the compounds in question 5, calculate the percent by mass of each element present in the compounds.

7. What does an empirical formula tell us about a compound? A molecular formula? What information must be known for a compound to calculate its molecular formula?

8. An oxide of iron is found to be 70.0% iron by mass. Determine the empirical formula for this compound and name it.

9. A compound that consists of nitrogen and oxygen is found to be 30.4% nitrogen by mass. The molar mass of this compound is between 90 and 100 g/mol. Determine the empirical and molecular formulas for this compound.

Chapter 6: Challenge Review Worksheet

1. How does the text define a *mole,* and why have chemists defined the mole in this manner?

2. How do we know that 16.00 g of oxygen contains the same number of atoms as 12.01 g of carbon and 22.99 g of sodium? How do we know that 106.0 g of Na_2CO_3 contains the same number of carbon atoms as does 12.01 g of carbon but three times as many oxygen atoms as in 16.00 g of oxygen and twice as many sodium atoms as in 22.99 g of sodium.

3. Define *molar mass*. Calculate the molar mass of $Al_2(SO_4)_3$ from the atomic masses of the elements.

4. Why must the molecular formula be an *integer multiple* of the empirical formula?

5. When chemistry teachers prepare an exam question on determining the empirical formula of a compound, they usually take a known compound and calculate the percent composition of the compound from the formula. They then give the students this percent composition data and have the students calculate the original formula. Using a compound of *your* choice, first use the molecular formula of the compound to calculate the percent composition of the compound. Then use this percent composition data to calculate the empirical formula of the compound.

6. How does the percent by mass of each element present in a compound depend on the mass of the sample?

7. A 151.9-mg sample of a new compound has been analyzed and found to contain the following masses of elements: carbon, 82.80 mg; hydrogen, 13.90 mg; oxygen, 55.15 mg. Calculate the empirical formula of this compound.

8. One way of determining the empirical formula of a hydrocarbon (a compound that consists of hydrogen and carbon) is to burn it in the air and measure the mass of carbon dioxide and water vapor that is produced. To do this, we must assume that all the carbon from the hydrocarbon ends up in the carbon dioxide and all the hydrogen from the hydrocarbon ends up in the water. Suppose that you burn 2.500 g of a hydrocarbon and you collect 3.66 g carbon dioxide and 1.50 g water. Determine the empirical formula for this hydrocarbon.

9. The molar mass of the compound in question 8 is found to be around 60 g/mol. Determine the molecular formula of the compound.

Chapter 7: Basic Review Worksheet

1. What kind of visual evidence indicates that a chemical reaction has occurred? Give a reaction that illustrates each type of evidence you have mentioned.

2. What are the substances indicated to the left of the arrow called in a chemical equation? To the right of the arrow?

3. How are the physical states of reactants and products indicated when writing chemical equations?

4. What does it mean to *balance* an equation?

5. What do the *coefficients* in a balanced chemical equation represent? What do the *subscripts* in a balanced chemical equation represent? Which can be changed when balancing a chemical equation?

6. Balance the following chemical equations:
   a. $FeCl_3(aq) + KOH(aq) \rightarrow Fe(OH)_3(s) + KCl(aq)$
   b. $AgC_2H_3O_2(aq) + HCl(aq) \rightarrow AgCl(s) + HC_2H_3O_2(aq)$
   c. $SnO(s) + C(s) \rightarrow Sn(s) + CO_2(g)$
   d. $K_2O(s) + H_2O(l) \rightarrow KOH(aq)$

Chapter 7: Standard Review Worksheet

1. Do all reactions produce visual evidence that they have taken place? If yes, explain why; if no, provide examples of reactions that do not provide visual evidence.

2. What, in general terms, does a chemical equation indicate?

3. Why is it so important that the equations be balanced? What does it mean to say that atoms must be *conserved* in a balanced chemical equation?

4. When balancing a chemical equation, why is it acceptable to adjust a substance's coefficient but not permissible to adjust the subscripts within the substance's formula? What would changing the subscripts within a formula do?

5. Balance the following chemical equations:

   a. $Na_2O_2(s) + H_2O(l) \rightarrow NaOH(aq) + O_2(g)$

   b. $Fe(s) + Br_2(l) \rightarrow FeBr_3(s)$

   c. $Na_2S(s) + HCl(aq) \rightarrow NaCl(aq) + H_2S(g)$

   d. $H_2SO_4(aq) + NaCl(s) \rightarrow Na_2SO_4(aq) + HCl(aq)$

   e. $N_2(g) + I_2(s) \rightarrow NI_3(s)$

Chapter 7: Challenge Review Worksheet

1. The text emphasizes balancing a chemical equation so that all the coefficients are lowest multiple whole numbers. This is called *standard form*. Although it is not standard, coefficients in a balanced equation can be fractions. However, subscripts can never be fractions. Explain why each of these statements is true.

2. Determine the sum of the coefficients for each of the following chemical equations when they are balanced in standard form:

   a. $NaBH_4 + BF_3 \rightarrow NaBF_4 + B_2H_6$
   b. $NO + H_2 \rightarrow N_2 + H_2O$
   c. $Fe_2O_3 + CO \rightarrow Fe + CO_2$

3. Potassium and sodium are highly reactive metals. Write balanced chemical equations (standard form) for the reaction of each of these metals with the following substances to give the indicated products:

   a. With water, producing aqueous sodium hydroxide or potassium hydroxide, and hydrogen gas
   b. With chlorine gas, producing sodium chloride or potassium chloride
   c. With phosphorus, producing sodium phosphide or potassium phosphide
   d. With nitrogen gas, producing sodium nitride or potassium nitride
   e. With hydrogen gas, producing sodium hydride or potassium hydride

4. You wish to make baking soda (sodium hydrogen carbonate). To do so, you bubble carbon dioxide into cold water that contains dissolved ammonia and sodium chloride. The other product is ammonium chloride, which remains dissolved in the water. The baking soda is not soluble, so you can collect it by filtration. Write a balanced chemical equation (standard form) for this reaction.

5. If table sugar ($C_{12}H_{22}O_{11}$) burns, it combines with oxygen gas to produce carbon dioxide and water. Write a balanced chemical equation in standard form for this reaction.

6. You suspect that a water supply near your home contains lead. This lead is in the form of lead(II) ions, $Pb^{2+}(aq)$. You add a sodium chloride solution to the water, and solid lead(II) chloride precipitates. The other product is sodium nitrate, which remains dissolved in solution. Write a balanced chemical equation in standard form for this reaction.

7. Corrosion involves the reaction of metal with materials in the environment, causing formation of metallic compounds that usually are not as strong as the original metals.

   a. Many iron items, such as metal trash cans and buckets, are covered with a thin coating of zinc metal to keep the iron from rusting. Write a balanced chemical equation in standard form for the reaction of iron and oxygen to form solid iron(III) oxide.
   b. Aluminum reacts with oxygen in the air to form a thin layer of aluminum oxide, which protects the metal under it. Write a balanced chemical equation in standard form for the reaction of aluminum metal with oxygen.

Name _____   Section _____   Date _____

Chapter 8: Basic Review Worksheet

1. What is meant by the *driving force* for a reaction?

2. What is a *precipitation reaction*? Provide an example.

3. Define the term *strong electrolyte*. Provide three formulas of strong electrolytes and name them.

4. Summarize the simple solubility rules for ionic compounds.

5. In general terms, what are the *spectator ions* in a precipitation reaction?

6. Describe some physical and chemical properties of *acids* and *bases*. What is meant by a *strong* acid or base?

7. What is a *salt*? Provide three formulas of salts and name them.

8. What is *oxidation*? What is *reduction*?

9. What is a *combustion* reaction? Write an equation that illustrates a combustion reaction.

10. Give an example of a *synthesis* reaction and of a *decomposition* reaction.

11. Classify the reaction represented by each of the following chemical equations in as *many* ways as possible based on what you have learned. Balance each equation.

    a. $NaOH(s) + CuSO_4(aq) \rightarrow Cu(OH)_2(s) + Na_2SO_4(aq)$
    b. $HI(aq) + KOH(aq) \rightarrow KI(aq) + H_2O(l)$
    c. $FeO(s) + HNO_3(aq) \rightarrow Fe(NO_3)_2(aq) + H_2O(l)$
    d. $C_{12}H_{22}O_{11}(s) \rightarrow C(s) + H_2O(g)$
    e. $B(s) + O_2(g) \rightarrow B_2O_3(s)$

Chapter 8: Standard Review Worksheet

1. Give some examples of driving forces that make reactants tend to form products. Write a balanced chemical equation illustrating each type of driving force you have named.

2. What would you see if a precipitation reaction were to take place in a beaker? Write a balanced chemical equation illustrating a precipitation reaction.

3. What types of substances tend to be strong electrolytes? What does a solution of a strong electrolyte contain? Give a way to determine if a substance is a strong electrolyte.

4. How do we use the solubility rules in determining the identity of the solid formed in a precipitation reaction? Give three examples including balanced complete and net ionic equations.

5. Why are the spectator ions not included in writing the net ionic equation for a precipitation reaction?

6. Write chemical equations showing the formation of three different salts. What other product is formed when an aqueous acid reacts with an aqueous base? Write the net ionic equation for the formation of this substance.

7. What is essential in an oxidation–reduction reaction? Write a balanced chemical equation illustrating an oxidation–reduction reaction between a metal and nonmetal. Indicate which species is oxidized and which is reduced.

8. Are combustion reactions a unique type of reaction, or are they a special case of a more general type of reaction?

9. Are synthesis and decomposition reactions always also oxidation–reduction reactions? Explain.

10. Classify the reaction represented by each of the following chemical equations in as *many* ways as possible based on what you have learned. Balance each equation.

    a. $Mg(s) + CO_2(g) + O_2(g) \rightarrow MgCO_3(s)$
    b. $C_3H_8(g) + O_2(g) \rightarrow CO_2(g) + H_2O(g)$
    c. $Co(NH_3)_6Cl_2(s) \rightarrow CoCl_2(s) + NH_3(g)$
    d. $HCl(aq) + Pb(C_2H_3O_2)_2(aq) \rightarrow HC_2H_3O_2(aq) + PbCl_2(s)$
    e. $Al(s) + HNO_3(aq) \rightarrow Al(NO_3)_3(aq) + H_2(g)$

Name _____ Section _____ Date _____

Chapter 8: Challenge Review Worksheet

1. Spectator ions are not included in writing the net ionic equation for a precipitation reaction. Does this mean that the spectator ions do not have to be present in the solution?

2. Are strong acids and bases also strong electrolytes? Give several examples of strong acids and strong bases.

3. Three common strong acids are HCl, HNO_3, and H_2SO_4, whereas NaOH and KOH are two common strong bases. Write the neutralization reaction equations for each of these strong acids with each of these strong bases in aqueous solution.

4. The reagent shelf in a general chemistry lab contains aqueous solutions of the following substances: silver nitrate, sodium chloride, acetic acid, nitric acid, sulfuric acid, potassium chromate, barium nitrate, phosphoric acid, hydrochloric acid, lead nitrate, sodium hydroxide, and sodium carbonate. Suggest how you might prepare the following pure substances using these reagents and any normal laboratory equipment. If it is *not* possible to prepare a substance using these reagents, indicate why.

   a. $BaCrO_4(s)$
   b. $NaC_2H_3O_2(s)$
   c. $AgCl(s)$
   d. $PbSO_4(s)$
   e. $Na_2SO_4(s)$
   f. $BaCO_3(s)$

5. Can an oxidation reaction take place without a reduction also taking place? Why?

6. List and define all the ways of classifying chemical reactions that have been discussed in the text. Give a balanced chemical equation as an example of each type of reaction, and show clearly how your example fits the definition you have given.

Chapter 9: Basic Review Worksheet

1. Considering the reaction represented by the (unbalanced) equation

$$N_2(g) + H_2(g) \rightarrow NH_3(g)$$

   determine the number of moles of $NH_3(g)$ that can be produced from the following:

   a. 0.20 mol $N_2(g)$ reacts completely with $H_2(g)$.
   b. 0.30 mol $H_2(g)$ reacts completely with $N_2(g)$.

2. Considering the reaction represented by the (unbalanced) equation

$$Mg(s) + HCl(aq) \rightarrow MgCl_2(aq) + H_2(g)$$

   determine the mass of $H_2(g)$ that can be produced from the following:

   a. 10.0 g $Mg(s)$ reacts completely with $HCl(aq)$.
   b. 20.0 g $HCl(aq)$ reacts completely with $Mg(s)$.

3. What is meant by a *limiting reactant* in a particular reaction? What does it mean to say that one or more of the reactants are present *in excess*?

4. Considering the reaction represented by the (unbalanced) equation

$$H_2(g) + O_2(g) \rightarrow H_2O(l)$$

   determine the limiting reactant in each of the following cases:

   a. 4.0 mol $H_2(g)$ reacts with 3.0 mol $O_2(g)$.
   b. 10.0 g $H_2(g)$ reacts with 10.0 g $O_2(g)$.
   c. 10.0 mol $H_2(g)$ reacts with 10.0 mol $O_2(g)$.
   d. 5.0 g $H_2(g)$ reacts with 30.0 g $O_2(g)$.

5. What do we mean by the *theoretical yield* for a reaction? What is meant by the *actual yield*?

Name _____   Section _____   Date _____

Chapter 9: Standard Review Worksheet

1. Balanced chemical equations give us information on the molecular level (individual molecules reacting in the proportions indicated by the coefficients), as well as on the macroscopic level (moles). Write a balanced chemical equation of your choice, and interpret in words the meaning of the equation on the molecular and macroscopic levels.

2. Consider the *unbalanced* equation for the combustion of ethyl alcohol, C_2H_5OH:

$$C_2H_5OH(l) + O_2(g) \rightarrow CO_2(g) + H_2O(g)$$

   For a given amount of ethyl alcohol, write the mole ratios that would enable you to calculate the number of moles of each product, as well as the number of moles of O_2 that would be required. Show how these mole ratios would be applied if 0.65 mol of ethyl alcohol is combusted.

3. When a limiting reactant is present, in what way is the reaction "limited"? What happens to a reaction when the limiting reactant is used up?

4. For each of the following balanced equations, calculate the mass of each product formed if 25.0 g of the reactant listed first reacts completely with the second:

   a. $2AgNO_3(aq) + CaSO_4(aq) \rightarrow Ag_2SO_4(s) + Ca(NO_3)_2(aq)$
   b. $2Al(s) + 6HNO_3(aq) \rightarrow 2Al(NO_3)_3(aq) + 3H_2(g)$
   c. $H_3PO_4(aq) + 3NaOH(aq) \rightarrow Na_3PO_4(aq) + 3H_2O(l)$
   d. $CaO(s) + 2HCl(aq) \rightarrow CaCl_2(aq) + H_2O(l)$

5. For the reactions in question 4, calculate the mass of each product formed if 12.5 g of the first reactant is combined with 10.0 g of the second reactant. Indicate which substance is the limiting reactant for each case.

6. Look at your answers to question 5. Is there a pattern to which reactant is limiting? That is, is the limiting reactant always the one that is present with the lowest mass in grams? Is it always the one that is present with the least number of moles? Explain.

7. In a problem, how do we determine the *theoretical yield*? Where do we get the *actual yield*? How do we use these to calculate the *percent yield*?

8. You have calculated the theoretical yield for a reaction to be 4.0 g Cu(s). You collect 2.8 g of Cu(s) in the lab. Determine your percent yield.

Chapter 9: Challenge Review Worksheet

1. In the practice of chemistry, one of the most important calculations concerns the masses of products expected when particular masses of reactants are used in an experiment. For example, chemists judge the practicality and efficiency of a reaction by seeing how close the amount of product actually obtained is to the expected amount. Using a balanced chemical equation and an amount of starting material of your choice, summarize and illustrate the various steps needed in such a calculation for the expected amount of product.

2. For a balanced chemical equation of your choice, and using 25.0 g of each of the reactants in your equation, illustrate and explain how you would determine which reactant is the limiting reactant. Indicate *clearly* in your discussion how the choice of limiting reactant follows from your calculations.

3. Chlorine gas is a very reactive substance and will combine with most metals. For example,

$$2K(s) + Cl_2(g) \rightarrow 2KCl(s)$$
$$Ca(s) + Cl_2(g) \rightarrow CaCl_2(s)$$
$$2Al(s) + 3Cl_2(g) \rightarrow 2AlCl_3(s)$$

Suppose that individual 25.0-g samples of these three metals are reacted with separate 50.0-g samples of $Cl_2(g)$. In each case, determine whether the metal or chlorine is the limiting reactant, and calculate the theoretical yield of metal chloride for each process.

4. Suppose that you run the reaction between potassium and chlorine (with the amounts given in question 3), and you collect 31.2 g of potassium chloride. Determine your percent yield.

5. Your teacher gives you 5.00 g of a mixture of the two salts silver nitrate and potassium nitrate and asks you to determine the percent silver nitrate by mass in the mixture. You dissolve the mixture in water and add an excess of aqueous sodium chloride. You collect and dry the white solid that precipitates and find that it has a mass of 1.48 g. Provide balanced equations for all reactions that occur in this process, and determine the percent silver nitrate by mass in the original mixture.

Chapter 10: Basic Review Worksheet

1. How is the concept of *energy* defined?

2. As a ball rolls down a hill, _____ energy decreases, _____ energy increases, and _____ energy remains the same.

3. What is meant by the term *state function*? Provide an example.

4. What does *temperature* measure?

5. Explain what is meant by the terms *exothermic* and *endothermic*.

6. Define the terms *system* and *surroundings*.

7. What are some common *units* of energy, and how are these units defined?

8. For each of the following amounts of energy, perform the indicated conversion of units:

   a. 459 J to calories
   b. 55.31 kJ to joules
   c. 84.1 kJ to kilocalories

9. Calculate ΔE for each of the following cases:

   a. $q = 34$ J, $w = -22$ J
   b. $q = -28$ J, $w = -23$ cal
   c. $q = -15$ J, $w = +12$ J

10. For an endothermic process, q is reported with a _____ sign, and for an exothermic process, q is reported with a _____ sign.

11. What is meant by the *specific heat capacity* of a material?

12. Calculate the *mass* (in grams) of each of the following substances that could be warmed over the indicated temperature range by application of exactly 1.0 kJ of energy:

   a. water, from 15 to 42°C
   b. iron, from 25 to 125°C
   c. carbon, from −10 to 47°C

13. What is meant by the term *enthalpy*?

Name _____   Section _____   Date _____

14. Why does the quality of energy decrease when we use it?

15. What is the driving force for every exothermic process?

16. Consider the combustion of propane

$$C_3H_8(g) + 5O_2(g) \rightarrow 3CO_2(g) + 4H_2O(l) \qquad \Delta H = -2221 \text{ kJ}$$

   a. Is the combustion of propane endothermic or exothermic?
   b. Is energy as heat released into the surroundings or absorbed by the system?
   c. How much energy as heat is released when 2 mol of propane are burned in excess oxygen?

17. Given the following data:

$$4CuO(s) \rightarrow 2Cu_2O(s) + O_2(g) \qquad \Delta H = 288 \text{ kJ}$$
$$Cu_2O(s) \rightarrow Cu(s) + CuO(g) \qquad \Delta H = 11 \text{ kJ}$$

determine ΔH for the reaction $2Cu(s) + O_2(g) \rightarrow 2CuO(s)$.

Name _____   Section _____   Date _____

Chapter 10: Standard Review Worksheet

1. There is no heat in an insulated system at a constant temperature of 400.°C. Explain.

2. Explain how Figure 10.1 in the text shows the law of conservation of energy.

3. For each of the following amounts of energy, perform the indicated conversion of units:
   a. 7031 cal to kilojoules
   b. 78.3 kcal to kilojoules
   c. 4541 cal to kilocalories

4. Energy is a state function. Why isn't heat a state function?

5. At the end of Section 10.3 in the text, an exothermic reaction is explained. Write an analogous explanation of an endothermic reaction.

6. You start a fire in a fireplace by striking a match and lighting crumpled paper under some logs. Explain all the energy transitions in this scenario using the terms *exothermic*, *endothermic*, *system*, *surroundings*, *potential energy*, and *kinetic energy* in the discussion.

7. How is specific heat capacity used to calculate the energy change when a substance is heated?

8. Calculate the *mass* (in grams) of each of the following substances that could be warmed over the indicated temperature range by application of exactly 1.0 kJ of energy:
   a. gold, from 56 to 74°F
   b. silver, from 289 to 385 K
   c. aluminum, from −10 to 85.0°F

9. Calculate ΔE for each of the following cases:
   a. A system releases 23 J of heat while 12 J of work is done on it.
   b. 14 J of work is done on a system, and 5.0 calories of heat are released.
   c. A system absorbs 87 J of heat and performs 32 J of work.

10. Consider the combustion of propane

$$C_3H_8(g) + 5O_2(g) \rightarrow 3CO_2(g) + 4H_2O(l) \qquad \Delta H = -2221 \text{ kJ}$$

   a. How much energy as heat is released when 100.0 g of propane is burned in excess oxygen?
   b. How much energy as heat is released when 100.0 g of carbon dioxide is produced?

11. Use the following data to calculate the value of ΔH for the reaction

$$I_2(s) + Cl_2(g) \rightarrow 2ICl(g)$$

	ΔH (kJ/mol)
$Cl_2(g) \rightarrow 2Cl(g)$	242.3
$I_2(g) \rightarrow 2I(g)$	151.0
$ICl(g) \rightarrow I(g) + Cl(g)$	211.3
$I_2(s) \rightarrow I_2(g)$	62.8

12. Is enthalpy a state function? Explain your answer.

13. Explain how we can have an "energy crisis" given that the law of conservation of energy is true.

14. What acts as a driving force for every endothermic process that occurs?

Chapter 10: Challenge Review Worksheet

1. According to the text, increasing entropy is a driving force, and steam has higher entropy than liquid water. So why doesn't all the liquid water on earth spontaneously turn to steam?

2. You heat a 5.00-g sample of iron in a boiling-water bath. You then quickly and carefully place the iron into 125.0 mL of water at 25.0°C in a coffee-cup calorimeter. Determine the final temperature of the water, and explain all assumptions.

3. Explain why the first law of thermodynamics cannot be used to explain why a ball cannot roll up a hill spontaneously but the second law can be used.

Chapter 11: Basic Review Worksheet

1. What is *electromagnetic radiation*?

2. Sketch a representation of a wave, and indicate on your drawing one wavelength of the wave.

3. Explain what it means for an atom to be in an excited state and what it means for an atom to be in its ground state.

4. What is a *photon*?

5. Describe Bohr's model of the hydrogen atom.

6. Explain what is meant by the term *orbital*.

7. What is the symbol for the lowest-energy hydrogen orbital?

8. Give the symbols for each of the orbitals that constitute the third and fourth principal energy levels of hydrogen.

9. Describe electron spin.

10. What does the Pauli exclusion principle tell us about electrons?

11. List the order in which the orbitals are filled as the atoms beyond hydrogen are built up.

12. How many electrons can be placed in a given *s* subshell? In a given *p* subshell? In a specific *p* orbital?

13. Define the valence electrons and the core electrons in an atom.

14. Sketch the overall shape of the periodic table and indicate the general regions of the table that represent the various *s, p, d,* and *f* orbitals being filled.

15. Write the electron configurations for the following atoms:

    a. Na   b. N   c. Be   d. Sr

16. What are the *representative elements*? In what region(s) of the periodic table are these elements found? In what general area of the periodic table are the *metallic* elements found? In what general area of the table are the *nonmetals* found? Where in the table are the *metalloids* located?

Name _____   Section _____   Date _____

17. Define the terms *ionization energy* and *atomic radius*.

18. How do the *ionization energies* and *atomic sizes* of elements vary both within a vertical group (family) of the periodic table and within a horizontal row (period)?

19. Arrange the following atoms from largest to smallest atomic radius and from highest to lowest ionization energy:

    a. Na, K, Rb   b. C, O, F   c. Na, Si, O

Chapter 11: Standard Review Worksheet

1. Give some examples of electromagnetic radiation.

2. Explain what the *wavelength* (λ) and *frequency* (ν) of electromagnetic radiation represent.

3. At what speed does electromagnetic radiation move through space? How is this speed related to λ and ν?

4. How does an excited atom *return* to its ground state?

5. How is the wavelength (color) of light related to the energy of the photons being emitted by an atom? How is the energy of the photons being *emitted* by an atom related to the energy changes taking place *within* the atom?

6. How did Bohr envision the relationship between the electron and the nucleus of the hydrogen atom? How did Bohr's model explain the emission of only discrete wavelengths of light by excited hydrogen atoms? Why did Bohr's model not stand up as more experiments were performed using elements other than hydrogen?

7. How does the wave mechanical picture of the atom fundamentally differ from the Bohr model?

8. How do wave mechanical *orbitals* differ from Bohr's *orbits*? What does it mean to say that an orbital represents a probability map for an electron?

9. Describe the general characteristics of the first (lowest-energy) hydrogen atomic orbital. Does this orbital have a sharp "edge"? Does the orbital represent a surface on which the electron travels at all times?

10. What do the *principal energy levels* and their sublevels represent for a hydrogen atom? How do we designate specific principal energy levels and sublevels in hydrogen?

11. Describe the sublevels and orbitals that constitute the third and fourth principal energy levels of hydrogen. What are the general shapes of their probability maps?

12. How does electron spin affect the total number of electrons that can be accommodated in a given orbital?

13. Why do we place unpaired electrons in the 2*p* orbitals of carbon, nitrogen, and oxygen?

Name _____   Section _____   Date _____

14. How many electrons overall can be accommodated in the first and second principal energy levels?

15. Why are the valence electrons more important to the atom's chemical properties than the core electrons? How is the number of valence electrons in an atom related to the atom's position on the periodic table?

16. Explain how the valence-electron configuration of most of the elements can be written just by knowing the relative *location* of the element on the table. Give specific examples.

17. Write the electron configurations for the following atoms:

 a. P
 b. Se
 c. Zr
 d. Ce

18. Arrange the following atoms from largest to smallest atomic radius and from highest to lowest ionization energy:

 a. Na, K, P
 b. Rb, N, Al
 c. Cs, I, O

Chapter 11: Challenge Review Worksheet

1. Do atoms in excited states emit radiation randomly, at any wavelength? Explain.

2. What does it mean to say that the hydrogen atom has only certain *discrete energy levels* available? How do we know this?

3. Why was the quantization of energy levels surprising to scientists when it was first discovered?

4. Schrodinger and de Broglie suggested a "wave-particle duality" for small particles—that is, if electromagnetic radiation showed some particle-like properties, then perhaps small particles might exhibit some wave-like properties. Explain this duality.

5. Use the wave mechanical picture of the hydrogen atom to describe what happens when the atom absorbs energy and moves to an "excited" state.

6. Summarize the postulates of the wave mechanical model of the atom.

7. Explain *why* the ionization energies and atomic sizes of the elements are related to the position on the periodic table.

8. Write an electron configuration for the following atoms that corresponds to an excited state:
   a. C
   b. Cr
   c. Br
   d. Os

Chapter 12: Basic Review Worksheet

1. In general, what do we mean by a *chemical bond*? Name the principal types of chemical bonds.

2. What do we mean by *ionic* bonding? Give an example of a substance whose particles are held together by ionic bonding.

3. What do we mean by *covalent* bonding and *polar covalent* bonding? How are these two bonding types similar, and how do they differ?

4. Define *electronegativity*.

5. What does it mean to say that a molecule has a *dipole moment*?

6. Give evidence that ionic bonds are very strong. Does an ionic substance contain discrete molecules?

7. Write the electron configuration for each of the following atoms and for the simple ion that the element most commonly forms. In each case, indicate which noble gas has the same electron configuration as the ion.

    a. sodium   b. iodine   c. calcium

8. On the basis of their electron configurations, predict the formula of the simple binary ionic compound likely to form when the following pairs of elements react with each other:

    a. barium and chlorine
    b. sodium and fluorine
    c. potassium and oxygen

9. What is the most important factor for the formation of a stable compound? How do we use this requirement when writing Lewis structures?

10. In writing Lewis structures for molecules, what is meant by the *duet rule*? To which element does the duet rule apply?

11. In writing Lewis structures for molecules, what do we mean by the *octet rule*? Why is attaining an octet of electrons important for an atom when it forms bonds to other atoms?

12. What is a bonding *pair* of electrons? What is nonbonding (or *lone*) pair of electrons?

Name _____ Section _____ Date _____

13. Write Lewis structures for the following molecules:

    a. PF_3 b. $SiCl_4$ c. H_2S

14. What does a *double* bond between two atoms represent in terms of the number of electrons shared? What does a *triple* bond represent?

15. What are resonance structures?

16. Determine the geometric shape for each of the following molecules:

    a. NCl_3 b. Cl_2O c. CF_4

Chapter 12: Standard Review Worksheet

1. What does the *bond energy* tell us about the strength of a chemical bond?

2. What experimental evidence do we have for the existence of ionic bonding? In general, what types of substances react to produce compounds having ionic bonding?

3. What circumstance must exist for a bond to be purely covalent? How does a polar covalent bond differ from an ionic bond?

4. How does the polarity of a bond depend on the *difference* in electronegativities of the two atoms participating in the bond? If two atoms have exactly the *same* electronegativity, what type of bond will exist between the atoms? If two atoms have vastly different electronegativities, what type of bond will exist between them?

5. What is the *difference* between a polar bond and a polar molecule (one that has a dipole moment)?

6. When atoms of a metal react with atoms of a nonmetal, what type of electron configurations do the resulting ions attain? Explain how the atoms in a covalently bonded compound can attain noble gas electron configurations.

7. With what general type of structure do ionic compounds occur? Sketch a representation of a general structure for an ionic compound.

8. Why is a cation always smaller and an anion always larger than the respective parent atom?

9. Write the electron configuration for each of the following atoms and for the simple ion that the element most commonly forms. In each case, indicate which noble gas has the same electron configuration as the ion.

    a. nitrogen   b. selenium   c. aluminum

10. On the basis of their electron configurations, predict the formula of the simple binary ionic compound likely to form when the following pairs of elements react with each other:

    a. aluminum and oxygen
    b. magnesium and nitrogen
    c. cesium and sulfur

11. When writing a Lewis structure, explain how we recognize when a molecule must contain double or triple bonds.

Name _____ Section _____ Date _____

12. Write Lewis structures for the following molecules. Draw all resonance structures when appropriate.

    a. C_2H_6 b. H_2SO_4 c. SO_2

13. Determine the geometric shape for each of the following ions:

    a.   chlorate ion   b. chlorite ion   c. perchlorate ion

Name _____   Section _____   Date _____

Chapter 12: Challenge Review Worksheet

1. Give an example of a molecule that has polar bonds and a dipole moment. Give an example of a molecule that has polar bonds but *not* a dipole moment. What are some implications of the fact that water has a dipole moment?

2. How is the attainment of a noble gas electron configuration important to our ideas of how atoms bond to each other?

3. Using an example, describe the bonding in an ionic compound containing polyatomic ions.

4. For three simple molecules of your own choosing, *apply* the rules for writing Lewis structures. Write the discussion as if you are explaining the method to someone who is *not* familiar with Lewis structures.

5. Although many simple molecules fulfill the octet rule, some common molecules are exceptions to this rule. Give three examples of molecules whose Lewis structures are exceptions to the octet rule and explain.

6. What do we mean by the *geometric structure* of a molecule? Draw the geometric structures of at least four simple molecules of your choosing, and indicate the bond angles in the structures. Explain the main ideas of the *valence shell electron pair repulsion* (VSEPR) *theory*. Using several examples, explain how you would *apply* the VSEPR theory to predict their geometric structures.

7. What bond angle results when there are only two valence electron pairs around an atom? What bond angle results when there are three valence pairs? What bond angle results when there are four pairs of valence electrons around the central atom in a molecule? Give examples of molecules containing these bond angles.

8. How do we predict the geometric structure of a molecule whose Lewis structure indicates that the molecule contains a double or triple bond? Give an example of such a molecule, write its Lewis structure, and show how the geometric shape is derived.

Chapter 13: Basic Review Worksheet

1. What are some of the general properties of gases that distinguish them from liquids and solids?

2. What is the SI unit of pressure? What units of pressure are commonly used in the United States? Why are these common units more convenient to use than the SI unit?

3. Convert 1.20 atm to units of mm Hg, torr, and pascals.

4. Your textbook gives several definitions and formulas for Boyle's law for gases. Write, in your *own* words, what this law really tells us about gases.

5. What does Charles's law tell us about how the volume of a gas sample varies as the temperature of the sample is changed?

6. What temperature scale is defined with its lowest point as the absolute zero of temperature? What is absolute zero in Celsius degrees?

7. What does Avogadro's law tell us about the relationship between the volume of a sample of gas and the number of molecules the gas contains?

8. What do we mean specifically by an *ideal* gas?

9. What is the numerical value and what are the specific units of the universal gas constant R? Why is close attention to *units* especially important when doing ideal gas law calculations?

10. A sample of gas in a 10.0-L container exerts a pressure of 565 mm Hg. Calculate the pressure exerted by the gas if the volume is changed to 15.0 L at constant temperature.

11. A sample of gas in a 5.00-L container at 35.0°C is heated at constant pressure to a temperature of 70.0°C at constant pressure. Determine the volume of the heated gas.

12. A 4.50-mol sample of a gas occupies a volume of 34.6 L at a particular temperature and pressure. What volume does 2.50 mol of the gas occupy at these same conditions of pressure and temperature?

13. A sample of gas at 24°C occupies a volume of 3.45 L and exerts a pressure of 2.10 atm. The gas is cooled to –12°C, and the pressure is increased to 5.20 atm. Determine the new volume occupied by the gas.

Name _____   Section _____   Date _____

14. What mass of helium gas exerts a pressure of 1.20 atm in a volume of 5.40 L at a temperature of 27°C?

15. Dalton's law of partial pressures concerns the properties of mixtures of gases. What is meant by the *partial pressure* of an individual gas in a mixture?

16. A 2.50-g sample of neon gas is added to a 5.00-g sample of argon gas in a 10.0-L container at 23°C. Calculate the partial pressure of each gas and the total pressure of the mixture.

17. A sample of oxygen gas is collected over water at 27°C. The total pressure is 0.95 atm, and the water vapor pressure at 27°C is 26.7 torr. Determine the partial pressure of the oxygen gas collected.

18. When calcium carbonate is heated strongly, carbon dioxide gas is evolved:

$$CaCO_3(s) \rightarrow CaO(s) + CO_2(g)$$

Determine the volume occupied by the carbon dioxide produced by the decomposition of 23.5 g of calcium carbonate. The carbon dioxide is collected at 1.10 atm and 24°C.

19. What does *STP* stand for? What conditions correspond to STP?

20. Under what conditions of pressure and temperature does a gas behave most ideally? Explain.

Chapter 13: Standard Review Worksheet

1. Describe a *manometer,* and explain how such a device can be used to measure the pressure of gas samples.

2. Write a mathematical expression for Boyle's law, and explain it. Sketch the general shape of a graph of pressure versus volume for an ideal gas, and explain it.

3. When using Boyle's law in solving problems in the textbook, you may have noticed that questions often were qualified by stating "the temperature and amount of gas remain the same." Why is this qualification necessary?

4. How does the volume-temperature relationship of Charles's law differ from the volume-pressure relationship of Boyle's law?

5. For Charles's law to hold true, why must the pressure and amount of gas remain the same?

6. Does Avogadro's law describe a direct or an inverse relationship between the volume and the number of moles of gas?

7. Why must the temperature and pressure be held constant for a valid comparison using Avogadro's law?

8. Explain how the *ideal gas law* is actually a combination of Boyle's, Charles's, and Avogadro's gas laws.

9. A sample of gas in a 25.0-L container exerts a pressure of 3.20 atm. Calculate the pressure exerted by the gas if the volume is changed to 45.0 L at constant temperature.

10. A sample of gas in a 21.5-L container at 45°C is cooled at constant pressure to a temperature of –37°C at constant pressure. Determine the volume of the cooled gas.

11. A 32.8-g sample of hydrogen gas occupies a volume of 21.6 L at a particular temperature and pressure. What volume does 12.3 g of hydrogen gas occupy at the same pressure and temperature?

12. A sample of gas at 38°C occupies a volume of 2.97 L and exerts a pressure of 3.14 atm. The gas is heated to 118°C, and the volume is decreased to 1.04 L. Determine the new pressure exerted by the gas.

13. What mass of oxygen gas exerts a pressure of 475 mm Hg in a volume of 1.25 L at a temperature of –22°C?

14. How does the *total pressure* of a gaseous mixture depend on the partial pressures of the individual gases in the mixture?

15. Many common laboratory preparations of gaseous substances involve collecting the gas produced by displacement of water from a receiving container. How is Dalton's law of partial pressures used in determining the partial pressure of the prepared gas in such an experiment?

16. A 12.5-g sample of oxygen gas is added to a 25.0-g sample of nitrogen gas in a 25.0-L container at 28°C. Calculate the partial pressure of each gas and the total pressure of the mixture.

17. A sample containing 0.80 mol of oxygen gas is collected over water at 30.0°C. The total pressure is 1.10 atm, and the water vapor pressure at 30.0°C is 31.8 torr. Determine the volume of the oxygen gas.

18. Without consulting your textbook, list and explain the main postulates of the kinetic molecular theory of gases. How do these postulates help us to account for the following properties of a gas: the pressure of the gas and why the pressure of the gas increases with increased temperature, the fact that a gas fills its entire container, and the fact that the volume of a given sample of gas increases as its temperature increased.

19. Zinc metal reacts with hydrochloric acid according to the following unbalanced equation:

$$Zn(s) + HCl(aq) \rightarrow ZnCl_2(aq) + H_2(g)$$

A 10.0-g sample of zinc is reacted with 0.200 mol of HCl. Determine the volume occupied by the hydrogen gas collected at 755 mm Hg and 22°C.

20. Do gases behave most ideally at STP? Explain.

Chapter 13: Challenge Review Worksheet

1. One of the most obvious properties of gaseous materials is the pressure they exert on their surroundings. In particular, the pressure exerted by the atmospheric gases is important. How does the pressure of the atmosphere arise, and how is this pressure commonly measured?

2. Explain how the concept of absolute zero came about through Charles's studies of gases. *Hint:* What would happen to the volume of a gas sample at absolute zero (if the gas did not liquefy first)?

3. A 12.4-g sample of helium gas occupies a volume of 23.5 L at a certain temperature and pressure. What volume does a 56.2-g sample of neon gas occupy at these conditions of temperature and pressure?

4. If the volume of a given amount of gas is doubled and the Celsius temperature is doubled, what will happen to the pressure? Explain using the gas laws and the kinetic molecular theory.

5. How does Dalton's law help us to realize that for an ideal gas sample the volume of an individual molecule is insignificant compared with the bulk volume of the sample?

6. Zinc and magnesium metal each react with hydrochloric acid according to the following equation (where M represents either Zn or Mg):

    $$M(s) + 2HCl(aq) \rightarrow MCl_2(aq) + H_2(g)$$

    A 10.00-g mixture of zinc and magnesium produces 5.74 L of hydrogen gas at 1.10 atm and 27°C. Determine the percent magnesium in the original mixture.

7. Why aren't gases ideal?

Name _____ Section _____ Date _____

Chapter 14: Basic Review Worksheet

1. Explain how the densities and compressibilities of solids and liquids contrast with those properties of gaseous substances.

2. Describe some of the physical properties of water.

3. Define the normal boiling point of water and the normal freezing point of water. Sketch a representation of a heating/cooling curve for water, marking clearly the normal freezing and boiling points.

4. Define the term *changes in state*.

5. What types of forces must be overcome to melt or vaporize a substance (are these forces *intra*molecular or *inter*molecular)?

6. Define *molar heat of fusion* and *molar heat of vaporization*.

7. The heat of fusion of aluminum is 3.95 kJ/g. What is the molar heat of fusion of aluminum?

8. What is a *dipole–dipole attraction*? What is *hydrogen bonding*?

9. Define *London dispersion forces*. Although London forces exist among all molecules, for what type of molecule are they the *only* major intermolecular force?

10. What is *vaporization*? What is *condensation*?

11. Define the *equilibrium vapor pressure* of a liquid. How is the magnitude of a liquid's vapor pressure related to the intermolecular forces?

12. What is the vapor pressure of water at 100.0°C? How do you know this?

13. Define *crystalline solid*.

14. What are metal *alloys*?

Chapter 14: Standard Review Worksheet

1. How do we know that the properties of the solid and liquid states of a substance are more similar than to the properties of the substance in the gaseous state?

2. Why is water one of the most important substances on earth?

3. Why does a sample of boiling water remain at the same temperature until all the water has been boiled away?

4. Are changes in state physical or chemical changes? Explain. Why is the molar heat of vaporization of water so much larger than its molar heat of fusion?

5. Why does the boiling point of a liquid vary with altitude?

6. How do the strengths of dipole–dipole forces compare with the strengths of typical covalent bonds?

7. What conditions are necessary for hydrogen bonding to exist in a substance or mixture? Provide a molecular-level sketch, and label the hydrogen bonding.

8. Explain how London forces arise. Are London forces relatively strong or relatively weak? Explain.

9. Why does the process of *vaporization* require an input of energy?

10. Calculate the total energy required to melt 55.1 g of ice at 0°C, to warm the resulting liquid water from 0 to 100°C , and to boil the water completely to vapor at 100°C.

11. Explain how the process of vaporization and condensation represent an *equilibrium* in a closed container.

12. Why is the magnitude of a liquid's vapor pressure related to its intermolecular forces?

13. Explain in your own words why the boiling point of a liquid is related to the atmospheric pressure.

14. Describe in detail some important types of crystalline solids, and name a substance that is an example of each type of solid. Explain how the particles are held together in each type of solid (the interparticle forces that exist).

15. Describe the bonding that exists in metals and how this model explains some of the unique physical properties of metals.

16. Identify the two main types of alloys, and describe how their structures differ. Give two examples of each type of alloy.

Chapter 14: Challenge Review Worksheet

1. What experimental evidence do we have for hydrogen bonding?

2. Why is it so important that water has a large heat of vaporization?

3 Describe an experiment that demonstrates vapor pressure.

4. How do the interparticle forces in a solid influence the bulk physical properties of the solid?

5. Which is the more ideal gas, CO or N_2? Explain.

6. Another name for an atomic solid is a network solid. Explain why the term *network solid* is an appropriate name for such substances.

7. You are on a camping trip and notice that water seems to boil more quickly than it does at home. You measure the temperature of the boiling water and find that it is 98°C. What are possible explanations for your observation? Why does the water seem to boil more quickly?

8. Plant material is a renewable energy source used extensively in many areas of the world. It includes peat from bogs, trees, and ethanol made from corn. Basically, it includes any plant materials that have water removed from them so that they will burn and release energy for heating, cooking, and other uses. Ethanol releases 2.34×10^4 kJ/L when it is burned. What volume of ethanol must burn to change 500.0 g of water to steam if the initial temperature of the water is 22.0°C?

Chapter 15: Basic Review Worksheet

1. Define a *solution*.

2. Describe how an ionic solute such as NaCl dissolves in water to form a solution. How does a molecular solid such as sugar dissolve in water?

3. List three ways to increase the rate of dissolution of a solute.

4. Define a *saturated* solution, an *unsaturated* solution, and a *supersaturated* solution.

5. Define *percent by mass*, *molarity,* and *normality*.

6. What is one *equivalent* of an acid? What does an equivalent of a base represent?

7. What is a one *normal* solution of an acid or a base?

8. A 12.5-g sample of glucose ($C_6H_{12}O_6$) is dissolved in 225 g of water. Calculate the percent by mass of glucose in the solution.

9. A chemist prepares some standard solutions for use in the lab using 500.0-mL volumetric flasks to contain the solutions. If the following masses of solutes are used, calculate the resulting molarity of each solution:

   a. 4.865 g NaCl b. 78.91 g $AgNO_3$

10. Suppose that each of the following solutions is diluted by adding the indicated amount of water. Calculate the new concentrations of the solutions.

    a. 255 mL of 3.02 M HCl; 375 mL water added
    b. 75.1 g of 1.51% $AgNO_3$; 125 g water added

11. Calculate the volume (in milliliters) of each of the following acid solutions that would be required to neutralize 36.2 mL of 0.259 M NaOH solution:

    a. 0.271 M HCl   b. 0.119 M H_2SO_4 c. 0.171 M H_3PO_4

12. What volume of 0.242 M H_2SO_4 can furnish the same number of moles of H^+ ions as each of the following?

    a. 41.5 mL of 0.118 M HCl
    b. 27.1 mL of 0.121 M H_3PO_4

13. Calculate the normality of the following solutions:

    a.   0.204 M HCl

    b.   0.328 M H_2SO_4

14. What volume of 0.10 M $Ba(NO_3)_2$ solution is required to react completely with 100.0 mL of 0.50 M NaCl solution to form $BaCl_2(s)$?

15. What is meant by the term *colligative property*?

Chapter 15: Standard Review Worksheet

1. How are the strong bonding forces in a crystal of ionic solute overcome to allow the solid to dissolve in water?

2. What forces between water molecules and the molecules of a molecular solid tend to help the solute dissolve?

3. Does the term *saturated* for a solution mean the same thing as *concentrated*? Explain.

4. When a solution is diluted by adding additional solvent, the *concentration* of solute changes, but the *amount* of solute present does not change. Explain.

5. Suppose 250.0 mL of water is added to 125.0 mL of 0.551 M NaCl solution. Explain *how* you would calculate the concentration of the solution after dilution.

6. How is the equivalent weight of an acid or a base related to the substance's molar mass?

7. Give an example of an acid and a base that have equivalent weights *equal* to their molar masses. Give an example of an acid and a base that have equivalent weights that are *not equal* to their molar masses.

8. How is the *normality* of an acid or a base solution related to its *molarity*?

9. Suppose that 4.25 g of NaCl and 7.50 g of KCl are both dissolved in 125 g of water. Calculate the percent by mass of each component of the solution.

10. Calculate the molarity of a solution in which enough water is added to 250.0 g of calcium chloride to make a solution with a volume of 2.25 L.

11. To prepare 125 mL of 0.100 M sulfuric acid (H_2SO_4) in the lab requires 0.69 mL of concentrated acid. What is the concentration of concentrated sulfuric acid?

12. Silver chromate (Ag_2CrO_4) is a blood red ionic solid that has very low solubility in water. What mass of silver chromate can be produced by mixing 100.0 mL of 0.100 M silver nitrate and 75.0 mL of 0.100 M sodium chromate?

13. Calculate the volume (in milliliters) of 0.104 M HCl that would be required to neutralize 25.2 mL of 0.00491 M barium hydroxide solution.

14. What volume (in milliliters) of 0.50 N NaOH is required to neutralize 15.0 mL of 0.35 N H_2SO_4?

15. Explain in your own words why adding a solute to water raises its boiling point.

Chapter 15: Challenge Review Worksheet

1. Why do some substances *not* dissolve in water to any appreciable extent?

2. Why does a solute dissolve only to a particular extent in water?

3. How does formation of a saturated solution represent an equilibrium?

4. The concentration of a solution may be expressed in various ways. Two means of expressing concentration were introduced in Chapter 15—mass percent and molarity. How are these two concentration expressions the same, and how do they differ? Suppose that 5.0 g of NaCl is dissolved in 15.0 g of water to give a solution volume of 16.1 mL. Explain how you would calculate the mass percent of NaCl and the molarity of NaCl in this solution. Which number did you *not* use for the mass percent calculation? Which number did you *not* use for the molarity calculation? Suppose that instead of being given the volume of the solution after mixing, you had been given the density of the solution. Explain how you would calculate the molarity of this solution with this information.

5. Give an example of a solution whose normality is equal to its molarity and an example of a solution whose normality is *not* the same as its molarity.

6. You make two solutions, one containing silver nitrate and one containing sodium chloride. You make these separate solutions by adding equal masses of the solid to enough water to make 1.0 L of each solution. You then mix these solutions together and note the formation of a white solid. You collect and dry the solid, and you find the mass to be 143.35 g. Determine the concentration of all the ions remaining in the solution.

7. What mass of glucose ($C_6H_{12}O_6$) must be dissolved in 1.0 L of water so that the solution has the same freezing point as a solution containing 10.0 g of NaCl in 1.0 L of water?

Chapter 16: Basic Review Worksheet

1. Compare the Arrhenius and Brønsted-Lowry definitions of an acid and a base.

2. Describe the relationship between a conjugate acid–base pair in the Brønsted-Lowry model.

3. Write balanced chemical equations showing the following molecules behaving as Brønsted-Lowry acids in water: HCl, H_2SO_4.

4. How is the *strength* of an acid related to the *position* of its ionization equilibrium?

5. Write the equations for the dissociation (ionization) of HCl, HNO_3, and $HClO_4$ in water.

6. Explain how water is an *amphoteric* substance.

7. What values does K_w have at 25°C? What are $[H^+]$ and $[OH^-]$ in pure water at 25°C?

8. How does $[H^+]$ compare with $[OH^-]$ in an acidic solution? How does $[H^+]$ compare with $[OH^-]$ in a basic solution?

9. How is the pH scale defined?

10. What range of pH values corresponds to acidic solutions? What range corresponds to basic solutions?

11. When the pH of a solution changes by one unit, by what factor does the hydrogen ion concentration change in the solution?

12. How is pOH defined?

13. Describe a *buffered* solution. Why is buffering so important in biologic systems?

14. Write the conjugate acid of each of the following bases:
    a. SO_3^{2-}
    b. HS^-
    c. F^-
    d. CH_3COO^-

15. Write the conjugate base of each of the following acids:

    a. H_2SO_4

    b. H_2S

    c. H_2CO_3

    d. $HC_2H_3O_2$

16. For each of the given items, calculate the indicated quantity:

    a. $[H^+] = 4.01 \times 10^{-3}\ M$; pH = ?

    b. $[OH^-] = 7.41 \times 10^{-8}\ M$; pOH = ?

    c. $[H^+] = 9.61 \times 10^{-6}\ M$; pOH = ?

17. Calculate the pH and pOH values for each of the following solutions:

    a. $0.00141\ M\ HNO_3$

    b. $2.13 \times 10^{-3}\ M\ NaOH$

18. A 25.0-mL sample of 0.50 M HCl is titrated to the endpoint with 12.4 mL of NaOH. Calculate the concentration of the NaOH solution.

Chapter 16: Standard Review Worksheet

1. Write balanced chemical equations showing the following molecules/ions behaving as Brønsted-Lowry acids in water: H_3PO_4, NH_4^+.

2. Acetic acid is a weak acid in water. What does this indicate about the affinity of the acetate ion for protons compared with the affinity of water molecules for protons? If a solution of sodium acetate is dissolved in water, the solution is basic. Explain. Write equilibrium reaction equations for the ionization of acetic acid in water and for the reaction of the acetate ion with water in a solution of sodium acetate.

3. Are aqueous solutions of NaCl, $NaNO_3$, or $NaClO_4$ acidic, basic, or neutral? Explain.

4. Write the chemical equation for the autoionization of water. Write the expression for the equilibrium constant K_w for this reaction.

5. Why is pH = 7.00 considered *neutral*?

6. How are pH and pOH for a given solution related? Explain.

7. Give three examples of buffered solutions. For each of your examples, write equations that explain how the components of the buffered solution consume added strong acids or bases.

8. Write the conjugate acid of each of the following bases:

   a. HSO_4^-
   b. HSO_3^-
   c. H_2O
   d. S^{2-}

9. Write the conjugate base of each of the following acids:

   a. H_3PO_4
   b. HS^-
   c. HCO_3^-
   d. NH_3

10. For each of the given items, calculate the indicated quantity:

   a. $[OH^-] = 6.62 \times 10^{-3}$ M; pH = ?
   b. pH = 6.325; $[OH^-]$ = ?
   c. pH = 9.413; $[H^+]$ = ?

11. Calculate the pH and pOH values for each of the following solutions:

   a.   0.00515 M HCl

   b. 5.65×10^{-5} M Ca(OH)$_2$

12. You titrate a 50.0-mL sample of HCl with 0.10 M NaOH. The titration requires 23.8 mL of the base. Calculate the concentration of the HCl solution.

Chapter 16: Challenge Review Worksheet

1. For each of the following species, write the equation for the reaction of each species with water if it acts like an acid and if it acts like a base:

   a. HS^-
   b. HCO_3^-
   c. HSO_4^-
   d. $H_2PO_4^-$
   e. HSO_3^-

2. At 35°C, the value of K_w is 2.09×10^{-14}. Determine the pH of water at this temperature. What does the term neutral mean at 35°C?

3. Determine the pH of a solution made by dissolving 1.0×10^{-12} mol HCl in enough water to make 1.0 L of solution.

4. An acidic solution is made by dissolving 1.0×10^{-13} mol HNO_3 in enough distilled water to make 1.0 L of solution.

   a. What is the pH of the solution?
   b. What is the pOH?
   c. What is the $[OH^-]$?

5. Normal rainwater is slightly acidic because carbon dioxide from the air dissolves in the water, forming a dilute carbonic acid. A sample of rainwater from an area is found to have a pH of 6.34.

   a. What is the pOH of the rainwater?
   b. What is the $[OH^-]$?
   c. What is the $[H^+]$?

6. You are titrating a 50.0-mL sample of HNO_3 with 0.20 M NaOH. After adding 45.3 mL of the base, you remember that you have not added phenolphthalein indicator. On adding the indicator, the solution turns bright pink. You decide to "backtitrate" by adding 0.10 M HCl to the solution. You reach the stoichiometric point by adding 11.6 mL of the 0.10 M HCl. Determine the concentration of the original HNO_3 solution.

7. Equal amounts of an acid and a base react completely, forming a salt and water. The pH of the resulting solution is checked, and rather than its being neutral, the solution is found to have a pH of 6.1. Using what you know about strong acids and bases, categorize the reacting acid and base as one of the following: strong acid and strong base, strong acid and weak base, or weak acid and strong base. Explain your answer.

Chapter 17: Basic Review Worksheet

1. Explain the *collision model* for chemical reactions. What "collides"?

2. Define *activation energy*.

3. Define *catalyst*. What do we call a biologic catalyst?

4. Explain what it means when a reaction "has reached a state of chemical equilibrium."

5. What do we mean by an *equilibrium position*? Is the equilibrium position always the same for a reaction regardless of the amounts of reactants present initially?

6. Compare *homogeneous* and *heterogeneous* equilibria.

7. Give Le Chatelier's principle in your own words.

8. Explain what is meant by *solubility product constant*.

9. Write the equilibrium constant expressions for each of the following reactions:
   a. $H_2(g) + Br_2(g) \rightleftharpoons 2HBr(g)$
   b. $SO_2Cl_2(g) \rightleftharpoons SO_2(g) + Cl_2(g)$
   c. $CaCO_3(s) \rightleftharpoons CaO(s) + CO_2(g)$

10. Write expressions for K_{sp} for each of the following sparingly soluble salts:
    a. ZnS
    b. $HgCl_2$
    c. LaF_3

11. Copper(II) sulfide (CuS) dissolves in water to give a solution that is 9.2×10^{-23} M at 25°C. Calculate K_{sp} for CuS at this temperature.

Chapter 17: Standard Review Worksheet

1. Do all collisions between molecules result in the breaking of bonds and the formation of products? Why?

2. How does the collision model account for the observation that higher concentrations and higher temperatures tend to make reactions occur faster?

3. Sketch a graph for the progress of a reaction illustrating the *activation energy* for the reaction.

4. Explain how an increase in temperature for a reaction affects the number of collisions that possess energy greater than E_a.

5. How does a *catalyst* speed up a reaction? Does a catalyst change E_a for the reaction?

6. Explain why equilibrium is a *dynamic* state.

7. What happens to the *rates* of the forward and reverse reactions as a system proceeds to equilibrium from a starting point where only reactants are present?

8. Although the equilibrium constant for a given reaction always has the same value at the same temperature, the actual *concentrations* present at equilibrium may differ from one experiment to another. Explain.

9. How does the fact that an equilibrium is *heterogeneous* influence the expression we write for the equilibrium constant for the reaction?

10. Suppose that the reaction system

$$2SO_2(g) + O_2(g) \rightleftharpoons 2SO_3(g)$$

has already reached equilibrium. Predict the effect of each of the following changes on the position of the equilibrium:

   a. $SO_2(g)$ is added to the system.
   b. The $SO_3(g)$ is liquefied and removed from the system.
   c. A very efficient catalyst is used.
   d. The volume of the container is reduced drastically.

11. Explain how dissolving a slightly soluble salt to form a saturated solution is an *equilibrium* process.

12. When writing expressions for K_{sp}, why is the concentration of the sparingly soluble salt itself not included in the expression?

13. Given the value for the solubility product for a slightly soluble salt, explain how the molar solubility, and the solubility in grams per liter, may be calculated.

14. Write the equilibrium constant expressions for each of the following reactions:
    a. $2NO(g) + O_2(g) \rightleftharpoons 2NO_2(g)$
    b. $N_2H_4(l) + O_2(g) \rightleftharpoons N_2(g) + 2H_2O(g)$
    c. $CO(g) + NO_2(g) \rightleftharpoons CO_2(g) + NO(g)$

15. For the reaction

$$2SO_2(g) + O_2(g) \rightleftharpoons 2SO_3(g)$$

at a particular temperature, the equilibrium system contains $[SO_3(g)] = 0.42\ M$, $[SO_2(g)] = 1.4 \times 10^{-3}\ M$, and $[O_2(g)] = 4.5 \times 10^{-4}\ M$. Calculate K for the process at this temperature.

16. Write expressions for K_{sp} for each of the following slightly soluble salts:
    a. $Fe(OH)_3$
    b. $Cd(OH)_2$
    c. $Ba_3(PO_4)_2$

17. Silver chloride (AgCl) dissolves in water to give a solution containing 9.0×10^{-4} g solute per liter at 10°C. Calculate K_{sp} for AgCl at this temperature.

Chapter 17: Challenge Review Worksheet

1. Explain why, once a chemical system has reached equilibrium, the concentrations of all reacts and products remain *constant* with time. Why does this *constancy* of concentration not contradict our picture of equilibrium as being *dynamic*?

2. Describe how we write the equilibrium expression for a reaction. Give three examples of balanced chemical equations and the corresponding expressions for their equilibrium constants.

3. Give balanced chemical equations and write the corresponding equilibrium constant expressions for examples of both homogeneous and heterogeneous equilibria.

4. Give an example (including a balanced chemical equation) of how each of the following changes can affect the position of equilibrium in favor of additional products for a system:

   a. The concentration of one of the reactants is increased.
   b. One of the products is selectively removed from the system.
   c. The reaction system is compressed to a smaller volume.
   d. The temperature is increased for an endothermic reaction.
   e. The temperature is decreased for an exothermic process.

5. Give three balanced chemical equations for solubility processes and write the expressions for K_{sp} corresponding to the reactions you have chosen.

6. Magnesium fluoride dissolves in water to give a solution containing 8.0×10^{-2} g solute per liter at 25°C. Calculate K_{sp} for magnesium fluoride at this temperature.

Chapter 18: Basic Review Worksheet

1. What is meant by the term *oxidation*? What is meant by the term *reduction*? Answer these in terms of electrons and in terms of oxidation states.

2. Determine the oxidation states of the atoms in the following substances:

   a. Cr_2O_3
   b. $FeCl_2$
   c. Na_3PO_4

3. What is meant by *oxidizing agent*? What is meant by *reducing agent*? Explain the statement, "An oxidizing agent is reduced, and a reducing agent is oxided."

4. What are *half-reactions*? Why do we use them?

5. Answer the following:

   a. When a half-reaction is reversed, what happens to its potential?
   b. When the coefficients of a half-reaction are multiplied by a factor, what happens to its potential?

6. How is balancing oxidation–reduction equations similar to the method for balancing equations you learned in Chapter 7? How is it different?

7. Balance the following oxidation–reduction equations:

   a. $Mg(s) + Hg^{2+}(aq) \rightarrow Mg^{2+}(aq) + Hg_2^{2+}(aq)$
   b. $Zn(s) + Ag^+(aq) \rightarrow Zn^{2+}(aq) + Ag(s)$

8. What is an *anode*? What is a *cathode*?

Chapter 18: Standard Review Worksheet

1. Identify the elements that are oxidized and the elements that are reduced in the following equations:

   a. $2Al(s) + 3Cl_2(g) \rightarrow 2AlCl_3(s)$
   b. $2K(s) + I_2(s) \rightarrow 2KI(s)$
   c. $2NO(g) + O_2(g) \rightarrow 2NO_2(g)$

2. Determine the oxidation states of the atoms in the following:

   a. $KMnO_4$
   b. $HCrO_4^-$
   c. BiO^+

3. Identify the oxidizing and reducing agents in the following equations:

   a. $CH_4(g) + 2O_2(g) \rightarrow CO_2(g) + 2H_2O(g)$
   b. $2Cu(s) + S(s) \rightarrow Cu_2S(s)$

4. Why must the number of electrons be balanced in an oxidation–reduction reaction?

5. Balance the following oxidation–reduction equations in acidic solution:

   a. $NO_3^-(aq) + Br^-(aq) \rightarrow NO(g) + Br_2(l)$
   b. $Ni(s) + NO_3^-(aq) \rightarrow Ni^{2+}(aq) + NO_2(g)$

6. Why must we separate the oxidizing agent from the reducing agent when constructing an electrochemical cell?

7. Consider the oxidation–reduction reaction

$$Cu(s) + Ag^+(aq) \rightarrow Cu^{2+}(aq) + Ag(s)$$

   a. Balance this oxidation–reduction equation.
   b. Label the oxidizing agent and the reducing agent.
   c. Sketch a galvanic cell that uses this reaction, and label the anode and the cathode.

Chapter 18: Challenge Review Worksheet

1. Determine the oxidation states of the atoms in the molecule OF_2.

2. Not all oxidation–reduction reactions involve a metal and nonmetal. Give an example that does not, and explain how it is an oxidation–reduction reaction.

3. Balance the following oxidation–reduction equations for the conditions specified:

   a. $S_2O_8^{2-}(aq) + Cr^{3+}(aq) \rightarrow SO_4^{2-}(aq) + Cr_2O_7^{2-}(aq)$ (acidic solution)
   b. $ClO_4^-(aq) + Cl^-(aq) \rightarrow ClO_3^-(aq) + Cl_2(g)$ (acidic solution)
   c. $Cl_2(g) \rightarrow Cl^-(aq) + ClO^-(aq)$ (basic solution)

Chapter 19: Basic Review Worksheet

1. What particles are present in the nucleus of an atom that account for its great density? List the relative masses and charges for these particles.

2. What does it mean when we say that a substance is *radioactive*?

3. How is balancing nuclear equations similar to balancing chemical equations? How is it different?

4. Provide an example of each of the following nuclear processes: alpha-particle production, beta-particle production, positron production, and electron capture.

5. Complete the following nuclear equations by supplying the missing particle:

   a. $^2_1H + {}^3_1H \rightarrow {}^4_2He + ?$

   b. $^{74}_{35}Br \rightarrow {}^0_{+1}\beta + ?$

6. Consider the isotopes of radium listed in Table 19.3 in the text. Which isotope is the most stable against decay? Which isotope is the "hottest"?

7. Define the term *half-life*.

8. How is radioactivity used in the medical field?

9. Compare and contrast *nuclear fission* and *nuclear fusion*.

10. What is meant by *chain reaction*?

Chapter 19: Standard Review Worksheet

1. What is the net effect of beta production? Positron production? Use examples to support your answer.

2. The Z does not supply new information in $_Z^A X$ notation. Why not?

3. Use $_Z^A X$ notation to show the net effect of alpha-particle production, beta-particle production, positron production, and electron capture. That is, each of the equations you write should have $_Z^A X$ on the left side and should be balanced.

4. Write a nuclear equation for each of the following:

   a. The nuclide $_{23}^{53} V$ undergoes radioactive decay by production of a beta particle.

   b. The nuclide $_{96}^{244} Cm$ undergoes radioactive decay by production of an alpha particle.

5. Complete the following nuclear equations by supplying the missing particle.

   a. $_{88}^{226} Ra \rightarrow {}_{86}^{222} Rn + ?$

   b. $_{86}^{222} Rn \rightarrow {}_{84}^{218} Po + ?$

6. Consider the following radioactive isotopes of krypton and their half-lives:

Isotope	Half-Life
krypton-73	27 s
krypton-74	11.5 min
krypton-76	14.8 h
krypton-81	2.1×10^5 yr

   a. Which of the isotopes is most stable?

   b. Which of the isotopes is "hottest"

   c. If we were to begin a half-life experiment with separate 125-μg samples of each isotope, approximately how much of each isotope would remain after 24 hours?

7. Explain the relevance of critical mass to the idea of a chain reaction.

8. How does a breeder reactor compare with a general nuclear reactor?

Chapter 19: Challenge Review Worksheet

1. There are four stable isotopes of iron with mass numbers 54, 56, 57, and 58. There are two radioactive isotopes: iron-53 and iron-59. Predict modes of decay for each of these isotopes and explain.

2. Neon consists primarily of two isotopes with mass numbers 20 and 22, with a small amount of a third isotope with mass number 21. Which of the neon isotopes predominates in nature? Explain.

3. The problems in the text have asked you to approximate the amount of radioactive sample after a certain amount of time given the half-life. Knowing that a half-life is the amount of time required for half of a sample of radioactive substance to decay, derive a formula to calculate this amount exactly. Then use the formula to calculate the percent of radioactive nuclei present after 73 years given a half-life of 21 years.

4. Define the term *third-life* in an analogous way to the term *half-life*. Determine the third-life of a sample that has a half-life of 15 years.

5. How do the chemical properties of radioactive isotopes compare with those of stable isotopes? Why? Why is this important for radiotracers?

Chapter 20: Standard Review Worksheet

1. When a carbon atom is bonded to four other carbon atoms, what geometric arrangement occurs around the carbon atom? Why?

2. Write the names and structural formulas of the first 10 straight-chain alkanes without looking in your textbook. By what group of atoms does each successive member of this family differ from the previous member?

3. How is the number of multiple substituents of the same type indicated in the systematic name of a hydrocarbon?

4. How is the root name of an alkane modified to indicate that a given hydrocarbon contains a double or triple bond?

5. How is the location of a double or triple bond in the longest continuous chain of an unsaturated hydrocarbon indicated?

6. What does a triple bond represent? How many pairs of electrons are shared between the atoms in a triple bond? Draw the Lewis structure of a molecule with a triple bond.

7. Draw structural formulas showing all possible molecules containing six carbon atoms and having one triple bond. Name each of these.

8. Sketch the general formula for the following functional groups without looking in your text: alcohols (primary, secondary, and tertiary), ethers, aldehydes, ketones, carboxylic acids, esters, and amines.

9. Name the following molecules:

   a.

   $$CH_3 - CH - CH_2 - CH_3$$
   $$\qquad\quad |$$
   $$\qquad CH_2 - CH_3$$

   b.

   $$CH_3 - CH = CH - CH - CH_2 - CH_3$$
   $$\qquad\qquad\qquad\quad |$$
   $$\qquad\qquad\qquad CH_3$$

   c.

   $$\qquad\qquad\qquad Cl$$
   $$\qquad\qquad\qquad |$$
   $$CH_3 - C \equiv C - CH - CH_3$$

d.

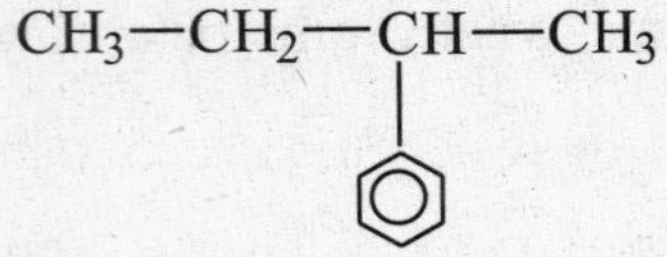

$$CH_3-CH_2-CH-CH_3$$

e.

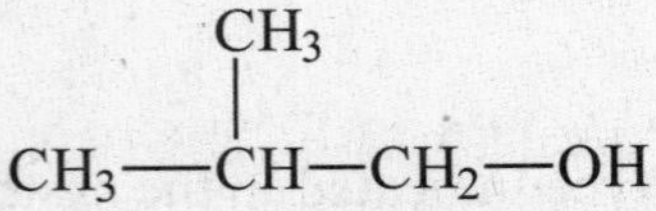

$$CH_3-CH-CH_2-OH$$
with CH_3 above the CH

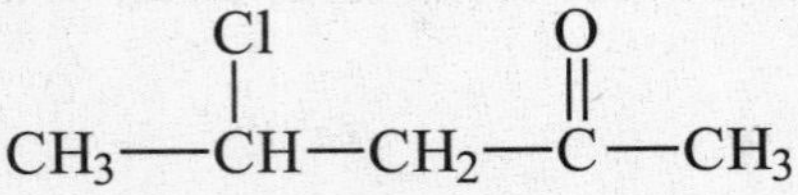

f.

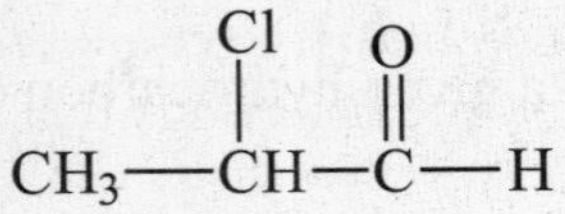

$$CH_3-CH-C-H$$
with Cl above the CH and O above the C

g.

$$CH_3-CH-CH_2-C-CH_3$$
with Cl above the CH and O above the C

h.

$$CH_3-CH_2-CH_2-CH-C-OH$$
with CH_3 above the CH and O above the C

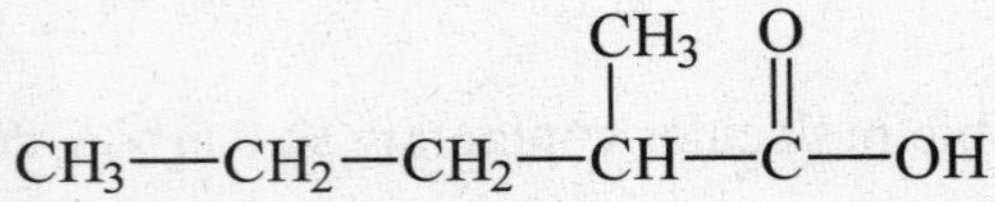

10. Sketch the following molecules:

   a. 2-methylbutane
   b. 3-methyl-2-pentene
   c. 3,3-dichloropropyne
   d. 1,3,5-trichlorobenzene
   e. 2-methyl-2-propanol
   f. 3-methylbutanal
   g. 2,5,6-trichloro-3-heptanone
   h. 3-iodopropanoic acid

Chapter 20: Challenge Review Worksheet

1. Petroleum is a mixture of hydrocarbons that is separated into its component parts by fractional distillation. Explain why the boiling points of the hydrocarbons contained in petroleum increase as their molecular masses increase.

2. Weak acids ionize to various extents as indicated by equilibrium constants. For the weak acid 4-chlorobutanoic acid ($ClCH_2CH_2CH_2COOH$), $K = 2.96 \times 10^{-5}$. For another weak acid with the same atoms arranged differently, 2-chlorobutanoic acid ($CH_3CH_2CHClCOOH$), $K = 1.39 \times 10^{-3}$. Why are more ions in solution for 2-chlorobutanoic acid?

3. Organic chemistry involves the study of carbon-containing compounds, but not all carbon-containing compounds are organic compounds. List at least four compounds that contain carbon but are not organic compounds.

Chapter 21: Standard Review Worksheet

1. The substance in the nucleus of the cell that stores and transmits genetic information is _____, which stands for _____.

2. The basic repeating monomer units of DNA and RNA are called _____.

3. The basic linkage in DNA or RNA between the sugar molecule and phosphoric acid is a phosphate _____ linkage

4. In a normal strand of DNA, the base _____ is always paired with adenine, and _____ is always paired with cytosine.

5. The codes specified by _____ are responsible for assembling the correct primary structure of a protein.

6. _____ are esters of the polyhydroxyalcohol glycerol with long-chain carboxylic acids.

7. Vegetable oils tend to contain _____ fatty acids, whereas animal fats tend to be _____.

8. The starting material in the body for the synthesis of other steroids is _____.

9. The protein _____ carries oxygen from the lungs to other body tissues.

10. Consider the amino acids shown in Figure 21.2 in the text. Based on your knowledge of intermolecular forces, indicate which amino acids you would expect to be hydrophilic and which would be hydrophobic. Explain your reasoning for each amino acid.

11. Sketch the basic ring structure common to all steroids. Sketch the structures of at least three common steroids and describe their functions.

12. What is a *phospholipid*? How does the structure of a phospholipid differ from that of a triglyceride? What common phospholipid behaves as an emulsifying agent and is used frequently in the food industry?

13. How many possible primary structures exist for a small polypeptide containing four individual amino acids?

14. In the formation of a polynucleotide, which adjacent nucleotides bond to each other?

15. What general name is given to sugars containing five carbon atoms? Six carbon atoms? Three carbon atoms?

16. What is the primary human bile acid, and what is its function in the body?

17. Describe the structure of a *wax*. Where do waxes occur in living creatures, and what functions do they serve?

Name _____   Section _____   Date _____

Chapter 21: Challenge Review Worksheet

1. a. Write the sequences of all possible tripeptides composed of the following amino acids: cysteine (cys), glutamine (gln), aspartic acid (asp), and arginine (arg).

   b. Does your list from part a include all possible tripeptides that contain these four amino acids? Explain.

2. Laundry detergents often advertise that they contain enzymes. Why might it be an advantage to have enzymes in laundry detergents?

Answer Key

Chapter 2: Basic Review Worksheet

1. Defining what scientists mean by "matter" often seems circular to students. Scientists say that matter is something that "has mass and occupies space" without ever really explaining what it means to "have mass" or to "occupy space"! The concept of matter is so basic and fundamental that it becomes difficult to give a good textbook definition other than to say that matter is the "stuff" of which everything is made.

2. Chemists tend to give a functional definition of what they mean by an "element": An element is a fundamental substance that cannot be broken down into any simpler substances by chemical methods. Compounds, on the other hand, can be broken down into simpler substances (the elements of which the compound is composed). Examples include water as a compound and gold as an element.

3. A gas is a substance that has no fixed volume or shape; in addition, the particles making up a gas are spread relatively far apart. A liquid is a substance that has a definite volume but takes the shape of its container; also, the particles making up a liquid are relatively close together. A solid is a substance that has a fixed shape and volume and is rigid; the particles making up a solid are generally packed together and orderly.

4. The chemical properties of a given substance indicate how that substance reacts with other substances. The physical properties of a substance are the inherent characteristics of the substance, which result in no change in the composition of the substance when we measure or study these properties.

5. A chemical change for a substance results in the substance being converted into another substance or substances. A physical change for a substance is a change in the substance that does not alter the identity or composition of the substance; physical changes typically represent changes in only the physical state (solid, liquid, vapor) of the substance.

6. An alloy is a substance that contains a mixture of elements and has metallic properties. Brass and steel are examples of alloys.

7. A mixture is a combination of two or more substances that may be varied in its composition. Most commonly in chemistry a mixture is a combination of two or more pure substances (either elements or compounds). Dirt is an example of a mixture.

8. A solution is a particular type of mixture that appears completely homogeneous throughout. A solution can be made by dissolving sugar in water, for example.

9. Pure substances are either elements or compounds. A pure substance always has the same composition. A pure substance cannot be a mixture.

10. A homogeneous mixture is a mixture that is the same throughout; a homogeneous mixture is also called a *solution*. A heterogeneous mixture is a mixture that contains regions with different properties.

11. Mixtures can be resolved into their components by distillation or filtration.

Chapter 2: Standard Review Worksheet

1. On the most fundamental basis, all matter is composed of tiny particles called *atoms*. Atoms may be combined to form molecules. Matter can be classified as to the physical state a particular substance happens to take. Some are gases, some liquids, and some solids. Matter also can be classified as to whether it is a pure substance or a mixture. If it is a mixture, it can be further classified as homogeneous or heterogeneous.

2. Physical properties include color, odor, physical state, density, solubility, melting point, boiling point, etc. For example, when we say that sodium is a grayish white, soft, low-density metal, we are describing some of sodium's physical properties. When we say that sodium metal reacts with chlorine gas to form sodium chloride, we are describing a chemical property of sodium.

3. For example, when we heat a piece of sodium metal in a sealed tube in a burner flame, the sodium melts and then vaporizes. The liquid and vapor are still sodium, however, and only physical changes have occurred. On the other hand, if we heat a piece of sodium in an open flame, the sodium reacts with oxygen in the air and is converted to a mixture of sodium oxides. The pure elemental substance sodium is converted into compounds and has undergone a chemical change.

4. a. physical; b. physical; c. chemical; d. chemical

5. For example, sulfur and oxygen are both elements (sulfur occurs as S_8 molecules and oxygen as O_2 molecules). When sulfur and oxygen are placed together and heated, the compound sulfur dioxide (SO_2) forms.

6. Although a solution is homogeneous in appearance, a solution is a mixture of two or more pure substances: If it were possible to see the individual particles of a solution, we would notice that different types of molecules are present.

7. Yes to both. Pure substances contain only one type of atom or molecule. Thus elements (composed of one type of atom) or compounds (composed of one type of molecule) will always be pure substances.

8. No to both. Pure substances contain only one type of atom or molecule. Mixtures contain more than one type of atom or molecule. Solutions are homogeneous mixtures. Thus we cannot say that a sugar–water solution is pure because it contains two types of molecules (sugar molecules and water molecules).

9. In filtration, a mixture is poured onto a mesh (such as filter paper) that allows the liquid to pass through but leaves the solid material behind. In distillation, the liquid is boiled off and collected in a separate container.

Chapter 2: Challenge Review Worksheet

1. Answers will vary.

2. Answers will vary.

3. No. Physical properties are not necessarily accompanied by chemical changes. However, chemical changes are always accompanied by physical changes.

4. No. Some elements can be composed of molecules. For example, the oxygen that we breathe is made of diatomic oxygen molecules (O_2).

5. When we analyze sulfur dioxide, for example, we notice that each and every molecule consists of one sulfur atom and two oxygen atoms, and on a mass basis, sulfur dioxide consists of 50% each of sulfur and oxygen. Thus sulfur dioxide has a constant composition. The reason the mass percent of all sulfur dioxide is constant is because of a constant number of atoms of each type present in the compound's molecules.

6. Yes. For example, if a scientist anywhere in the universe analyzed sulfur dioxide, he or she would find the same composition. If a scientist finds something that does not have the same composition, then the substance cannot be sulfur dioxide.

7. Answers will vary. Examples may include dirt, sand, paper, and chunky peanut butter.

8. All solutions are mixtures, but not all mixtures are solutions. Only homogeneous mixtures are solutions.

9. Answers will vary. Examples include: a. a sugar–water solution, homogeneous; b. air, homogeneous (although air consists of more than two gases, it is mainly oxygen and nitrogen); c. rubbing alcohol, homogeneous; d. brass, homogeneous.

10. Filtration and distillation are both physical methods. They do not involve a change in the chemical makeup of the substances that are separated.

Chapter 3: Basic Review Worksheet

1. An element is a pure substance that cannot be broken down into simpler substances by chemical means. There are presently more than 110 elements recognized, of which 88 occur in nature (the remaining have been synthesized by nuclear processes). The most abundant elements (by mass) on the earth are oxygen (49.2%), silicon (25.7%), and aluminum (7.50%), with less than 5% of each of the other elements present.

2. The three fundamental particles from which atoms are composed are electrons, protons, and neutrons. The properties of these particles are summarized below:

Particle	Relative Mass	Relative Charge	Location
proton	1836	1+	nucleus
neutron	1839	none	nucleus
electron	1	1–	outside the nucleus

3. The expression *nuclear* atom indicates that we view the atom as having a dense center of positive charge (called the *nucleus*) around which the electrons move through primarily empty space.

4. Isotopes represent atoms of the same element that have different atomic masses. Isotopes are atoms of a given element that have different numbers of neutrons in their nuclei.

5. Most elements are too reactive to be found in nature in other than the combined form. Aside from the noble metals gold, silver, and platinum, the only other elements commonly found in nature in the uncombined state are some of the gaseous elements (such as O_2,. N_2, He, Ar, etc.), and the solid nonmetals carbon and sulfur.

6.

Group	Family Name
1	Alkali metals
2	Alkaline earth elements
6	Chalcogens (not used commonly)
7	Halogens
8	Noble gases

7. Based on arrangement by electronic structure, the metallic elements tend to be toward the left-hand side of the chart, whereas the nonmetallic elements are found toward the right-hand, upper side. Since metallic nature increases going downward within any vertical column (as the outermost shell gets farther from the nucleus), there are also some metallic elements among the lower members of groups at the right-hand side of the table (many periodic tables indicate the dividing line between metallic and nonmetallic elements with a colored "stairstep").

8. Ions are electrically charged particles formed from atoms or molecules that have gained or lost one or more electrons. Positively charged ions are called *cations*, whereas negative ions are termed *anions*.

9. Ionic compounds typically are hard, crystalline solids with high melting and boiling points. Ionic substances such as sodium chloride, when dissolved in water or when melted, conduct electric currents. Chemists have taken this evidence to mean that ionic substances consist of positively and negatively charged particles (ions).

10.

Name	Symbol	Atomic Number
magnesium	Mg	12
tin	Sn	50
lead	Pb	82
sodium	Na	11
hydrogen	H	1
chlorine	Cl	17
silver	Ag	47

11. a. helium, 2; b. boron, 5; c. selenium, 34; d. barium, 56; e. phosphorus 15; f. strontium 38.

12. a. potassium, K; b. magnesium, Mg; c. hydrogen, H; d. carbon, C; e. lead, Pb; f. helium, He.

13. a. 2p, 2n, 2e; b. 17p, 20n, 17e; c. 20p, 20n, 20e

14. a. Mg^{2+}; b. F^-; c. Ba^{2+}; d. Na^+; e. O^{2-}; f. Cl^-

15. a. 19p, 18e; b. 35p, 36e; c. 11p, 10e

Chapter 3: Standard Review Worksheet

1. The symbols for some elements may refer to an archaic name for the element or to the element's name in a modern language other than English. Here are some examples:

Element	English Name	Derivation of Name
Na	sodium	Latin: *natrium*
K	potassium	Latin: *kalium*
Fe	iron	Latin: *ferrum*
W	tungsten	German: *wolfram*

2. A compound is a distinct, pure substance that is composed of two or more elements held together by chemical bonds. Carbon dioxide and water are two examples, but answers will vary.

3. Rutherford's experiment involved shooting a beam of particles at a thin sheet of metal foil. According to the then-current "plum pudding" model of the atom, most of these positively charged particles should have passed right through the foil. However, Rutherford detected that a significant number of particles effectively bounced off something and were deflected backwards to the source of particles and that other particles were deflected from the foil at large angles. Rutherford realized that his observations could be explained if the atoms of the metal foil had a small, dense, positively charged nucleus with a significant amount of empty space between nuclei. The empty space between nuclei would allow most of the particles to pass through the atom. However, if a particle hit a nucleus head-on, it would be deflected backwards at the source. If a positively charged particle passed near a positively charged nucleus (but did not hit the nucleus head-on), then the particle would be deflected by the repulsive forces between the positive charges. Rutherford's experiment conclusively disproved the "plum pudding" model for the atom, which envisioned the atom as a uniform sphere of positive charge with enough negatively charged electrons scattered through the atom to balance the positive charge.

4. It is the number and arrangement of the *electrons* in an atom that are responsible for the chemical behavior of the atom. The electrons are found in nearly the entire region of space occupied by an atom, from just outside the nucleus all the way out to the outermost *edge* of the atom. When two atoms approach each other in space prior to a reaction taking place, the electrons from one atom interact with the electrons of the other atom. The nucleus is so small compared with the overall size of the atom that the nuclei of atoms do not interact with each other.

5. Isotopes have the same atomic number (number of protons in the nucleus) but have different mass numbers (total number of protons and neutrons in the nucleus). The different isotopes of an atom are indicated by symbolism of the form $^A_Z X$, in which Z represent the atomic number and A the mass number of element X. For example, $^{13}_6 C$ represents a nuclide of carbon with atomic number 6 (6 protons in the nucleus) and mass number 13 (reflecting 6 protons plus 7 neutrons in the nucleus).

6. The periodic table arranges the elements in order of increasing atomic number. The table is further arranged by placing elements with similar electronic structure (and hence similar chemical properties) into the same vertical column (group). Since the periodic table is arranged with the elements in the same vertical column having *similar* electronic

structures, the mere *location* of an element in the periodic table can be an indication of what simple ions the element forms. For example, the Group 1 elements all form 1+ ions (Li^+, Na^+, K^+, Rb^+, and Cs^+), whereas the Group 7 elements all form 1– ions (F^-, Cl^-, Br^-, and I^-). You will learn more about how the charge of an ion is related to an atom's electronic structure in a later chapter.

7. A positive ion forms when an atom or molecule loses one or more of its electrons (negative charges). For example, sodium atoms and magnesium atoms form ions as indicated below:

   Na (atom) → Na^+ (ion) + e^- 　　　　　　　　　 Mg (atom) → Mg^{2+} (ion) + $2e^-$

   The resulting ions contain the same number of protons and neutrons in their nuclei as do the atoms from which they are formed because the only change that has taken place involves the electrons (which are not in the nucleus). These ions contain fewer electrons than the atoms from which they are formed. A negative ion forms when an atom or molecule *gains* one or more electrons from an outside source (another atom or molecule). For example, chlorine atoms and oxygen atoms form ions as indicated below:

   Cl (atom) + e^- → Cl^- (ion) 　　　　　　　　 O (atom) + $2e^-$ → O^{2-} (ion)

8. Although an ionic substance is made up of positively and negatively charged particles, there is no net electrical charge on a sample of such a substance because the total number of positive charges is balanced by an equal number of negative charges.

9.
Name	Symbol	Atomic Number
potassium	K	19
calcium	Ca	20
bromine	Br	35
neon	Ne	10
aluminum	Al	13
gold	Au	79
mercury	Hg	80
iodine	I	53

10. a. silicon, 14; b. carbon, 12; c. fluorine, 9; d. beryllium, 4; e. oxygen, 8; f. chromium, 24.

11. a. krypton, Kr; b. uranium, U; c. phosphorus, P; d. gold, Au; e. copper, Cu; f. oxygen, O.

12. a. 35p, 44n, 35e; b. 92p, 146n, 92e; c. 1p, 0n, 1e

13. a. Ag^+; b. Al^{3+}; c. Br^-; d. K^+; e. S^{2-}; f. Ca^{2+}

14. a. 1p, 0e; b. 7p, 10e; c. 9p, 10e

Chapter 3: Challenge Review Worksheet

1. While students certainly don't have to memorize all the elements, they should at least be able to give the symbols and names for the most common elements.

2. Dalton's atomic theory as presented in this text consists of five main postulates. Although Dalton's theory was exceptional scientific thinking for its time, some of the postulates have been modified as our scientific instruments and calculation methods have become increasingly more sophisticated. The main postulates of Dalton's theory are as follows: (1) Elements are made up of tiny particles called *atoms;* (2) all atoms of a given element are

identical; these atoms are different from the atoms of all other elements; (4) atoms of one element can combine with atoms of another element to form a compound, and such a compound will always contain the same relative numbers and types of atoms; and (5) atoms are rearranged into new groupings during an ordinary chemical reaction, and no atom is ever destroyed and no new atom is ever created during such a reaction. Students should explain these in their own words.

3. A given compound always contains exactly the same relative masses of its constituent elements. This statement is termed the *law of constant composition*. The law of constant composition is a result of the fact that a given compound always contains the same types and numbers of each constituent atom. For example, water's composition by mass (88.8% oxygen, 11.2% hydrogen) is a result of the fact that each water molecule contains one oxygen atom (relative mass 16.0) and two hydrogen atoms (relative mass 1.008 each). The law of constant composition is important to our study of chemistry because it means that we can always assume that any sample of a given pure substance, from whatever source, will be identical to any other sample.

4. The various isotopes of an element have virtually identical chemical properties because the chemical properties of an atom are a function of the electrons in the atom (*not* the nucleus). The physical properties of the isotopes of an element (and compounds containing those isotopes) may differ because of the difference in mass of the isotopes.

5. Isolated atoms do not form ions on their own but are induced to gain or lose electrons by some other species (which loses or gains the electrons).

6. An ionic compound could not possibly exist of just cations or just anions. There must be a balance of charge, or the compound would be very unstable (like charges repel each other).

7. a. 9p, 10n, 10e; b. 12p, 12n, 10e; c. 26p, 30n, 23e

8. a. 37p, 36e; b. 26p, 24e; c. 1p, 2e; d. 13p, 10e; e. 17p, 18e; f. 8p, 10e

9. RbH, $RbCl$, Rb_2O; FeH_2, $FeCl_2$, FeO; AlH_3, $AlCl_3$, Al_2O_3

Chapter 4: Basic Review Worksheet

1. When naming ionic compounds, we name the positive ion (cation) first. Sodium chloride is an example.

2. For simple binary Type I ionic compounds, the ending *-ide* is added to the root name of the element that is the negative ion (anion). For example, the Type I ionic compound formed between potassium and sulfur, K_2S, is named *potassium sulfide*. Potassium is the cation, and sulfur is the anion (with the suffix *-ide* added).

3. Type II compounds involve elements that form more than one stable ion, and so it is necessary to specify which ion is present in a given compound.

4. Type II compounds are named by either of two systems, the "ous-ic" system (which is falling out of use), and the "Roman numeral" system, which is preferred by most chemists. For example, iron forms two types of stable ions: Fe^{2+} and Fe^{3+}. Iron can react with oxygen to form either of two stable oxides, FeO or Fe_2O_3, depending on which cation is involved. Under the Roman numeral naming system, FeO would be named iron(II) oxide to show that it contains Fe^{2+} ions; Fe_2O_3 would be named iron(III) oxide to indicate that it contains

Fe^{3+} ions. The Roman numeral used in a name corresponds to the charge of the specific ion present in the compound. Under the less-favored "ous-ic" system, for an element that forms two stable ions, the ending *-ous* is used to indicate the lower charged ion, so FeO and Fe_2O_3 would be named *ferrous oxide* and *ferric oxide,* respectively. The "ous-ic" system has fallen out of favor because it does not indicate the actual charge on the ion but only that it is the lower or higher charged of the two. This can lead to confusion. For example, Fe^{2+} is called *ferrous* ion in this system, but Cu^{2+} is called *cupric* ion (because there is also a Cu^+ ion).

5. In writing the names for such compounds, the element listed first in the formula is named first (using the full name of the element), and then the second element in the formula is named as though it were an anion (with the *-ide* ending). Since there often may be more than one compound possible involving the same two nonmetallic elements, the naming system for Type III compounds goes one step further than the system for ionic compounds by explicitly stating (by means of a numerical prefix) the number of atoms of each of the nonmetallic elements present in the molecules of the compound. For example, carbon and oxygen (both nonmetals) form two common compounds, CO and CO_2. To indicate clearly which compound is being discussed, the names of these compounds indicate explicitly the number of oxygen atoms present by using a numerical prefix.

CO	carbon *monoxide*	(*mon-* or *mono-* is the prefix meaning "one")
CO_2	carbon *dioxide*	(*di-* is the prefix meaning "two")

The prefix *mono-* is not normally used for the first element named in a compound when there is only one atom of the element present, but numerical prefixes are used for the first element if there is more than one atom of that element present. For example, nitrogen and oxygen form many binary compounds:

NO	nitrogen *mon*oxide	
NO_2	nitrogen *di*oxide	
N_2O	*di*nitrogen *mon*oxide	
N_2O_4	*di*nitrogen *tetr*oxide	(*tetra-* or *tetr-* means "four")

6. Several families of polyatomic anions contain an atom of a given element combined with differing numbers of oxygen atoms. Such anions are called *oxyanions*. For example, sulfur forms two common oxyanions, SO_3^{2-} and SO_4^{2-}.

7. Acids in general are substances that produce protons (H^+ ions) when dissolved in water. HCl and H_2SO_4 are two examples.

8. a. sodium chloride; b. potassium oxide; c. magnesium bromide; d. aluminum iodide; e. calcium sulfide; f. strontium oxide.

9. a. ammonium ion; b. sulfite ion; c. nitrate ion; d. hydroxide ion; e. perchlorate ion; f. phosphate ion.

10. a. nitrogen dioxide; b. iodine monochloride; c. carbon monoxide

11. a. K_2S; b. HCl; c. $CaSO_4$; d. $CuBr_2$

Chapter 4: Standard Review Worksheet

1. Type III binary compounds represent compounds involving only nonmetallic elements. In writing the names for such compounds, the element listed first in the formula is named first (using the full name of the element), and then the second element in the formula is named as though it were an anion (with the *-ide* ending). This is similar, thus far, to the method used for naming ionic compounds (Type I). Since there may be more than one compound possible involving the same two nonmetallic elements, the naming system for Type III compounds goes one step further than the system for ionic compounds by explicitly stating (by means of a numerical prefix) the number of atoms of each of the nonmetallic elements present in the molecules of the compound.

2. When there are two oxyanions in such a series (as for sulfur), the name of the anion with fewer oxygen atoms ends in *-ite,* and the name of the anion with more oxygen atoms ends in *-ate*. Under this method, SO_3^{2-} is named *sulfite,* and SO_4^{2-} is named *sulfate*. When there are more than two members of such a series, the prefixes *hypo-* and *per-* are used to indicate the members of the series with the *fewest* and *largest* number of oxygen atoms, respectively. For example, bromine forms four common oxyanions as listed below:

Formula	Name
BrO^-	*hypo*brom*ite* (fewest number of oxygens)
BrO_2^-	brom*ite*
BrO_3^-	brom*ate*
BrO_4^-	*per*brom*ate* (largest number of oxygens)

3. For acids that do not contain oxygen, the prefix *hydro-* and the suffix *-ic* are used with the root name of the element present in the acid (for example, HCl, hydrochloric acid; H_2S, hydrosulfuric acid; HF, hydrofluoric acid).

4. The nomenclature of acids whose anions contain oxygen is more complicated. A series of prefixes and suffixes is used with the name of the nonoxygen atom in the anion of the acid. These prefixes and suffixes indicate the relative (not actual) number of oxygen atoms present in the anion. Most of the elements that form oxyanions form two such anions. For example, sulfur froms sulfite ion (SO_3^{2-}) and sulfate ion (SO_4^{2-}), and nitrogen forms nitrite ion (NO_2^-) and nitrate ion (NO_3^-). For an element that forms two oxyanions, the acid containing the anions will have the ending *-ous* if the anion is the *-ite* anion and the ending *-ic* if the anion is the *-ate* anion. For example, HNO_2 is nitr*ous* acid, and HNO_3 is nitr*ic* acid; H_2SO_3 is sulfur*ous* acid, and H_2SO_4 is sulfur*ic* acid. The halogen elements (Group 7) each form four oxyanions and, consequently, four oxyacids. The prefix *hypo-* is used for the oxyacid that contains fewer oxygen atoms than the *-ite* anion, and the prefix *per-* is used for the oxyacid that contains more oxygen atoms than the *-ate* anion. For example:

Acid	Name	Anion	Anion Name
HBrO	*hypo*brom*ous*	BrO^-	*hypo*brom*ite*
$HBrO_2$	brom*ous*	BrO_2^-	*hypo*brom*ite*
$HBrO_3$	brom*ic* acid	BrO_3^-	brom*ate*
$HBrO_4$	*per*brom*ic* acid	BrO_4^-	*per*brom*ate*

5. a. iron(III) chloride; b. nickel(II) sulfide; c. aluminum oxide; d. copper(II) oxide; e. barium chloride; f. iron(II) oxide

6. a. incorrect; should be Na_2S; b. correct; c. incorrect; should be NaCl; d. incorrect; should be $CaBr_2$

7. a. nitrite ion; b. hypochlorite ion; c. sulfate ion; d. cyanide ion

8. a. phosphorus pentachloride; b. dinitrogen tetroxide; c. sulfur hexafluoride

9. a. HNO_3; b. NaH; c. Ag_2SO_3; d. $NH_4C_2H_3O_2$

Chapter 4: Challenge Review Worksheet

1. The principle we use when writing the formula of an ionic compound is sometimes called the *principle of electroneutrality*. This means that a chemical compound must have an overall net electrical charge of zero. For ionic compounds, this means that the total number of positive charges on the positive ions present must equal the total number of negative charges on the negative ions present. For example, with sodium chloride, if we realize that an individual sodium ion has a 1+ charge and that an individual chloride ion has a 1– charge, then if we combine one of each of these ions, the compound will have an overall net charge of zero: $(1+) + (1–) = 0$. On the other hand, for magnesium iodide, when we realize that an individual magnesium ion has a 2+ charge, then clearly one iodide ion with its 1– charge will not lead to a compound with an overall charge of zero. We would need *two* iodide ions, each with its 1– charge, to balance the 2+ charge of the magnesium ion: $(2+) + 2(1–) = 0$. If we consider magnesium oxide, however, we would need only one oxide ion, with its 2– charge, to balance with one magnesium with its 2+ charge $[(2+) + (2–) = 0]$, so the formula of magnesium oxide is just MgO.

2. A polyatomic is an ion containing more than one atom. Parentheses are used in writing formulas containing polyatomic ions to indicate unambiguously how many of the polyatomic ions are present in the formula while making certain that there is no mistake as to what is meant by the formula. For example, consider calcium phosphate. The correct formula for this substance is $Ca_3(PO_4)_2$, which indicates that three calcium ions are combined for every two phosphate ions (check the total number of positive and negative charges to see why this is so). If we did not write the parenthesis around the formula for the phosphate ion, that is, if we had written Ca_3PO_{42}, people reading this formula might think that there were 42 oxygen atoms present.

3. a. chromium(III) sulfide; b. copper(I) sulfide; c. iron(III) oxide; d. gold(III) iodide; e. manganese(IV) oxide; f. cobalt(II) bromide

4. a. correct; b. incorrect; should be CsCl; c. incorrect; should be Ba_3P_2; d. correct

5. a. diboron trioxide; b. tetraphosphorus decoxide; c. dinitrogen trioxide

6. a. H_2S; b. $Ba_3(PO_4)_2$; c. $Mg(ClO_4)_2$; d. $MnCl_2$

Chapter 5: Basic Review Worksheet

1. Uncertainty in measurement means that we can never take an exact measurement (except for counting). The last digit of a recorded measurement is estimated and therefore uncertain.

2. A unit tells us what scale or standard is being used to represent the results of the measurement.

3. Dimensional analysis is a method of problem solving that pays particular attention to the units of measurements and uses these units as if they were algebraic symbols that multiply, divide, and cancel. Consider the following example. A dozen of eggs costs $1.25. Suppose we want to know how much one egg costs and also how much three dozen eggs will cost. To solve these problems, we need to make use of two equivalence statements:

$$1 \text{ dozen eggs} = 12 \text{ eggs}$$
$$1 \text{ dozen eggs} = \$1.25$$

The first of these equivalence statements is obvious: Everyone knows that 12 eggs are "equivalent" to one dozen. The second statement also expresses an equivalence: If you give the grocer $1.25, he or she will give you a dozen eggs. From these equivalence statements we can construct the conversion factors we need to answer the two questions. For the first question (what does one egg cost), we can set up the calculation as follows:

$$\frac{\$1.25}{12 \text{ eggs}} = \$0.104 = \$0.10$$

as the cost of one egg. Similarly, for the second question (the cost of 3 dozen eggs), we can set up the conversion as follows:

$$3 \text{ dozen} \times \frac{\$1.25}{1 \text{ dozen}} = \$3.75$$

as the cost of three dozen eggs. See Section 5.6 of the text for how we construct conversion factors from equivalence statements.

4. a. $122.4 \times 10^5 = (1.224 \times 10^2) \times 10^5 = 1.224 \times 10^7$
   b. $5.993 \times 10^{-4} = 0.0005993$

5. a. $6.0 \text{ pt} \times \frac{1 \text{ qt}}{2 \text{ pt}} \times \frac{1 \text{ L}}{1.0567 \text{ qt}} = 2.8 \text{ L}$

   b. $6.0 \text{ pt} \times \frac{1 \text{ qt}}{2 \text{ pt}} \times \frac{1 \text{ gal}}{4 \text{ qt}} = 0.75 \text{ gal}$

   c. $5.91 \text{ yd} \times \frac{1 \text{ m}}{1.0936 \text{ yd}} = 5.40 \text{ m}$

   d. $62.5 \text{ mi} \times \frac{1 \text{ km}}{0.62137 \text{ mi}} = 101 \text{ km}$

   e. $88.5 \text{ cm} \times \frac{10 \text{ mm}}{1 \text{ cm}} = 885 \text{ mm}$

6. a. $10.20 + 4.1 + 26.001 + 2.4 = 42.701 = 42.7$ (one decimal place)
   b. $[1.091 - 0.991] + 1.2 = 1.3$ (one decimal place)
   c. $(4.06 + 5.1)(2.032 - 1.02) = (9.16)(1.012) = (9.2)(1.01) = 9.3$
   d. $(67.21)(1.003)(2.4) = 161.8 = 1.6 \times 10^2$ (only 2 significant figures)

7. a. $541 \text{ K} - 273 = 268°C$
   b. $221°C + 273 = 494 \text{ K}$

8. a. Density = 212.4 g/42.4 cm^3 = 2.86 g/cm^3
   b. 0.721 lb = 327 g
      Density = 327 g/241 cm^3 = 1.36 g/cm^3

Chapter 5: Standard Review Worksheet

1. Whenever a scientific measurement is made, we always employ the instrument or measuring device we are using to the limits of its precision. On a practical basis, this usually means that we *estimate* our reading of the last significant figure of the measurement. Scientists appreciate the limits of experimental techniques and instruments and always assume that the last digit in a number representing a measurement has been estimated.

2. We need to include a unit in order to be able to communicate. If we report, for example, that we have "1.4 of water," this is not very helpful. Is this amount 1.4 cups? 1.4 liters? The unit is just as important as the number.

3. Answers will vary.

4. a. $0.0004321 \times 10^4 = (4.321 \times 10^{-4}) \times 10^4 = 4.321 \times 10^0 = 4.321$
   b. $5.241 \times 10^2 = 524.1$

5. a. $16.0 \text{ L} \times \dfrac{1 \text{ qt}}{0.94633 \text{ L}} \times \dfrac{32 \text{ fl. oz.}}{1 \text{ qt}} = 541 \text{ fl. oz.}$

   b. $5.25 \text{ L} \times \dfrac{1 \text{ gal}}{3.7854 \text{ L}} = 1.39 \text{ gal}$

   c. $8.25 \text{ m} \times \dfrac{1.0936 \text{ yd}}{1 \text{ m}} \times \dfrac{36 \text{ in}}{1 \text{ yd}} = 325 \text{ in}$

   d. $4.25 \text{ kg} \times \dfrac{2.2046 \text{ lb}}{1 \text{ kg}} = 9.37 \text{ lb}$

   e. $4.21 \text{ in} \times \dfrac{2.54 \text{ cm}}{1 \text{ in}} = 10.7 \text{ cm}$

6. a. $[(7.815 + 2.01)(4.5)]/(1.9001) = 23$
   b. $(1.67 \times 10^{-9})(1.1 \times 10^{-4}) = 1.837 \times 10^{-13} = 1.8 \times 10^{-13}$
   c. $[(4.02 \times 10^{-4})(2.91 \times 10^3)]/(9.102 \times 10^{-1}) = 1.29$
   d. $[(1.04 \times 10^2) + (2.1 \times 10^1)]/(4.51 \times 10^3) = 2.77 \times 10^{-2}$
   e. $(1.51 \times 10^{-3})^2/(1.074 \times 10^{-7}) = 21.2$
   f. $(1.89 \times 10^2)/[(7.01 \times 10^{-3})(4.1433 \times 10^4)] = 0.651$

7. a. $1.80(-50.1°C) + 32 = -58.2°F$
   b. $[(-30.7°F) - 32]/1.80 = -34.8°C$

8. a. Mass = $124.1 \text{ mL} \times 0.821 \text{ g} \cdot \text{mL} = 102 \text{ g}$
   b. $4.51 \text{ L} = 4,510 \text{ cm}^3$
      Mass = $4,510 \text{ cm}^3 \times 1.15 \text{ g/cm}^3 = 5.19 \times 10^3 \text{ g}$

Chapter 5: Challenge Review Worksheet

1. Since the last significant figure in every measurement is assumed to be estimated, it is never possible to exclude uncertainty from measurements. The best we can do is to try to

improve our techniques and instruments so that we get more significant figures for our measurements.

2. Scientists are careful about reporting their measurements to the appropriate number of significant figures to indicate to their colleagues the precision with which the experiments were performed. That is, the number of significant figures reported indicates how *carefully* measurements were made. Suppose you were considering buying a new home, and the real estate agent told you that a prospective new house was "between 1000 and 2000 square feet of space" and had "five or six rooms, more or less" and stood on "maybe an acre or two of land." Would you buy the house, or would you look for another real estate agent? When a scientist says that a sample of material "has a mass of 3.126 grams," he or she is narrowing down the limits as to the actual, true mass of the sample: The mass is clearly slightly more than halfway between 3.12 and 3.13 grams.

   The rules for significant figures are covered in the text. In brief, these rules for experimentally measured numbers are as follows: (1) Nonzero integers are *always* significant; (2) leading zeroes are *never* significant, captive zeroes are *always* significant, and trailing zeroes *may* be significant (if a decimal point is indicated); and (3) exact numbers (for example, definitions) have an infinite number of significant figures.

   When we have to round off an answer to the correct number of significant figures (as limited by whatever measurement was least precise), we do this in a particular manner. If the digit to be removed is equal to or greater than 5, the preceding digit is increased by 1. If the digit to be removed is less than 5, the preceding digit is not changed. To perform a series of calculations involving a set of data, retain all the digits in the intermediate calculations until arriving at the final answer, and then round off to the appropriate number of significant figures.

   When doing arithmetic with experimentally determined numbers, the final answer is limited by the least precise measurement. In doing multiplication or division calculations, the number of significant figures in the result should be the same as the measurement with the fewest significant figures. In performing addition or subtraction, the number of significant figures in the result is limited by the measurement with the fewest decimal places.

3. a. $0.0000009814 = 9.814 \times 10^{-7}$
   b. $14.2 \times 10^{0} = 14.2$

4. a. $351 \text{ K} - 273 = 78°C$
      $1.80(78°C) + 32 = 172.4 = 172°F$

   b. $[(72°F) - 32]/1.80 = 22.2°C$
      $22.2°C + 273 = 295.2 = 295 \text{ K}$

5. $-40°C = -40°F$; $1.8C + 32 = F$; if $C = F$, $1.8C + 32 = C$; thus $32 = -0.8C$ and $-40 = C$

6. a. Volume $= 142.4 \text{ g}/0.915 \text{ g/mL} = 156 \text{ mL}$
   b. $4.2 \text{ lb} = 1.9 \times 10^{3} \text{ g}$
      Volume $= 1.9 \times 10^{3} \text{ g}/3.75 \text{ g/cm}^{3} = 507 \text{ cm}^{3} = 5.1 \times 10^{2} \text{ cm}^{3}$

7. $5.27 \pm 0.03 \text{ g/mL}$

128.1 g/24.3 mL = 5.27 g/mL. We can get the extremes of the densities by dividing the maximum mass by the minimum volume and the minimum mass by the maximum volume. Doing so, we get 128.2 g/24.2 mL = 5.30 g/mL and 128.0 g/24.4 mL = 5.25 g/mL.

Chapter 6: Basic Review Worksheet

1. The average atomic mass of an element represents the weighted average mass, on the relative atomic scale, of all the isotopes of an element. Average atomic masses are usually given in terms of atomic mass units

2. The molar mass of a compound is the mass in grams of one mole of the compound (6.022×10^{23} molecules of the compound) and is calculated by summing the average atomic masses of all the atoms present in a molecule (or empirical formula unit for an ionic substance) of the compound. For example, a unit of the compound K_2O contains two potassium atoms and one oxygen atom. The molar mass is obtained by adding up the average atomic masses of these atoms: Molar mass K_2O = 2(39.10 g) + 1(16.00 g) = 94.20 g.

3. The percent composition (by mass) of a compound shows the relative amount of each element present in the compound on a mass basis. For compounds whose formulas are known (and whose molar masses therefore are known), the percentage of a given element present in the compound is given by

$$\frac{\text{Mass of the element present in 1 mol of the compound}}{\text{Mass of 1 mol of the compound}} \times 100$$

The percent composition of water, therefore, is 11.2% hydrogen and 88.8% oxygen.

4.   a.   Cu (molar mass = 63.55 g)

$$\text{Mol Cu} = 5.00 \text{ g} \times \frac{1 \text{ mol}}{63.55 \text{ g}} = 0.0787 \text{ mol}$$

$$\text{Atoms Cu} = 0.0787 \text{ mol} \times \frac{6.022 \times 10^{23} \text{ atoms}}{1 \text{ mol}} = 4.74 \times 10^{22} \text{ atoms}$$

      b. NH_3 (molar mass = 17.03 g)

$$\text{Mol NH3} = 5.00 \text{ g} \times \frac{1 \text{ mol}}{17.03 \text{ g}} = 0.294 \text{ mol}$$

$$\text{Molecules NH}_3 = 0.294 \text{ mol} \times \frac{6.022 \times 10^{23} \text{ molecules}}{1 \text{ mol}} = 1.77 \times 10^{23} \text{ molecules}$$

$$\text{Atoms N} = 1.77 \times 10^{23} \text{ molecules} \times \frac{1 \text{ N atom}}{1 \text{ molecule}} = 1.77 \times 10^{23} \text{ atoms N}$$

$$\text{Atoms H} = 1.77 \times 10^{23} \text{ molecules} \times \frac{3 \text{ H atoms}}{1 \text{ molecule}} = 5.31 \times 10^{23} \text{ atoms H}$$

      c. $KClO_3$ (molar mass = 122.6 g)

$$\text{Mol KClO}_3 = 5.00 \text{ g} \times \frac{1 \text{ mol}}{122.6 \text{ g}} = 0.0408 \text{ mol KClO}_3$$

$$0.0408 \text{ mol KClO}_3 \times \frac{6.022 \times 10^{23} \text{ formula units}}{1 \text{ mol}} = 2.46 \times 10^{22} \text{ formula units KClO}_3$$

$$\text{Atoms K} = 2.46 \times 10^{22} \text{ formula units} \times \frac{1 \text{ K atom}}{1 \text{ formula unit}} = 2.46 \times 10^{22} \text{ atoms K}$$

Atoms Cl = 2.46×10^{22} formula units T $\dfrac{1 \text{ Cl atoms}}{1 \text{ formula unit}}$ = 2.46×10^{22} atoms Cl

Atoms O = 2.46×10^{22} formula units × $\dfrac{3 \text{ O atoms}}{1 \text{ formula unit}}$ = 7.38×10^{22} atoms O

d. $Ca(OH)_2$ (molar mass = 74.096 g)

Mol $Ca(OH)_2$ = 5.00 g × $\dfrac{1 \text{ mol}}{74.096 \text{ g}}$ = 0.0675 mol $Ca(OH)_2$

0.0675 mol $Ca(OH)_2$ × $\dfrac{6.022 \times 10^{23} \text{ formula units}}{1 \text{ mol}}$ = 4.06×10^{22} formula units $Ca(OH)_2$

Atoms Ca = 4.06×10^{22} formula units × $\dfrac{1 \text{ Ca atom}}{1 \text{ formula unit}}$ = 4.06×10^{22} atoms Ca

Atoms O = 4.06×10^{22} formula units × $\dfrac{2 \text{ O atoms}}{1 \text{ formula unit}}$ = 8.12×10^{22} atoms O

Atoms H = 4.06×10^{22} formula units × $\dfrac{2 \text{ H atoms}}{1 \text{ formula unit}}$ = 8.12×10^{22} atoms H

5. a. 100% Cu

  b. NH_3: %N = $\dfrac{14.01 \text{ g N}}{17.03 \text{ g}}$ × 100% = 82.27% N

  %H = $\dfrac{3(1.008 \text{ g H})}{17.03 \text{ g}}$ × 100% = 17.76% H

  c. $KClO_3$: %K = $\dfrac{39.10 \text{ g K}}{122.6 \text{ g}}$ × 100% = 31.89% K

  %Cl = $\dfrac{35.45 \text{ g Cl}}{122.6 \text{ g}}$ × 100% = 28.92% Cl

  %O = $\dfrac{3(16.00 \text{ g O})}{122.6 \text{ g}}$ × 100% = 39.15% O

  d. $Ca(OH)_2$: %Ca = $\dfrac{40.08 \text{ g Ca}}{74.096 \text{ g}}$ × 100% = 54.09% Ca

  %O = $\dfrac{2(16.00 \text{ g O})}{74.096 \text{ g}}$ × 100% = 43.19% O

  %H = $\dfrac{2(1.008 \text{ g H})}{74.096 \text{ g}}$ × 100% = 2.721% H

6. The empirical formula of a compound represents the smallest ratio of the relative number of atoms of each type present in a molecule of the compound, whereas the molecular formula represents the actual number of atoms of each type present in a real molecule of the compound. For example, both acetylene (molecular formula C_2H_2) and benzene (molecular formula C_6H_6) have the same relative number of carbon and hydrogen atoms (one hydrogen for each carbon atom) and so have the same empirical formula (CH).

7. 7.99 g C × $\dfrac{1 \text{ mol}}{12.01 \text{ g}}$ = 0.665 mol C

2.01 g H × $\dfrac{1 \text{ mol}}{1.008 \text{ g}}$ = 1.99 mol H

1.99/0.665 = 2.99. Thus there are three hydrogen atoms for every one carbon atom. The empirical formula is CH_3.

8. The molar mass of the empirical formula CH_3 is 15.034 [12.01 + 3(1.008)]. This is half the molar mass of the compound; thus the compound must have the molecular formula C_2H_6.

Chapter 6: Standard Review Worksheet

1. 1 amu = 1.66×10^{-24} g. For example, the average atomic mass of sodium is 22.99 amu, which represents the average mass of all the sodium atoms in the world (including all the various isotopes and their relative abundances). So that we will be able to use the mass of a sample of sodium to count the number of atoms of sodium present in the sample, we consider that every sodium atom in a sample has exactly the same mass (the *average atomic mass*). The average atomic mass of an element is typically *not* a whole number of amu's because of the presence of the different isotopes of the element, each with its own relative abundance. Since the relative abundance of an element can be any number, when the weighted average atomic mass of the element is calculated, the average is unlikely to be a whole number.

2. On a microscopic basis, one mole of a substance represents Avogadro's number (6.022×10^{23}) of individual units (atoms or molecules) of the substance. On a macroscopic basis, one mole of a substance represents the amount of substance present when the molar mass of the substance in grams is taken (for example, 12.01 g of carbon will be one mole of carbon).

3. The molar mass of a compound is the mass in grams of one mole of the compound (6.022×10^{23} molecules of the compound) and is calculated by summing the average atomic masses of all the atoms present in a molecule of the compound. For example, a molecule of the compound H_3PO_4 contains three hydrogen atoms, one phosphorus atom, and four oxygen atoms. The molar mass is obtained by adding up the average atomic masses of these atoms:
Molar mass H_3PO_4 = 3(1.008 g) + 1(30.97 g) + 4(16.00 g) = 97.99 g.

4. When a new compound is prepared (the formula is not known), the percent composition must be determined on an experimental basis. An elemental analysis must be done of a sample of the new compound to see what mass of each element is present in the sample. For example, if a 1.000-g sample of a hydrocarbon is analyzed, and it is found that the sample contains 0.7487 g of C, then the percent by mass of carbon present in the compound is

$$\frac{0.7487 \text{ g C}}{1.000\text{-g sample}} \times 100\% = 74.87\% \text{ C}$$

Since we can use the formula of a known compound to calculate the percent composition by mass of the compound, it is not surprising that we can go in the opposite direction—from experimentally determined percent compositions for an unknown compound, we can calculate the formula of the compound.

5.   a. K_2CrO_4 (molar mass = 194.2 g)

Mol K_2CrO_4 = 5.00 g $\times \dfrac{1 \text{ mol}}{194.2 \text{ g}}$ = 0.0257 mol K_2CrO_4

0.0257 mol $\times \dfrac{6.022 \times 10^{23} \text{ formula units}}{1 \text{ mol}}$ = 1.55×10^{22} formula units K_2CrO_4

Atoms K = 1.55×10^{22} formula units $\times \dfrac{2 \text{ K atoms}}{1 \text{ formula unit}}$ = 3.10×10^{22} atoms K

Atoms Cr = 1.55×10^{22} formula units $\times \dfrac{1 \text{ Cr atom}}{1 \text{ formula unit}} = 1.55 \times 10^{22}$ atoms Cr

Atoms O = 1.55×10^{22} formula units $\times \dfrac{4 \text{ O atoms}}{1 \text{ formula unit}} = 6.20 \times 10^{22}$ atoms O

b. $AuCl_3$ (molar mass = 303.4 g)

Mol $AuCl_3$ = $5.00 \text{ g} \times \dfrac{1 \text{ mol}}{303.4 \text{ g}} = 0.0165$ mol $AuCl_3$

0.0165 mol $AuCl_3 \times \dfrac{6.022 \times 10^{23} \text{ formula units}}{1 \text{ mol}} = 9.94 \times 10^{21}$ formula units $AuCl_3$

Atoms Au = 9.94×10^{21} formula units $\times \dfrac{1 \text{ Au atom}}{1 \text{ formula unit}} = 9.94 \times 10^{21}$ atoms Au

Atoms Cl = 9.94×10^{21} formula units $\times \dfrac{3 \text{ Cl atoms}}{1 \text{ formula unit}} = 2.98 \times 10^{22}$ atoms Cl

c. SiH_4 (molar mass = 32.12 g)

Mol SiH_4 = $5.00 \text{ g} \times \dfrac{1 \text{ mol}}{32.12 \text{ g}} = 0.156$ mol SiH_4

0.156 mol $SiH_4 \times \dfrac{6.022 \times 10^{23} \text{ molecules}}{1 \text{ mol}} = 9.39 \times 10^{22}$ molecules SiH_4

Atoms Si = 9.39×10^{22} molecules $\times \dfrac{1 \text{ Si atom}}{1 \text{ molecule}} = 9.39 \times 10^{22}$ atoms Si

Atoms H = 9.39×10^{22} molecules $\times \dfrac{4 \text{ H atoms}}{1 \text{ molecule}} = 3.76 \times 10^{23}$ atoms H

d. $Ca_3(PO_4)_2$ (molar mass = 310.18 g)

Mol $Ca_3(PO_4)_2$ = $5.00 \text{ g} \times \dfrac{1 \text{ mol}}{310.18 \text{ g}} = 0.0161$ mol $Ca_3(PO_4)_2$

0.0161 mol $Ca_3(PO_4)_2 \times \dfrac{6.022 \times 10^{23} \text{ formula units}}{1 \text{ mol}} = 9.70 \times 10^{21}$ formula units

$Ca_3(PO_4)_2$

Atoms Ca = 9.70×10^{21} formula units $\times \dfrac{3 \text{ Ca atoms}}{1 \text{ formula unit}} = 2.91 \times 10^{22}$ atoms Ca

Atoms P = 9.70×10^{21} formula units $\times \dfrac{2 \text{ P atoms}}{1 \text{ formula unit}} = 1.94 \times 10^{22}$ atoms P

Atoms O = 9.70×10^{21} formula units $\times \dfrac{8 \text{ O atoms}}{1 \text{ formula unit}} = 7.76 \times 10^{22}$ atoms O

6. a. K_2CrO_4: %K = $\dfrac{2(39.10 \text{ g K})}{194.2 \text{ g}} \times 100\% = 40.27\%$ K

%Cr = $\dfrac{52.00 \text{ g Cr}}{194.2 \text{ g}} \times 100\% = 26.78\%$ Cr

%O = $\dfrac{4(16.00 \text{ g O})}{194.2 \text{ g}} \times 100\% = 32.96\%$ O

b. $AuCl_3$: %Au = $\dfrac{197.0 \text{ g Au}}{303.4 \text{ g}} \times 100\% = 64.93\%$ Au

%Cl = $\dfrac{3(35.45 \text{ g Cl})}{303.4 \text{ g}} \times 100\% = 35.05\%$ Cl

c. SiH_4: %Si = $\dfrac{28.09 \text{ g Si}}{32.12 \text{ g}} \times 100\% = 87.45\%$ Si

$$\%H = \frac{4(1.008 \text{ g H})}{32.12 \text{ g}} \times 100\% = 12.55\% \text{ H}$$

d. $Ca_3(PO_4)_2$: $\%Ca = \dfrac{3(40.08 \text{ g Ca})}{310.18 \text{ g}} \times 100\% = 38.76\% \text{ Ca}$

$$\%P = \frac{2(30.97 \text{ g P})}{310.18 \text{ g}} \times 100\% = 19.97\% \text{ P}$$

$$\%O = \frac{8(16.00 \text{ g O})}{310.18 \text{ g}} \times 100\% = 41.27\% \text{ O}$$

7. The empirical formula of a compound represents the smallest ratio of the relative number of atoms of each type present in a molecule of the compound, whereas the molecular formula represents the actual number of atoms of each type present in a real molecule of the compound. Once the empirical formula of a compound has been determined, it is also necessary to determine the molar mass of the compound before the actual molecular formula can be calculated.

8. Assume 100.0 g.

$$70.0\% \text{ Fe} = 70.0 \text{ g Fe} \times \frac{1 \text{ mol}}{55.85 \text{ g}} = 1.25 \text{ mol Fe}$$

$$30.0\% \text{ O} = 30.0 \text{ g O} \times \frac{1 \text{ mol}}{16.00 \text{ g}} = 1.88 \text{ mol O}$$

$1.88/1.25 = 1.50 = 3/2$. Thus the empirical formula is Fe_2O_3.

9. Assume 100.0 g.

$$30.4\% \text{ N} = 30.4 \text{ g N} \times \frac{1 \text{ mol}}{14.01 \text{ g}} = 2.17 \text{ mol N}$$

$$69.6\% \text{ O} = 69.6 \text{ g O} \times \frac{1 \text{ mol}}{16.00 \text{ g}} = 4.35 \text{ mol O}$$

$4.35/2.17 = 2$. The empirical formula is NO_2. The molar mass of NO_2 is about 46 g/mol, which falls in the range of half the molar mass of the compound. The molecular formula must be N_2O_4.

Chapter 6: Challenge Review Worksheet

1. Chemists have chosen these definitions so that there will be a simple relationship between measurable amounts of substances (grams) and the actual number of atoms or molecules present and so that the number of particles present in samples of *different* substances can be compared easily. For example, it is known that carbon and oxygen react according to the equation

$$C(s) + O_2(g) \rightarrow CO_2(g)$$

Chemists understand this equation to mean that one carbon atom reacts with one oxygen molecule to produce one molecule of carbon dioxide and also that one mole (12.01 g) of carbon will react with one mole (32.00 g) of oxygen to produce one mole (44.01 g) of carbon dioxide.

2. It's all relative. The mass of each substance mentioned in this question happens to be the molar mass of that substance. Each of the three samples of elemental substances mentioned (O, C, and Na) contains Avogadro's number (6.022×10^{23}) of atoms of its respective

element. For the compound Na_2CO_3 given, since each unit of Na_2CO_3 contains two sodium atoms, one carbon atom, and three oxygen atoms, then it's not surprising that a sample having a mass equal to the molar mass of Na_2CO_3 should contain one molar mass of carbon, two molar masses of sodium, and three molar masses of oxygen:
$12.01 \text{ g} + 2(22.99 \text{ g}) + 3(16.00 \text{ g}) = 106.0 \text{ g}$.

3. The molar mass of a compound is the mass in grams of one mole of the compound (6.022×10^{23} molecules of the compound) and is calculated by summing the average atomic masses of all the atoms present in a molecule of the compound (or empirical formula unit of an ionic substance). For example, a formula unit of the compound $Al_2(SO_4)_3$ contains two aluminum atoms, three sulfur atoms, and twelve oxygen atoms. The molar mass is obtained by adding up the average atomic masses of these atoms: Molar mass
$Al_2(SO_4)_3 = 2(26.98 \text{ g}) + 3(32.07 \text{ g}) + 12(16.00 \text{ g}) = 342.2 \text{ g}$.

4. The subscripts in an empirical formula represent the relative numbers of each type of atom in the molecule. The ratios of these numbers must be the same in the molecular formula (which represents the actual numbers of each type of atom in the molecule). Thus the molecular formula is always a multiple of the empirical formula. The subscripts must be integers because we cannot have fractions of atoms.

5. Answers will vary, but consider the "known" compound phosphoric acid (H_3PO_4). First, we will calculate the percentage composition (by mass) for H_3PO_4, and then we will use our results to calculate the empirical formula.

    Molar mass $= 3(1.008 \text{ g}) + 1(30.97 \text{ g}) + 4(16.00 \text{ g}) = 97.99 \text{ g}$

    $\%H = \dfrac{3(1.008 \text{ g H})}{97.99 \text{ g}} \times 100\% = 3.086\% \text{ H}$

    $\%P = \dfrac{30.97 \text{ g P}}{97.99 \text{ g}} \times 100\% = 31.60\% \text{ P}$

    $\%O = \dfrac{4(16.00 \text{ g O})}{97.99 \text{ g}} \times 100\% = 65.31\% \text{ O}$

Now we will use this percentage composition data to calculate the empirical formula. We will pretend that we did not know the formula and were just presented with a question of the type: "A compound contains 3.086% hydrogen, 31.60% phosphorus, and 65.31% oxygen by mass; calculate the empirical formula."

First, we will assume, as usual, that we have 100.0 g of the compound so that the percentages turn into masses in grams. Thus our sample will contain 3.086 g H, 31.60 g P, and 65.31 g O. Next, we can calculate the number of moles of each element these masses represent.

$\text{Mol H} = 3.086 \text{ g H} \times \dfrac{1 \text{ mol H}}{1.008 \text{ g H}} = 3.062 \text{ mol H}$

$\text{Mol P} = 31.60 \text{ g P} \times \dfrac{1 \text{ mol P}}{30.97 \text{ g P}} = 1.020 \text{ mol P}$

$\text{Mol O} = 65.31 \text{ g O} \times \dfrac{1 \text{ mol O}}{16.00 \text{ g O}} = 4.082 \text{ mol O}$

To get the empirical formula, divide each of these numbers of moles by the smallest number of moles. This puts things on a relative basis.

$$\frac{3.062 \text{ mol H}}{1.020} = 3.002 \text{ mol H}$$

$$\frac{1.020 \text{ mol P}}{1.020} = 1.000 \text{ mol P}$$

$$\frac{4.082 \text{ mol O}}{1.020} = 4.002 \text{ mol O}$$

And this gives us as the empirical formula—H_3PO_4.

6. It doesn't. The percent by mass of hydrogen in water, for example, is only dependent on the fact that there are two hydrogen atoms for every oxygen atom in a molecule of water and that hydrogen has an average atomic mass of 1.008 compared with 16.00 for oxygen. Whether we have a cup of water, a gallon of water, or an ocean of water does not change the percent by mass of hydrogen and oxygen.

7. Millimol C $= 82.80 \text{ mg} \times \dfrac{1 \text{ millimol}}{12.01 \text{ mg}} = 6.894 \text{ millimol C}$

Millimol H $= 13.90 \text{ mg} \times \dfrac{1 \text{ millimol}}{1.008 \text{ mg}} = 13.79 \text{ millimol H}$

Millimol O $= 55.15 \text{ mg} \times \dfrac{1 \text{ millimol}}{16.00 \text{ g}} = 3.477 \text{ millimol O}$

Dividing each of these numbers of millimoles by the smallest number of millimoles (3.447 millimol O) gives the empirical formula as C_2H_4O.

8. $3.66 \text{ g CO}_2 \times \dfrac{12.01 \text{ g C}}{44.01 \text{ g CO}_2} = 0.999 \text{ g C}$

$1.50 \text{ g H}_2\text{O} \times \dfrac{2.016 \text{ g H}}{18.016 \text{ g H}_2\text{O}} = 0.168 \text{ g H}$

$2.500 \text{ g} - 0.999 \text{ g} - 0.168 \text{ g} = 1.333 \text{ g O}$

$0.999 \text{ g C} \times \dfrac{1 \text{ mol C}}{12.01 \text{ g C}} = 0.0833 \text{ mol C}$

$0.168 \text{ g C} \times \dfrac{1 \text{ mol H}}{1.008 \text{ g H}} = 0.167 \text{ mol H}$

$1.332 \text{ g O} \times \dfrac{1 \text{ mol O}}{16.00 \text{ g O}} = 0.08331 \text{ mol O}$

Since $0.0833 : 0.167 : 0.08331 = 1 : 2 : 1$, the empirical formula is CH_2O.

9. The molar mass of CH_2O is about 30 g/mol. This is half the molar mass of the compound. Thus the molecular formula is $C_2H_4O_2$.

Chapter 7: Basic Review Worksheet

1. There are numerous ways we can recognize that a chemical reaction has taken place.

In some reactions there may be a *color change*. For example, the ions of many of the transition metals are brightly colored in aqueous solution. If one of these ions undergoes a reaction in which the oxidation state changes, however, the characteristic color of the ion *may* be changed. For example, when a piece of zinc is added to an aqueous copper(II) ion solution (which is bright blue), the Cu^{2+} ions are reduced to copper metal, and the blue color of the solution fades as the reaction takes place.

$$Zn(s) + Cu^{2+}(aq) \rightarrow Zn^2(aq) + Cu(s)$$

  blue solution   red/black solid

In many reactions of ionic solutes, a solid precipitate forms when the ions are combined. For example, when a clear, colorless aqueous solution of sodium chloride is added to a clear, colorless solution of silver nitrate, a white solid of silver chloride forms and settles out of the mixture.

$$AgNO_3(aq) + NaCl(aq) \rightarrow NaNO_3(aq) + AgCl(s)$$

In some reactions, particularly in the combustion of organic chemical substances with oxygen, gas, heat, and light (a flame) may be produced. For example, when methane (natural gas) is burned in oxygen, a luminous flame is produced, and heat energy is released:

$$CH_4(g) + 2O_2(g) \rightarrow CO_2(g) + 2H_2O(g) + energy$$

2. The substances to the left of the arrow in a chemical equation are called the *reactants;* those to the right of the arrow are referred to as the *products*.

3. The physical states are indicated by using italic letters in parentheses after the formula: (*s*), (*l*), (*g*), or (*aq*).

4. When we "balance" a chemical equation, we adjust the *coefficients* of the reactants and products in the equation so that the same total numbers of atoms of each element are present both before and after the reaction has taken place.

5. Coefficients in a balanced chemical equation represent the relative numbers of each type of molecule involved in the reaction. Subscripts represent the numbers of each type of atom in a particular molecule. When we balance a chemical equation, it is permitted only to adjust the coefficients of a formula because changing a coefficient merely changes the number of molecules of a substance being used in the reaction without changing the identity of the substance.

6.
    a. $FeCl_3(aq) + 3KOH(s) \rightarrow Fe(OH)_3(s) + 3KCl(aq)$

    b. $AgC_2H_3O_2(aq) + HCl(aq) \rightarrow AgCl(s) + HC_2H_3O_2(aq)$

    c. $2SnO(s) + C(s) \rightarrow 2Sn(s) + CO_2(g)$

    d. $K_2O(s) + H_2O(l) \rightarrow 2KOH(aq)$

Chapter 7: Standard Review Worksheet

1. All chemical reactions do produce some evidence that the reaction has occurred, but sometimes this evidence may *not* be visual and may not be very obvious. For example, when very dilute aqueous solutions of acids and bases are mixed, the neutralization reaction

$$H^+(aq) + OH^-(aq) \rightarrow H_2O(l)$$

takes place. However, the only evidence for this reaction is the release of heat energy, which should be evident as a temperature change for the mixture. Since water has a relatively high specific heat capacity, however, if the acid and base solutions are very dilute, the temperature may change only by a fraction of a degree and may not be noticed.

2. A chemical equation indicates the substances necessary for a chemical reaction to take place, as well as what is produced by that chemical reaction. In addition, if a chemical equation has been balanced, then the equation indicates the relative proportions in which the reactant molecules combine to form the product molecules.

3. Balancing chemical equations is so important because a balanced chemical equation shows us not only the identities of the reactants and products but also the relative numbers of each involved in the process. This information is necessary if we are to do any sort of calculation involving the amounts of reactants required for a process or are to calculate the yield expected from a process. When we say that atoms must be conserved when writing balanced chemical equations, we mean that the number of atoms of each element must be the same after the reaction as before the reaction. Atoms are not created or destroyed during a chemical reaction; they are just arranged into new products

4. It is never permissible to change the subscripts of a formula when balancing a chemical equation. Changing the subscripts changes the identity of a substance from one chemical to another. For example, consider the unbalanced chemical equation

$$H_2(g) + O_2(g) \rightarrow H_2O(l)$$

If you changed the *formula* of the product from $H_2O(l)$ to $H_2O_2(l)$, the equation would appear to be "balanced." However, H_2O is water, whereas H_2O_2 is hydrogen peroxide—a completely different chemical substance (which is not prepared by reaction of the elements hydrogen and oxygen).

5.   a. $2Na_2O_2(s) + 2H_2O(l) \rightarrow 4NaOH(aq) + O_2(g)$
     b. $2Fe(s) + 3Br_2(l) \rightarrow 2FeBr_3(s)$

     c. $Na_2S(s) + 2HCl(aq) \rightarrow 2NaCl(aq) + H_2S(g)$

     d. $H_2SO_4(aq) + 2NaCl(s) \rightarrow Na_2SO_4(aq) + 2HCl(aq)$

     e. $N_2(g) + 3I_2(s) \rightarrow 2NI_3(s)$

Chapter 7: Challenge Review Worksheet

1. The coefficients represent the relative numbers of molecules involved in the reaction. They also can represent the relative numbers of moles of molecules (in fact, this is the most convenient way of thinking about coefficients). Since we can have fractions of moles, the coefficients can be fractions. Subscripts represent numbers of each type of atom in a molecule. Since we cannot have fractions of atoms, the subscripts cannot be fractions.

2. The balance equations are given as follows:

   a. $3NaBH_4 + 4BF_3 \rightarrow 3NaBF_4 + 2B_2H_6$ sum of coefficients = 12
   b. $2NO + 2H_2 \rightarrow N_2 + 2H_2O$ sum of coefficients = 7
   c. $Fe_2O_3 + 3CO \rightarrow 2Fe + 3CO_2$ sum of coefficients = 9

3.   a. $2Na(s) + 2H_2O(l) \rightarrow 2NaOH(aq) + H_2(g)$
             $2K(s) + 2H_2O(l) \rightarrow 2KOH(aq) + H_2(g)$

      b. $2Na(s) + Cl_2(g) \rightarrow 2NaCl(s)$
             $2K(s) + Cl_2(g) \rightarrow 2KCl(s)$

      c. $3Na(s) + P(s) \rightarrow Na_3P(s)$
             $3K(s) + P(s) \rightarrow K_3P(s)$

      d. $6Na(s) + N_2(g) \rightarrow 2Na_3N(s)$
             $6K(s) + N_2(g) \rightarrow 2K_3N(s)$

      e. $2Na(s) + H_2(g) \rightarrow 2NaH(s)$
             $2K(s) + H_2(g) \rightarrow 2KH(s)$

4. $CO_2(g) + H_2O(l) + NH_3(aq) + NaCl(aq) \rightarrow NaHCO_3(s) + NH_4Cl(aq)$

5. $C_{12}H_{22}O_{11}(s) + 12O_2(g) \rightarrow 12CO_2(g) + 11H_2O(g)$ (Water might be listed as a liquid.)

6. $Pb(NO_3)_2(aq) + 2NaCl(aq) \rightarrow PbCl_2(s) + 2NaNO_3(aq)$

7.   a. $4Fe(s) + 3O_2(g) \rightarrow 2Fe_2O_3(s)$
      b. $4Al(s) + 3O_2(g) \rightarrow 2Al_2O_3(s)$

Chapter 8: Basic Review Worksheet

1. The concept of a "driving force" for chemical reactions, at this point, is a rather nebulous idea. Clearly, there must be some reason why certain substances react when combined and why other substances can be combined without anything happening. Because there are driving forces, we can use some generalizations about what sorts of events tend to make a reaction take place.

2. A precipitation reaction is one in which a *solid* forms when the reactants are combined. The solid is called a *precipitate*. An example is $Pb(NO_3)_2(aq) + 2NaI(aq) \rightarrow PbI_2(s) + 2NaNO_3(aq)$.

3. A strong electrolyte is one that completely dissociates into ions when dissolved in water. That is, each unit of the substance that dissolves in water produces separated, free ions. For example, NaCl (sodium chloride), KNO_3 (potassium nitrate), and NaOH (sodium hydroxide) are strong electrolytes.

4. In summary, nearly all compounds containing the nitrate, sodium, potassium, and ammonium ions are soluble in water. Most salts containing the chloride and sulfate ions are soluble in water, with specific exceptions (see Table 8.1 for these exceptions). Most compounds containing the hydroxide, sulfide, carbonate, and phosphate ions are not soluble in water, unless the compound also contains one of the cations mentioned earlier (Na^+, K^+, or NH_4^+).

5. The spectator ions in a precipitation reaction are the ions in the solution that do *not* precipitate.

6. Acids (such as the citric acid found in citrus fruits and the acetic acid found in vinegar) were first noted primarily because of their sour taste. The first bases noted were

characterized by their bitter taste and slippery feel on the skin. Acids and bases chemically react with (neutralize) each other forming water. The net ionic equation is

$$H^+(aq) + OH^-(aq) \rightarrow H_2O(l)$$

The strong acids and bases are those that fully ionize when they dissolve in water. Since these substances fully ionize, they are strong electrolytes.

7. A salt can be thought of as any ionic compound that contains ions other than H^+ and OH^- (compounds containing these ions are called *acids* and *bases,* respectively). In particular, a salt is formed in the neutralization reaction between an acid and a base. Examples will vary but could include NaCl (sodium chloride), KNO_3 (potassium nitrate), and Na_2SO_4 (sodium sulfate).

8. *Oxidation* represents a loss of electrons by an atom, molecule, or ion, whereas *reduction* is the gain of electrons by such a species.

9. Combustion reactions represent processes involving oxygen gas that release energy rapidly enough that a flame is produced. An example is the burning of methane (natural gas):

$$CH_4(g) + 2O_2(g) \rightarrow CO_2(g) + 2H_2O(g) + energy$$

10. In general, a synthesis reaction represents the reaction of elements or simple compounds to produce more complex substances. There are many examples of synthesis reactions. For example:

$$N_2(g) + 3H_2(g) \rightarrow 2NH_3(g)$$

Decomposition reactions represent the breakdown of a more complex substance into simpler substances. There are many examples of decomposition reactions. For example:
$$2H_2O_2(aq) \rightarrow 2H_2O(l) + O_2(g)$$

11.
   a. $2NaOH(s) + CuSO_4(aq) \rightarrow Cu(OH)_2(s) + Na_2SO_4(aq)$
   precipitation, double-displacement

   b. $HI(aq) + KOH(aq) \rightarrow KI(aq) + H_2O(l)$
   acid–base, double-displacement

   c. $FeO(s) + 2HNO_3(aq) \rightarrow Fe(NO_3)_2(aq) + H_2O(l)$
   acid–base, double-displacement

   d. $C_{12}H_{22}O_{11}(s) \rightarrow 12C(s) + 11H_2O(g)$
   decomposition, oxidation–reduction

   e. $4B(s) + 3O_2(g) \rightarrow 2B_2O_3(s)$
   synthesis, oxidation–reduction

Chapter 8: Standard Review Worksheet

1. A reaction is likely if any of the following things occur as a result of the reaction: formation of a solid, formation of water (or another non-ionized molecule), formation of a gas, or the transfer of electrons from one species to another. Examples of reactions illustrating each of these include

Formation of a solid:

$$BaCl_2(aq) + K_2CrO_4(aq) \rightarrow 2KCl(aq) + BaCrO_4(s)$$
$$Pb(NO_3)_2(aq) + 2NaCl(aq) \rightarrow PbCl_2(s) + 2NaNO_3(aq)$$

Formation of water:

$$HCl(aq) + NaOH(aq) \rightarrow NaCl(aq) + H_2O(l)$$
$$HC_2H_3O_2(aq) + KOH(aq) \rightarrow KC_2H_3O_2(aq) + H_2O(l)$$

Formation of a gas:

$$2NI_3(s) \rightarrow N_2(g) + 3I_2(s)$$
$$CaCO_3(s) \rightarrow CaO(s) + CO_2(g)$$

Transfer of electrons:

$$Zn(s) + 2Ag^+(aq) \rightarrow Zn^{2+}(aq) + 2Ag(s)$$
$$Mg(s) + Cu^{2+}(aq) \rightarrow Mg^{2+}(aq) + Cu(s)$$

2. If you were to perform such a reaction, the mixture would turn cloudy as the reactants are combined, and a solid eventually would settle from the mixture on standing. One example would be to combine barium nitrate and sodium carbonate solutions. A precipitate of barium carbonate would form.

$$Ba(NO_3)_2(aq) + Na_2CO_3(aq) \rightarrow BaCO_3(s) + 2NaNO_3(aq)$$

3. Ionic compounds, since they already consist of ions in the solid state, are strong electrolytes if they are soluble in water. Certain acids and bases also behave as strong electrolytes. A solution of a strong electrolyte consists of free, separated ions moving through the solvent independently of one another (there are no molecules or clusters of combined positive and negative ions). An apparatus for experimentally determining whether or not a substance is an electrolyte is shown in Figure 8.2 in the text.

4. Examples will vary. The solubility rules are phrased as if you had a sample of a given solute and wanted to see if you could dissolve it in water. These rules also can be applied, however, to predict the identity of the solid produced in a precipitation reaction. A given combination of ions will not be soluble in water whether you take a pure compound out of a reagent bottle or if you generate the insoluble combination of ions during a chemical reaction. For example, the solubility rules say that $BaSO_4$ is not soluble in water. This means not only that a pure sample of $BaSO_4$ taken from a reagent bottle will not dissolve in water but also that if Ba^{2+} ion and SO_4^{2-} ion end up together in the same solution, they will precipitate as $BaSO_4$. For example, solid barium sulfate forms when we combine barium chloride and sulfuric acid solutions:

$$BaCl_2(aq) + H_2SO_4(aq) \rightarrow BaSO_4(s) + 2HCl(aq)$$

Also, if a barium nitrate solution were combined with a sodium sulfate solution, a precipitate of $BaSO_4$ would form. Barium sulfate is insoluble in water regardless of its source.

5. Since we take the actual chemical reaction in a precipitation process to be the formation of the solid, and since the spectator ions are not found in and do not participate in the formation of the solid, we leave them out of the net ionic equation for the reaction.

6. The textbook describes acid–base neutralization reactions as reactions that result in the formation of water. The water results from the combination of the $H^+(aq)$ ion from the acid with the $OH^-(aq)$ ion from the base:

$$H^+(aq) + OH^-(aq) \rightarrow H_2O(l)$$

However, the H^+ ion must have been paired with some negative ion in the original acid solution, and the OH^- ion must have been paired with some positive ion in the original base solution. These counterions to the acid–base ions are what constitute the salt that is formed during the neutralization. Below are three acid–base neutralization reactions, with the salts that are formed indicated:

$$HCl(aq) + NaOH(aq) \rightarrow H_2O(l) + NaCl(aq)$$
$$\text{acid} \qquad \text{base} \qquad \text{water} \qquad \text{a salt}$$
$$HNO_3(aq) + KOH(aq) \rightarrow H_2O(l) + KNO_3(aq)$$
$$\text{acid} \qquad \text{base} \qquad \text{water} \qquad \text{a salt}$$
$$HC_2H_3O_2(aq) + NaOH(aq) \rightarrow H_2O(l) + NaC_2H_3O_2(aq)$$
$$\text{acid} \qquad \text{base} \qquad \text{water} \qquad \text{a salt}$$

7. Oxidation–reduction reactions are electron-transfer reactions. An example of a simple oxidation–reduction reaction between a metal and a nonmetal could be the following:

$$Mg(s) + F_2(g) \rightarrow MgF_2(s)$$

In this process, Mg atoms lose two electrons each to become Mg^{2+} ions in MgF_2: Mg is oxidized. Each F atom of F_2 gains one electron to become an F^- ion, for a total of two electrons gained for each F_2 molecule: F_2 is reduced.

$$Mg \rightarrow Mg^{2+} + 2e^- \quad \rightarrow \quad 2(F + e^- \rightarrow F^-)$$

8. Combustion reactions are a special subclass of oxidation–reduction reactions (the fact that elemental oxygen gas is a reactant but combined oxygen is a product shows this). The most common combustion reactions are those we make use of through the burning of petroleum products as sources of heat, light, or other forms of energy.

9. Synthesis and decomposition reactions are very often also oxidation–reduction reactions, especially if an elemental substance reacts or is generated. It is not necessary, however, for synthesis and decomposition reactions to always involve oxidation–reduction. For example, the reaction between NaOH and CO_2 as shown below does not represent oxidation–reduction.

$$NaOH(aq) + CO_2(g) \rightarrow NaHCO_3(s)$$

10. a. $2Mg(s) + 2CO_2(g) + O_2(g) \rightarrow 2MgCO_3(s)$
       synthesis, oxidation–reduction

   b. $C_3H_8(g) + 5O_2(g) \rightarrow 3CO_2(g) + 4H_2O(g)$
       combustion, oxidation–reduction

   c. $Co(NH_3)_6Cl_2(s) \rightarrow CoCl_2(s) + 6NH_3(g)$
       decomposition

   d. $2HCl(aq) + Pb(C_2H_3O_2)_2(aq) \rightarrow 2HC_2H_3O_2(aq) + PbCl_2(s)$
       precipitation, double-displacement

   e. $2Al(s) + 6HNO_3(aq) \rightarrow 2Al(NO_3)_3(aq) + 3H_2(g)$
       oxidation–reduction, single-displacement

Chapter 8: Challenge Review Worksheet

1. Just because we leave the spectator ions out when writing a net ionic equation for a reaction does not mean that the spectator ions do not have to be present. The spectator ions are needed to provide a balance of charge in the reactant compounds for the ions that combine to form the precipitate. For a reaction in which silver chloride is formed, it would not be possible to have a reagent bottle containing just silver ions (there would have to be some negative ions present) or just chloride ions (there would have to be some positive ions present).

2. Yes, strong acids and bases are also strong electrolytes. The common strong acids are HCl (hydrochloric), HNO_3 (nitric), H_2SO_4 (sulfuric), and $HClO_4$ (perchloric). The most common strong bases are the alkali metal hydroxides, particularly NaOH (sodium hydroxide) and KOH (potassium hydroxide).

3. $HCl(aq) + NaOH(aq) \rightarrow NaCl(aq) + H_2O(l)$
   $HNO_3(aq) + NaOH(aq) \rightarrow NaNO_3(aq) + H_2O(l)$
   $H_2SO_4(aq) + 2NaOH(aq) \rightarrow Na_2SO_4(aq) + H_2O(l)$
   $HCl(aq) + KOH(aq) \rightarrow KCl(aq) + H_2O(l)$
   $HNO_3(aq) + KOH(aq) \rightarrow KNO_3(aq) + H_2O(l)$
   $H_2SO_4(aq) + 2KOH(aq) \rightarrow K_2SO_4(aq) + 2H_2O(l)$

4.   a. $Ba(NO_3)_2(aq) + K_2CrO_4(aq) \rightarrow BaCrO_4(s) + 2KNO_3(aq)$

      b. $NaOH(aq) + HC_2H_3O_2(aq) \rightarrow H_2O(l) + NaC_2H_3O_2(aq)$
   (then evaporate the water from the solution)

      c. $AgNO_3(aq) + NaCl(aq) \rightarrow AgCl(s) + NaNO_3(aq)$

      d. $Pb(NO_3)_2(aq) + H_2SO_4(aq) \rightarrow PbSO_4(s) + 2HNO_3(aq)$

      e. $2NaOH(aq) + H_2SO_4(aq) \rightarrow Na_2SO_4(aq) + 2H_2O(l)$
   (then evaporate the water from the solution)

      f. $Ba(NO_3)_2(aq) + Na_2CO_3(aq) \rightarrow BaCO_3(s) + 2NaNO_3(aq)$

5. No. Since an oxidation–reduction process represents the transfer of electrons between species, you can't have one without the other also taking place. The electrons lost by one species must be gained my some other species.

6. The different ways of classifying chemical reactions that have been discussed in the text are listed below, along with an example of each type of reaction:

   Formation of a solid (precipitation):
      $FeCl_3(aq) + 3NaOH(aq) \rightarrow Fe(OH)_3(s) + 3NaCl(aq)$

   Formation of water (acid–base):
      $H_2SO_4(aq) + 2NaOH(aq) \rightarrow Na_2SO_4(aq) + 2H_2O(l)$

   Transfer of electrons (oxidation–reduction):
      $2Na(s) + Cl_2(g) \rightarrow 2NaCl(s)$

   Combustion:
      $2C_2H_6(g) + 7O_2(g) \rightarrow 4CO_2(g) + 6H_2O(g) + energy$

Synthesis (combination):

$$Ca(s) + Cl_2(g) \rightarrow CaCl_2(s)$$

Decomposition:

$$2HgO(s) \rightarrow 2Hg(l) + O_2(g)$$

Single displacement:

$$Mg(s) + 2AgNO_3(aq) \rightarrow Mg(NO_3)_2(aq) + 2Ag(s)$$

Double displacement:

$$Na_2SO_4(aq) + BaCl_2(aq) \rightarrow 2NaCl(aq) + BaSO_4(s)$$

Chapter 9: Basic Review Worksheet

1. The balanced equation is $N_2 + 3H_2 \rightarrow 2NH_3$

   a. $0.20 \text{ mol } N_2 \times \dfrac{2 \text{ mol } NH_3}{1 \text{ mol } N_2} = 0.40 \text{ mol } NH_3$

   b. $0.30 \text{ mol } H_2 \times \dfrac{2 \text{ mol } NH_3}{3 \text{ mol } H_2} = 0.20 \text{ mol } NH_3$

2. The balanced equation is $Mg + 2HCl \rightarrow MgCl_2 + H_2$

   a. $10.0g \text{ Mg} \times \dfrac{1 \text{ mol Mg}}{24.31g \text{ Mg}} \times \dfrac{1 \text{ mol } H_2}{1 \text{ mol Mg}} \times \dfrac{2.016 \text{ } H_2}{1 \text{ mol } H_2} = 0.829g \text{ } H_2$

   b. $20.0g \text{ HCl} \times \dfrac{1 \text{ mol HCl}}{36.458g \text{ HCl}} \times \dfrac{1 \text{ mol } H_2}{2 \text{ mol HCl}} \times \dfrac{2.016 \text{ } H_2}{1 \text{ mol } H_2} = 0.553g \text{ } H_2$

3. Although we can calculate specifically the exact amounts of each reactant needed for a chemical reaction, often reaction mixtures are prepared using more or less arbitrary amounts of the reagents. However, regardless of how much of each reagent may be used for a reaction, the substances still react stoichiometrically, according to the mole ratios derived from the balanced chemical equation for the reaction. When arbitrary amounts of reactants are used, there will be one reactant that, stoichiometrically, is present in the least amount. This substance is called the *limiting reactant* for the experiment. We say that the other reactants in the experiment are present in the excess, which means that a portion of these reactants will still be present unchanged after the reaction has ended and the limiting reactant has been used up completely.

4. The balanced equation is $2H_2 + O_2 \rightarrow 2H_2O$.

   a. $4.0 \text{ mol } H_2 \times \dfrac{1 \text{ mol } O_2}{2 \text{ mol } H_2} = 2.0 \text{ mol } O_2$; H_2 is limiting.

   b. $10.0g \text{ } H_2 \times \dfrac{1 \text{ mol } H_2}{2.016g \text{ } H_2} \times \dfrac{1 \text{ mol } O_2}{2 \text{ mol } H_2} \times \dfrac{32.00g \text{ } O_2}{1 \text{ mol } O_2} = 79.4g \text{ } O_2$; O_2 is limiting.

   c. $10.0 \text{ mol } H_2 \times \dfrac{1 \text{ mol } O_2}{2 \text{ mol } H_2} = 5.00 \text{ mol } O_2$; H_2 is limiting.

   d. $5.0g \text{ } H_2 \times \dfrac{1 \text{ mol } H_2}{2.016g \text{ } H_2} \times \dfrac{1 \text{ mol } O_2}{2 \text{ mol } H_2} \times \dfrac{32.00g \text{ } O_2}{1 \text{ mol } O_2} = 40.g \text{ } O_2$; O_2 is limiting.

5. The theoretical yield for an experiment is the mass of product calculated based on the limiting reactant for the experiment being completely consumed. The actual yield for an experiment is the mass of product actually collected by the experimenter.

Chapter 9: Standard Review Worksheet

1. Answers will vary. An example is included below:

$$2H_2O_2(aq) \rightarrow 2H_2O(l) + O_2(g)$$

This describes the decomposition reaction of hydrogen peroxide.
Microscopic: Two molecules of hydrogen peroxide (in aqueous solution) decompose to produce two molecules of liquid water and one molecule of oxygen gas.
Macroscopic: Two moles of hydrogen peroxide (present in aqueous solution) decompose to produce two moles of liquid water and one mole of oxygen gas.

2. The mole ratios for a reaction are based on the coefficients of the balanced chemical equation for the reaction. These coefficients show in what proportions molecules (or moles of molecules) combine. From the balanced equation

$$C_2H_5OH(l) + 3O_2(g) \rightarrow 2CO_2(g) + 3H_2O(g)$$

(and assuming a given amount of C_2H_5OH) various mole ratios can be constructed.

To calculate mol CO_2 produced: $\dfrac{2 \text{ mol } CO_2}{1 \text{ mol } C_2H_5OH}$

To calculate mol H_2O produced: $\dfrac{3 \text{ mol } H_2O}{1 \text{ mol } C_2H_5OH}$

To calculate mol O_2 required: $\dfrac{3 \text{ mol } O_2}{1 \text{ mol } C_2H_5OH}$

We could calculate the number of moles of the other substances if 0.65 mol C_2H_5OH were to be combusted as follows:

Mol CO_2 produced = (0.65 mol C_2H_5OH) × $\dfrac{2 \text{ mol } CO_2}{1 \text{ mol } C_2H_5OH}$ = 1.3 mol CO_2

Mol H_2O produced = (0.65 mol C_2H_5OH) × $\dfrac{3 \text{ mol } H_2O}{1 \text{ mol } C_2H_5OH}$ = 1.95 = 2.0 mol H_2O

Mol O_2 required = (0.65 mol C_2H_5OH) × $\dfrac{3 \text{ mol } O_2}{1 \text{ mol } C_2H_5OH}$ = 1.95 = 2.0 mol O_2

3. It is the limiting reactant that controls how much product is formed, regardless of how much of the other reactants are present. The limiting reactant limits the amount of product that can form in the experiment because once the limiting reactant has reacted completely, the reaction must stop.

4.   a. $2AgNO_3(aq) + CaSO_4(aq) \rightarrow Ag_2SO_4(s) + Ca(NO_3)_2(aq)$
Molar masses: $AgNO_3$, 169.9 g; Ag_2SO_4, 311.9 g; $Ca(NO_3)_2$, 164.1 g

25.0 g $AgNO_3$ × $\dfrac{1 \text{ mol}}{169.9 \text{ g}}$ = 0.147 mol $AgNO_3$

0.147 mol $AgNO_3$ × $\dfrac{1 \text{ mol } Ag_2SO_4}{2 \text{ mol } AgNO_3}$ = 0.0735 mol Ag_2SO_4

0.0735 mol Ag_2SO_4 × $\dfrac{311.9 \text{ g}}{1 \text{ mol}}$ = 22.9 g Ag_2SO_4

$$0.147 \text{ mol AgNO}_3 \times \frac{1 \text{ mol Ca(NO}_3)_2}{2 \text{ mol AgNO}_3} = 0.0735 \text{ mol Ca(NO}_3)_2$$

$$0.0735 \text{ mol Ca(NO}_3)_2 \times \frac{164.1 \text{ g}}{1 \text{ mol}} = 12.1 \text{ g Ca(NO}_3)_2$$

b. $2Al(s) + 6HNO_3(aq) \rightarrow 2Al(NO_3)_3(aq) + 3H_2(g)$
Molar masses: Al, 26.98 g; $Al(NO_3)_3$, 213.0 g; H_2, 2.016 g

$$25.0 \text{ g Al} \times \frac{1 \text{ mol}}{26.98 \text{ g}} = 0.927 \text{ mol Al}$$

$$0.927 \text{ mol Al} \times \frac{2 \text{ mol Al(NO}_3)_3}{2 \text{ mol Al}} = 0.927 \text{ mol Al(NO}_3)_3$$

$$0.927 \text{ mol Al(NO}_3)_3 \times \frac{213.0 \text{ g}}{1 \text{ mol}} = 197 \text{ g Al(NO}_3)_3$$

$$0.927 \text{ mol Al} \times \frac{3 \text{ mol H}_2}{2 \text{ mol Al}} = 1.39 \text{ mol H}_2$$

$$1.39 \text{ mol H}_2 \times \frac{2.016 \text{ g}}{1 \text{ mol}} = 2.80 \text{ g H}_2$$

c. $H_3PO_4(aq) + 3NaOH(aq) \rightarrow Na_3PO_4(aq) + 3H_2O(l)$
Molar masses: H_3PO_4, 97.99 g; Na_3PO_4, 163.9 g; H_2O, 18.02 g

$$25.0 \text{ g H}_3PO_4 \times \frac{1 \text{ mol}}{97.99 \text{ g}} = 0.255 \text{ mol H}_3PO_4$$

$$0.255 \text{ mol H}_3PO_4 \times \frac{1 \text{ mol Na}_3PO_4}{1 \text{ mol H}_3PO_4} = 0.255 \text{ mol Na}_3PO_4$$

$$0.255 \text{ mol Na}_3PO_4 \times \frac{163.9 \text{ g}}{1 \text{ mol}} = 41.8 \text{ g Na}_3PO_4$$

$$0.255 \text{ mol H}_3PO_4 \times \frac{3 \text{ mol H}_2O}{1 \text{ mol H}_3PO_4} = 0.765 \text{ mol H}_2O$$

$$0.765 \text{ mol H}_2O \times \frac{18.02 \text{ g}}{1 \text{ mol}} = 13.8 \text{ g H}_2O$$

d. $CaO(s) + 2HCl(aq) \rightarrow CaCl_2(aq) + H_2O(l)$
Molar masses: CaO, 56.08 g; $CaCl_2$, 111.0 g; H_2O, 18.02 g

$$25.0 \text{ g CaO} \times \frac{1 \text{ mol}}{56.08 \text{ g}} = 0.446 \text{ mol CaO}$$

$$0.446 \text{ mol CaO} \times \frac{1 \text{ mol CaCl}_2}{1 \text{ mol CaO}} = 0.446 \text{ mol CaCl}_2$$

$$0.446 \text{ mol CaCl}_2 \times \frac{111.0 \text{ g}}{1 \text{ mol}} = 49.5 \text{ g CaCl}_2$$

$$0.446 \text{ mol CaO} \times \frac{1 \text{ mol H}_2O}{1 \text{ mol CaO}} = 0.446 \text{ mol H}_2O$$

$$0.446 \text{ mol H}_2O \times \frac{18.02 \text{ g}}{1 \text{ mol}} = 8.04 \text{ g H}_2O$$

5. a. $2AgNO_3(aq) + CaSO_4(aq) \rightarrow Ag_2SO_4(s) + Ca(NO_3)_2(aq)$
Molar masses: $AgNO_3$, 169.9 g; $CaSO_4$, 136.2 g; Ag_2SO_4, 311.9 g; $Ca(NO_3)_2$, 164.1 g

$$12.5 \text{ g AgNO}_3 \times \frac{1 \text{ mol}}{169.9 \text{ g}} = 0.0736 \text{ mol AgNO}_3$$

$$10.0 \text{ g CaSO}_4 \times \frac{1 \text{ mol}}{136.2 \text{ g}} = 0.0734 \text{ mol CaSO}_4$$

AgNO$_3$ is the limiting reactant.

$$0.0736 \text{ mol AgNO}_3 \times \frac{1 \text{ mol Ag}_2\text{SO}_4}{2 \text{ mol AgNO}_3} \times \frac{311.9 \text{ g Ag}_2\text{SO}_4}{1 \text{ mol Ag}_2\text{SO}_4} = 11.5 \text{ g Ag}_2\text{SO}_4$$

$$0.0736 \text{ mol AgNO}_3 \times \frac{1 \text{ mol Ca(NO}_3)_2}{2 \text{ mol AgNO}_3} \times \frac{164.1 \text{ g}}{1 \text{ mol}} = 6.04 \text{ g Ca(NO}_3)_2$$

b. $2\text{Al}(s) + 6\text{HNO}_3(aq) \rightarrow \text{Al(NO}_3)_3(aq) + 3\text{H}_2(g)$

Molar masses: Al, 26.98 g; HNO$_3$, 63.02 g, Al(NO$_3$)$_3$, 213.0 g; H$_2$, 2.016 g

$$12.5 \text{ g Al} \times \frac{1 \text{ mol}}{26.98 \text{ g}} = 0.463 \text{ mol Al}$$

$$10.0 \text{ g HNO}_3 \times \frac{1 \text{ mol}}{63.02 \text{ g}} = 0.159 \text{ mol HNO}_3$$

HNO$_3$ is the limiting reactant.

$$0.159 \text{ mol HNO}_3 \times \frac{2 \text{ mol Al(NO}_3)_3}{6 \text{ mol HNO}_3} \times \frac{213.0 \text{ g}}{1 \text{ mol}} = 11.3 \text{ g Al(NO}_3)_3$$

$$0.159 \text{ mol HNO}_3 \times \frac{3 \text{ mol H}_2}{6 \text{ mol HNO}_3} \times \frac{2.016 \text{ g}}{1 \text{ mol}} = 0.160 \text{ g H}_2$$

c. $\text{H}_3\text{PO}_4(aq) + 3\text{NaOH}(aq) \rightarrow \text{Na}_3\text{PO}_4(aq) + 3\text{H}_2\text{O}(l)$

Molar masses: H$_3$PO$_4$, 97.99 g; NaOH, 40.00 g, Na$_3$PO$_4$, 163.9 g; H$_2$O, 18.02 g

$$12.5 \text{ g H}_3\text{PO}_4 \times \frac{1 \text{ mol}}{97.99 \text{ g}} = 0.128 \text{ mol H}_3\text{PO}_4$$

$$10.0 \text{ g NaOH} \times \frac{1 \text{ mol}}{40.00 \text{ g}} = 0.250 \text{ mol NaOH}$$

NaOH is the limiting reactant.

$$0.250 \text{ mol NaOH} \times \frac{1 \text{ mol Na}_3\text{PO}_4}{3 \text{ mol NaOH}} \times \frac{163.9 \text{ g}}{1 \text{ mol}} = 13.7 \text{ g Na}_3\text{PO}_4$$

$$0.250 \text{ mol NaOH} \times \frac{3 \text{ mol H}_2\text{O}}{3 \text{ mol NaOH}} \times \frac{18.02 \text{ g}}{1 \text{ mol}} = 4.51 \text{ g H}_2\text{O}$$

d. $\text{CaO}(s) + 2\text{HCl}(aq) \rightarrow \text{CaCl}_2(aq) + \text{H}_2\text{O}(l)$

Molar masses: CaO, 56.08 g; HCl, 36.46 g, CaCl$_2$, 111.0 g; H$_2$O, 18.02 g

$$12.5 \text{ g CaO} \times \frac{1 \text{ mol}}{56.08 \text{ g}} = 0.222 \text{ mol CaO}$$

$$10.0 \text{ g HCl} \times \frac{1 \text{ mol}}{36.458 \text{ g}} = 0.274 \text{ mol HCl}$$

Since twice as many moles of HCl (compared with CaO) are required, HCl is the limiting reactant.

$$0.274 \text{ mol HCl} \times \frac{1 \text{ mol CaCl}_2}{2 \text{ mol HCl}} \times \frac{111.0 \text{ g}}{1 \text{ mol}} = 15.2 \text{ g CaCl}_2$$

$$0.274 \text{ mol HCl} \times \frac{1 \text{ mol H}_2\text{O}}{2 \text{ mol HCl}} \times \frac{18.02 \text{ g}}{1 \text{ mol}} = 2.47 \text{ g H}_2\text{O}$$

6. There is no pattern. For example, in part a, AgNO$_3$ is present with the highest mass and greatest number of moles, and it is the limiting reactant. In part b, HNO$_3$ limits the reaction and is present in the least amount (of mass and moles). Students need to understand that they must figure out the limiting reactant, not just memorize an incorrect shortcut such as "the limiting reactant is present in least amount."

7. We determine the theoretical yield by stoichiometric calculations. The actual yield is determined by experiment. The percent yield is calculated by taking the actual yield, dividing by the theoretical yield, and multiplying this number by 100%.

8. $(2.8 \text{ g})/(4.0 \text{ g}) \times 100\% = 70.\% \text{ yield}$.

Chapter 9: Challenge Review Worksheet

1. Answers will vary. An example is provided showing the decomposition of calcium carbonate, producing calcium oxide and carbon dioxide.

$$CaCO_3(s) \rightarrow CaO(s) + CO_2(g)$$

Let's suppose that 50.0 g of $CaCO_3$ is to be decomposed.
Molar masses: $CaCO_3$, 100.09 g; CaO, 56.08; CO_2, 44.01 g

$$\text{Mol } CaCO_3 = 50.0 \text{ g} \times \frac{1 \text{ mol}}{100.09 \text{ g}} = 0.4995 \text{ mol } CaCO_3$$

$$\text{Mol } CaO = 0.4995 \text{ mol } CaCO_3 \times \frac{1 \text{ mol } CaO}{1 \text{ mol } CaCO_3} = 0.4995 \text{ mol } CaO$$

$$\text{Mass } CaO = 0.4995 \text{ mol } CaO \times \frac{56.08 \text{ g}}{1 \text{ mol}} = 28.0 \text{ g } CaO$$

$$\text{Mol } CO_2 = 0.4995 \text{ mol } CaCO_3 \times \frac{1 \text{ mol } CO_2}{1 \text{ mol } CaCO_3} = 0.4995 \text{ mol } CO_2$$

$$\text{Mass } CO_2 = 0.4995 \text{ mol } CO_2 \times \frac{44.01 \text{ g}}{1 \text{ mol}} = 22.0 \text{ g } CO_2$$

The results illustrate an important point: The sum of the masses of the two products (28.0 g + 22.0 g) equals the mass of the reactant (50.0 g).

2. Answers will vary. An example of hydrogen and oxygen reacting to form water is provided.

$$2H_2(g) + O_2(g) \rightarrow 2H_2O(l)$$

Molar masses: H_2, 2.016 g; O_2, 32.00 g

To determine which reactant is limiting, we first need to realize that the masses of the reactants (25.0 g of each) tell us nothing. We need to calculate how many moles of each reactant is present.

$$\text{Mol } H_2 = 25.0 \text{ g } H_2 \times \frac{1 \text{ mol } H_2}{2.016 \text{ g } H_2} = 12.0 \text{ mol } H_2$$

$$\text{Mol } O_2 = 25.0 \text{ g } O_2 \times \frac{1 \text{ mol } O_2}{32.00 \text{ g } O_2} = 0.781 \text{ mol } O_2$$

Considering now these numbers of moles, it is clear that there is considerably more hydrogen present than oxygen. Chances are that the hydrogen is present in excess, and oxygen is the limiting reactant. We need to prove this, however, by calculation. If we consider that the 0.7813 mol of oxygen may be the limiting reactant, we can calculate how much hydrogen would be needed for complete reaction. This requires the mole ratio as determined by the coefficients of the balanced chemical equation.

$$0.781 \text{ mol } O_2 \times \frac{2 \text{ mol } H_2}{1 \text{ mol } O_2} = 1.56 \text{ mol } H_2 \text{ required for reaction}$$

Since only 1.56 mol of H_2 is required to react with 0.781 mol of O_2, and since we have considerably more hydrogen present in our sample than this amount, clearly hydrogen is present in excess, and oxygen is indeed the limiting reactant.

Suppose we had not initially considered that oxygen was the limiting reactant (because there is so much less oxygen present on a mole basis) and had wondered if H_2 was the limiting reactant. For the given amount of H_2 (12.4 mol), we could calculate how much oxygen would be required to react:

$$12.4 \text{ mol } H_2 \times \frac{1 \text{ mol } O_2}{2 \text{ mol } H_2} = 6.20 \text{ mol } O_2 \text{ would be required}$$

Since we do not have 6.20 mol of O_2 (we have only 0.781 mol O_2), clearly there is not enough oxygen present to react with all the hydrogen, and we would conclude again that oxygen must be the limiting reactant.

3. For potassium: $2K(s) + Cl_2(g) \rightarrow 2KCl(s)$
   Molar masses: K, 39.10 g; Cl_2, 70.90 g; KCl, 74.55 g

   $$25.0 \text{ g } K \times \frac{1 \text{ mol}}{39.10 \text{ g}} = 0.639 \text{ mol } K$$

   $$50.0 \text{ g } Cl_2 \times \frac{1 \text{ mol}}{70.90 \text{ g}} = 0.705 \text{ mol } Cl_2$$

   K is the limiting reactant.
   $$0.639 \text{ mol } K \times \frac{2 \text{ mol } KCl}{2 \text{ mol } K} \times \frac{74.55 \text{ g}}{1 \text{ mol}} = 47.6 \text{ g } KCl$$

   For calcium: $Ca(s) + Cl_2(g) \rightarrow CaCl_2(s)$
   Molar Masses: Ca, 40.08 g; Cl_2, 70.90 g; $CaCl_2$, 111.0 g

   $$25.0 \text{ g } Ca \times \frac{1 \text{ mol}}{40.08 \text{ g}} = 0.624 \text{ mol } Ca$$

   $$50.0 \text{ g } Cl_2 \times \frac{1 \text{ mol}}{70.90 \text{ g}} = 0.705 \text{ mol } Cl_2$$

   Ca is the limiting reactant.
   $$0.624 \text{ mol } Ca \times \frac{1 \text{ mol } CaCl_2}{1 \text{ mol } Ca} \times \frac{111.0 \text{ g}}{1 \text{ mol}} = 69.3 \text{ g } CaCl_2$$

   For aluminum: $2Al(s) + 3Cl_2(g) \rightarrow 2AlCl_3(s)$
   Molar masses: Al, 26.98 g; Cl_2 70.90 g; $AlCl_3$, 133.3 g

   $$25.0 \text{ g } Al \times \frac{1 \text{ mol}}{26.98 \text{ g}} = 0.927 \text{ mol } Al$$

   $$50.0 \text{ g } Cl_2 \times \frac{1 \text{ mol}}{70.90 \text{ g}} = 0.705 \text{ mol } Cl_2$$

   Cl_2 is the limiting reactant.
   $$0.705 \text{ mol } Cl_2 \times \frac{2 \text{ mol } AlCl_3}{3 \text{ mol } Cl_2} \times \frac{133.3 \text{ g}}{1 \text{ mol}} = 62.7 \text{ g } AlCl_3$$

4. (31.2 g KCl/47.6 g KCl) × 100% = 65.6% yield.

5. The relevant reaction is $Ag^+(aq) + Cl^-(aq) \rightarrow AgCl(s)$

   $$1.48 \text{ AgCl} \times \frac{1 \text{ mol } AgCl}{143.35 \text{ g } AgCl} \times \frac{1 \text{ mol } Ag^+}{1 \text{ mol } AgCl} = 0.0103 \text{ mol } Ag^+$$

The 0.0103 mol Ag^+ comes from $AgNO_3$; thus we started with 0.0103 mol $AgNO_3$ in the mixture.

$$0.0103 \text{ mol } AgNO_3 \times \frac{169.91g}{1 \text{ mol } AgNO_3} = 1.75g \text{ } AgNO_3$$

$$\frac{1.75 \text{ g } AgNO_3}{5.00 \text{ g mixture}} \times 100\% = 35.0\%$$

The mixture is 35.0% $AgNO_3$.

Chapter 10: Basic Review Worksheet

1. Scientists define *energy* as "the capacity to do work or to produce heat." As with *matter*, energy is such a fundamental concept that it is hard to define.

2. potential; kinetic; total

3. A state function is a property that is independent of pathway. Energy and elevation are examples of state functions. Heat and work are not state functions.

4. Temperature is a measure of the average kinetic energy of the particles of a system.

5. An exothermic reaction or process is one in which energy as heat is released to the surroundings; an endothermic reaction or process is one in which the system absorbs energy as heat from the surroundings.

6. The system is the part of the universe on which we focus attention; the surroundings are the rest of the universe.

7. Although the SI unit of energy is the joule, until relatively recently energies were more commonly given in terms of the calorie: One calorie is defined to be the amount of heat required to raise the temperature of one gram of water by one Celsius degree. The calorie is a "working" definition, and we can more easily appreciate this amount of energy. In terms of the SI unit, 1 calorie = 4.184 joule, so it takes 4.184 J to raise the temperature of one gram of water by one Celsius degree.

8.   a. $459 \text{ J} \times \frac{1 \text{ cal}}{4.184 \text{ J}} = 109.7 = 110. \text{ cal}$

       b. $55.31 \text{ kJ} = 55,310 \text{ J} = 5.531 \times 10^4 \text{ J}$

       c. $84.1 \text{ kJ} \times \frac{1 \text{ kcal}}{4.184 \text{ kJ}} = 20.1 \text{ kcal}$

9. $\Delta E = q + w$
     a. $34 \text{ J} + (-22 \text{ J}) = 12 \text{ J}$

     b. $(-28 \text{ J}) + (-23 \text{ cal}) = (-28 \text{ J}) + (-96 \text{ J}) = -124 \text{ J}$

     c. $(-15 \text{ J}) + 12 \text{ J} = -3 \text{ J}$

10. positive; negative

11. The specific heat capacity of a substance is the amount of energy required to raise the temperature of one gram of a substance by one Celsius degree. Therefore, the specific heat capacity of water must be 1.000 cal/g°C or 4.184 J/g °C.

12.   a. Temperature change = 27°C

Mass $= 1.0 \times 10^3$ J/$(4.184$ J/g°C$)(27°C) = 8.9$ g

b. Temperature change $= 100.°C$
Mass $= 1.0 \times 10^3$ J/$(0.45$ J/g°C$)(100.°C) = 22$ g

c. Temperature change $= 57°C$
Mass $= 1.0 \times 10^3$ J/$(0.71$ J/g°C$)(57°C) = 25$ g

13. Enthalpy H has a mathematical definition $H = E + PV$. However, at constant pressure, it turns out that the change in enthalpy is equal to the energy flow as heat.

14. The quality of energy is decreasing because of entropy as a driving force. For example, the amount of energy before and after a car consumes a gallon of gasoline is the same. However, the energy is more "spread out" once it has been burned and is less able to perform useful work. Thus the quantity is constant, but the quality is always decreasing.

15. The driving force is entropy or, more specifically, "energy spread." That is, for an exothermic reaction, energy is spread from more concentrated (in the system) to less concentrated (in the surroundings).

16.   a. Since ΔH is given with a negative sign, the reaction is exothermic.

    b. Energy as heat is released into the surroundings.

    c. $2(-2221$ J$) = -4442$ J. Thus 4442 J of energy as heat is released when 2 mol of propane is burned in excess oxygen.

17. Reverse the two given reactions, multiply the second by 2, and add

$$
\begin{array}{ll}
2Cu_2O(s) + O_2(g) \rightarrow 4CuO(s) & \Delta H = -288 \text{ kJ} \\
\underline{2Cu(s) + 2CuO(g) \rightarrow 2Cu_2O(s)} & \underline{\Delta H = -22 \text{ kJ}} \\
2Cu(s) + O_2(g) \rightarrow 2CuO(s) & \Delta H = -310. \text{ kJ}
\end{array}
$$

Chapter 10: Standard Review Worksheet

1. Heat is defined as a flow of energy due to a temperature difference. In an insulated system at constant temperature there is no temperature difference and thus no energy flow as heat. This can confuse students because 400°C seems "hot," and this equates to thinking of the system as "containing heat." However, heat is not a substance. If we were to stick our hands in such a system, there would be a difference in temperature between the system and our hand, and there would be energy flow as heat.

2. In Figure 10.1(a), ball A has greater potential energy than ball B. As ball A rolls down the hill, the potential energy decreases, but its kinetic energy increases. When ball A hits ball B, the kinetic energy of ball A is transferred to ball B. The potential energy of ball B is increased. Assuming that all the energy was transferred from ball A to ball B (no frictional heating, for example), the potential energy of ball B in Figure 10.1(b) is the same as the potential energy of ball A in Figure 10.1(a).

3.   a. 7031 cal $\times \dfrac{4.184 \text{ J}}{1 \text{ cal}} \times \dfrac{1 \text{ kJ}}{1000 \text{ J}} = 29.42$ kJ

    b. 78.3 kcal $\times \dfrac{4.184 \text{ J}}{1 \text{ cal}} = 327.6 = 328$ kJ

c. 4541 cal = 4.541 kcal

4. Heat is only one way that energy is transferred. For example, if a ball rolls down a hill, the amount of heat involved literally depends on the pathway (for example, if the pathway is rough, there is more friction and thus more heat involved). However, the work the ball can do once it rolls down the hill depends on the pathway as well. These factors are opposite of one another, and thus energy is conserved even though heat and work vary.

5. In any endothermic reaction, some of the thermal energy (random kinetic energy) via heat is converted to potential energy stored in the chemical bonds.

6. Answers will vary. However, crumpling paper and striking a match are endothermic (although the burning of a match is overall an exothermic process). The paper and logs are the system, whereas the room makes up the surroundings. Potential energy is stored in the match, the paper, and the logs. Kinetic energy is released as thermal energy via heat.

7. To see how specific heat capacities may be used to calculate the energy change for a process, consider this example: "How much energy is required to warm 25.0 g of water from 15.1 to 35.2°C?" The specific heat capacity of water is 1.000 cal/g°C. This is the quantity of energy required to raise the temperature of only one gram of water by only one Celsius degree. In this example, we are raising the temperature by (35.2 – 15.1) = 20.1°C. Thus, using the specific heat capacity as a conversion factor, we can say

$$\text{Energy required} = \left(\frac{1.00 \text{ cal}}{\text{g °C}} \right) \times (25.0 \text{ g}) \times (20.1°C) = 503 \text{ cal}$$

Notice how the units of g and °C cancel, leaving the answer in energy units only. This sort of calculation of energy change can be done for any substance, using the substance's own specific heat capacity.

8. a. 56°F = 13.3°C; 75°F = 23.9°C
Temperature change = 24 –13 = 11°C
Mass = 1.0×10^3 J/[(0.13 J/g°C)(11°C)] = 7.3×10^2 g

b. Temperature change = 385 K – 289 K = 96 K = 96°C
Mass = 1.0×10^3 J/[(0.24 J/g°C)(96°C)] = 43 g

c. 85.0°F = 29.4°C
Temperature change = 29.4°C – (–10.0°C) = 39.4°C
Mass = 1.0×10^3 J/[(0.89 J/g°C)(39.4°C)] = 29 g

9. $E = q + w$
a. (–23 J) + 12 J = –11 J

b. 14 J + (–5 cal) = 14 J + (–21 J) = –7 J

c. 87 J + (–32 J) = 55 J

10. a. $100.0 \text{ g C}_3\text{H}_8 \times \dfrac{1 \text{ mol C}_2\text{H}_8}{44.094 \text{ g C}_3\text{H}_8} \times \dfrac{-2221 \text{ kJ}}{1 \text{ mol C}_3\text{H}_8} = -5037 \text{ kJ}$

b. $100.0 \text{ g CO}_2 \times \dfrac{1 \text{ mol CO}_2}{44.01 \text{ g CO}_2} \times \dfrac{-2221 \text{ kJ}}{3 \text{ mol CO}_2} = -1682 \text{ kJ}$

11.

	ΔH (kJ/mol)
$I_2(s) \rightarrow I_2(g)$	62.8
$I_2(g) \rightarrow 2I(g)$	151.0
$Cl_2(g) \rightarrow 2Cl(g)$	242.3
$2I(g) + 2Cl(g) \rightarrow 2ICl(g)$	$-2(211.3)$
$I_2(s) + Cl_2(g) \rightarrow 2ICl(g)$	33.5

12. Yes, enthalpy is a state function. The definition of enthalpy H is $H = E + PV$. Since E, P, and V are all state functions, H is a state function as well.

13. The energy crisis has to do with the fact that the quality of the energy is decreasing (owing to entropy or, more specifically "energy spread"). The amount of energy is constant, but the amount of useful work that can be done with this energy is decreasing.

14. One driving force is "energy spread," which occurs in exothermic processes as energy goes from more to less concentrated. However, if an endothermic process occurs, this must be because of "matter spread" (for example, when a gas is produced from a solid, matter is "spread").

Chapter 10: Challenge Review Worksheet

1. We have to consider both "matter spread" and "energy spread" as driving forces. While water turning to steam is favored owing to matter spread, it is disfavored by energy spread. This is so because energy must flow via heat into water in order to make the conversion to steam. This is one example of many processes in which the two driving forces are counter to each other, therefore making spontaneity temperature-dependent.

2. We will assume the following:

    a. All the heat lost by the iron is gained by the water.

    b. The iron has an initial temperature of 100.0°C.

    c. The density of water is 1.00 g 1 mL over the temperature.

    d. The iron and water achieve the same final temperature.

    To make both signs positive, we will define the change in temperature of the iron as $100.0°C - t_f$ and the change in temperature of the water as $t_f - 25.0°C$.
    Heat lost by iron = heat gained by water
    $(5.00)(0.45 \text{ J/g°C})(100.0 - t_f) = (125.0 \text{ g})(4.184 \text{J/g°C})(t_f - 25.0)$
    $225 - 2.25t_f = 523t_f - 13,075$
    $13,300 = 525.25t_f$
    $25.3°C = t_f$

3. The first law of thermodynamics tells us that energy is conserved. Thus, when a ball rolls down a hill, potential energy is converted to kinetic energy owing to the motion of the ball and to frictional heating of the ball and hill. There is nothing in the first law, however, that states that the energy that has been "spread" cannot "reconcentrate" to the ball and cause the ball to roll back up the hill. The second law of thermodynamics tells us that entropy (or disorder) is constantly increasing. Thus energy spread as the ball rolls down the hill is a driving force, and energy will not "reconcentrate" spontaneously.

Chapter 11: Basic Review Worksheet

1. *Electromagnetic radiation* represents the propagation of energy through space in the form of waves.

2. A representative wave is depicted in Figure 11.3 in the text.

3. An atom is said to be in its ground state when it is in its lowest possible energy state. When an atom possesses more energy than in its ground state, the atom is said to be in an *excited state*.

4. Photons are discrete quantities of radiation. Atoms do not gain or emit radiation randomly but rather do so only in discrete bundles of radiation called *photons*.

5. Bohr pictured the electron moving in only certain circular orbits around the nucleus. Each particular orbit (corresponding to a particular distance from the nucleus) had associated with it a particular energy (resulting from the attraction between the nucleus and the electron).

6. When we draw a picture of a given orbital, we are saying that there is a 90% probability of finding the electron within the region indicated in the drawing.

7. The lowest-energy hydrogen atomic orbital is called the $1s$ orbital.

8. The third principal energy level of hydrogen is divided into three sublevels, the $3s$, $3p$, and $3d$ sublevels. The fourth principal energy level of hydrogen is divided into four sublevels, the $4s$, $4p$, $4d$, and $4f$ orbitals.

9. In simple terms, in addition to moving around the nucleus of the atom, we picture the electron rotating (spinning) on its own axis. There are only two ways a body spinning on its own axis can rotate (often described as "clockwise" and "counterclockwise" motions) to the right or to the left (for example, the earth is rotating on its axis to the right).

10. The Pauli exclusion principle summarizes our theory about intrinsic electron spin: A given atomic orbital can hold a maximum of two electrons, and those two electrons must have opposite spins.

11. The order in which the orbitals fill with electrons is indicated by the periodic table according to atomic number and the "block". Thus we get $1s$, $2s$, $2p$, $3s$, $3p$, $4s$, $3d$, $4p$, etc. It is not intuitively obvious why electrons fill the $4s$ orbitals before the $3d$ orbitals, but this is indicated by the known form of the periodic table.

12. A particular s subshell can hold two electrons. Since any p subshell consists of three orbitals, a given p subshell can hold a maximum of six electrons. A particular p orbital (like any orbital) can hold only two electrons (of opposite spin).

13. The valence electrons of an atom are the electrons in the outermost shell of the atom. The core electrons are those in principal energy levels closer to the nucleus than the outermost shell (the core electrons are the electrons that are not valence electrons).

14. This general periodic table is shown in the text as Figure 11.31. Students should not have to memorize of exactly where each element is found in the table, but they should know that the table is arranged in terms of the electronic structure of the atoms. For example, the first horizontal row of the table corresponds to the $n = 1$ shell, which consists of only the $1s$

orbital, so there are only two elements in the row. However, the second row of the table contains eight elements, since the $n = 2$ shell contains a total of four orbitals (the $2s$ and the three $2p$ orbitals).

15.   a. Na: $1s^2 2s^2 2p^6 3s^1$

b. N: $1s^2 2s^2 2p^3$

c. Be: $1s^2 2s^2$

d. Sr: $1s^2 2s^2 2p^6 3s^2 3p^6 4s^2 3d^{10} 4p^6 5s^2$ or $[Kr]5s^2$

16. The representative elements are the elements in Groups 1–8 of the periodic table whose valence electrons are in s and p subshells. There are two groups of representative elements at the left side of the periodic table (corresponding to the s subshells) and six groups of representative elements at the right side of the periodic table (corresponding to the p subshells). Metallic character is largest at the left-hand end of any horizontal row of the periodic table and largest at the bottom of any vertical group. Overall, these two trends mean that the most metallic elements are at the lower left of the periodic table, and the least metallic (that is, the nonmetals) are at the top right of the periodic table. The metalloids, which have both metallic and nonmetallic properties, are found in the "stairstep" region indicated on most periodic tables.

17. The ionization energy of an atom represents the energy required to remove an electron from the atom. The atomic radius is the distance from the center of the nucleus to the outer "edge" of the valence electrons.

18. As one goes from top to bottom in a vertical group in the periodic table, the ionization energies decrease (it becomes easier to remove an electron). Within a given vertical group, the atoms get progressively larger (increase in atomic radius) when going from the top of the group to the bottom. In going from left to right within a horizontal row of the elements in the periodic table, the atoms get progressively smaller.

19.   a. Atomic radius: Rb > K > Na; ionization energy: Na > K > Rb

b. Atomic radius: C > O > F; ionization energy: F > O > C

c. Atomic radius: Na > Si > O; ionization energy: O > Si > Na

Chapter 11: Standard Review Worksheet

1. Visible light, radio and television transmissions, microwaves, X rays, and radiant heat are all examples of electromagnetic radiation.

2. The waves by which electromagnetic radiation is propagated have several characteristic properties. The wavelength λ represents the distance between two corresponding points (peaks or troughs) on consecutive waves and is measured in units of length (meters, centimeters, etc.). The frequency ν of electromagnetic radiation represents how many complete waves pass a given point in space per second and is measured in waves per second (hertz).

3. The speed c or propagation velocity of electromagnetic radiation represents how fast a given wave itself moves through space and is equal to 3×10^8 m/s in a vacuum. For electromagnetic radiation, these three properties are related by the formula $\lambda \times \nu = c$.

4. An atom is promoted from its ground state to an excited state by absorbing energy. When the atom returns from an excited state to its ground state, it emits the excess energy as electromagnetic radiation.

5. The photons of radiation emitted by atoms are characterized by the wavelength (color) of the radiation: Longer-wavelength photons carry less energy than shorter-wavelength photons. The energy of a photon emitted by an atom corresponds exactly to the difference in energy between two allowed energy states in an atom. Thus we can use an observable phenomenon (emission of light by excited atoms) to gain insight into the energy changes taking place within the atom.

6. For Bohr, when an atom absorbs energy, the electron moves from its ground state in the orbit closest to the nucleus ($n = 1$) to an orbit father away from the nucleus ($n = 2, 3, 4, . . .$). When an excited atom returns to its ground state, corresponding to the electron moving form an outer orbit to the orbit nearest the nucleus, the atom emits the excess energy as radiation. Since the Bohr orbits correspond to fixed distances from the nucleus and from each other, when an electron moves form one fixed orbit to another, the energy change is of a definite amount. This corresponds to a photon being emitted of a particular characteristic wavelength and energy. The original Bohr theory worked very well for hydrogen. Bohr even predicted emission wavelengths for hydrogen, which had not yet been seen and were subsequently found at the exact wavelengths Bohr had calculated. However, when the simple Bohr model for the atom was applied to the emission spectra of other elements, the theory could not predict or explain the observed emission spectra.

7. The wave-mechanical theory for atomic structure developed by Schrodinger provided a model for the structure of the hydrogen atom that was consistent with all the observed properties of the hydrogen atom. Unlike Bohr's theory, however, which failed completely for atoms other than hydrogen, the wave-mechanical model was able to be extended to describe other atoms with considerable success. Rather than the fixed "orbits" that Bohr had postulated, the wave-mechanical model for the atom pictures the electrons of an atom as being distributed in regions of space called *orbitals*.

8. The wave-mechanical model for the atom does not describe in classical terms the exact motion or trajectory of an electron as it moves around the nucleus but rather predicts the probability of finding the electron in a particular location within the atom. The orbitals that constitute the solutions to the mathematical formulation of the wave-mechanical model for the atom represent probability contour maps for finding the electrons. When we draw a particular picture of a given orbital, we are saying that there is a 90% probability of finding the electron within the region indicated in the drawing.

9. The $1s$ orbital is spherical in shape (that is, the electron density around the nucleus is uniform in all directions from the nucleus). The $1s$ orbital represents a probability map of electron density around the nucleus for the first principal energy level. The orbital does not have a sharp edge (it appears fuzzy) because the probability of finding the electron does not ever go to zero with distance from the nucleus. The orbital does not represent just a spherical surface on which the electron moves (this would be similar to Bohr's original theory). When we draw a picture to represent the $1s$ orbital, we are indicating that the probability of finding the electron within this region of space is about 90%. We know that

the likelihood of finding the electron within this orbital is very high, but we still don't know exactly where in this region the electron is at a given instant in time.

10. The principal energy levels (for hydrogen) correspond fairly well with the "orbits" of the Bohr theory and are designated by an integer n called the *principal quantum number* ($n = 1$, 2, 3, . . .). In the wave-mechanical model, however, these principal energy levels are further subdivided into sets of equivalent orbitals called *subshells*. For example, the $n = 2$ principal level of hydrogen is further subdivided into an s and a p subshell (indicated as the $2s$ and $2p$ subshells, respectively). These subshells, in turn, consist of the individual orbitals in which the electrons reside. The $2s$ subshell consists of the single, spherically shaped $2s$ orbital, whereas the $2p$ subshell consists of a set of three equivalent, dumbbell-shaped $2p$ orbitals (which are often designated as $2p_x$, $2p_y$, and $2p_z$ to indicate their orientation in space). Similarly, the $n = 3$ principal energy level of hydrogen is subdivided into three subshells: the $3s$ subshell (one orbital), the $3p$ subshell (a set of three orbitals), and the $3d$ subshell (a set of five orbitals).

11. The $3s$ subshell consists of the single $3s$ orbital. Like the other s orbitals, the $3s$ orbital is spherical in shape. The $3p$ subshell consists of a set of three equal-energy $3p$ orbitals. Each of these $3p$ orbitals has the same shape ("dumbbell"), but each of the $3p$ orbitals is oriented in a different direction in space. The $3d$ subshell consists of a set of five $3d$ orbitals. The $3d$ orbitals have the shapes indicated in Figure 11.23 and are oriented in different directions around the nucleus (students sometimes say that four of the $3d$ orbitals have the shape of a four-leaf clover). The $4s$ subshell consists of the single $4s$ orbital. The $4p$ subshell consists of a set ot three $4p$ orbitals. The $4d$ subshell consists of a set of five $4d$ orbitals. The shapes of the $4s$, $4p$, and $4d$ orbitals are the same as the shapes of the orbitals of the third principal energy level (the orbitals of the fourth principal energy level are larger and further from the nucleus than the orbitals of the third level, however). The fourth principal energy level also contains a $4f$ subshell, consisting of seven $4f$ orbitals (the shapes of the $4f$ orbitals are beyond the scope of this text).

12. Since there are only two possible orientations for an electron's intrinsic spin, this results in a given orbital being able to accommodate only two electrons (one spinning in each direction).

13. Since the three orbitals within a given p subshell are of exactly the same energy and differ only in their orientation in space, when we write the electron configuration of an element such as N or O that has a partially-filled p subshell, we place the electrons in separate p orbitals to minimize the interelectronic repulsion. Thus the configuration of nitrogen could be written as $1s^2 2s^2 2p_x^1 2p_y^1 2p_z^1$ to emphasize this.

14. Since the first principal level consists only of the $1s$ orbital, the $n = 1$ level can contain only two electrons. Since the second principal level consists of the $2s$ orbital and the set of three $2p$ orbitals, the $n = 2$ level can hold a maximum of $[2 + 3(2)] = 8$ electrons.

15. Since the valence electrons are those in the outermost filled shell of the atom, it is these electrons that are affected by the presence of other atoms and which are gained, lost, or shared with other atoms. The periodic table is basically arranged in terms of the valence electronic configurations of the elements (elements in the same vertical group have similar configurations). For example, all the elements in Group 1 have one valence electron.

16. Just from the column and row location of an element, one can determine the expected valence shell electronic configuration. For example, the element in the third horizontal row in the second vertical column has a $3s^2$ for an atom valence configuration. We know that the valence electrons are in the $n = 3$ shell because the element is in the third horizontal row. We know that the valence electrons are s electrons because the first two electrons in a horizontal row are always in an s subshell. We know that there are two electrons because the element is the second element in the horizontal row. As an additional example, the element in the seventh vertical column of the second horizontal row in the periodic table has the valence configuration $2s^2 2p^5$.

17. a. P: $1s^2 2s^2 2p^6 3s^2 3p^3$

 b. Se: $1s^2 2s^2 2p^6 3s^2 3p^6 4s^2 3d^{10} 4p^4$ or $[Ar]4s^2 3d^{10} 4p^4$

 c. Zr: $1s^2 2s^2 2p^6 3s^2 3p^6 4s^2 3d^{10} 4p^6 5s^2 4d^2$ or $[Kr]5s^2 4d^2$

 d. Ce: $1s^2 2s^2 2p^6 3s^2 3p^6 4s^2 3d^{10} 4p^6 5s^2 4d^{10} 5p^6 6s^2 5d^1 4f^1$ or $[Xe]6s^2 5d^1 4f^1$

18. a. Atomic radius: K > Na > P; ionization energy: P > Na > K

 b. Atomic radius: Rb > Al > N; ionization energy: N > Al > Rb

 c. Atomic radius: Cs > I > O; ionization energy: O > I > Cs

Chapter 11: Challenge Review Worksheet

1. Excited atoms definitely do not emit their excess energy in a random or continuous manner. Rather, an excited atom of a given element emits only discrete photons of characteristic wavelength and energy when going back to its ground state.

2. Since an excited atom of a given element always emits photons of exactly the same energy, we take this to mean that the internal structure of the atom is such that there are only certain discrete allowed energy states for the electrons in atoms and that the wavelengths of radiation emitted by an atom correspond to the exact energy differences between these allowed energy states. For example, excited hydrogen atoms always display the visible spectrum shown in Figure 11.11 of the text. We take this spectrum as evidence for the existence of only certain discrete energy levels within the hydrogen atom, and we describe this by saying that the energy levels of hydrogen are *quantized*.

3. Previously, scientists had thought that atoms emitted energy continuously.

4. De Broglie and Schrodinger took the new idea that electromagnetic radiation behaved as if it were a steam of small particles (photons), as well as a traditional wave, and basically reversed the premise. That is, if something that had previously been considered to be entirely wave-like also had a particle-like nature, then perhaps small particles also have a wave-like nature under some circumstances.

5. When an atom (hydrogen, for example) absorbs energy, the electron moves to a higher energy state, which corresponds in the wave-mechanical model to a different type of orbital. The orbitals are arranged in a hierarchy of principal energy levels, as well as sublevels of these principal levels.

6. Atoms have a series of principal energy levels symbolized by the letter n. The $n = 1$ level is the closest to the nucleus, and the energies of the levels increase as the value of n increases

going out from the nucleus. Each principal energy level is divided into a set of sublevels of different characteristic shapes (designated by the letters *s, p, d,* and *f*). Each sublevel is further subdivided into a set of orbitals. Each *s* subshell consists of a single s orbital; each *p* subshell consists of a set of three *p* orbitals; each *d* subshell consists of a set of five *d* orbitals; etc. A given orbital can be empty, or it can contain one or two electrons but never more than two electrons (if an orbital contains two electrons, then the electrons must have opposite intrinsic spins). The shape we picture for an orbital represents only a probability map for finding electrons. The shape does not represent a trajectory or pathway for electron movements.

7. Students often find it easier to make sense of the atomic radius trends and to use these to explain the trends in ionization energy. The relative sizes of atoms vary systematically with the location of an element in the periodic table. Within a given vertical group, the atoms get progressively larger when going from the top of the group to the bottom. The valence electrons of the atoms are in progressively higher principal energy shells (and are progressively further from the nucleus) as we go down a group. In going from left to right within a horizontal row of the elements in the periodic table, the atoms get progressively smaller. Although in a given row all valence electrons are in the same principal energy shell, the nuclear charge is progressively increasing from left to right, making the given valence shell progressively smaller as the electrons are drawn more closely to the nucleus. The ionization energy of an atom represents the energy required to remove an electron from the atom. As one goes from top to bottom in a vertical group in the periodic table, the ionization energies decrease (it becomes easier to remove an electron). As one goes down a group, the valence electrons are farther and farther from the nucleus (larger atomic radius) and are less tightly held. The ionization energies increase when going from left to right within a horizontal row of the periodic table. The left-hand side of the periodic table is where the metallic elements are found, which lose electrons relatively easily. The right-hand side of the periodic table is where the nonmetallic elements are found. Rather than losing electrons, these elements tend to gain electrons. Within a given horizontal row in the periodic table, the valence electrons are all in the same principal energy shell. However, in going from left to right in the horizontal row, the nuclear charge that holds onto the electrons is increasing one unit with each successive element, making it that much more difficult to remove an electron (and the atomic radius is smaller).

8. Answers will vary. The excited-state electron configuration must have the same number of electrons as the ground-state electron configuration. However, the highest-energy electron is not in the ground state. The ground-state electron configurations are provided below:

   a. C: $1s^2 2s^2 2p^2$

   b. Cr: $1s^2 2s^2 2p^6 3s^2 3p^6 4s^1 3d^5$ or $[Ar]4s^1 3d^5$

   c. Br: $1s^2 2s^2 2p^6 3s^2 3p^6 4s^2 3d^{10} 4p^5$ or $[Ar]4s^2 3d^{10} 4p^5$

   d. Os: $1s^2 2s^2 2p^6 3s^2 3p^6 4s^2 3d^{10} 4p^6 5s^2 4d^{10} 5p^6 6s^2 4f^{14} 5d^6$ or $[Xe]6s^2 4f^{14} 5d^6$

Chapter 12: Basic Review Worksheet

1. A *chemical bond* is a force that holds two or more atoms together and makes them function as a unit. The principal types of chemical bonding are ionic bonding, pure covalent bonding, and polar covalent bonding.

2. Ionic bonding results when elements of very different electronegativities react with each other. Sodium chloride (NaCl) is an example of a typical ionic compound.

3. A bond between two atoms is, in general, covalent if the atoms share a pair of electrons in mutually completing their valence electron shells. Covalent bonds can be subclassed as to whether they are pure (nonpolar) covalent or polar covalent. In a nonpolar covalent bond, two atoms of the same elecronegativity (often this means the same type of atom) equally share a pair of electrons. The electron cloud of the bond is symmetrically distributed along the bond axis. In a polar covalent bond, one of the atoms of the bond has a higher electronegativity than the other atom and draws the shared pair of electrons more closely toward itself (pulling the electron cloud along the bond axis closer to the more electronegative atom). Because the more electronegative atom of a polar covalent bond ends up with a higher electron density than normal, there is a center of partial negative charge at this end of he bond. Conversely, because the less electronegative element of a polar covalent bond has some of its valence electrons pulled partly away from the atom, a center of positive charge develops at this end of the bond.

4. Electronegativity represents the relative ability of an atom in a molecule to attract shared electrons toward itself.

5. A molecule is said to possess an overall dipole moment if the centers of positive and negative charge in the molecule do not coincide.

6. The properties of typical ionic substances (hardness, rigidity, high melting and boiling points, etc.) suggest that the ionic bond is a very strong one. The formulas we write for ionic substances are really only empirical formulas, showing the relative numbers of each type of atom present in the substance. For example, when we write $CaCl_2$ as the formula for calcium chloride, we are only saying that there are two chloride ions for each calcium ion in the substance and not that there are distinct molecules of $CaCl_2$.

7.   a. Na: $1s^2 2s^2 2p^6 3s^1$ or $[Ne]3s^1$ or Na^+: $1s^2 2s^2 2p^6$ or $[Ne]$

      b. I: $1s^2 2s^2 2p^6 3s^2 3p^6 4s^2 3d^{10} 4p^6 5s^2 4d^{10} 5p^5$ or $[Kr]5s^2 4d^{10} 5p^5$

         I^-: $1s^2 2s^2 2p^6 3s^2 3p^6 4s^2 3d^{10} 4p^6 5s^2 4d^{10} 5p^6$ or $[Xe]$

      c. Ca: $1s^2 2s^2 2p^6 3s^2 3p^6 4s^2$ or $[Ar]4s^2$; Ca^{2+}: $1s^2 2s^2 2p^6 3s^2 3p^6$ or $[Ar]$

8.   a. $BaCl_2$ b. NaF   c. K_2O

9. Bonding between atoms to form a molecule involves only the valence electrons of the atoms [not the inner (core) electrons]. Thus, when we draw the Lewis structure of a molecule, we show only the valence electrons (both bonding valence electrons and nonbonding valence electrons). The most important requisite for the formation of a stable compound (and which we try to demonstrate when we write Lewis structures) is that each atom of a molecule attains a noble gas electron configuration. When we write Lewis

structures, we arrange the bonding and nonbonding valence electrons to try to complete the octet (or duet) for as many atoms as is possible.

10. The "duet" rule applies only for the element hydrogen: When a hydrogen atom forms a bond to another atom, the single electron of the hydrogen atom pairs up with an electron from the other atom to give the shared electron pair (that is, two electrons—a duet) that constitutes the covalent bond. By sharing this additional electron, the hydrogen atom attains effectively the $1s^2$ configuration of the noble gas helium.

11. The "octet" rule applies for the representative elements other than hydrogen. When one of these atoms forms bonds to other atoms, the atom shares enough electrons to end up with the ns^2np^6 (that is, eight electrons—an octet) electron configuration of a noble gas.

12. Bonding electrons are those electrons used in forming a covalent bond between atoms. The bonding electrons in a molecule represent the electrons that are shared between atoms. Nonbonding (or lone pair) electrons are those valence electrons which are not used in covalent bonding and which "belong" exclusively to one atom in a molecule. For example, in the molecule ammonia (NH_3), the Lewis structure shows that there are three pairs of bonding electrons (each pair constitutes a covalent bond between the nitrogen atom and one of the hydrogen atoms) as well as one nonbonding pair of electrons that belongs exclusively to the nitrogen atom. The presence of nonbonding pairs of electrons on an atom in a molecule has a significant effect on the geometric shape of the molecule and on the molecule's properties.

13.   a.

$$:\!F\!-\!P\!-\!F\!:$$
$$|$$
$$:\!F\!:$$

   b.

$$:\!Cl\!:$$
$$|$$
$$:\!Cl\!-\!Si\!-\!Cl\!:$$
$$|$$
$$:\!Cl\!:$$

   c.

$$H\!-\!S\!-\!H$$

14. A double bond between two atoms represents the atoms sharing two pairs of electrons (four electrons) between them. A triple bond represents two atoms sharing three pairs (six electrons) between them.

15. If it is possible to draw more than one valid Lewis structure for a molecule, differing only in the location of the double bonds, we say that the molecule exhibits *resonance*.

16.   a. trigonal pyramid   b. bent or V-shaped   c. tetrahedral

Chapter 12: Standard Review Worksheet

1. The strength of a chemical bond is commonly described in terms of the *bond energy,* which is the quantity of energy required to break the bond.

2. We know that ionically bonded solids do not conduct electricity in the solid state (because the ions are held tightly in place by all the attractive forces), but such substances are strong electrolytes when melted or when dissolved in water (either of which process sets the ions free to move around). Ionic bonds are formed when a metallic element reacts with a nonmetallic element, with the metallic element losing electrons and forming positive ions and the nonmetallic element gaining electrons and forming negative ions.

3. For a bond to be purely covalent, the electronegativity values of the atoms in the bond must be the same. A polar covalent bond represents a partial transfer of electron density from one atom to another, but with the atoms still held together as a unit. This is in contrast with an ionic bond, in which one atom completely transfers one or more electrons to a more electronegative atom, but with the resulting positive and negative ions able to separate and behave independently of one another (for example, in solution).

4. In order for a bond to be polar, one of the atoms in the bond must attract the shared electron pair toward itself and away from the other atom of the bond. This can happen only if one atom of the bond is more electronegative than the other (that is, that there is a considerable difference in electronegativities for the two atoms of the bond). If two atoms in a bond have the same electronegativity, then the two atoms pull the electron pair equally, and the bond is nonpolar covalent. If two atoms sharing a pair of electrons have vastly different electronegativities, the electron pair will be pulled so strongly by the more electronegative atom that a negative ion may be formed (as well as a positive ion for the second atom), and ionic bonding will result. If the difference in electronegativities between two atoms sharing an electron pair is somewhere in between these two extremes (equal sharing of the electron pair and formation of ions), then a polar covalent bond results.

5. A distinction must be made between whether or not individual bonds within a molecule are polar and whether or not individual bonds within a molecule are polar and whether the molecule possesses a net dipole moment. Sometimes the geometric shape of a molecule is such that individual bond dipoles effectively cancel each other out, leaving the molecule nonpolar overall.

6. In general, when atoms of a metal react with atoms of a nonmetal, the metal atoms lose electrons until they have the configuration of the preceding noble gas, and the nonmetal atoms gain electrons until they have the configuration of the following noble gas. Covalently and polar covalently bonded molecules also strive to attain noble gas electronic configurations. For a covalently bonded molecule such as F_2, in which neither fluorine atom has a greater tendency than the other to gain or lose electrons completely, each F atom provides one electron of the pair of electrons that constitutes the covalent bond. Each F atom feels also the influence of the other F atom's electron in the shared pair, and each F atom effectively fills its outermost shell. Similarly, in polar covalently bonded molecules such as HF or HCl, the shared pair of electrons between the atoms effectively completes the outer electron shell of each atom simultaneously to give each atom a noble gas electronic configuration.

7. Ionic substances in the bulk consist of crystals containing an extended lattice array of positive and negative ions in a more or less alternating pattern (that is, a given positive ion typically has several negative ions as its nearest neighbors in the crystal). A typical ionic crystal lattice is shown in Figure 12.8 in the text.

8. When an atom forms a positive ion (cation), it sheds its outermost electron shell (the valence electrons), giving a positive ion a smaller size than the atom from which it was formed. When an atom forms a negative ion, the atoms takes additional electrons into its outermost shell, which causes the outermost shell to increase in size because of the additional repulsive forces. This results in a negative ion that is larger than the atom from which it was formed.

9.
   a. N: $1s^22s^22p^3$; N^{3-}: $1s^22s^22p^6$ or [Ne]

   b. Se: $1s^22s^22p^63s^23p^64s^23d^{10}4p^4$ or $[Ar]4s^23d^{10}4p^4$

   Se^{2-}: $1s^22s^22p^63s^23p^64s^23d^{10}4p^6$ or [Kr]

   c. Al: $1s^22s^22p^63s^23p^1$ or $[Ne]3s^23p^1$; Al^{3+}: $1s^22s^22p^6$ or [Ne]

10.
   a. Al_2O_3

   b. Mg_3N_2

   c. Cs_2S

11. When writing a Lewis structure for a molecule, if (after placing a pair of bonding electrons between each of the atoms to be connected) there are not enough valence electrons remaining to complete the octet (or duet) for each atom, then this strongly suggests that there must be multiple bonding present in the molecule. For example, if a molecule seems to be two electrons short of enough to complete independently the octet, this suggests that there must be a second bond between two of the atoms (a double bond exists between those atoms). If a molecule seems to be four electrons short, this could mean either that a triple bond exists between two of the atoms or that there are two double bonds present in the molecule.

12.   a.

   b.

c.

$$:\ddot{O}\!=\!\ddot{S}\!-\!\ddot{O}: \longleftrightarrow :\ddot{O}\!-\!\ddot{S}\!=\!\ddot{O}$$

13.　　a. trigonal pyramid　b. bent or V-shaped　c. tetrahedral

Chapter 12: Challenge Review Worksheet

1. For example, compare the two molecules H_2O and CO_2. The water molecule is nonlinear (bent or V-shaped), whereas the CO_2 molecule is linear because of the double bonds. Both the O—H and the C=O bonds are themselves polar (because the atoms involved have different electronegativities). However, since the CO_2 molecule is linear, the two individual bond dipoles lie in opposite directions on the same axis and cancel each other out, leaving CO_2 as a nonpolar molecule overall. Water has polar bonds that lie at an angle of about 105° and thus do not cancel each other out. This means that water is a very polar molecule. Bond dipoles are in actuality vector quantities, and the overall dipole moment of the molecule represents the resultant of all the individual bond dipole vectors. The high polarity of the water molecule, combined with the existence of hydrogen bonding among water molecules, is responsible for the fact that water is a liquid at room temperature.

2. It has been observed over many, many experiments that when an active metal such as sodium or magnesium reacts with a nonmetal, the sodium atoms always form Na^+ ions, and the magnesium atoms always form Mg^{2+} ions. It has been further observed that aluminum always forms only the Al^{3+} ion, and that when nitrogen, oxygen, and fluorine form simple ions, the ions are always N^{3-}, O^{2-}, and F^-, respectively. Clearly, the facts that these elements always form the same ions and that those ions all contain eight electrons in the outermost shell led scientists to speculate that there must be something very fundamentally stable about a species that has eight electrons in its outermost shell (such as the noble gas neon). The repeated observation that so many elements, when reacting, tend to attain an electronic configuration that is isoelectronic with a noble gas led chemists to speculate that all elements try to attain such a configuration for their outermost shells. However, knowing that species *do* attain a noble gas electron configuration does not explain *why* they do.

3. In the case of ionic compounds involving polyatomic ions, more than one type of bonding force is involved. First of all, ionic bonding exists between the positive and negative ions. However, within the polyatomic ions themselves, the atoms are held together by covalent bonds.

4. Answers will vary. Let's illustrate the method for ammonia (NH_3). First, count up the total number of valence electrons available in the molecule (without regard to which atom they originally come from). Remember that for the representative elements, the group in which the element is found on the periodic table indicates the number of valence electrons. For NH_3, since nitrogen is in Group 5, one nitrogen atom would contribute five valence electrons. Since hydrogen atoms only have one electron each, the three hydrogen atoms provide an additional three valence electrons, for a total of eight valence electrons overall. Next, write down the symbols for the atoms in the molecule, and use one pair of electrons (represented by a line) to form a bond between each pair of bound atoms.

$$H-N-H$$
$$|$$
$$H$$

These three bonds use six of the eight valence electrons. Since each hydrogen already has its duet in what we have drawn so far, whereas the nitrogen atom has only six electrons around it so far, the final two valence electrons must represent a lone pair on the nitrogen.

$$H-\overset{..}{N}-H$$
$$|$$
$$H$$

5. There are several types of exceptions to the octet rule described in the text. The octet rule is really a "rule of thumb" that we apply to molecules. There are some common molecules that from experimental measurements we know do not follow the octet rule. Boron and beryllium compounds usually do not fit the octet rule. For example, in BF_3, the boron atom has only six valence electrons, whereas in BeF_2, the beryllium atom has only four valence electrons. Other molecules that are exceptions to the octet rule include any molecule with an odd number of valence electrons (such as NO or NO_2). You can't get an octet (an even number) of electrons around each atom in a molecule with an odd number of valence electrons.

6. The general geometric structure of a molecule is determined by how many electron pairs surround the central atom in the molecule and how many of those electron pairs are used for bonding to the other atoms of the molecule. As examples, let's show how we would determine the geometric structure of the molecules CH_4, NH_3, and H_2O. First, we must draw the Lewis structures for each of these molecules:

$$\begin{array}{ccc} & H & \\ & | & \\ H-C-H & H-\overset{..}{N}-H & H-\overset{..}{\underset{..}{O}}-H \\ & | & | \\ & H & H \end{array}$$

In each of these structures, the central atom (C, N, or O) is surrounded by four pairs (an octet) of electrons. According to the VSEPR theory, the four pairs of electrons repel each other and orient themselves in space as far away from each other as possible. This leads to a tetrahedron orientation of the electron pairs, separated by angles of 109.5°. For CH_4, each of the four pairs of electrons around the C atom is a bonding pair. We therefore say that CH_4 itself has a tetrahedral geometry, with H—C—H bond angles of 109.5°. For NH_3, however, although there are four tetrahedrally arranged electron pairs around the nitrogen atom, only three of these pairs are bonding pairs. There is a lone pair on the nitrogen atom. We describe the geometry of NH_3 as a trigonal pyramid. The three hydrogen atoms lie below the nitrogen atom in space as a result of the presence of the lone pair on nitrogen. The H—N—H bond angles are slightly less than the tetrahedral angle of 109.5°. Finally, only two of these pairs are bonding pairs. There are two lone electron pairs on the oxygen atom. We describe the geometry of H_2O as bent, V-shaped, or nonlinear. The presence of the lone pairs makes the H—O—H bond angle not 180° (linear) but somewhat less than the tetrahedral angle of 109.5°.

7.

Number of Valence Pairs	Bond Angle	Example(s)
2	180°	BeF_2, BeH_2
3	120°	BCl_3
4	109.5°	CH_4, CCl_4, GeF_4

8. In predicting the geometric structure of a molecule, we treat a double (or triple) bond as a single entity (as if it were a single pair of electrons). This approach is reasonable because all the bonding electrons between two atoms must be present in the same region of space between the atoms (whether one, two, or three electron pairs). For example, if we write the Lewis structure of acetylene (C_2H_2)

$$H: C:::C:H$$

we realize that each carbon atom in the molecule has effectively only two "things" (termed *repulsive units* in the text) attached to it: a bonding pair of electrons (that bonds the H atom) and a triple bond (that bonds the other C atom). Since there are effectively only two things (repulsive units) attached to each carbon atom, we would expect the bond angles for each carbon atom to be 180°, which makes the molecule linear.

Chapter 13: Basic Review Worksheet

1. Gases have no fixed volume or shape but take on the shape and volume of the container in which they are confined. This is in contrast to solids and liquids. A sample of solid has its own intrinsic volume and shape and is very incompressible. A sample of liquid has an intrinsic volume but does not take on the shape of its container.

2. The SI unit of pressure is the pascal, but this unit is almost never used in everyday situations because it is too small to be practical. Rather, we tend to use units of pressure that are based on the simple instruments used to measure pressures, the mercury barometer and manometer. The mercury barometer, used for measuring the pressure of the atmosphere, consists of a column of mercury that is held in a vertical glass tube by the atmosphere. The pressure of the atmosphere is indicated by the height of the mercury in the long tube (relative to the surface of the mercury in the reservoir). As the atmospheric pressure changes, the height of the mercury column changes. The height of the mercury column is given in radio and TV weather reports in inches in mercury, but most scientific applications would quote the height in millimeters of mercury (mm Hg, torr). Pressures are also quoted in standard atmospheres, where 1 atm is equivalent to a pressure of 760 mm Hg.

3. $1.20 \text{ atm} \times \frac{760 \text{ mm Hg}}{1 \text{ atm}} = 912 \text{ mm Hg}$

   $1.20 \text{ atm} \times \frac{760 \text{ torr}}{1 \text{ atm}} = 912 \text{ torr}$

   $1.20 \text{ atm} \times \frac{101,325 \text{ Pa}}{1 \text{ atm}} = 122,000 \text{ Pa}$

4. Answers will vary, but consider the following: Boyle's law basically says that the volume of a gas sample will decrease if you squeeze harder on it. Imagine squeezing hard on a tennis ball with your hand. The ball collapses as the gas inside it is forced into a smaller volume by your hand. Students should remember that the temperature and amount of gas (moles) must remain the same for Boyle's law to hold true.

5. Charles's law basically says that if you heat a sample of gas, the volume of the sample will increase. That is, when the temperature of a gas is increased, the volume of the gas also increases (assuming the pressure and amount of gas remain the same).

6. The Kelvin or absolute temperature scale is defined with absolute zero as its lowest temperature, with all temperature positive relative to this point. The size of the Kelvin degree was chosen to be the same size as the Celsius degree. Absolute zero (0 K) corresponds to $-273°C$.

7. Avogadro's law tells us that with all other things being equal, two moles of gas have twice the volume of one mole of gas. That is, the volume of a sample of gas is directly proportional to the number of moles or molecules of gas present (at constant temperature and pressure).

8. An *ideal gas* is defined to be a gas that obeys the ideal gas law.

9. $R = \dfrac{0.08206 \text{ L atm}}{\text{mol K}}$

Although it is always important to pay attention to the units when solving a problem, this is especially important when solving gas problems involving the universal gas constant R. The numerical value of 0.08206 for R applies only when the properties of the gas sample are given in the units specified for the constant: the volume in liters (not mL) the pressure in atmospheres (not mm Hg, torr, or Pa), the amount of gas in moles (not g), and the temperature in units of Kelvin (not °F or °C).

10. Use $P_1 V_1 = P_2 V_2$

(565 mm Hg)(10.0 L) = P_2 (15.0 L)
377 mm Hg = P_2

11. Use $\dfrac{V_1}{T_1} = \dfrac{V_2}{T_2}$

$\dfrac{5.00 \text{ L}}{[(35 + 273) \text{ K}]} = \dfrac{V_2}{[(70 + 273) \text{ K}]}$

5.57 L = V_2

12. Use $\dfrac{V_1}{n_1} = \dfrac{V_2}{n_2}$

$\dfrac{34.6 \text{ L}}{4.50 \text{ mol}} = \dfrac{V_2}{2.50 \text{ mol}}$

19.2 L = V_2

13. Use $\dfrac{P_1 V_1}{T_1} = \dfrac{P_2 V_2}{T_2}$

$\dfrac{(2.10 \text{ atm}) (3.45 \text{ L})}{[(24 + 273) \text{ K}]} = \dfrac{(5.20 \text{ atm}) (V_2)}{[(-12 + 273) \text{ K}]}$

1.22 L = V_2

14. Use $PV = nRT$, $n = \dfrac{PV}{RT}$

$$n = \frac{(1.20 \text{ atm}) \, (5.40 \text{ L})}{(0.08206 \, \frac{\text{L atm}}{\text{mol K}})[(27 + 273) \text{ K}]} = 0.263 \text{ mol He}$$

$0.263 \text{ mol He} \times \dfrac{4.003 \text{ g He}}{1 \text{ mol He}} = 1.05 \text{g He}$

15. The "partial" pressure of an individual gas in a mixture of gases represents the pressure the gas would have in the same container at the same temperature if it were the only gas present.

16. $2.50 \text{ g Ne} \times \dfrac{1 \text{ mol Ne}}{20.18 \text{ g Ne}} = 0.124 \text{ mol Ne}$

$5.00 \text{ g Ar} \times \dfrac{1 \text{ mol Ar}}{39.95 \text{ g Ar}} = 0.125 \text{ mol Ar}$

$$P_{Ne} = \frac{(0.124 \text{ mol}) \, (0.08206 \, \frac{\text{L atm}}{\text{mol K}})[(23 + 273) \text{ K}]}{(10.0 \text{ L})} = 0.301 \text{ atm}$$

$$P_{Ar} = \frac{(0.125 \text{ mol}) \, (0.08206 \, \frac{\text{L atm}}{\text{mol K}})[(23 + 273) \text{ K}]}{(10.0 \text{ L})} = 0.304 \text{ atm}$$

$$P_{total} = 0.605 \text{ atm}$$

17. $0.95 \text{ atm} \times \dfrac{760 \text{ torr}}{1 \text{ atm}} = 722 \text{ torr}$

$$P_{total} = P_{O_2} + P_{H_2O}$$

$$722 \text{ torr} = P_{O_2} + 26.7 \text{ torr}$$

$$P_{O_2} = 695 \text{ torr}$$

18. $23.5 \text{ g CaCO}_3 \times \dfrac{1 \text{ mol CaCO}_3}{100.09 \text{ g CaCO}_3} \times \dfrac{1 \text{ mol CO}_2}{1 \text{ mol CaCO}_3} = 0.235 \text{ mol CO}_2$

$$V = \frac{(0.235 \text{ mol CO}_2) \, (0.08206 \, \frac{\text{L atm}}{\text{mol K}})[(24 + 273) \text{ K}]}{(1.10 \text{ atm})} = 5.21 \text{ L}$$

19. The abbreviation *STP* stands for "standard temperature and pressure." STP corresponds to a temperature of 0°C and a pressure of 1 atm. These conditions were chosen for comparisons of gas samples because they are easy to reproduce in any laboratory (an equilibrium mixture of ice and water has a temperature of 0°C, and the pressure in most laboratories is very near to 1 atm).

20. Gases behave most ideally at conditions of low pressure and high temperature. Two of the premises of the kinetic-molecular theory are that gas particles exert no forces on each other and that the volume of gas particles is negligible compared with the volume of the container. These conditions are more closely approached as the pressure of the gas is decreased (less gas per volume) and the temperature of the gas is increased (greater average kinetic energy results in faster-moving particles).

Chapter 13: Standard Review Worksheet

1. While the barometer is used to measure atmospheric pressure, a device called a *mercury manometer* is used to measure the pressure of samples of gas in the laboratory. A manometer consists basically of a U-shaped tube filled with mercury, with one arm of the U open to the atmosphere. If the pressure of the gas sample equals atmospheric pressure, then the mercury levels will be the same in both sides of the U. If the pressure of the gas is not the same as the atmospheric pressure, then the difference in height of the mercury levels can be sued to determine by how many mm Hg the pressure of the gas sample differs from atmospheric pressure.

2. The expression $P \times V = $ constant is Boyle's law. In order for the product ($P \times V$) to remain constant, if one of these terms increases, the other must decrease. A second formulation of Boyle's law is one more commonly used in solving problems:

    $$P_1 \times V_1 = P_2 \times V_2$$

    With this second formulation, we can determine pressure–volume information about a given sample under two sets of conditions. These two mathematical formulas are just two different ways of saying the same thing: If the pressure on a sample of gas is increased, the volume of the sample of gas will decrease. A graph of Boyle's law data is given in Figure 13.5. This sort of graph ($xy = k$) is known to mathematicians as a *hyperbola*.

3. The qualification is necessary because the volume of a gas sample depends on all its properties. The properties of a gas are all interrelated (as shown by the ideal gas law, $PV = nRT$). If we want to use one of the derivative gas laws (Boyle's, Charles's, or Avogadro's gas laws), which isolate how the volume of a gas sample varies with just one of its properties, then we must keep all the other properties constant while that one property is studied.

4. Charles's law is a direct proportionality when the temperature is expressed in Kelvins (if you increase T, this increases V), whereas Boyle's law is an inverse proportionality (if you increase P, this decreases V).

5. Charles's law holds true only if the amount of gas remains the same (for example, the volume of a gas sample would increase if there were more gas present) and also if the pressure remains the same (a change in pressure also changes the volume of a gas sample).

6. Avogadro's law is a direct proportionality: The greater the number of gas molecules in a sample, the larger the sample's volume will be.

7. Comparing the volumes of two samples of the same gas to determine the relative amount of gas present in the samples requires that the two samples of gas are at the same pressure and temperature. The volume of a sample of gas would vary with either temperature (according to Charles's law) or pressure (according to Boyle's law) or both. Avogadro's law holds true for comparing gas samples that are under the same conditions of pressure and temperature.

8. Boyle's law states that the volume of a gas is inversely proportional to its pressure (at constant temperature for a fixed amount of gas):

    $$V = (\text{constant})/P$$

Copyright © Houghton Mifflin Company.

Charles's law indicates that the volume of a gas sample is related to its temperature (at constant pressure for a fixed amount of gas):

$$V = (\text{constant}) \times T$$

Avogadro's law states that the volume of a gas sample is proportional to the number of moles of gas (at constant pressure and temperature):

$$V = (\text{constant}) \times n$$

We can combine all these relationships (and constants) to show how the volume of a gas is proportional to all its properties simultaneously:

$$V = (\text{constant}) \times \frac{T \times n}{P}$$

This can be arranged to the familiar form of the ideal gas law: $PV = nRT$.

9. Use $P_1V_1 = P_2V_2$.

   (3.2 atm)(25.0 L) = P_2 (45.0 L)
   1.78 atm = P_2

10. Use $\frac{V_1}{T_1} = \frac{V_2}{T_2}$.

    $$\frac{21.5 \text{ L}}{[(45 + 273) \text{ K}]} = \frac{V_2}{[(-37 + 273) \text{ K}]}$$
    16.0 L = V_2

11. Since both samples are hydrogen, the number of moles is directly related to mass; thus use

    $$\frac{V_1}{\text{Mass}_1} = \frac{V_2}{\text{mass}_2}$$

    $$\frac{21.6 \text{ L}}{32.8 \text{ g}} = \frac{V_2}{12.3 \text{ g}}$$
    8.10 L = V_2

12. Use $\frac{P_1V_1}{T_1} = \frac{P_2V_2}{T_2}$.

    $$\frac{(3.14 \text{ atm}) (2.97 \text{ L})}{[(38 + 273) \text{ K}]} = \frac{(P_2) (1.04 \text{ L})}{[(118 + 273) \text{ K}]}$$
    11.3 atm = P_2

13. Use $PV = nRT$, $n = \frac{PV}{RT}$.

    $$P = 475 \text{ mm Hg} \times \frac{1 \text{ atm}}{760 \text{ mm Hg}} = 0.625 \text{ atm}$$

    $$n = \frac{(0.625 \text{ atm}) (1.25 \text{ L})}{(0.08206 \frac{\text{L atm}}{\text{mol K}}) [(-22 + 273) \text{ K}]} = 0.0379 \text{ mol O}_2$$

    $$0.0379 \text{ mol O}_2 \times \frac{32.00 \text{ g O}_2}{1 \text{ mol O}_2} = 1.21 \text{ g O}_2$$

14. The total pressure in a mixture of gases is the sum of the individual partial pressures of the gases present in a mixture.

15. When a gas is collected by displacement of water from a container, the gas becomes saturated with water vapor. The collected gas is actually a mixture of the desired gas and water vapor. To determine the partial pressure of the desired gas in the mixture, it is necessary to subtract the pressure of water vapor from the total pressure of the sample:

$$P_{gas} = P_{total} - P_{water\ vapor}$$

Dalton's law of partial pressures states that the total pressure in a mixture of gases is the sum of the partial pressures of the components of the mixture. Since the saturation pressure of water vapor is a function only of temperature, such water vapor pressures are conveniently tabulated (see Table 13.2 in the text).

16. $12.5 \text{ g O}_2 \times \dfrac{1 \text{ mol O}_2}{32.00 \text{ g O}_2} = 0.391 \text{ mol O}_2$

$25.0 \text{ g N}_2 \times \dfrac{1 \text{ mol N}_2}{28.02 \text{ g N}_2} = 0.892 \text{ mol N}_2$

$P_{O_2} = \dfrac{(0.391 \text{ mol})\,(0.08206\,\frac{\text{L atm}}{\text{mol K}})[(28+273)\text{ K}]}{(25.0 \text{ L})} = 0.386 \text{ atm}$

$P_{N_2} = \dfrac{(0.892 \text{ mol})\,(0.08206\,\frac{\text{K atm}}{\text{mol K}})[(28+273)\text{ K}]}{(25.0 \text{ L})} = 0.881 \text{ atm}$

$P_{total} = 1.267 \text{ atm}$

17. $P_{H_2O} = 31.8 \text{ torr} \times \dfrac{1 \text{ atm}}{760 \text{ torr}} = 0.0418 \text{ atm}$

$P_{O_2} = 1.10 \text{ atm} - 0.0418 \text{ atm} = 1.06 \text{ atm}$

$V = \dfrac{(0.80 \text{ mol})\,(0.08206\,\frac{\text{K atm}}{\text{mol K}})[(30+273)\text{ K}]}{(1.06 \text{ atm})}$

$V = 18.8 \text{ L}$

18. The main postulates of the kinetic-molecular theory for gases are as follows: (a) Gases consist of tiny particles (atoms or molecules), and the size of these particles themselves is negligible compared with the bulk volume of a gas sample; (b) the particles in a gas are in constant random motion, colliding with the walls of the container; (c) the particles in a gas sample do not exert any attractive or repulsive forces on one another; and (d) the average kinetic energy of the particles in a sample of gas is directly related to the absolute temperature of the gas sample. The pressure exerted by a gas is a result of the molecules colliding with (and pushing on) the walls of the container. The pressure increases with temperature because at a higher temperature the molecules are moving faster and hit the walls of the container with greater force. A gas fills whatever volume is available to it because the molecules in a gas are in constant random motion. If the motion of the molecules is random, they eventually will move out into whatever volume is available until the distribution of molecules is uniform. At constant pressure, the volume of a gas sample increases as the temperature is increased because with each collision having greater force, the container must expand so that the molecules hit the walls less frequently to maintain the same pressure.

19. The balanced equation is $Zn + 2HCl \rightarrow ZnCl_2 + H_2$.

$$10.0 \text{ g Zn} \times \frac{1 \text{ mol Zn}}{65.38 \text{ g Zn}} \times \frac{1 \text{ mol } H_2}{1 \text{ mol Zn}} = 0.153 \text{ mol } H_2$$

$$0.200 \text{ mol HCl} \times \frac{1 \text{ mol } H_2}{2 \text{ mol HCl}} = 0.100 \text{ mol } H_2$$

Thus 0.100 mol H_2 is produced because HCl is limiting.

$$V = \frac{(0.100 \text{ mol}) (0.08206 \frac{\text{K atm}}{\text{mol K}})[(22 + 273) \text{ K}]}{(755 \text{ atm} \times \frac{1 \text{ atm}}{760 \text{ mm Hg}})}$$

$V = 2.44$ L

20. Gases do not behave most ideally at STP. Standard temperature and pressure (0°C, 1 atm) is chosen as standard because it is easy to produce these conditions in the lab, not because gases behave most ideally at these conditions. Many students believe this to be the case, however.

Chapter 13: Challenge Review Worksheet

1. The pressure exerted by the atmosphere is due to the several-mile-thick layer of gases above the surface of the earth pressing down on us. Atmospheric pressure traditionally has been measured with a mercury barometer. A mercury barometer usually consists of a glass tube that is sealed at one end and filled with mercury. The tube is then inverted into an open reservoir also containing mercury. When the tube is inverted, most of the mercury does not fall out of the tube. Since the reservoir of mercury is open to the atmosphere, the atmospheric pressure on the surface of the mercury in the reservoir is enough pressure to hold the bulk of the mercury in the glass tube. The pressure of the atmosphere is sufficient, on average, to support a column of mercury 76 cm (760 mm) high in the tube.

2. The volume of a gas sample changes by the same factor (that is, linearly) for each Celsius degree its temperature is changed (for a fixed amount of gas at a constant pressure). Charles realized that if a gas were cooled, the volume of a gas sample would decrease by a constant factor for each degree the temperature was lowered. When Charles plotted his experimental data and extrapolated the linear data to very low temperatures that he could not measure experimentally, he realized that there would be an ultimate temperature no matter what gas sample was used for the experiment. This temperature—where the volume of an ideal gas sample would approach zero as a limit—is called the *absolute zero* of temperature. Unlike the Fahrenheit and Celsius temperature scales, which were defined by humans with experimentally convenient reference points, the absolute zero of temperature is a fundamental, natural reference point for the measurement of temperatures.

3. $12.4 \text{ g He} \times \frac{1 \text{ mol He}}{4.003 \text{ g He}} = 3.10 \text{ mol He}$

    $56.2 \text{ g Ne} \times \frac{1 \text{ mol Ne}}{20.18 \text{ g Ne}} = 2.78 \text{ mol Ne}$

    Use $\frac{V_1}{n_1} = \frac{V_2}{n_2}$ (the identity of the gas does not matter).

    $\frac{23.5 \text{ L}}{3.10 \text{ mol}} = \frac{V_2}{2.78 \text{ mol}}$

    $21.1 \text{ L} = V_2$

4. Doubling the volume should cut the pressure in half (Boyle's law), and doubling the Celsius temperature will increase the pressure but not double it (the Kelvin temperature must be doubled to double the pressure). Thus, doubling the volume and Celsius temperature will cause a decrease in pressure. Boyle's law holds true because at twice the volume the gas particles will make half the number of impacts with the walls; thus the pressure is halved. As the temperature is increased, the average kinetic energy of the particles is increased (although not doubled because average kinetic energy is related to the Kelvin temperature). Thus the particles move faster and hit the walls with a greater force and frequency, and the pressure is increased.

5. Because the partial pressures of the gases in a mixture are additive (that is, the total pressure is the sum of the partial pressures), this suggests that the total pressure in a container is a function only of the number of molecules present and not of the identity of the molecules or any other property of the molecules (such as their inherent atomic size).

6. $\text{Mol } H_2 = \dfrac{(1.10 \text{ atm}) (5.74 \text{ L})}{(0.08206 \frac{\text{L atm}}{\text{mol K}}) [(27 + 273) \text{ K}]} = 0.256 \text{ mol } H_2$

   Mass Zn + mass Mg = 10.0 g
   Mol Zn + mol Mg = 0.256 mol
   $\dfrac{\text{Mass Zn}}{\text{Mol Zn}} = 65.38 \text{ g/mol}; \dfrac{\text{mass Mg}}{\text{mol Mg}} = 24.31 \text{ g/mol}$
   (a) (65.38)(mol Zn) + (24.31)(mol Mg) = 10.00
   (b) mol Zn + mol Mg = 0.256
   Multiply (b) by 24.31 and subtract from (a):
   (41.07)(mol Zn) = 3.78

   Mol Zn = 0.0920 mol

   Mol Mg = 0.164 mol

   $\text{Mass Mg} = 0.164 \text{ mol Mg} \times \dfrac{24.31 \text{ g}}{1 \text{ mol}} = 3.99 \text{ g Mg}$

   $\dfrac{3.99 \text{ g Mg}}{10.00 \text{g}} \times 100\% = 39.9\% \text{ Mg}$

7. Gases are not ideal because the particles making up a sample of gas exert forces on each other and have a finite volume.

Chapter 14: Basic Review Worksheet

1. Solids and liquids have much greater densities than do gases and are much less compressible, because there is so little room between the particles in the solid and liquid states (solids and liquids have definite volumes of their own, and their volumes are not affected much by the temperature or pressure).

2. Water is a colorless, odorless, tasteless liquid that freezes at 0°C and boils at 100°C at 1 atm pressure.

3. The normal boiling point of water, that is, water's boiling point at a pressure of exactly 760 mm Hg, is 100°C (the boiling point of water was used to set one of the reference temperatures of the Celsius temperature scale). The normal (760 mm Hg) freezing point of

water is exactly 0°C (again, this property of water was used as one of the reference points for the Celsius temperature scale). A cooling curve for water is given in Figure 14.7. Notice how the curve shows that the amount of heat needed to boil the sample is much larger than the amount needed to melt the sample.

4. Changes in state refer to changes from solid to liquid (or vice versa), liquid to gas (or vice versa), or solid to gas (or vice versa).

5. In order to melt or vaporize a substance, intermolecular forces must be overcome. Intramolecular forces are also known as *chemical bonds*.

6. The quantities of energy required to melt and to boil one mole of a substance are called the *molar heat of fusion* and *molar heat of vaporization,* respectively.

7. $(3.95 \text{ kJ/g}) \times (26.98 \text{ g/mol}) = 107 \text{ kJ/mol}$

8. Dipole–dipole forces are a type of intermolecular force that can exist between molecules with permanent dipole moments. Molecules with permanent dipole moments try to orient themselves so that the positive end of one polar molecule can attract the negative end of another polar molecule. Hydrogen bonding is an especially strong sort of dipole–dipole attractive force that can exist when hydrogen atoms are directly bonded to the most electronegative atoms (N, O, and F).

9. London dispersion forces are the relatively weak forces that must exist to explain the fact that substances consisting of single atoms or of nonpolar molecules can be liquefied and solidified. They arise from instantaneous dipole moments. Although an instantaneous dipole can arise in any molecule, in most cases other, much stronger intermolecular forces predominate. However, for substances that exist as single atoms (for example, the noble gases) or that exist as nonpolar molecules (for example, H_2 and O_2), London forces are the only intermolecular forces.

10. *Vaporization* refers to the process by which molecules in the liquid state form a vapor. Condensation is the opposite process to vaporization. *Condensation* refers to the process by which molecules in the vapor state form a liquid.

11. The pressure of the vapor over the liquid in a closed container at equilibrium is characteristic for the liquid at each particular temperature. Typically, liquids with strong intermolecular forces have small vapor pressures (they have more difficulty in evaporating) than do liquids with very weak intermolecular forces. For example, the components of gasoline (weak forces) have much higher vapor pressures than water (strong forces) and evaporate more easily.

12. The vapor pressure of water at 100.0°C is 1 atm. Recall that the normal boiling point of water is 100.0°C and that the boiling point of a liquid is the point at which the vapor pressure of the liquid is equal to the atmoshpheric pressure.

13. Cyrstalline solids consist of a regular lattice array that extends in three dimensions of the components of the solid (atoms, molecules, or ions).

14. An alloy is a material (which has metallic properties) that contains a mixture of elements.

Chapter 14: Standard Review Worksheet

1. Solids and liquids are much more condensed states of matter than are gases. The molecules are much closer together in solids and liquids and interact with each other to a much greater extent. Although solids are more rigid than liquids, the solid and liquid states have much more in common with each other than either of these states has with the gaseous state. We know this is true because it typically only takes a few kilojoules of energy to melt one mole of solid (because not much change has to take place in the intermolecular forces), whereas it may take 10 times more energy to vaporize a liquid (because there is such a great change in the intermolecular forces in going from the liquid to the gaseous state).

2. Water is one of the most important substances on earth. Water forms the solvent for all the biochemical processes necessary for plant and animal life. Water in the oceans moderates the temperature of the earth. Because of its relatively large specific heat capacity and its great abundance, water is used as the primary coolant for industrial machinery. Water provides a medium for transportation across vast distances on the earth. Water provides a medium for the smallest plants and animals in many food chains.

3. Water remains at 100°C while boiling, until all the water has boiled away, because the additional heat energy being added to the sample is used to overcome attractive forces among the water molecules as they go from the condensed, liquid state to the gaseous state.

4. Changes in state are only physical changes. No chemical bonds are broken during the change, and no new substances result (no changes in the intramolecular forces take place). The molar heat of vaporization of water (or any substance) is much larger than the molar heat of fusion because in order to form a vapor, the molecules have to be moved much farther apart, and virtually all the intermolecular forces must be overcome (when a solid melts, the intermolecular forces remaining in the liquid are still relatively strong).

5. The boiling point of a liquid decreases with altitude because the atmospheric pressure (against which the vapor must be expanded during boiling) decreases with altitude (the atmosphere is "thinner").

6. Dipole–dipole forces are not nearly as strong as ionic or covalent bonding forces (typically only about 1% as strong as covalent bonding forces) because electrostatic attraction is related to the magnitude of the charges of the attracting species. Since polar molecules have only a "partial" charge at each end of the dipole, the magnitude of the attractive force is not as large. The strength of such forces also drops rapidly as molecules move farther apart and is important only in the solid and liquid states (such forces are negligible in the gaseous state because the molecules are too far apart).

7. Hydrogen bonding is an especially strong sort of dipole–dipole attractive force that can exist when hydrogen atoms are directly bonded to the most strongly electronegative atoms (N, O, and F). Because the hydrogen atom is so small, dipoles involving N—H, O—H, and F—H bonds can approach each other much more closely than can dipoles involving other atoms. Since the magnitude of dipole–dipole forces depends on distance, unusually strong attractive forces can exist in such molecules. Molecular-level sketches will vary, but an example is provided below. Students should understand that hydrogen-bonding interactions are intermolecular forces, not intramolecular bonds.

H
|
H—C—O—H
|
H

Hydrogen bonding

H   O—H
\ /
 C
/ \
H   H

8. London forces are instantaneous dipole forces that come about as the electrons of an atom move around the nucleus. Although we usually consider that the electrons are uniformly distributed in space around the nucleus, at any given instant there may be more electronic charge on one side of the nucleus than on the other, which results in an instantaneous separation of charge and a small dipole moment. Such an instantaneous dipole can induce a similar instantaneous dipole in a neighboring atom, which then results in an attractive force between the dipoles.

9. Vaporization of a liquid requires an input of energy because the intermolecular forces that hold the molecules together in the liquid state must be overcome.

10. Total energy = energy to melt ice + energy to heat water + energy to boil water.

Energy to melt ice $= 55.1 \text{ g} \times \dfrac{1 \text{ mol}}{18.016 \text{ g}} \times \dfrac{6.02 \text{ kJ}}{1 \text{ mol}} = 18.4 \text{ kJ}$

Energy to heat water $= 55.1 \text{ g} \times (4.184 \text{ J/g°C}) \times 100°\text{C} = 23{,}100 \text{ J} = 23.1 \text{ kJ}$

Energy to boil water $= 55.1 \text{ g} \times \dfrac{1 \text{ mol}}{18.016 \text{ g}} \times \dfrac{40.6 \text{ kJ}}{1 \text{ mol}} = 124 \text{ kJ}$

Total energy = 166 kJ

11. In a closed container containing a liquid and some empty space above the liquid, an equilibrium is set up between vaporization and condensation. The liquid in such a sealed container never completely evaporates. When the liquid is first placed in the container, the liquid phase begins to evaporate into the empty space. As the number of molecules in this space accumulate, some reenter the liquid phase. Eventually, every time a molecule of liquid somewhere in the container enters the vapor phase, somewhere else in the container a molecule of vapor reenters the liquid phase. There is no further net change in the amount of liquid or vapor phases (although molecules are continually moving between the liquid and vapor phases).

12. As the strength of the intermolecular forces increases, the vapor pressure decreases. The more particles in a liquid are attracted to one another, the less likely the particles are to escape into the vapor; that is, the less likely they are to evaporate. Therefore, the vapor pressure will be smaller.

13. A liquid boils when its vapor pressure is equal to atmospheric pressure. As the temperature of the liquid is increased, the particles of the liquid are more likely to have enough energy to escape the liquid. However, this amount of energy depends on the pressure around the liquid. Thus, as the atmospheric pressure decreases, less energy is required, and the boiling point of the liquid is decreased.

14. The three important types of crystalline solids are ionic solids, molecular solids, and atomic solids. Sodium chloride is a typical ionic solid. Its crystals consist of an alternating array of positive Na^+ ions and negative Cl^- ions. Each positive ion is surrounded by several negative ions, and each negative ion is surrounded by several positive ions. The electrostatic forces that develop in such an arrangement are very large, and the resulting substance is very stable and has very high melting and boiling points.

Ice is a molecular solid. The crystals consist of polar water molecules arranged in three dimensions so as to maximize dipole–dipole interactions (hydrogen bonding). Figure 14.18(c) shows a representation of an ice crystal, showing how the negative end of one water molecule is oriented toward the positive end of another water molecule and how this arrangement repeats. Since dipole–dipole forces are weaker than ionic bonding forces, substances that exist as molecular solids typically have much lower melting and boiling points.

Atomic solids vary as to how the atoms are held together in the crystal. Substances such as the noble gases are held together in the solid only by very weak London dispersion forces. Such substances have extremely low melting and boiling points because these forces are so weak. In other atomic solids, such as the diamond form of carbon, adjacent atoms actually may form covalent bonds with each other, causing the entire crystal to be one giant molecule. Such atomic solids have much higher boiling and melting points than those substances held together by only London forces. Finally, the metallic substances are also atomic solids, in which there are strong but nondirectional bonding leading to the properties associated with metals. Metals are envisioned in terms of the "electron sea" model in which a regular array of metal atoms exist in a "sea" of freely moving valence electrons.

15. The simple model we use to explain many properties of metallic elements is called the *electron sea model*. In this model we picture a regular lattice array of metal cations in a "sea" of mobile valence electrons. The electrons can move easily to conduct heat or electricity through the metal, and the lattice of cations can be deformed fairly easily, allowing the metal to be hammered into a sheet or stretched to make a wire.

16. Substitutional alloys consist of a host metal in which some of the atoms in the metal's crystalline structure are replaced by atoms of other metallic elements of comparable size to the atoms of the host metal. For example, sterling silver consists of an alloy in which approximately 7% of the silver atoms have been replaced by copper atoms. Brass and pewter are also substitutional alloys. An interstitial alloy is formed when other smaller atoms enter the interstices (holes) between atoms in the host metal's crystal structure. Steel is an interstitial alloy in which carbon atoms occupy the interstices of a crystal of iron atoms. The presence of the interstitial carbon atoms markedly changes the properties of the iron, making it much harder and tougher. Depending on the amount of carbon introduced into the iron crystal, the properties of the resulting steel can be carefully controlled.

Chapter 14: Challenge Review Worksheet

1. The fact that the boiling point of water is so much higher than that of the other covalent hydrogen compounds of the Group 6 elements is evidence for the special strength of

hydrogen bonding (it takes more energy to vaporize water because of the extrastrong forces between the molecules in the liquid state).

2. The high heat of vaporization of water is essential to life on earth because much of the excess energy striking the earth from the sun is dissipated in vaporizing water.

3. A simple experiment to determine vapor pressure is shown in Figure 14.11. Samples of a liquid are injected into a sealed tube containing mercury. Since mercury is so dense, the liquids float to the top of the mercury, where they evaporate. As the vapor pressures of the liquids develop to the saturation point, the level of mercury in the tube changes as an index of the magnitude of the vapor pressures.

4. The stronger the interparticle forces in a solid, the higher are the melting and boiling points.

5. N_2 is a more ideal gas than CO. The carbon monoxide molecule is polar, whereas N_2 is a nonpolar molecule. Thus the intermolecular forces for CO are greater than those for N_2. One of the premises of the kinetic-molecular theory is that the gas particles exert no forces on each other. This is more true for N_2 than for CO; thus N_2 is a more ideal gas than CO.

6. Networks connect like items. Network solids contain like atoms bonded together.

7. You are camping at an altitude higher than that at home. The higher altitude has a lower atmospheric pressure; therefore, the pressure pushing on the surface of the water is less. You do not have to heat the water to as high a temperature to enable bubbles to form in the interior of the water.

8. Total energy to turn water to steam = energy to heat water + energy to boil water
    Energy to heat water = 500.0 g × (4.184 J/g°C) × (100°C − 22.0°C) = 163,176 J = 163.176 kJ
    Energy to boil water = 500.0 g × $\frac{1\ mol}{18.016\ g}$ × $\frac{40.6\ kJ}{1\ mol}$ = 1127 kJ

    Total energy = 163.176 kJ + 1127 kJ = 1289.96 kJ
    Volume of ethanol needed = 1289.96 kJ × $\frac{1\ L}{2.34 \times 10^4\ kJ}$ = 0.0551 L or 55.1 mL

Chapter 15: Basic Review Worksheet

1. A *solution* is a homogeneous mixture, a mixture in which the components are uniformly intermingled.

2. In a crystal of sodium chloride there is a negative chloride ion at one of the corners of the crystal. When this crystal is placed in water, water molecules surround the chloride ion and orient themselves with the positive end of their dipoles aimed at the negative chloride ion. When enough water molecules have so arranged themselves, the resulting attraction of the several water molecules for the chloride ion becomes stronger than the attractive forces from the positive sodium ions in the crystal, and the chloride ion separates from the crystal and enters the solution (still surrounded by the group of water molecules). Similarly, a positive sodium ion in a similar position would be attracted by a group of water molecules arranged with the negative ends of their dipoles oriented toward the positive ion. When enough water molecules are present to surpass the attractive forces from negative ions in the crystal, the sodium ion enters the solution. Once the chloride ion and the sodium ion are in solution, they remain surrounded by water molecules (called a *hydration sphere*), which

diminishes the effective charge each ion would feel from the other and prevents them from recombining easily. For a molecular solid (such as sugar) to dissolve in a solvent, there must be some portion or portions of the molecule that can be attracted by molecules of solvent. For example, common table sugar (sucrose) contains many hydroxyl groups (—OH). These hydroxyl groups on a sugar molecule are attractive to water molecules (naturally, the —OH groups also can hydrogen bond with water). When the attractive forces between water molecules and solute molecules are strong enough, the solid dissolves.

3. To increase the rate of dissolution, we can heat the solution, stir the solution, or increase the surface area of the solute (in all cases we expose more solute to fresh solvent).

4. A saturated solution is one that contains as much solute as can dissolve at a particular temperature. An unsaturated solution is one that contains less solute than can dissolve at a particular temperature. A supersaturated solution is one in which more solute is dissolved than is normally possible at a particular temperature.

5. *Percent by mass* (or *mass percent*) is defined as (mass of solute)/(mass of solution) × 100%. *Molarity* is defined as the number of moles of solute per liter of solution. *Normality* is defined as the number of equivalents per liter of solution.

6. One equivalent of an acid is the amount of acid that can furnish one mole of H^+ ions. One equivalent of a base is the amount of a base that can furnish one mole of OH^- ions.

7. The normality of a solution is defined as the number of equivalents of solute contained in 1 liter of the solution. A 1 N solution of an acid contains 1 mole of H^+ per liter; a 1 N solution of a base contains 1 mole of OH^- per liter.

8. 12.5 g glucose/237.5 g solution × 100% = 5.26% glucose.

9.   a. 500.0 mL = 0.5000 L
      Molar mass NaCl = 58.44 g

$$4.865 \text{ g NaCl} \times \frac{1 \text{ mol}}{58.44 \text{ g NaCl}} = 0.08325 \text{ mol NaCl}$$

$$M = \frac{0.08325 \text{ mol NaCl}}{0.5000 \text{ L}} = 0.1665 \; M$$

  b. Molar mass $AgNO_3$ = 169.9 g

$$78.91 \text{ g AgNO}_3 \times \frac{1 \text{ mol}}{169.9 \text{ g AgNO}_3} = 0.4644 \text{ mol AgNO}_3$$

$$M = \frac{0.4644 \text{ mol AgNO}_3}{0.5000 \text{ L}} = 0.9288 \; M$$

10.   a. $\dfrac{(3.02 \; M)(255 \text{ mL})}{(255 + 375) \text{ mL}} = 1.22 \; M$

  b. $\dfrac{(1.51\%)(75.1 \text{ g})}{(75.1 + 125) \text{ g}} = 0.567\%$

11. It would be convenient to first calculate the number of moles of NaOH present in the sample because this information will be needed for each part of the answer.

    36.2 mL = 0.0362 L

$$\text{Mol NaOH} = 0.0362 \text{ L} \times \frac{0.259 \text{ mol NaOH}}{1 \text{ L}} = 9.38 \times 10^{-3} \text{ mol NaOH}$$

a. $HCl + NaOH \rightarrow NaCl + H_2O$

$$9.38 \times 10^{-3} \text{ mol NaOH} \times \frac{1 \text{ mol HCl}}{1 \text{ mol NaOH}} = 9.38 \times 10^{-3} \text{ mol HCl}$$

$$9.38 \times 10^{-3} \text{ mol HCl} \times \frac{1 \text{ L}}{0.271 \text{ mol HCl}} = 0.0346 \text{ L} = 34.6 \text{ mL}$$

b. $H_2SO_4 + 2NaOH \rightarrow Na_2SO_4 + 2H_2O$

$$9.38 \times 10^{-3} \text{ mol NaOH} \times \frac{1 \text{ mol H}_2\text{SO}_4}{2 \text{ mol NaOH}} = 4.69 \times 10^{-3} \text{ mol H}_2\text{SO}_4$$

$$4.69 \times 10^{-3} \text{ mol H}_2\text{SO}_4 \times \frac{1 \text{ L}}{0.119 \text{ mol H}_2\text{SO}_4} = 0.0394 \text{ L} = 39.4 \text{ mL}$$

c. $H_3PO_4 + 3NaOH \rightarrow Na_3PO_4 + 3H_2O$

$$9.38 \times 10^{-3} \text{ mol H}_3\text{PO}_4 \times \frac{1 \text{ mol H}_3\text{PO}_4}{3 \text{ mol NaOH}} = 3.13 \times 10^{-3} \text{ mol H}_3\text{PO}_4$$

$$3.13 \times 10^{-3} \text{ mol H}_3\text{PO}_4 \times \frac{1 \text{ L}}{0.171 \text{ mol H}_3\text{PO}_4} = 0.0183 \text{ L} = 18.3 \text{ mL}$$

12. a. $\dfrac{(41.5 \text{ mL})(0.118 \, M)(1)}{(0.242 \, M)(2)} = 10.1 \text{ mL H}_2\text{SO}_4$

b. $\dfrac{(27.1 \text{ mL})(0.121 \, M)(3)}{(0.242 \, M)(2)} = 20.3 \text{ mL H}_2\text{SO}_4$

13. a. $0.204 \, M \text{ HCl} = 0.204 \, N \text{ HCl}$

b. $0.328 \, M \text{ H}_2\text{SO}_4 = 0.656 \, N \text{ H}_2\text{SO}_4$

14. The balanced equation is $Ba(NO_3)_2 + 2NaCl \rightarrow BaCl_2 + 2NaNO_3$

$$\frac{0.50 \text{ mol NaCl}}{1000 \text{ mL}} \times \frac{1 \text{ mol Ba(NO}_3)_2}{2 \text{ mol NaCl}} \times \frac{1000 \text{ mL}}{0.10 \text{ mol Ba(NO}_3)_2} = 250.0 \text{ mL } 0.10 \, M \text{ Ba(NO}_3)_2$$

15. A colligative property is a property of a solution that depends on the number of particles in solution, not the nature (or identity) of the particles.

Chapter 15: Standard Review Worksheet

1. When an ionic substance is dissolved in water to form a solution, the water plays an essential role in overcoming the strong interparticle forces in the ionic crystal. Water is a highly polar substance. One end of the water molecule dipole is partially negative, and the other is partially positive.

2. In order for a substance to dissolve, the molecules of the substance must be capable of being dispersed among water molecules. (See the discussion of question 2, Chapter 15: Basic Review Worksheet.)

3. To say that a solution is saturated does not necessarily mean that the solute is present at a high concentration. For example, magnesium hydroxide only dissolves to a very small extent before the solution is saturated, whereas it takes a great deal of sugar to form a saturated solution (the saturated sugar solution is extremely concentrated).

4. Adding additional solvent to a solution so as to dilute the solution does not change the number of moles of solute present but only changes the volume in which the solute is dispersed. If we are using the molarity of the solution to describe its concentration, the

number of liters is changed when we add solvent, and the number of moles per liter (the molarity) changes, but the actual number of moles of solute does not change.

5. For example, 125 mL of 0.551 M NaCl contains 68.9 millimol NaCl. The solution will still contain 68.9 millimol NaCl after the 250 mL water is added to it; only now the 68.9 millimol NaCl will be dispersed in a total volume of 375 mL. This gives the new molarity as 68.9 mmol/375 mL = 0.184 M. The volume and the concentration have changed, but the number of moles of solute in the solution has not changed.

6. The equivalent weight of an acid or base is related to the molar mass of the substance by taking into account how many H^+ or OH^- ions the substance furnishes per molecule.

7. HCl and NaOH have equivalent weights equal to their molar masses because each of these substances furnishes one H^+ or OH^- ion per unit, respectively

$$HCl \rightarrow H^+ + Cl^- \qquad NaOH \rightarrow Na^+ + OH^-$$

However, sulfuric acid (H_2SO_4) has an equivalent weight that is half the molar mass because each H_2SO_4 molecule can produce two H^+ ions. Therefore, only half a mole of H_2SO_4 is needed to provide one mole of H^+ ion. Similarly, the equivalent weight of phosphoric acid (H_3PO_4) is one-third its molar mass because each H_3PO_4 molecule can provide three H^+ ions (and so only one-third mole of H_3PO_4 is needed to provide one mole of H^+ ions).

$$H_2SO_4 \rightarrow 2H^+ + SO_4^{2-} \qquad H_3PO_4 \rightarrow 3H^+ + PO_4^{3-}$$

Similarly, bases such as $Ca(OH)_2$ and $Mg(OH)_2$ have equivalent weights that are half their molar masses because each of these substances produces two moles of OH^- ion per mole of base (and so only half a mole of base is needed to provide one mole of OH^-).

8. Since the equivalent weight and the molar mass of a substance are related by small whole numbers (representing the number of H^+ or OH^- ions a unit of the substance furnishes), the normality and molarity of a solution are also simply related by these same numbers. In fact, $N = n \times M$ for a solution, where n represents the number of H^+ or OH^- ions furnished per molecule of solute.

9. Mass of solution = 4.25 g + 7.50 g + 125 g = 136.75 g (137 g)

$$\frac{4.25 \text{ g NaCl}}{136.75 \text{ g}} \times 100 = 3.11\% \text{ NaCl} \qquad \frac{7.50 \text{ g KCl}}{136.75 \text{ g}} \times 100 = 5.48\% \text{ KCl}$$

10. $250.0 \text{ g CaCl}_2 \times \frac{1 \text{ mol CaCl}_2}{110.98 \text{ g CaCl}_2} = 2.253 \text{ mol CaCl}_2$

$$\frac{2.253 \text{ mol}}{2.25 \text{ L}} = 1.00 \ M$$

11. $125 \text{ mL} \times \frac{0.100 \text{ mol}}{1000 \text{ mL}} = 0.0125 \text{ mol } H_2SO_4$

$$\frac{0.0125 \text{ mol } H_2SO_4}{0.00069 \text{ L}} = 18 \ M \ H_2SO_4$$

12. The balanced equation is $2AgNO_3(aq) + Na_2CrO_4(aq) \rightarrow Ag_2CrO_4(s) + 2NaNO_3(aq)$.

First, we need to find which reactant is limiting:

$$100.0 \text{ mL} \times \frac{0.100 \text{ mol AgNO}_3}{1000 \text{ mL}} \times \frac{1 \text{ mol Ag}_2\text{CrO}_4}{2 \text{ mol AgNO}_3} \times \frac{331.8 \text{ g Ag}_2\text{CrO}_4}{1 \text{ mol Ag}_2\text{CrO}_4} = 1.66 \text{ g Ag}_2\text{CrO}_4$$

$$75.0 \text{ mL} \times \frac{0.100 \text{ mol Na}_2\text{CrO}_4}{1000 \text{ mL}} \times \frac{1 \text{ mol Ag}_2\text{CrO}_4}{1 \text{ mol Na}_2\text{CrO}_4} \times \frac{331.8 \text{ g Ag}_2\text{CrO}_4}{1 \text{ mol Ag}_2\text{CrO}_4} = 2.49 \text{ g Ag}_2\text{CrO}_4$$

Thus 1.66 g Ag_2CrO_4 can be produced (the amount of $AgNO_3$ is limiting).

13. The balanced equation is $2HCl + Ba(OH)_2 \rightarrow BaCl_2 + 2H_2O$.

$$25.2 \text{ mL} \times \frac{0.00491 \text{ mol Ba(OH)}_2}{1000 \text{ mL}} \times \frac{2 \text{ mol HCl}}{1 \text{ mol Ba(OH)}_2} \times \frac{1000 \text{ mL}}{0.104 \text{ mol HCl}} = 2.38 \text{ mL HCl}$$

14. The balanced equation is $H_2SO_4 + 2NaOH \rightarrow Na_2SO_4 + 2H_2O$.

$$15.0 \text{ mL} \times \frac{0.35 \text{ eq. H}_2\text{SO}_4}{1000 \text{ mL}} \times \frac{1 \text{ eq. NaOH}}{1 \text{ eq. H}_2\text{SO}_4} \times \frac{1000 \text{ mL}}{0.50 \text{ eq. NaOH}} = 10.5 \text{ mL } 0.50 \text{ } N \text{ NaOH}$$

15. This is explained in the text, but students should phrase the answer in their own words. Basically adding a solute decreases the vapor pressure of the water (students should include their own phrasing of the "bubbles" that form in the water). Recall as well that the boiling point is the point at which the vapor pressure of the solution is equal to the atmospheric pressure. Thus, at 100°C, the vapor pressure of an aqueous solution is less than 1 atm, so the solution must be heated to a higher temperature in order for the solution to boil.

Chapter 15: Challenge Review Worksheet

1. If the water–solute interactions are not comparable to the water–water interactions, the substance will not dissolve. (See the discussion of question 2, Chapter 15: Basic Review Worksheet.)

2. A saturated solution is one that is in equilibrium with undissolved solute. As molecules of solute dissolve from the solid in one place in the solution, dissolved molecules rejoin the solid phase in another place in the solution.

3. As with the development of vapor pressure above a liquid, formation of a solution reaches a state of dynamic equilibrium. Once the rates of dissolving and "undissolving" become equal, there will be no further net change in the concentration of the solution, and the solution will be saturated.

4. The mass percent and the molarity are similar in that both methods of expressing the concentration of a solution represent ratios; that is, they both express the amount of solute per unit of solution. The mass percent for a solution represents the number of grams of solute that would be present in 100. g of the solution. Since the mass percent is based only on mass, it is invariant for a given solution under all conditions. The molarity of a solution represents the number of moles of solute that would be present in 1 L of the solution. Since the volume of a liquid varies slightly with temperature, the molarity of a solution also varies with temperature.

If 5.0 g NaCl were dissolved in 15.0 g water, the mass percent composition of the solution could be calculated as

$$\frac{5.00 \text{ g NaCl}}{(15.0 \text{ g H}_2\text{O} + 5.0 \text{ g NaCl})} \times 100\% = 25\% \text{ NaCl}$$

Since the mass percent is based only on the masses of the components of the solution, the volume of the solution is not needed for this calculation.

If 5.0 g NaCl (molar mass 58.4 g) were dissolved in enough water to give a total solution volume of 16.1 mL, the molarity of the solution could be calculated as

$$5.0 \text{ g NaCl} \times \frac{1 \text{ mol}}{58.4 \text{ g}} = 0.0856 \text{ mol NaCl}$$

$$16.1 \text{ mL} = 0.0161 \text{ L}$$

$$M = \frac{0.0856 \text{ mol NaCl}}{0.0161 \text{ L solution}} = 5.3 \text{ } M$$

Since the molarity is based on the amount of solute per liter of solution, the mass of solvent present is not needed for the calculation. If the density (1.24 g.mL) of the solution had been given rather than the explicit volume, the volume could be calculated as

$$V = m/d = \frac{(5.0 \text{ g} + 15.0 \text{ g})}{1.24 \text{ g/mL}} = \frac{20.0 \text{ g}}{1.24 \text{ g/mL}} = 16.1 \text{ mL}$$

5. For example, a 0.521 M HCl solution is also 0.521 N because each HCl furnishes one H^+ ion. However, a 0.475 M H_2SO_4 solution would have a normality equal to

$$N = n \times M = 2 \times 0.475 \text{ } M = 0.950 \text{ } N$$

because each H_2SO_4 molecule furnishes two H^+ ions.

6. The relevant balanced equation is

$$AgNO_3(aq) + NaCl(aq) \rightarrow AgCl(s) + NaNO_3(aq)$$

$$143.35 \text{ g AgCl} \times \frac{1 \text{ mol AgCl}}{143.35 \text{ g AgCl}} = 1 \text{ mol AgCl}$$

Thus, 1 mol AgCl is formed. Therefore, we must have at least 1 mol $AgNO_3$ (169.91 g) and 1 mol NaCl (58.44 g). Since we are told that we have equal masses of each reactant, we must have 169.91 g of each.

$$169.91 \text{ g NaCl} \times \frac{1 \text{ mol NaCl}}{58.44 \text{ g NaCl}} = 2.91 \text{ mol NaCl}$$

Using the net ionic equation,

	Ag^+	+	Cl^-	$\rightarrow$	AgCl
Initial	1.00 mol		2.91 mol		
Change	−1.00 mol		−1.00 mol		
End	0		1.91 mol		

When the reaction is complete, we have

0 mol Ag^+

1.00 mol NO_3^-

2.91 mol Na^+

1.91 mol Cl^-

Since our total volume is 2.00 L,

$[NO_3^-] = 0.500\ M$

$[Na^+] = 1.46\ M$

$[Cl^-] = 0.955\ M$

7. Freezing-point depression depends on the number of particles.

$$10.0\text{ g NaCl} \times \frac{1\text{ mol NaCl}}{58.44\text{ g NaCl}} \times \frac{2\text{ mol ions}}{1\text{ mol NaCl}} = 0.342\text{ mol ions (particles)}$$

$$0.342\text{ mol }C_6H_{12}O_6 \times \frac{180.156\text{ g}}{1\text{ mol }C_6H_{12}O_6} = 61.6\text{ g glucose}$$

Chapter 16: Basic Review Worksheet

1. Arrhenius defined acids and bases in terms of the ions that show acidic and basic properties in aqueous solution: An acid is a substance that produces H^+ ions in aqueous solution, and a base is a substance that produces OH^- ions in aqueous solution. This definition is too restrictive because it only considers aqueous systems. For example, Arrhenius recognized HCl as an acid when it is dissolved in water, but what about gaseous hydrogen chloride? Or how about HCl dissolved in some other solvent? The Arrhenius theory also only allows for only one kind of base, the hydroxide ion.

The Brønsted–Lowry model for acids and bases extends some of the concepts of the Arrhenius theory and adapts them to more general situation. Acids and bases are defined in a more fundamental manner. In the Brønsted–Lowry model, an acid still represents a source of H^+ ions (specifically, a Brønsted–Lowry acid is a proton donor), but there is no restriction as to the solvent being only water. Thus, in the Brønsted–Lowry model, if HCl transfers H^+ to another species, then HCl is an acid regardless of any other consideration. Where the Brønsted–Lowry theory really extends our idea of acid–base chemistry is in defining what represents a base. A Brønsted–Lowry base is any species that accepts a proton from an acid. According to the Brønsted–Lowry theory, the hydroxide ion in aqueous solution is a base because if an acid is added to a hydroxide ion solution, the hydroxide ions would accept protons from the acid

$$HCl + OH^- \rightarrow H_2O + Cl^-$$

The Brønsted–Lowry theory allows for other bases, however, and does not require water to be the solvent. For example, ammonia and hydrogen chloride react with each other in the gas phase.

$$HCl(g) + NH_3(g) \rightarrow NH_4Cl(s)$$

This is an acid–base reaction because in the Brønsted–Lowry model a proton has been transferred from the acid (HCl) to the base (NH_3) to form NH_4^+.

2. A conjugate acid–base pair consists of two species related to each other by the donating or accepting of a single proton, H^+. An acid has one more H^+ than its conjugate base; a base has one less H^+ than its conjugate acid.

3. $HCl(aq) + H_2O(l) \rightarrow Cl^-(aq) + H_3O^+(aq)$

$H_2SO_4(aq) + H_2O(l) \rightarrow HSO_4^-(aq) + H_3O^+(aq)$

4. The strength of an acid is a direct result of the position of the acid's ionization equilibrium. We call an acid for which the ionization equilibrium position lies far to the right a *strong acid,* and we call an acid whose equilibrium position lies only slightly to the right a *weak acid.* For example, HCl, HNO$_3$, and HClO$_4$ are all strong acids, which means that they are completely ionized in aqueous solution (the position of the ionization equilibrium is very far to the right).

5. $HCl(aq) + H_2O(l) \rightarrow Cl^-(aq) + H_3O^+(aq)$
   $HNO_3(aq) + H_2O(l) \rightarrow NO_3^-(aq) + H_3O^+(aq)$
   $HClO_4(aq) + H_2O(l) \rightarrow ClO_4^-(aq) + H_3O^+(aq)$

6. When we say that water is an amphoteric substance, we are just recognizing that water will behave as a Brønsted–Lowry base if a strong acid is added to it but will behave as a Brønsted–Lowry acid if a strong base is added to it. For example, water behaves as a base when HCl is dissolved in it:

$$HCl + H_2O \rightarrow Cl^- + H_3O^+$$

However, water would behave as an acid if the strong base NaNH$_2$ were added to it:

$$NH_2^- + H_2O \rightarrow NH_3 + OH^-$$

7. The equilibrium constant K_w has the value 1.0×10^{-14} at 25°C. Because of the fact that hydronium ions and hydroxide ions are produced in equal numbers when water molecules undergo autoionization, and with the value for the equilibrium constant given, we know that in pure water $[H_3O^+] = [OH^-] = 1.0 \times 10^{-7}\ M$.

8. If a solution has a higher concentration of H$_3$O$^+$ ion than OH$^-$ ion, we say the solution is acidic. If a solution has a lower concentration of H$_3$O$^+$ ion than OH$^-$ ion, we say the solution is basic.

9. The pH of a solution is defined as the negative of the base 10 logarithm of the hydrogen ion concentration in the solution; that, is pH $= -\log[H^+]$.

10. Solutions in which the hydrogen ion concentration is greater than $1.0 \times 10^{-7}\ M$ (pH < 7.00) are acidic; solutions in which the hydrogen ion concentration is less than $1.0 \times 10^{-7}\ M$ (pH > 7.00) are basic.

11. Since the pH scale is logarithmic, when the pH changes by one unit, this corresponds to a change in the hydrogen ion concentration by a factor of 10.

12. In some instances it may be more convenient to speak directly about the hydroxide ion concentration present in a solution, and so an analogous logarithmic expression is defined for the hydroxide ion concentration: pOH $= -\log[OH^-]$.

13. A buffered solution is one that resists a change in its pH even when a strong acid or base is added to it. Buffered solutions consist of approximately equal amounts of two components: a weak acid (or base) and its conjugate base (or acid). The weak acid component of the buffered solution is capable of reacting with added strong base. The conjugate base component of the buffered solution is able to react with added strong acid. By reacting with (and effectively neutralizing) the added strong acid or strong base, the buffer is able to maintain its pH at a relatively constant level.

Buffered solutions are crucial to the reactions in biologic systems because many of these reactions are extremely pH-dependent. A change in pH of only one or two units can make some reactions impossible or extremely slow. Many biologic molecules have three-dimensional structures that are extremely dependent on the pH of their surroundings. For example, protein molecules can lose part of their necessary structure and shape if the pH of their environment changes (if a protein's structure is changed, it may not work correctly). For example, if a small amount of vinegar is added to whole mile, the milk instantly curdles. The solid that forms is the protein portion of the milk, which becomes less soluble at lower pH values.

14.   a. HSO_3^-

        b. H_2S

        c. HF

        d. CH_3COOH

15.   a. HSO_4^-

        b. HS^-

        c. HCO_3^-

        d. $C_2H_3O_2^-$

16.   a. $[H^+] = 4.01 \times 10^{-3}$ M, pH $= -\log(4.01 \times 10^{-3}) = 2.397$

        b. $[OH^-] = 7.41 \times 10^{-8}$ M, pOH $= -\log(7.41 \times 10^{-8}) = 7.130$

        c. $[H^+] = 9.61 \times 10^{-6}$ M, pH $= -\log[9.61 \times 10^{-6}] = 5.017$, pOH $= 14.00 - 5.017 = 8.98$

17.   a. $[HNO_3] = [H^+] = 0.00141$ M, pH $= -\log(0.00141) = 2.851$, pOH $= 14.00 - 2.851 = 11.15$

        b. $[NaOH] = [OH^-] = 2.13 \times 10^{-3}$ M, pOH $= -\log(2.13 \times 10^{-3}) = 2.672$, pH $= 14.00 - 2.672 = 11.33$

18. The equation is $HCl + NaOH \rightarrow H_2O + NaCl$

$$25.0 \text{ mL} \times \frac{0.50 \text{ mol HCl}}{1000 \text{ mL}} \times \frac{1 \text{ mol NaOH}}{1 \text{ mol HCl}} = 0.0125 \text{ mol NaOH}$$

$$\frac{0.0125 \text{ mol NaOH}}{0.0124 \text{ L}} = 1.01 \text{ } M \text{ NaOH}$$

Chapter 16: Standard Review Worksheet

1. $H_3PO_4(aq) + H_2O(l) \rightleftharpoons H_2PO_4^-(aq) + H_3O^+(aq)$

     $NH_4^+(aq) + H_2O(l) \rightleftharpoons NH_3(aq) + H_3O^+(aq)$

2.   When we say that acetic acid is a weak acid, we can take either of two points of view. Usually we say that acetic acid is a weak acid because it doesn't ionize very much when dissolved in water. We say that not very many acetic acid molecules dissociate. However, we can describe this situation from another point of view. We could say that the reason acetic acid doesn't dissociate much when we dissolve it in water is because the acetate ion

(the conjugate base of acetic acid) is extremely effective at holding onto protons and specifically is better at holding onto protons than water is in attracting them.

$$HC_2H_3O_2 + H_2O \rightleftharpoons H_3O^+ + C_2H_3O_2^-$$

Now what would happen if we had a source of free acetate ions (for example, sodium acetate) and placed them into water? Since acetate ion is better at attracting protons than is water, the acetate ions would pull protons out of water molecules, leaving hydroxide ions. That is,

$$C_2H_3O_2^- + H_2O \rightleftharpoons HC_2H_3O_2 + OH^-$$

Since an increase in hydroxide ion concentration would take place in the solution, the solution would be basic. Because acetic acid is a weak acid, the acetate ion is a base in aqueous solution.

3. Since HCl, HNO_3, and $HClO_4$ are all strong acids, we know that their anions (Cl^-, NO_3^-, and ClO_4^-) must be very weak bases and that solutions of the sodium salts of these anions would not be basic. Since these acids have a strong tendency to lose protons, there is very little tendency for the anions (bases) to gain protons.

4. $H_2O + H_2O \rightleftharpoons H_3O^+ + OH^-$

   Because this reaction is so important to our understanding the relative acidity and basicity of aqueous solution, the equilibrium constant for the autoionization of water is given a special symbol, $K_w = [H_3O^+][OH^-]$.

5. Since in pure water the amount of $H^+(aq)$ ion present is equal to the amount of $OH^-(aq)$ ion present, we say that pure water is neutral. Since $[H^+] = 1.0 \times 10^{-7}$ M in pure water, this means that the pH of pure water is $-\log(1.0 \times 10^{-7}$ M$) = 7.00$.

6. The concentrations of hydrogen ion and hydroxide ion in water (and in aqueous solutions) are not independent of one another but rather are related by the dissociation equilibrium constant for water:

$$K_w = [H^+][OH^-] = 1.0 \times 10^{-14} \text{ at } 25°C.$$

From this constant we can see that pH + pOH = 14.00 for water (or an aqueous solution) at 25°C.

7. Answers will vary, but consider the following three buffered solutions:

   0.10 M $HC_2H_3O_2$/0.10 M $NaC_2H_3O_2$

   0.50 M HF/0.50 M KF

   0.25 M NH_4Cl/0.25 M NH_3

The acidic component of each of these buffered solutions can neutralize added OH^- ion as shown below:

   $HC_2H_3O_2 + OH^- \rightarrow C_2H_3O_2^- + H_2O$

   $HF + OH^- \rightarrow F^- + H_2O$

   $NH_4^+ + OH^- \rightarrow NH_3 + H_2O$

Notice that in each case the added hydroxide ion has been neutralized and converted to a water molecule. The basic component of the buffered solutions can neutralize added H^+ ions as shown below:

$$C_2H_3O_2^- + H^+ \rightarrow HC_2H_3O_2$$

$$F^- + H^+ \rightarrow HF$$

$$NH_3 + H^+ \rightarrow NH_4^+$$

Notice that in each case the added hydrogen ion is converted to some other species.

8. a. H_2SO_4

    b. H_2SO_3

    c. H_3O^+

    d. HS^-

9. a. $H_2PO_4^-$

    b. S^{2-}

    c. CO_3^{2-}

    d. NH_2^-

10. a. $[OH^-] = 6.62 \times 10^{-3}$ M, pOH $= -\log(6.62 \times 10^{-3}) = 2.179$, pH $= 14.00 - 2.179 = 11.82$

    b. pH $= 6.325$, pOH $= 14.00 - 6.325 = 7.68$, $[OH^-] = $ (inv)log$(-7.68) = 2.1 \times 10^{-8}$

    c. pH $= 9.413$, $[H^+] = $ (inv)log$(-9.413) = 3.86 \times 10^{-10}$

11. a. $[HCl] = [H^+] = 0.00515$ M, pH $= -\log(0.00515) = 2.288$, pOH $= 14 - 2.288 = 11.71$

    b. $[OH^-] = 2 \times 5.65 \times 10^{-5}$ $M = 1.13 \times 10^{-4}$ M, pOH $= -\log(1.13 \times 10^{-4}) = 3.947$, pH $= 14.00 - 3.947 = 10.05$

12. The equation is HCl + NaOH $\rightarrow$ H_2O + NaCl.

$$23.8 \text{ mL} \times \frac{0.10 \text{ mol NaOH}}{1000 \text{ mL}} \times \frac{1 \text{ mol HCl}}{1 \text{ mol NaOH}} = 0.00238 \text{ mol HCl}$$

$$\frac{0.00238 \text{ mol HCl}}{0.0500 \text{ L}} = 0.0476 \text{ } M \text{ HCl}$$

Chapter 16: Challenge Review Worksheet

1. a. Acid: $HS^- + H_2O \rightleftharpoons S^{2-} + H_3O^+$
       Base: $HS^- + H_2O \rightleftharpoons H_2S + OH^-$

    b. Acid: $HCO_3^- + H_2O \rightleftharpoons H_3O^+ + CO_3^{2-}$
       Base: $HCO_3^- + H_2O \rightleftharpoons H_2CO_3 + OH^-$

    c. Acid: $HSO_4^- + H_2O \rightleftharpoons SO_4^{2-} + H_3O^+$
       Base: $HSO_4^- + H_2O \rightleftharpoons H_2SO_4 + OH^-$

    d. Acid: $H_2PO_4^- + H_2O \rightleftharpoons H_3O^+ + HPO_4^{2-}$
       Base: $H_2PO_4^- + H_2O \rightleftharpoons H_2PO_4^- + H_3O^+$

e. Acid: $HSO_3^- + H_2O \rightleftharpoons SO_3^{2-} + H_3O^+$
   Base: $HSO_3^- + H_2O \rightleftharpoons H_2SO_3 + OH^-$

2. $[H^+][OH^-] = 2.09 \times 10^{-14}$
   $[H^+] = [OH^-] = 1.45 \times 10^{-7}$
   $pH = 6.84$
   The solution is neutral because $[H^+] = [OH^-]$. The pH varies with temperature because the value of K_w varies with temperature.

3. The answer is 7.00. Many students will claim that the answer is 12.00 because $[HCl] = [H^+] = 1.0 \times 10^{-12}\ M$, and $-\log(1.0 \times 10^{-12}) = 12.00$. However, we must realize that water is also in the solution and contributes $1.0 \times 10^{-7}\ M\,H^+$. While it is true that the additional H^+ from the HCl affects the autoionization of water equilibrium, the amount of H^+ from the HCl is too small to have a detectable effect. Students also should see that it doesn't make sense that the pH becomes basic when a tiny amount of a strong acid is added to water.

4. a. $pH = 7.00$. Water is also in the solution and contributes $1.0 \times 10^{-7}\ M\,H^+$. While it is true that the additional H^+ from the HNO_3 affects the autoionization of water equilibrium, the amount of H^+ from the HNO_3 is too small to have a detectable effect.

    b. $pOH = 14.00 - pH = 14.00 - 7.00 = 7.00$

    c. $10^{-7.00} = 1.0 \times 10^{-7}\ M$

5. a. $pOH = 14.00 - pH = 14.00 - 6.34 = 7.66$

    b. $[OH^-] = 10^{-7.66} = 2.19 \times 10^{-8}\ M$

    c. $1.0 \times 10^{-14} = [H^+][OH^-] = [H^+][2.19 \times 10^{-8}] = 4.57 \times 10^{-8}\ M$

6. The equation is $HNO_3 + NaOH \rightarrow NaNO_3 + H_2O$.

   Thus moles acid = moles base (1:1 ratio).

   Total moles base $= 45.3\ mL \times \dfrac{0.20\ \text{mol NaOH}}{1000\ mL} = 0.00906$ mol base

   Mol HCl $= 11.6\ mL \times \dfrac{0.10\ \text{mol HCl}}{1000\ mL} = 0.00116$ mol HCl

   0.00906 mol (base) $=$ mol $HNO_3 + 0.00116$ mol (HCl)
   Mol $HNO_3 = 0.0079$ mol HNO_3

   $\dfrac{0.0079\ \text{mol } HNO_3}{0.0500\ L} = 0.158\ M\ HNO_3$

7. When a salt is in solution, a strong acid or base will completely ionize. Ions from a weak acid or base will react somewhat with water, and the corresponding $[H^+]$ for a weak acid or $[OH^-]$ for a weak base will decrease. In this solution the $[OH^-] < [H^+]$, so the original base was weak and the acid was strong.

Chapter 17: Basic Review Worksheet

1. Chemists envision that a reaction can only take place between molecules if the molecules physically collide with each other.

2. The *activation energy* for a reaction represents the minimum energy the reactant molecules must possess for a reaction to occur when the molecules collide.

3. A *catalyst* is a substance that speeds up a reaction without being consumed. Biologic catalysts are called *enzymes*.

4. Chemists define *equilibrium* as the balancing of two exactly opposing processes. When a chemical reaction is started by combining pure reactants, the only process possible initially is

   Reactants → products

   However, as the concentration of product molecules increases, it becomes more and more likely that product molecules will collide and react with each other

   Products → reactants

   giving back molecules of the original reactants. At some point in the process the rates of the forward and reverse reactions become equal, and the system attains chemical equilibrium.

5. Consider this example: Suppose we have a reaction for which $K = 4$, and we begin this reaction with 100 reactant molecules. At the point of equilibrium, there should be 80 molecules of product and 20 molecules of reactant remaining (80/20 = 4). Suppose we perform another experiment involving the same reaction, only this time we begin the experiment with 500 molecules of reactant. This time, at the point of equilibrium, there will be 400 molecules of product present and 100 molecules of reactant remaining (400/100 = 4). Since we began the two experiments with different numbers of reactant molecules, it's not troubling that there are different absolute numbers of product and reactant molecules present at equilibrium. However, the ratio K is the same for both experiments. We say that these two experiments represent two different positions of equilibrium. An equilibrium position corresponds to a particular set of equilibrium concentrations that fulfill the value of the equilibrium constant. Any experiment that is performed with a different amount of starting material will come to its one unique equilibrium position, but the equilibrium constant ratio K will be the same for a given reaction regardless of the starting amounts taken.

6. In a homogeneous equilibrium, all the reactants and products are in the same phase and have the same physical state (solid, liquid, or gas). For a heterogeneous equilibrium, however, one or more of the reactants or products exists in a phase or physical state different from the other substances.

7. Answers will vary, but a paraphrase of Le Châtelier's principle should go something like this: "When you make any change to a system at equilibrium, this throws the system temporarily out of equilibrium, and the system responds by reacting in whichever direction is necessary to reach a new position of equilibrium".

8. The solubility product constant is the constant for the equilibrium expression representing the dissolving of an ionic solid in water.

9. a. $K = [HBr(g)]^2/[H_2(g)][Br_2(g)]$

    b. $K = [SO_2(g)][Cl_2(g)]/[SO_2Cl_2(g)]$

    c. $K = [CO_2(g)]$

10.   a. $K_{sp} = [Zn^{2+}][S^{2-}]$

      b. $K_{sp} = [Hg^{2+}][Cl^-]^2$

      c. $K_{sp} = [La^{3+}][F^-]^3$

11. $K_{sp} = [Cu^{2+}][S^{2-}] = (9.2 \times 10^{-23})(9.2 \times 10^{-23}) = 8.5 \times 10^{-45}$

Chapter 17: Standard Review Worksheet

1. No. When molecules collide, the molecules must collide with enough force for the reaction to be successful (there must be enough energy to break bonds in the reactants), and the colliding molecules must be positioned with the correct relative orientation for the products (or intermediates) to form.

2. Reactions are faster if higher concentrations are used for the reaction because if there are more molecules present per unit volume, there will be more collisions between molecules in a given time period. Reactions are faster at higher temperatures because at higher temperatures the reactant molecules have higher average kinetic energy, and the number of molecules that will collide with sufficient force to break bonds increases.

3. A graph illustrating the activation energy barrier for a reaction is given as Figure 17.4 in the text.

4. Although an increase in temperature does not change the activation energy for a reaction itself, at higher temperatures the reactant molecules have higher energies and more collisions are effective. Recall that in the kinetic-molecular theory, temperature is a direct measure of average kinetic energy.

5. A catalyst speeds up a reaction by providing an alternate mechanism (pathway) having a lower activation energy than the original pathway.

6. To an outside observer, the system appears to have stopped reacting. On a microscopic basis, though, both the forward and reverse processes are still going on. Every time additional molecules of the product form, somewhere else in the system molecules of product react to give back molecules of reactant.

7. A graph showing how the rates of the forward and reverse reactions change with time is given in the text as Figure 17.8. At the start of the reaction, the rate of the forward reaction is at its maximum, whereas the rate of the reverse reaction is zero. As the reaction proceeds, the rate of the forward reaction gradually decreases as the concentrations of reactants decrease, whereas the rate of the reverse reaction increases as the concentrations of products increase. Once the two rates have become equal, the reaction has reached a state of equilibrium.

8. The equilibrium constant for a reaction is a special ratio of the concentration of products present at the point of equilibrium to the concentration of reactants still present. A ratio means that we have one number divided by another number. Since the equilibrium constant is a ratio, there are an infinite number of sets of data that can give the same ratio. For example, the ratios 8:4, 6:3, and 100:50 all have the same value, 2. The actual concentrations of products and reactants will differ from one experiment to another involving a particular chemical reaction, but the ratio of the amount of product to reactant at equilibrium should be the same for each experiment.

9. For a heterogeneous equilibrium, the concentrations of solids and pure liquids are left out of the expression for the equilibrium constant for the reaction. The concentration of a solid or pure liquid is constant.

10.   a. The equilibrium position is shifted to the right.

   b. The equilibrium position is shifted to the right.

   c. The equilibrium position is not shifted.

   d. The equilibrium position is shifted to the right.

11. When a slightly soluble salt is placed in water, ions begin to leave the crystals of salt and enter the solvent to form a solution. As the concentration of ions in solution increases, eventually ions from the solution are attracted to and rejoin the crystals of undissolved salt. Eventually, things get to the point that every time ions leave the crystals to enter the solution in one place in the system, somewhere else ions are leaving the solution to rejoin the solid. At the point where dissolving and "undissolving" are going on at the same rate, we arrive at a state of dynamic equilibrium.

12. We write the equilibrium constant (the solubility product) K_{sp} for the dissolving of a slightly soluble salt in the usual manner. Because the concentration of the solid material is constant, we do not include it in the expression for K_{sp}.

13. If the solubility product constant for a slightly soluble salt is known, the solubility of the salt in mol/L or g/L can be calculated. For example, for $BaSO_4$, $K_{sp} = 1.5 \times 10^{-9}$ at 25°C. Suppose x moles of $BaSO_4$ dissolve per liter; since the stoichiometric coefficients for the dissolving of $BaSO_4$ are all 1, this means that x moles of $Ba^{2+}(aq)$ and x moles of $SO_4^{2-}(aq)$ will be produced per liter when $BaSO_4$ dissolves.

$$K_{sp} = [Ba^{2+}][SO_4^{2-}] = [x][x] = 1.5 \times 10^{-9}$$

$$x^2 = 1.5 \times 10^{-9} \quad \text{and therefore} \quad x = 3.9 \times 10^{-5} \ M$$

Thus the molar solubility of $BaSO_4$ is $3.9 \times 10^{-5} \ M$. This could be converted to the number of grams of $BaSO_4$ (233.4 g/mol):

$$(3.9 \times 10^{-5} \ \text{mol/L})(233.4 \ \text{g/mol}) = 9.10 \times 10^{-3} \ \text{g/L}$$

14.   a. $K = [NO_2(g)]^2/[NO(g)]^2[O_2(g)]$

   b. $K = [N_2(g)][H_2O(g)]^2/[O_2(g)]$

   c. $K = [CO_2(g)][NO(g)]/[CO(g)][NO_2(g)]$

15. $2SO_2(g) + O_2(g) \rightleftharpoons 2SO_3(g)$

$$K = \frac{[SO_3]^2}{[SO_2]^2[O_2]} = \frac{(0.42)^2}{(1.4 \times 10^{-3})^2(4.5 \times 10^{-4})} = 2.0 \times 10^8$$

16.   a. $K_{sp} = [Fe^{3+}][OH^-]^3$

   b. $K_{sp} = [Cd^{2+}][OH^-]^2$

   c. $K_{sp} = [Ba^{2+}]^3[PO_4^{3-}]^2$

17. $9.0 \times 10^{-4} g \times \dfrac{1 \text{ mol}}{143.35 \text{ g AgCl}} = 6.3 \times 10^{-6} \text{ mol}$

$K_{sp} = [Ag^+][Cl^-] = (6.3 \times 10^{-6})(6.3 \times 10^{-6}) = 4.0 \times 10^{-11}$ at 10°C

Chapter 17: Challenge Review Worksheet

1. Once the point is reached that product molecules are reacting at the same speed at which they are forming, there is no further net change in concentration. However, the constancy of concentration is a macroscopic property. Microscopically, both the forward and reverse reactions are occurring, and the system is dynamic.

2. The expression for the equilibrium constant for a reaction has as its numerator the concentrations of the products (raised to the powers of their stoichiometric coefficients in the balanced chemical equation for the reaction) and as its denominator the concentrations of the reactants (also raised to the powers of their stoichiometric coefficients). In general terms, for a reaction

$$a A + b B \rightleftharpoons c C + d D$$

the equilibrium constant expression has the form

$$K = \frac{[C]^c [D]^d}{[A]^a [B]^b}$$

in which the square brackets indicate molar concentration. For example, here are three simple reactions and the expression for their equilibrium constants:

$$N_2(g) + O_2(g) \rightleftharpoons 2NO(g) \qquad K = [NO]^2/[N_2][O_2]$$
$$2SO_2(g) + O_2(g) \rightleftharpoons 2SO_3(g) \qquad K = [SO_3]^2/[SO_2]^2[O_2]$$
$$N_2(g) + 3H_2(g) \rightleftharpoons 2NH_3(g) \qquad K = [NH_3]^2/[N_2][H_2]^3$$

3. Answers will vary. Examples include

$$C(s) + O_2(g) \rightleftharpoons CO_2(g) \qquad \text{heterogeneous (solid, gases)}$$
$$K = [CO_2]/[O_2]$$

$$2CO(g) + O_2(g) \rightleftharpoons 2CO_2(g) \qquad \text{homogeneous (all gases)}$$
$$K = [CO_2]^2/[CO]^2[O_2]$$

4. There are various changes that can be made to a system in equilibrium. Here are examples of some of them:

   a. The concentration of one of the reactants is increased.
   Consider the reaction $2SO_2(g) + O_2(g) \rightleftharpoons 2SO_3(g)$.
   Suppose the reactants have already reacted, and a position of equilibrium has been reached that fulfills the value of K for the reaction. At this point there will be present particular amounts of each reactant and of the product. Suppose one additional mole of O_2 is added to the system from outside. At the instant the O_2 is added, the system will not be in equilibrium. There will be too much O_2 present in the system to be compatible with the amount of SO_2 and SO_3 present. The system will respond by reacting to get rid of some of the excess O_2 until the value of the ratio K is again fulfilled. As the system reacts to reduce the excess of O_2, additional

SO_3 will form. The net result is more SO_3 produced than if the change had not been made.

b. The concentration of one of the products is decreased by selectively removing it from the system.
Consider the reaction $CH_3COOH + CH_3OH \rightleftharpoons H_2O + CH_3COOCH_3$.
This reaction is typical of reactions involving organic chemical substances, in which two organic molecules react to form a larger molecule, with a molecule of water split out during the combination. This type of reaction on its own tends to come to equilibrium with only part of the starting materials being converted to the desired organic product (which effectively would leave the experimenter with a mixture of materials). A technique that is used by organic chemists to increase the effective yield of the desired organic product is to separate the two products. If the products are separated, they cannot react to give back the reactants. One method used is to add a drying agent to the mixture that chemically or physically absorbs the water from the system, removing it from the equilibrium. If the water is removed, the reverse reaction cannot take place, and the reaction proceeds to a greater extent in the forward direction than if the drying agent had not been added. In other situations, an experimenter may separate the products of the reaction by distillation (if the boiling points make this possible). Again, if the products have been separated, then the reverse reaction will not be possible, and the forward reaction will occur to a greater extent.

c. The reaction system is compressed to a smaller volume.
Consider the example $3H_2(I) + N_2(g) \rightleftharpoons 2NH_3(g)$.
For equilibria involving gases, when the volume of the reaction system is decreased suddenly, the pressure in the system increases. However, if the reacting system can relieve some of this increased pressure by reacting, it will do so. This will happen by the reaction occurring in whichever direction will give the smaller number of moles of gas (if the number of moles of gas is decreased in a particular volume, the pressure will decrease).
    For the reaction above, there are two moles of the gas on the right side, but there is a total of four moles on the left side. If this system at equilibrium were to be suddenly compressed to a smaller volume, the reaction would proceed further to the right (in favor of more ammonia being produced).

d. The temperature is increased for an endothermic reaction.
Consider the reaction $2NaHCO_3 + heat \rightleftharpoons Na_2CO_3 + H_2O + CO_2$.
Although a change in temperature actually does change the value of the equilibrium constant, we can simplify reactions involving temperature changes by treating heat energy as if it were a chemical substance. For this endothermic reaction, assume heat is one of the reactants. As we saw in the example in part a of this question, increasing the concentration of one of the reactants for a system at equilibrium causes the reaction to proceed further to the right, forming additional product. Similarly, for the endothermic reaction given above, increasing the temperature causes the reaction to proceed further in the direction of products than if no change had been made. It is as if there were too much "heat" to be compatible with the

amount of substances present. The substances react in a direction to consume some of the energy.

   e. The temperature is decreased for an exothermic process.
   Consider the reaction $PCl_3 + Cl_2 \rightleftharpoons PCl_5 + heat$.
   As discussed in part d above, although changing the temperature at which a reaction is performed does change the numerical value of K, we can simplify our discussion of this situation by treating heat energy as if it were a chemical substance. Heat is a product of this reaction. If we are going to lower the temperature of this reaction system, the only way to accomplish this is to remove energy from the system. Lowering the temperature of the system "encourages" the system to produce more heat. Thus lowering the temperature will favor the product.

5. Examples will vary. Consider the following:

   $AgCl(s) \rightleftharpoons Ag^+(aq) + Cl^-(aq)$ $\qquad K_{sp} = [Ag^+][Cl^-]$

   $PbCl_2(s) \rightleftharpoons Pb^{2+}(aq) + 2Cl^-(aq)$ $\qquad K_{sp} = [Pb^{2+}][Cl^-]^2$

   $BaSO_4(s) \rightleftharpoons Ba^{2+}(aq) + SO_4^{2-}(aq)$ $\qquad K_{sp} = [Ba^{2+}][SO_4^{2-}]$

6. $8.0 \times 10^{-2} \text{ g} \times \dfrac{1 \text{ mol}}{62.31 \text{ g MgF}_2} = 1.3 \times 10^{-3} \text{ mol}$

   $K_{sp} = [Mg^{2+}][F^-]^2 = (1.3 \times 10^{-3})(2.6 \times 10^{-3})^2 = 8.8 \times 10^{-9}$

Chapter 18: Basic Review Worksheet

1. *Oxidation* may be defined as the loss of electrons by an atom or as an increase in the oxidation state of the atom. *Reduction* may be defined as the gain of electrons by an atom or as a decrease in the oxidation state of the atom.

2.   a. $Cr = +3$, $O = +2$

   b. $Fe = +2$, $Cl = -1$

   c. $Na = +1$, $P = +5$, $O = -2$

3. An oxidizing agent is a molecule, atom, or ion that causes the oxidation of some other species; it does so by accepting one or more electrons. A reducing agent is a molecule, atom, or ion that causes reduction of some other species; it does so by giving up one or more electrons. Therefore, an oxidizing agent, by taking electrons, is reduced. A reducing agent, by giving electrons, is oxidized.

4. A half-reaction is the partial equation of an overall oxidation–reduction equation that represents either oxidation or reduction. We use them because they make it easier to balance oxidation–reduction equations.

5.   a. When a half-reaction is reversed, the cell potential is reversed.

   b. When the coefficients of a half-reaction are multiplied by a factor, the cell potential is unchanged.

6. Like those covered in Chapter 7, oxidation–reduction equations must be balanced by atoms (the total number of each type of atom on each side of the equation must be the same).

With oxidation–reduction equations, we also must balance the charge (the number of electrons gained by one species must be lost by another; there are no "free" electrons).

7.   a. $Mg(s) + 2Hg^{2+}(aq) \rightarrow Mg^{2+}(aq) + Hg_2^{2+}(aq)$

       b. $Zn(s) + 2Ag^+(aq) \rightarrow Zn^{2+}(aq) + 2Ag(s)$

8. The anode is the electrode where oxidation occurs in a galvanic cell; the cathode is the electrode where reduction occurs in a galvanic cell.

Chapter 18: Standard Review Worksheet

1.   a.   Aluminum is oxidized; chlorine is reduced.

       b.   Potassium is oxidized; iodine is reduced.

       c.   Nitrogen is oxidized; oxygen is reduced.

2.   a. $K = +1$, $Mn = +7$, $O = -2$

       b. $H = +1$, $Cr = +6$, $O = -2$

       c. $Bi = +3$, $O = -2$

3.   a. CH_4 is the reducing agent, O_2 is the oxidizing agent.

       b.   Cu is the reducing agent, S is the oxidizing agent.

4. Under ordinary conditions it is not possible to have "free" electrons that are not part of some atom, molecule, or ion. Thus the number of electrons lost by one species must be gained by another species (the electrons must be balanced).

5.   a. $8H^+(aq) + 2NO_3^-(aq) + 6Br^-(aq) \rightarrow 2NO(g) + 3Br_2(l) + 4H_2O(l)$

       b. $4H^+(aq) + Ni(s) + 2NO_3^-(aq) \rightarrow Ni^{2+}(aq) + 2NO_2(g) + 2H_2O(l)$

6. By separating the oxidizing agent and reducing agent, the electron that transfers from the reducing agent to the oxidizing agent must go through a wire. The current produced in the wire can do useful work.

7.   a. $Cu(s) + 2Ag^+(aq) \rightarrow Cu^{2+}(aq) + 2Ag(s)$

       b.   Cu is the reducing agent, and Ag^+ is the oxidizing agent.

       c.   The cell should look similar to Figure 18.5 in the text with Cu as the anode and Ag as the cathode.

Chapter 18: Challenge Review Worksheet

1. $O = +2$, $F = -1$. Normally, the oxidation state of O is -2. However, the fluorine atom is more electronegative than the oxygen atom, so the oxidation state of F must be lower than that of O.

2. Answers will vary. The combustion of methane is discussed in Section 18.3 of the text; students should choose a different example.

3.   a. $7H_2O(l) + 3S_2O_8^{2-}(aq) + 2Cr^{3+}(aq) \rightarrow 6SO_4^{2-}(aq) + Cr_2O_7^{2-}(aq) + 14H^+(aq)$

       b. $2H^+(aq) + ClO_4^-(aq) + 2Cl^-(aq) \rightarrow ClO_3^-(aq) + Cl_2(g) + H_2O(l)$

c. $2OH^-(aq) + Cl_2(g) \rightarrow Cl^-(aq) + ClO^-(aq) + H_2O(l)$

Chapter 19: Basic Review Worksheet

1. The protons and neutrons are present in the nucleus.

Particle	Relative Mass	Relative Charge
proton	1.0000	1+
neutron	1.0016	none

2. If a nucleus is radioactive, it spontaneously decomposes, forming a different nucleus and producing one or more particles.

3. In Chapter 7 we saw that chemical equations must be balanced by mass by having the total number of each type of atom on each side of the equation be the same. In nuclear reactions, the atomic number and mass number must be conserved, but the numbers of each type of atom are not the same on both sides of the equation.

4. Answers will vary. These processes are discussed in Section 19.1 of the text.

5. a. ^1_0n

    b. $^{74}_{34}Se$

6. $^{226}_{88}Ra$ is the most stable (longest half-life), and $^{224}_{88}Ra$ is the "hottest" (shortest half-life).

7. A *half-life* is the time required for half of a sample of radioactive material to decay.

8. Radiotracers are used in the medical field. These are radioactive nuclides introduced into the body. This allows the pathway to be traced in order to study organs and systems in the body.

9. Nuclear *fusion* is combining two light nuclei to form a heavier, more stable nucleus. Nuclear *fission* is the splitting of a heavy nucleus into smaller nuclei. In both cases new elements are produced.

10. A *chain reaction* is a self-sustaining fission process caused by the production of neutrons that proceed to split other nuclei.

Chapter 19: Standard Review Worksheet

1. The net effect of beta production is to change a neutron to a proton. The net effect of positron production is to change a proton to a neutron. Examples will vary, and some are given in Section 19.1 of the text.

2. The Z is the atomic number (number of protons). A given element always has the same atomic number. For example, carbon always has an atomic number of 6, regardless of the isotope of carbon we are considering.

3.

$$^A_Z X \longrightarrow\ ^4_2 He + ^{A-4}_{Z-2} Y$$

$$_Z^A X \longrightarrow {}_{-1}^0 e + {}_{Z+1}^A Y$$

$$_Z^A X \longrightarrow {}_1^0 e + {}_{Z-1}^A Y$$

$$_Z^A X + {}_{-1}^0 e \longrightarrow {}_{Z-1}^A Y$$

4.   a.

$$_{23}^{53} V \longrightarrow {}_{-1}^0 e + {}_{24}^{53} Cr$$

   b.

$$_{96}^{244} Cm \longrightarrow {}_2^4 He + {}_{94}^{240} Pu$$

5.   a. ${}_2^4 He$

   b. ${}_2^4 He$

6.   a. Kr-81 (it has the longest half-life)

   b. Kr-73 (it has the shortest half-life)

   c. <u>Kr-73:</u>

$$24 \text{ h} \times \frac{60 \text{ min}}{1 \text{ h}} \times \frac{60 \text{ s}}{1 \text{ min}} = 86{,}400 \text{ s}$$

$$\frac{86{,}400}{27 \text{ s}} = 3200 \text{ half-lives}$$

Essentially no Kr-73 is left after 24 hours.

<u>Kr-74:</u>

$$24 \text{ h} \times \frac{60 \text{ min}}{1 \text{ h}} = 1440 \text{ min}$$

$$\frac{1440 \text{ min}}{11.5 \text{ min}} = 125 \text{ half-lives}$$

Essentially no Kr-74 is left after 24 hours.

<u>Kr-76:</u>

$$\frac{24 \text{ h}}{14.48 \text{ h}} = 1.7 \text{ half-lives, almost 2 half-lives}$$

About ¼ (or 31 mg) Kr-76 is left after 24 hours.

<u>Kr-81:</u>

$$24 \text{ h} \times \frac{1 \text{ day}}{24 \text{ h}} \times \frac{1 \text{ year}}{365 \text{ days}} = 2.7 \times 10^{-3} \text{ years}$$

$$\frac{2.7 \times 10^{-3} \text{ yr}}{2.1 \times 10^5 \text{ yr}} = 1.3 \times 10^{-8} \text{ half lives}$$

Essentially all 125 mg of the Kr-81 remains.

7. For a chain reaction to occur, sufficient neutrons must be produced and captured by other nuclides to sustain a reaction. The critical mass is the amount of material needed to provide these conditions.

8. In a breeder reactor, fissionable fuel material is produced as the reactor runs (nonfissionable U-238 is changed to fissionable Pu-239).

Chapter 19: Challenge Review Worksheet

1. Fe-53 has "too many protons" (compared with the stable isotopes) and will undergo positron production, electron capture, and/or alpha-particle production. These will increase the neutron:proton ratio. Fe-59 has "too many neutrons" (compared with the stable isotopes) and will undergo beta-particle production (which effectively changes a neutron to a proton).

2. The average atomic mass of neon is given on the periodic table as 20.18. This suggests that Ne-20 predominates in nature. The average atomic mass is a weighted average that includes the masses of the isotopes and their relative abundances.

3. The general formulas is

$$\frac{A_0}{2^{\text{number of half-lives}}} = A$$

where A_0 = initial amount of radioactive nuclei
   A = amount of radioactive nuclide after a given time

$$\text{Number of half-lives} = \frac{\text{time}}{\text{time for one half-life}}$$

$73/21 = 3.5$ half lives

$$\frac{100\%}{2^{3.5}} = A = \frac{100\%}{11.31} = 8.8\%$$

4. Third-life = time required for one-third of the original sample of a nuclei to decay.

Given the formula from question 3,

$$\frac{100}{2^{t/t_{1/2}}} = A$$

In this case, t = time required for one-third of the sample to decay.

$$\frac{100\%}{2^{t/15}} = 66.7\% \text{ (Thus 66.7\%, or two-thirds, of the sample remains.)}$$

$$\frac{100}{66.7} = 2^{t/15}$$

$$\log\left(\frac{100}{66.7}\right) = \frac{t}{15} \log 2$$

$t = 8.8$ years

5. The chemical properties of isotopes (radioactive or not) of a given element are the same. This is so because the chemical properties are governed by the electrons, not the nucleus (although mass effects can be important for light elements). An example of the importance of this fact for radiotracers is I-131. Iodine is taken in by the thyroid gland, and I-131 is

used to monitor this uptake. If I-131 was chemically different from the more common I-127, it might not be taken in by the thyroid gland and would not be a useful radiotracer.

Chapter 20: Standard Review Worksheet

1. The geometric arrangement is a tetrahedral. This allows the four electron pairs coming off the carbon atom to be as far apart from each other as possible.

2. The extended formulas are shown in Table 20.1 in the text. Each successive member differs from the previous member by a —CH₂— unit.

3. The total number of substituents is indicated by a prefix before the name of the substituent [*di-* (2); *tri-* (3); *tetra-* (4); etc.].

4. To indicate a double bond, the ending of the longest chain containing the double bond is changed to *-ene;* to indicate a triple bond, the ending of the longest chain containing the triple bond is changed to *-yne.*

5. The location of the double or triple bond is indicated by giving the number of the lowest-number carbon atom involved in the double or triple bond.

6. A triple bond represents three pairs of electrons shared between atoms. An example of a molecule with a triple bond is C_2H_2. The Lewis structure is

$$H: C:::C:H \quad \text{or} \quad HC\equiv CH$$

7. Shown are carbon skeletons:

C≡C—C—C—C—C   C—C≡C—C—C—C   C—C—C≡C—C—C
1-hexene   2-hexene   3-hexene

C≡C—C—C—C
       |
       C
3-methyl-1-pentyne

C—C≡C—C—C
          |
          C
4-methyl-2-pentyne

C≡C—C—C—C
          |
          C
4-methyl-1-pentyne

          C
          |
C≡C—C—C
          |
          C
3,3-dimethyl-1-butyne

8.

alcohols: R—C—OH   primary

with H above and H below the C.

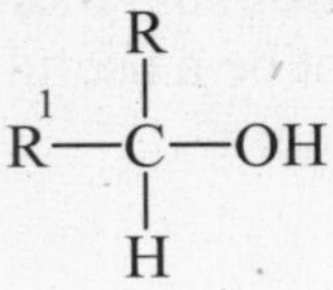

$$R^1-\overset{\displaystyle R}{\underset{\displaystyle H}{C}}-OH \qquad \text{secondary}$$

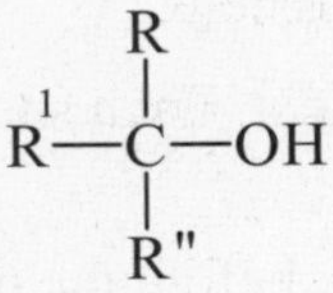

$$R^1-\overset{\displaystyle R}{\underset{\displaystyle R''}{C}}-OH \qquad \text{tertiary}$$

ethers: $\qquad R-O-R^1$

aldehydes: $\qquad R-\overset{\displaystyle O}{\overset{\|}{C}}-H$

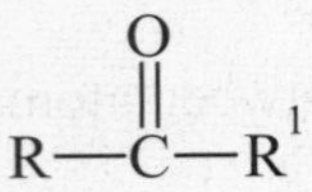

ketones: $\qquad R-\overset{\displaystyle O}{\overset{\|}{C}}-R^1$

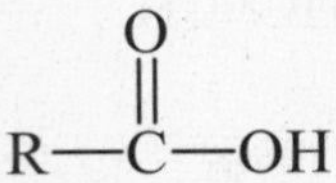

carboxylic acids: $\quad R-\overset{\displaystyle O}{\overset{\|}{C}}-OH$

esters: $\qquad R-\overset{\displaystyle O}{\overset{\|}{C}}-O-R^1$

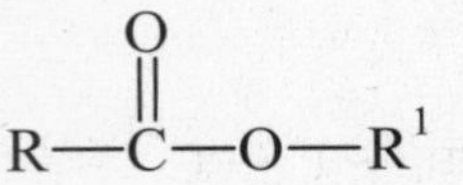

amines: $\qquad R-NH_2$

9. a. 3-methyl pentane   e. 2-methyl-1-propanol
    b. 4-methyl-2-hexene   f. 2-chloropropanal
    c. 4-chloro-2-pentyne   g. 4-chloro-2-pentanone
    d. 2-phenylbutane   h. 2-methylpentanoic acid

10. a.

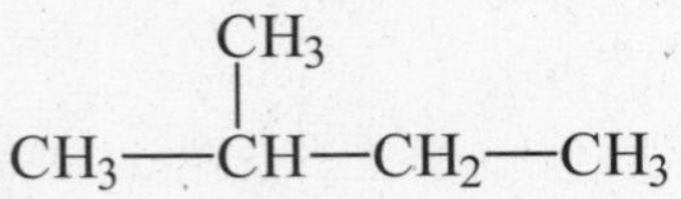

$$CH_3-\overset{\displaystyle CH_3}{\underset{}{CH}}-CH_2-CH_3$$

b.

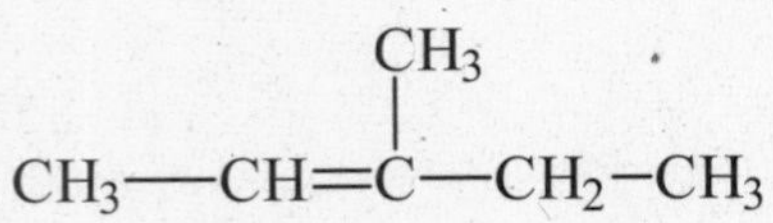

$$CH_3-CH=\overset{\displaystyle CH_3}{\underset{}{C}}-CH_2-CH_3$$

c.

$$HC \equiv C - \overset{\displaystyle Cl}{\underset{\displaystyle Cl}{CH}}$$

d.

e.

$$CH_3 - \overset{\displaystyle CH_3}{\underset{\displaystyle OH}{C}} - CH_3$$

f.

$$CH_3 - \overset{\displaystyle CH_3}{CH} - CH_2 - \overset{\displaystyle O}{CH}$$

g.

$$CH_3 - \overset{}{\underset{\displaystyle Cl}{CH}} - \overset{\displaystyle O}{C} - CH_2 - \overset{}{\underset{\displaystyle Cl}{CH}} - \overset{}{\underset{\displaystyle Cl}{CH}} - CH_3$$

h.

$$\overset{\displaystyle I}{CH_2} - CH_2 - \overset{\displaystyle O}{C} - OH$$

Chapter 20: Challenge Review Worksheet

1. More energy is needed to overcome the attraction between heavier molecules. Heavier molecules contain more electrons, which increase the chances of induced dipoles, therefore making the London dispersion forces greater.

2. In 2-chlorobutanoic acid the chlorine atom is closer to the carboxyl group and attracts the electrons from the O—H bond more strongly. Thus the hydrogen atom is held more loosely and will ionize more readily.

3. Answers might include CO_2, CO, or any carbonate, hydrogen carbonate, or cyanide compound.

Chapter 21: Standard Review Worksheet

1. DNA, deoxyribonucleic acid
2. nucleotides
3. ester
4. thymine, guanine
5. DNA
6. triglycerides
7. unsaturated, saturated
8. cholesterol
9. hemoglobin

10. Figure 21.2 shows the amino acids separated into hydrophilic and hydrophobic subgroupings. The hydrophobic amino acids contain R groups that are typically hydrocarbon (or substituted hydrocarbon) in nature. This makes the R groups nonpolar and unlikely to interact with the very polar water molecules. The hydrophilic amino acids contain a polar functional group (—OH, —SH, —C=O, for example) that enables the amino acid R groups to interact with water.

11. These are shown and described in Section 21.9 (common steroids are shown in Figure 21.25 of the text).

12. Phospholipids have a similar structure to triglycerides, except that one of the fatty acids attached to the glycerol backbone is replaced by a phosphate group. An important phospholipid is lecithin.

13. 24 (assuming no amino acid repeats)

14. The phosphate group and the sugar molecule of adjacent nucleotides become bonded to each other.

15. pentoses (5 carbons); hexoses (6 carbons); trioses (3 carbons)

16. The primary human bile acid is cholic acid, which helps to emulsify fats in the intestinal tract.

17. A wax is an ester of a fatty acid with a long-chain monohydroxy alcohol. Waxes are solids that provide waterproof coatings on the fruits and leaves of plants and on the skins and feathers of animals.

Chapter 21: Challenge Review Worksheet

1.   a. cys-gln-asp, cys-gln-arg, cys-asp-arg, cys-asp-gln, cys-arg-gln, cys-arg-asp, gln-asp-arg, gln-asp-cys, gln-arg-cys, gln-arg-asp, gln-cys-asp, gln-cys-arg, asp-arg-cys, asp-arg-gln, asp-cys-gln, asp-cys-arg, asp-gln-arg, asp-gln-cys, arg-cys-gln, arg-cys-asp, arg-gln-asp, arg-gln-cys, arg-asp-gln, arg-asp-cys

    b. No. Tripeptides could contain more than one unit of the same amino acid.

2. Enzymes can break down lipid or protein stains and remove them from laundry.

Section 4: Chapter Summaries

This section offers easy-to-read chapter summaries and additional active reading questions to help students who are having difficulty comprehending a chapter or section of the text.

Contents

Chapter 1... CS–1

Chapter 2... CS–4

Chapter 3... CS–7

Chapter 4..CS–10

Chapter 5..CS–13

Chapter 6..CS–16

Chapter 7..CS–19

Chapter 8..CS–21

Chapter 9..CS–23

Chapter 10..CS–25

Chapter 11..CS–28

Chapter 12..CS–32

Chapter 13..CS–35

Chapter 14..CS–38

Chapter 15..CS–41

Chapter 16..CS–44

Chapter 17..CS–47

Chapter 18..CS–50

Chapter 19..CS–53

Chapter 20..CS–56

Chapter 21..CS–60

Chapter 1   Chemistry: An Introduction

1.1   The Science of Chemistry

Key Term

chemistry

Summary

A knowledge of chemistry is useful to almost everyone. Chemistry is central to people's efforts to create new products; to produce cleaner, more abundant sources of energy; and to cure diseases that harm people as well as animals and plants that provide food. However, the knowledge of chemicals sometimes results in problems for people, other living things, and the environment. Studying chemistry can help solve these problems. Studying chemistry has other important benefits. It broadens a person's understanding of how the natural world operates, and it can make a person a better problem solver. The logical, step-by-step approach used to solve complicated chemistry problems can be applied to the solution of problems in many areas of life.

Chemistry can be defined as "the science that deals with the materials of the universe and the changes that these materials undergo." Most of the natural events that occur involve chemical changes in which one or more substances transform into different substances. Chemists "look inside" ordinary objects to see how their most basic parts—atoms and molecules—work.

1.2   Using Science to Solve Problems

Key Terms

scientific method   theory   natural law
measurement

Summary

Almost everyone uses similar steps to solve problems. First, people recognize the problem and state it clearly. Next, they propose possible solutions to the problem or suggest possible explanations for what they know about the problem. Finally, they decide which solutions to the problem are the best or which explanation is the most reasonable.

Scientists solve complex problems by breaking them down into manageable parts. Scientific thinking involves three main activities: making observations to collect information and help define the problem; forming a hypothesis, or educated guess, as to what the observations mean; and testing the hypothesis by performing experiments. After these three steps are completed, a scientist may come up with a theory, or an overall explanation of the findings that summarizes the hypothesis and agrees with the results of the experiment. This process can be used to solve most kinds of problems, not just scientific ones.

Science is a framework for gaining knowledge of nature and putting it together in a way that makes sense. Science is based on facts, but it is also a plan of action for studying and understanding certain types of information. When scientists use scientific thinking specifically to understand how the world of nature works, the step-by-step process of problem solving is called the *scientific method*. The scientific method has three steps:

1. State the problem and then collect data by making observations.

2. Formulate a hypothesis, or a possible explanation for the observations.

3. Perform experiments to test the hypothesis. Experiments produce new observations and allow scientists to gather new information. Such new information leads scientists to restate the problem, and the process begins again.

Steps in the Scientific Method

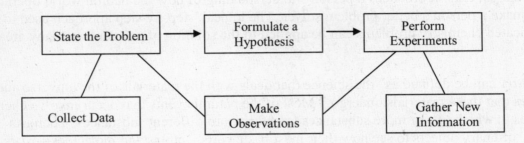

Once the observations, experiments, and hypothesis support one another, a theory can be formed. A *theory* is a possible explanation of some part of nature. Theories are not permanent. They are being changed constantly as new information becomes available. When the same observation applies to many different natural systems, this observation may be summarized in a statement called a *natural law*. A law and a theory differ in the following way: A *law* is a summary of observed behavior that tells what happens. A *theory* is an explanation of why it happens.

1.3   Learning Chemistry

Summary

Learning chemistry involves understanding nature on a level so tiny that we do not ordinarily see it—the microscopic level. Chemistry involves memorizing many unfamiliar terms and definitions and working hard to understand basic ideas and models that explain how complex chemical processes work. To achieve this, someone learning chemistry should be patient with trial and error. Even an experienced chemist does not expect to be right the first time he or she tackles a difficult problem in chemistry.

Additional Active Reading Questions

1. How can studying chemistry make a person a better problem solver?

2. What is the definition of chemistry?

3. What is the first step in solving a problem using a scientific approach?

4. What is a theory?

5. What is the difference between a law and a theory?

6. Why do you think trial and error is important in learning chemistry?

Chapter 2   Matter

2.1   The Nature of Matter

Key Terms

matter   atoms   compounds
molecule   element   solid
liquid   gas

Summary

Matter is all the "stuff" that makes up the universe. Anything that has mass and takes up space is matter. All matter is made up of tiny particles called *atoms*.

Atoms are the basic building blocks of elements. About 100 types of atoms make up all matter. Different types of matter—for example, air, minerals, plastics, and living cells—are formed when atoms join in various ways. Matter that is made up of just one kind of atom is called an *element*. When elements combine chemically, *compounds* are formed. Compounds always have the same composition—they always contain the same types and relative numbers of atoms.

Matter can exist in three states: solid, liquid, and gas. These states each have unique properties. A *solid* has a definite shape and volume. For example, if you put a solid in a container, the solid will not change shape or size. A *liquid* has a definite volume but no definite shape. A liquid takes the shape of the container it is in but always occupies the same amount of space. A *gas* has neither a definite shape nor a definite volume. A gas not only takes the shape of any container but also will spread out to fill any container.

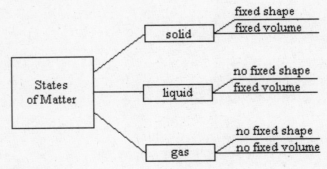

2.2   Properties of Matter

Key Terms

physical properties   chemical properties   physical change
chemical change

Summary

Matter has both physical and chemical properties and undergoes both physical and chemical changes. *Physical properties* include such obvious characteristics as odor, color, volume, state, density, boiling point, and melting point. A *physical change* involves a change in one or more of these properties but no change in a substance's composition. *Chemical properties* describe the way one substance can change into a different substance. In a *chemical change,* one substance actually turns into one or more new substances in which the atoms are organized in different ways.

2.3   Classifying Matter

Key Terms

mixtures	alloys	pure substances
homogeneous mixture	solution	heterogeneous mixture
distillation	filtration	

Summary

Almost all matter is made up of mixtures of substances. *Mixtures* can be a blend of elements or compounds or both. A mixture's composition—type and amount of "ingredients"—can vary. Scientists divide mixtures into two types. A *homogeneous mixture,* also called a *solution,* has the same properties throughout. Seawater, for example, contains various dissolved minerals that are spread evenly throughout the mixture. A *heterogeneous mixture* has areas of differing properties. For example, a shovel full of soil may contain a mixture of lumps of clay, sand, and tiny particles of decayed plant and animal matter. Each of these areas has its own properties.

Unlike mixtures, *pure substances* are always made up of the same ingredients in the same amounts. Compounds and elements are the two types of pure substances. Compounds can be broken down chemically into elements. Elements cannot be broken down chemically into simpler substances.

The substances that make up mixtures can be separated into pure substances. Two of the most common separation methods are *distillation* and *filtration.* Both distillation and filtration result in physical changes only. Distillation can separate the substances in a solution. In distillation the liquid part of a mixture is boiled away, separated, and collected; any dissolved solids are left behind. Filtration is useful for separating a liquid from a solid. The solid–liquid mixture is poured through a mesh that collects the solid but allows the liquid to pass through.

Additional Active Reading Questions

1. What are the two main properties of matter?

2. What is all matter made of?

3. How do elements and compounds differ?

4. Name the three states of matter.

5. Which state of matter has no definite volume or shape?

6. Which properties of a substance describe its ability to form new substances?

7. The changing of ice into water is an example of what type of change?

8. What type of change does burning cause in a substance?

9. What are the two classes of mixtures?

10. How is a pure substance different from a mixture?

11. Which method of separating mixtures involves the use of heat?

12. Can a pure substance be separated by filtration? Why or why not?

Chapter 3   Chemical Foundations: Elements, Atoms, and Ions

3.1   The Elements

Key Term

element symbols

Summary

About 115 different elements are known. Of these, 88 are natural, and the rest have been created in laboratories. Of all the elements, nine are by far the most abundant. These nine – oxygen, silicon, aluminum, iron, calcium, sodium, potassium, magnesium, and hydrogen— make up 98 percent of all substances on Earth.

To make writing names of the elements simple, chemists use abbreviations, or *element symbols.* Many of these symbols consist of the first letter or the first two letters of the element name.

3.2   Atoms and Compounds

Key Terms

law of constant composition   Dalton's atomic theory   atoms
compound   chemical formula

Summary

In the early 1800s, English scientist John Dalton came up with an explanation of how *atoms* combine to form *compounds. Dalton's atomic theory* has five main points: (1) Elements are made up of atoms. (2) Each atom of an element is exactly the same as all the others. (3) The atoms of a particular element are different from those of any other element. (4) Atoms of elements can combine with atoms of other elements to form compounds, and any single compound always contains the same elements in the same amount in relation to one another. This principle is called the *law of constant composition.* (5) A chemical reaction changes only the way the atoms are grouped and never creates or destroys atoms.

Many compounds contain molecules. Molecules are described by a *chemical formula,* or set of element symbols and numbers. The types of atoms are indicated by element symbols. A number called a subscript tells how many atoms of each element the molecule contains.

3.3   Atomic Structure

Key Terms

electrons	nuclear atom	nucleus
protons	neutrons	isotopes
atomic number	mass number	

Summary

All types of atoms are made up of smaller particles. *Electrons* are negatively charged particles, *protons* are positively charged particles, and *neutrons* have no charge. Protons and neutrons are grouped together in a dense mass in the center of the atom, called the *nucleus*. Electrons move around the nucleus. The number of protons in an atom is equal to the number of electrons. As a result, the atom's positive and negative charges are balanced, and its charge is zero, or neutral.

An atom's electrons move around the nucleus at an average distance of about 63,000 times the diameter of the nucleus. Thus most of an atom is really empty space. The number and arrangement of its electrons give each element unique chemical properties. When atoms of different elements combine to form molecules, the atoms' electrons interact.

Chemists describe an element by assigning it an atomic number and a mass number. The *atomic number* is the number of protons. The *mass number* is the sum of protons and neutrons. The number of neutrons in atoms of the same element may differ. Atoms with the same number of protons but a different number of neutrons are called *isotopes*.

3.4   Using the Periodic Table

Key Terms

periodic table	groups	alkali metals
alkaline earth metals	halogens	noble gases
transition metals	metals	nonmetals
metalloids (semimetals)	diatomic molecules	

Summary

Chemists have organized all the known elements into a chart called the *periodic table*. The periodic table is made up of rows of boxes. Each box contains the symbol for an element below the element's atomic number. The elements are listed in order of increasing atomic number. They are also listed in horizontal rows and vertical columns. Elements with similar chemical properties that lie in the same column in the periodic table are called *groups*.

Most elements react easily with other elements. Few elements are found in nature in their pure state. Instead, they exist in combination with other elements in the form of compounds. Elements exist in different forms in their natural state at normal temperatures. Most elements are solids. Several are gaseous. Only two elements are liquid at 25°C. Some elements form *diatomic molecules*—two atoms combined into a molecule.

3.5   Ions and Their Compounds

Key Terms

ion   cation   anion
ionic compounds

Summary

A charged particle, called an *ion,* can be produced by adding or removing one or more electrons from an atom. Removing an electron produces a positively charged ion, called a *cation.* Adding an electron produces a negatively charged ion, called an *anion.*

Many substances contain ions. Whenever a nonmetal and a metal combine to form a compound, it is likely to contain ions. Such a compound is called an *ionic compound.* The cations and anions in a compound must balance out to result in a charge of zero.

Additional Active Reading Questions

1. What are the nine most common elements on earth?

2. Write the symbols for the following elements: helium, argon, potassium, gold, boron, copper.

3. State the law of constant composition.

4. Write the chemical formula for a compound with one carbon atom and two oxygen atoms.

5. Which two types of particles make up the nucleus of an atom?

6. What is the source of an element's chemical properties?

7. How do you find the number of neutrons in an isotope?

8. What is the name for elements with similar chemical properties that lie in the same column in the periodic table?

9. Why are few elements found in nature in their pure form?

10. What is the name for a positively charged ion? a negatively charged ion?

11. What is an ionic compound?

Chapter 4   Nomenclature

4.1   Naming Binary Compounds

Key Terms

binary compound   binary ionic compound

Summary

A compound that is made up of two elements is called a *binary compound*. When a metal combines with a nonmetal, the compound that is formed is called a *binary ionic compound*. A binary ionic compound contains ions. The metal loses one or more electrons to become a cation, and the nonmetal gains one or more electrons to become an anion. The positive ion is always written first in the formula, and the negative ion is written second.

It is convenient to group binary ionic compounds into two types: Type I binary ionic compounds and Type II binary ionic compounds. Type I binary ionic compounds contain metal atoms that can form only one type of cation. Type II binary ionic compounds are formed from metal atoms that can form two or more types of cations with different charges.

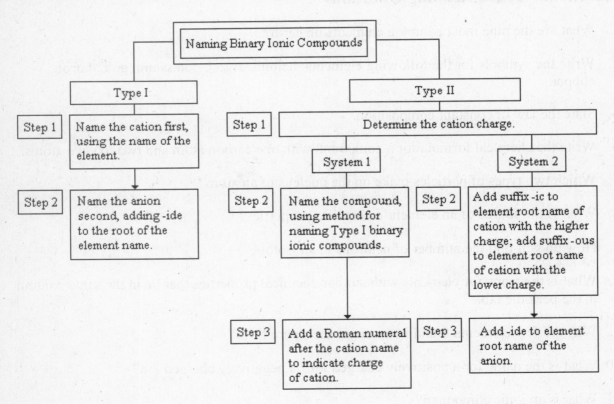

Type III binary compounds contain only nonmetals. In naming these compounds, the first element in the formula is named first, and the full element name is used. The second element is named as though it were an anion according to the rules summarized above. Prefixes (word beginnings) are used to tell how many atoms are present.

Each of the three types of binary compounds has a specific strategy for naming it. *Type I binary ionic compounds* are formed from metals that always form a cation with the same charge. *Type II binary ionic compounds* are formed from metals that form cations with various charges. *Type III binary compounds* contain only nonmetals. When determining which type of compound you are naming, use the periodic table to help you identify metals and nonmetals and to find out which elements form only one type of cation and which form more than one.

4.2   Naming and Writing Formulas for More Complex Compounds

Key Terms

polyatomic ions   oxyanions   acids

Summary

Polyatomic ions consist of several atoms bound together and carry an overall positive or negative charge. The names and charges of polyatomic ions must be memorized in order to name the compounds that contain them. Table 4.4 lists the most common polyatomic ions. One type of polyatomic anion contains an element plus different numbers of oxygen atoms. These anions are called *oxyanions*. The rules for naming ionic compounds that contain polyatomic ions are similar to those for naming binary ionic compounds. These rules are summarized in section 4.1 above.

Acids are substances that produce H^+ ions when dissolved in water. An acid is a molecule with one or more H^+ ions attached to an anion. The rules for naming acids depend on whether the anion contains oxygen. If the anion does not contain oxygen, the acid is named with the prefix *hydro-* and the suffix *–ic* attached to the root of the element name. When the anion contains oxygen, the acid name is formed from the root of the central element name of the anion or the anion name, with the suffix *–ic* or *–ous*. When the anion name ends in *–ate,* the suffix *–ic* is used. When the anion's suffix is *–ite,* the suffix *–ous* is used in the acid name.

It is necessary to learn the name, composition, and charge of each of the common polyatomic anions and the NH_4^+ cation by formula and by name in order to be able to write the compound's name given its formula or the compound's formula given its name.

Additional Active Reading Questions

1. What types of elements make up a binary ionic compound?

2. What kind of metal atoms form Type I binary ionic compounds?

3. What are two names for $FeCl_2$?

4. Which type of binary compound uses prefixes to indicate how many atoms of the elements are present?

5. For each item below, use Table 4.4 to find the chemical formula that matches the name or the name that matches the chemical formula.

a. _____ sulfate
c. _____ carbonate

b. _____ $C_2H_3O_2^-$
d. _____ ammonium

6. Describe an acid molecule.

7. What acid is formed from the sulfate (SO_4^{2-}) anion? the sulfite (SO_3^{2-}) anion?

Chapter 5   Measurements and Calculations

5.1   Scientific Notation and Units

Key Terms

measurement	scientific notation	units
English system	metric system	International System (SI)
volume	liter	milliliter
mass	gram	

Summary

Scientific notation is a method for making very large or very small numbers more compact and easier to write. It expresses a number as a product of a number between 1 and 10 and the appropriate power of 10. A power of 10 is 10 multiplied by itself. Powers of 10 are indicated by exponents, which are small numbers above and to the right of the number 10. To express a large number in scientific notation, we count the number of places the decimal point must be moved to get a number between 1 and 10. For numbers smaller than 10, the decimal point is moved to the right, and the power of 10 is written with a negative exponent. Thus 0.00093 would be written 9.3×10^{-4}.

To have meaning, a *measurement* must contain not only numbers but also words (*units*) that tell in which scale or standard the measurement is being expressed. Feet, meters, and inches are called units of measurements. Units of the *metric system* have long been preferred for most scientific work. The units used for scientific work are called SI units. The fundamental, or basic, SI units are the meter, kilogram, second, and Kelvin. The *International System (SI)* uses prefixes to indicate changes in the size of the units.

The fundamental SI unit of length is the meter, which is equal to about 39 inches, or 3 feet, 3 inches. The fundamental SI unit of volume is the cubic meter. *Volume* is the amount of three-dimensional space a substance takes up. A cubic meter is based on the volume of a cube that measures 1 meter on all sides. The fundamental SI unit of mass is the kilogram. *Mass* describes the amount of matter contained in an object.

5.2   Uncertainty in Measurement and Significant Figures

Key Terms

significant figures   rounding off

Summary

All measurements have some degree of uncertainty. Often objects or samples being measured do not correspond exactly to the graduations (lines of measurement) provided on a measuring device. For example, we might use a ruler with 1-mm graduations to measure the length of a pin. If the end of the pin appears to reach halfway between 2.8 and 2.9 cm, we might estimate that the pin is 2.85 cm long. However, another person might make an estimate of 2.86 cm. In this case, the first two digits (numbers) in each measurement are the same. These digits are called the certain numbers of the measurement. The third digit, which varies depending on who made the measurement, is called the uncertain number. When making measurements, scientists usually use all the certain numbers plus the first uncertain number.

In a measurement, all the certain numbers together with the first uncertain number are called *significant figures.* In doing calculations, it is important to know how much uncertainty is present in the measurements being used. Scientists have established rules for counting significant figures. If the result of a calculation has too many significant figures, we reduce it to fewer digits by a process known as *rounding off..*

5.3   Problem Solving and Unit Conversions

Key Terms

conversion factor	equivalence statement	dimensional analysis
Fahrenheit scale	Celsius scale	Kelvin (absolute) scale
density	specific gravity	

Summary

To change a measurement from one unit to another, we use a *conversion factor,* which is a number that shows the relationship between two different units of measurement. Table 5.7 shows some conversion factors between English units and metric units. To convert a measure from one unit to another, we generally multiply or divide the known unit by the correct conversion factor.

The three temperature scales are the *Fahrenheit, Celsius,* and *Kelvin (absolute)* scales. On the Fahrenheit scale, water boils at 212°F and freezes at 32°F. On the Celsius scale, water boils at 100°C and freezes at 0°C. On the Kelvin scale, water boils at 373 K and freezes at 273 K. The size of the degrees is the same in the Kelvin and Celsius scales. The Fahrenheit degree is smaller than the Celsius and Kelvin unit, and the zero points are different on all three scales.

To convert a Celsius temperature to a Kelvin temperature, add 273 to the Celsius temperature. To convert a Kelvin temperature to a Celsius temperature, subtract 273 from the Kelvin temperature. To convert Celsius to Fahrenheit, multiply the Celsius temperature by 1.80 and add 32. To convert Fahrenheit to Celsius, subtract 32 from the Fahrenheit temperature and then divide the result by 1.80.

Density is the amount of matter present in a given volume of a substance. Another way to express density is mass per unit volume. To calculate density, divide mass by volume. The common unit of density is grams per cubic centimeter (g/cm^3). The density of a liquid is sometimes described as *specific gravity,* the ratio of the density of a given liquid to the density of water at 4°C.

Additional Active Reading Questions

1. What is scientific notation?

2. Express the following numbers in scientific notation: 150, 0.000263, 129,000,000.

3. Name the four fundamental SI units.

4. What is the fundamental SI unit of volume?

5. Which numbers in the following pair are certain numbers? Which are uncertain numbers? 578.43, 578.42

6. Which digits in a number are always counted as significant figures?

7. Round off the following numbers to two digits: 1.657, 75.1, 0.352

8. What is a conversion factor?

9. How do you convert a Kelvin temperature to Celsius? Fahrenheit temperature to Celsius?

10. What is the density of an object with a mass of 30 g and a volume of 6 cm^3?

Chapter 6   Chemical Composition

6.1   Atoms and Moles

Key Terms

atomic mass unit   average atomic mass   mole
Avogadro's number

Summary

A large collection of individual objects can be counted by weighing if the average mass of the objects is known. The principle also applies to atoms.

If the average mass of the atoms of an element is known, the number of atoms in any sample of that element can be determined by weighing the sample. The opposite calculation works as well. If we know the number of atoms in a sample, we can calculate the sample's mass.

Because atoms are so tiny, the units of grams and kilograms are much too large to be convenient. Scientists have defined a much smaller unit of mass to describe the mass of a single atom. This unit is called the *atomic mass unit,* or amu. One amu equals 1.66×10^{-24} g. Every element has an *average atomic mass* in amu.

Two samples whose masses in grams have the same ratio (relation to each other) as the ratio of their average atomic masses in amu always contain the same number of atoms. *Avogadro's number* is 6.022×10^{23}. A *mole* is defined as a unit of measure equal to the number of carbon atoms in 12.01 g of carbon, which equals 6.022×10^{23}.

6.2   Molar Mass and Percent Composition

Key Terms

molar mass   mass percent

Summary

One mole of an element has a mass equal to the element's atomic mass expressed in grams. The *molar mass* of any compound is the mass (in grams) of 1 mol of the compound and is the sum of the masses of the atoms that make it up.

Percent composition consists of the mass percent of each element in a compound. *Mass percent* equals the mass of a given element in 1 mol of compound divided by the mass of 1 mol of that compound multiplied by 100%. To calculate the mass percent of an element in a compound, first we find the individual mass of that element by dividing the mass of that element contained in 1 mol of the compound by the total mass of 1 mol of the compound. Then, to convert the mass fraction to the mass percent, multiply by 100%.

6.3 Formulas of Compounds

Key Terms

empirical formula   molecular formula

Summary

When a chemical reaction gives an unknown product, a chemist can determine what compound
has been formed by figuring out which elements and how many atoms of each element form
the compound. However, when we break a compound down into its separate elements and then
count the atoms present, we learn only the numbers of atoms relative to one another. The
formula that expresses this ratio is called the *empirical formula*. The formula of the compound
that tells how many atoms of each element actually are present in each of the compound's
molecules is called the *molecular formula*. The molecular formula is always a whole-number
multiple of the empirical formula.

There are four basic steps in the calculation of empirical formulas.

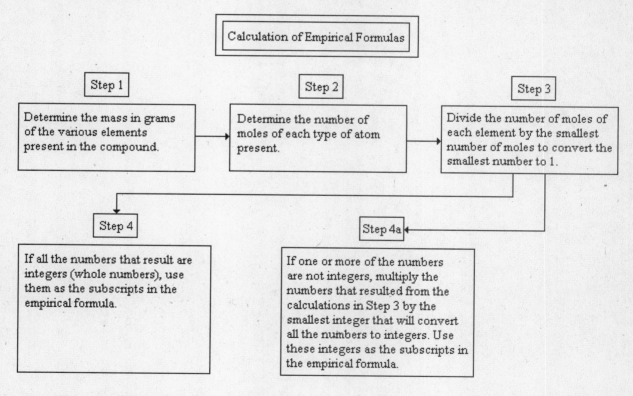

To determine the molecular formula of a compound, we compare the empirical formula mass
to the molar mass. The empirical formula mass is the mass of 1 mol of an empirical formula
unit. The unknown molecular formula is equal to the known empirical formula multiplied by
an unknown whole number. To find the value of the unknown whole number, we divide the
molar mass of the molecular formula by the empirical formula mass. This calculation tells us

the number of empirical formula masses that are present in one molar mass. The subscripts in the empirical formula then are multiplied by that number to get the molecular formula.

Additional Active Reading Questions

1. What factor must be known in order to count the units in a sample by weighing it?

2. What is an atomic mass unit? What is its value?

3. What are the two names for the number 6.022×10^{23}?

4. What is the molar mass of a compound? How is it determined?

5. Which type of formula describes the numbers of atoms in a compound relative to one another?

6. When the molar mass of a compound which has the empirical unit, C_5H_4, is divided by the empirical formula mass, the result is 2. What is the compound's molecular formula?

Chapter 7   Chemical Reactions: An Introduction

7.1   Evidence for a Chemical Reaction

Summary

We sometimes can see when a chemical reaction (change) has occurred because chemical reactions often result in visible effects. However, not every chemical reaction produces visible changes. Sometimes the only sign that a chemical reaction has occurred is a change in temperature.

7.2   Chemical Equations

Key Terms

chemical reaction	chemical equation	reactants
products	balanced the chemical equation	

Summary

A *chemical reaction* is a chemical change that occurs when compounds or elements interact with one another. A chemical reaction always involves a rearrangement of the ways in which the atoms are grouped. A *chemical equation* is used to represent a chemical reaction. A chemical equation shows the chemicals present before the reaction, called the *reactants,* and the chemicals formed by the reaction, called the *products,* as well as the relative numbers of atoms of each. An arrow indicates the direction of the change. The reactants are written to the left of the arrow, and the products are written to the right of the arrow. A chemical equation also often shows the physical states of the reactants and products, that is, whether the chemicals are solids, liquids, gases or aqueous (dissolved in water).

7.3   Balancing Chemical Equations

Key Terms

coefficients

Summary

A chemical reaction changes only the way the atoms in the reactants are grouped. Atoms are neither created nor destroyed. Therefore, a chemical equation must show the same number of each type of atom on the product side as on the reactant side. An equation that obeys this rule is a *balanced chemical equation.*

A chemical equation can be balanced by means of the following four-step process: (1) Identify the reactants and products and write the formulas. (2) Write the unbalanced equation. (3) Balance by trial and error, starting with the most complicated molecules. Without changing the formulas of any of the molecules, determine how many of each type of molecules needs to be on each side of the equation. The numbers that show the numbers of molecules are called *coefficients.* The best balanced equation has the smallest coefficients. (4) Double-check to make sure that the number and types of atoms are the same on each side of the equation.

Additional Active Reading Questions

1. What are some of the signs indicating that a chemical reaction has taken place?

2. What is a chemical reaction?

3. Identify the reactant(s) and the product(s) in the following reaction:
   $P_4(s) + 10 Br_2(l) \rightarrow 4 PBr_5(s)$. Is the equation balanced?

4. What does the arrow stand for in a chemical equation?

5. Describe a balanced equation.

6. What is the name for the numbers that show how many molecules need to be on each side of an equation for the equation to be balanced?

Chapter 8   Reactions in Aqueous Solutions

8.1   Understanding Reactions in Aqueous Solutions

Key Terms

precipitation	precipitate	precipitation reaction
strong electrolyte	soluble solid	molecular equation
complete ionic equation	spectator ions	net ionic equation
insoluble solid (slightly soluble solid)		

Summary

Reactants have several basic tendencies, or ways of behaving, when they are brought into contact with one another: the tendency to form a solid, to form water, to transfer electrons, or. to form a gas. Chemists consider these tendencies as driving forces for chemical reactions because two or more chemical compounds are likely to react with one another if any of these results can occur. Knowing these driving forces can help chemists make predictions about whether a reaction will take place between chemicals and what products may form. .

Solids can form in chemical reactions in a process called *precipitation*. The solid that forms is called a *precipitate*, and the reaction is called a *precipitation reaction*. Understanding the general rules on how substances dissolve in water helps chemists predict whether and what type of solid might form when two solutions are mixed.

Three types of equations are used to describe chemical reactions in solution: a *molecular equation*, a *complete ionic equation*, and a *net ionic equation*.

Equations for Reactions in Aqueous Solution		
Molecular Equation	Complete Ionic Equation	Net Ionic Equation
Shows complete formulas for all reactants and products	Shows all reactants and products that are strong electrolytes as ions	Includes only those parts of the solution that undergo a chemical change
$NaCl(aq) + AgNO_3(aq) \rightarrow$ $AgCl(s) + NaNO_3(aq)$	$Na^+(aq) + Cl^-(aq) + Ag^+(aq) +$ $NO_3^-(aq) \rightarrow AgCl(s) + Na^+(aq) +$ $NO_3^-(aq)$	$Cl^-(aq) + Ag^+(aq) \rightarrow AgCl(s)$

8.2   Other Reactions in Aqueous Solutions

Key Terms

acid	strong acid	base
strong base	salt	oxidation–reduction reaction

Summary

A *strong acid* is a compound in which almost every molecule dissociates (separates) to produce an H^+ ion and an anion when it dissolves in water. A *strong base* is a compound that dissolves in water to produce OH^- (hydroxide) ions and cations. When a strong acid and a strong base react, the H^+ ions from the *acid* combine with the OH^- ions from the *base* to produce water. The other ions react to produce an ionic compound called a *salt*. The reaction of H^+ and OH^- is often called an acid–base reaction.

Reactions of metals with nonmetals, called *oxidation–reduction reactions,* involve a transfer of electrons. In this type of reaction, an ionic compound is formed. The ions are formed when the metal transfers one or more electrons to the nonmetal. As a result, the metal atom becomes a cation, and the nonmetal atom becomes an anion. Two nonmetals also can undergo an oxidation–reduction reaction. When two nonmetals react, the compound formed is not ionic.

8.3 Classifying Reactions

Key Terms

double-displacement reaction   acid–base reaction   single-replacement reaction
combustion reactions   decomposition reaction   synthesis (combination) reaction

Summary

In one type of chemical reaction, the atoms of an element replace the atoms of another element that is part of a compound. This type of reaction is called a *single-replacement reaction* because only one type of anion is exchanged. A single-replacement reaction can be expressed this way: $A + BC \rightarrow B + AC$. In another type of reaction, a precipitation reaction, compounds exchange their anions to form two new compounds. For this reason, a precipitation reaction is also called a *double-displacement reaction.* Such a reaction can be represented this way: $AB + CD \rightarrow AD + CB$.

Oxidation–reduction reactions that involve oxygen and produce heat and flame are called *combustion reactions.* When a compound is formed from simpler materials, such as elements, the reaction is called a *synthesis reaction,* or a *combination reaction.* The opposite also can occur. A reaction can break a compound down into the elements that make it up. This type of reaction is called a *decomposition reaction.*

Additional Active Reading Questions

1. Name four driving forces for chemical reactions.

2. What is the product of a precipitation reaction?

3. How do a complete ionic equation and a net ionic equation differ?

4. Which two types of ions are involved in an acid–base reaction?

5. When are ions formed in an oxidation–reduction reaction?

6. What type of reaction can be represented $A + BC \rightarrow B + AC$? $AB + CD \rightarrow AD + CB$?

7. What is a synthesis reaction?

Chapter 9   Chemical Quantities

9.1   Using Chemical Equations

Key Term

mole ratio

Summary

The equation for a chemical reaction shows the relative numbers of reactant and product molecules needed for the reaction to take place. Using the equation makes it possible to determine the amounts of reactants needed to give a certain amount of product or to predict how much product we can make from a certain amount of reactants.

A balanced equation uses coefficients (numbers) to show the relative numbers of molecules or moles of molecules. We can use a balanced equation to predict the moles of products that a given number of moles of reactants will yield using conversion factors or mole ratios. The *mole ratio* is the ratio of moles of one substance to moles of another substance in a balanced equation. The mole ratios then can be used in calculations.

9.2   Using Chemical Equations to Calculate Mass

Key Term

stoichiometry

Summary

Converting between moles and masses is often used in dealing with chemical reactions. If we know the balanced equation for a reaction and the mass of one of the substances involved, we can perform calculations to determine various unknown quantities.

To calculate the amount, in grams, of one reactant that is needed to react exactly with a known amount of another reactant, we follow three steps: (1) Convert the known mass of the substance from grams to moles by using the substance's molar mass. (2) Use the coefficients in the balanced equation to determine how many moles of the other reactant are required. (3) Use the molar mass of the reactant in step 2 to convert that measurement from moles to grams.

The steps for calculating the masses of reactants and products in chemical reactions are as follows: (1) Balance the equation for the reaction. (2) Convert the masses of reactants or products to moles. (3) Use the balanced equation to set up the appropriate mole ratio or ratios. (4) Use the mole ratio or ratios to calculate the number of moles of the desired reactant or product. (5) Convert from moles back to mass.

The process of using a chemical equation to calculate the relative masses of reactants and products involved in a reaction is called *stoichiometry*. Chemists say that the balanced equation for a chemical reaction describes the stoichiometry of the reaction.

Comparing the stoichiometry of two reactions means comparing the moles of reactants and products involved in the chemical reactions. This process can be useful in determining the amounts of different reactants needed to react with a certain amount of another reactant. For example, both baking soda, $NaHCO_3$, and milk of magnesia, $Mg(OH)_2(s)$, can neutralize hydrochloric acid, HCl. Stoichiometric calculations can determine which substance can neutralize more hydrochloric acid per gram.

9.3 Limiting Reactants and Percent Yield

Key Terms

limiting reactant (limiting reagent)   theoretical yield   percent yield

Summary

Often reactants are not mixed in stoichiometric quantities. They do not "run out" at the same time, and the reaction stops when one of the reactants runs out. In this case, we must use the *limiting reactant (limiting reagent),* the reactant that runs out first, to calculate the amounts of products formed. Chemists solve stoichiometry problems involving limiting reactants using the following steps: (1) Write and balance the equation for the reaction. (2) Convert the known masses of reactants to moles. (3) Using the numbers of moles of reactants and the appropriate mole ratios, determine which reactant is limiting. (4) Using the amount of the limiting reactant and the appropriate mole ratios, compute the number of moles of the desired product. (5) Convert from moles of product to grams of product using the molar mass (if this is required by the problem).

In a chemical reaction, products stop forming when the limiting reactant runs out. The amount of product that is predicted to be formed as a result of calculations using the limiting reactant is known as the reaction's *theoretical yield*. The actual yield of a reaction, which is the amount of product actually obtained, is usually less than its theoretical yield. The actual yield of product often is compared with the theoretical yield. This comparison, usually expressed as a percentage, is called the *percent yield*. The actual yield divided by the theoretical yield all times 100% equals the percent yield.

Additional Active Reading Questions

1. Describe the basic information given by a chemical equation.

2. What is the term for the ratio of moles of one substance to moles of another substance in a balanced chemical equation?

3. The molar mass of manganese is 54.94 g/mol. How many moles does a 219.76-g sample of manganese contain?

4. What is the process of using a chemical equation to calculate the relative amounts of reactants and products involved in a reaction?

5. When does a chemical reaction stop?

6. If the actual yield of a reaction is 22.5 g of titanium(II) oxide and the theoretical yield is 25.0 g, what is the percent yield?

Chapter 10   Energy

10.1   Energy, Temperature, and Heat

Key Terms

energy

law of conservation of energy

temperature

surroundings

potential energy

work

heat

exothermic

kinetic energy

state function

system

Summary

Energy is the ability to do *work* (a force acting over a distance) or produce heat. It can be classified as *potential energy* (energy that results from an object's or substance's position or composition) or as *kinetic energy* (energy of motion). The *law of conservation of energy* states that energy can be changed from one form to another but can be neither created nor destroyed.

A *state function* is a property of a *system* (the part of the universe in which a process occurs) that changes independently of its pathway (the specific conditions under which the change occurs). A state function depends only on the beginning and final states of the system. Energy is a state function. Other functions, such as heat and work, depend on the specific pathway followed and are not state functions.

Temperature is a measure of the random motions of the particles that make up a substance. *Heat* is defined as the flow of energy that results from a temperature difference. The thermal energy of an object is the energy content of the object as produced by the random motions of its particles.

In an *exothermic* process, heat flows out of a system into its *surroundings*. In an endothermic process, heat flows from the surroundings into a system. In any exothermic chemical reaction, some of the potential energy stored in the substances' chemical bonds is converted to thermal energy (random kinetic energy) by means of heat.

10.2   The Flow of Energy

Key Terms

thermodynamics

calorie

first law of thermodynamics

joule

internal energy

Summary

Thermodynamics is the study of energy and its changes. The *first law of thermodynamics* states that the energy of the universe is constant. The *internal energy* (E) of a system is the sum of the kinetic and potential energies of all the particles in the system. The internal energy can be changed by a flow of work, heat, or both.

The heat required to change the temperature of a substance depends on the number of grams of the substance being heated, the temperature change, and the type of substance.

A substance's specific heat is the amount of energy required to change the temperature of one gram of the substance by one degree Celsius. The energy required equals the specific heat capacity times the mass of the sample in grams times the change in temperature in degrees Celsius. This is represented by the equation $Q = s \times m \times \Delta T$.

10.3   Energy and Chemical Reactions

Key Terms

enthalpy   calorimeter   Hess's law

Summary

Enthalpy (H) is the heat flow that occurs for a process carried out at constant pressure, For this case, the change in enthalpy equals the energy flow as heat. This is represented by the equation ΔH_p = heat.

Enthalpy is a state function. The change in enthalpy in a particular process is unrelated to the pathway for the process. As a result, during the change from a certain set of reactants to a certain set of products, the change in enthalpy is the same whether the reaction takes place in one step or in a series of steps. This principle is known as *Hess's law*. Hess's law allows chemists to calculate the heat of a reaction from known heats of related reactions.

10.4   Using Energy in the Real World

Key Terms

fossil fuels	petroleum	natural gas
coal	greenhouse effect	energy spread
matter spread	entropy	second law of thermodynamics

Summary

Although energy is conserved in every process, the quality (usefulness) of the energy decreases with each use. Energy is more useful when it is concentrated, such as the energy stored in gasoline.

Our world has many sources of energy. *Petroleum* is made up mostly of compounds called hydrocarbons. *Natural gas* consists mostly of methane. *Coal* was formed when plant material containing cellulose was chemically changed by heat and pressure. All these energy sources are *fossil fuels*.

The use of fossil fuels affects the environment in various ways. As we have burned increasing amounts of fossil fuels, the carbon dioxide concentration in the atmosphere has increased.

Carbon dioxide traps the sun's heat energy near earth's surface, a condition called the *greenhouse effect*. The increase in CO_2 eventually might raise the earth's average temperature enough to cause dramatic changes in climate.

Natural processes occur in the direction that leads to an increase in the *entropy* (*S*), or disorder of the universe. The principal driving forces for processes are energy spread and matter spread. *Energy spread* means that in a given process, concentrated energy is spread out widely. Energy spread occurs in every exothermic process. In *matter spread,* the molecules of a substance are spread out over a larger volume. Energy spread and matter spread lead to greater *entropy*. This fact leads to the *second law of thermodynamics:* The entropy of the universe is always increasing.

Additional Active Reading Questions

1. State the law of conservation of energy.

2. What is the difference between temperature and heat?

3. In what type of process does heat flow out of a system into its surroundings?

4. What is the term for the sum of the kinetic and potential energies of all the particles in a system?

5. What concept is expressed by the equation $Q = s \times m \times \Delta T$?

6. Define *enthalpy*.

7. What law provides a way for chemists to calculate the heat of a reaction from known heats of related reactions?

8. Why is it important to develop sources of energy other than the burning of fossil fuels?

9. What are the relationships among energy spread, matter spread, and entropy?

Chapter 11   Modern Atomic Theory

11.1 Atoms and Energy

Key Terms

electromagnetic radiation   wavelength   frequency
photons

Summary

In Rutherford's concept of the nuclear atom, negatively charged electrons move around the nucleus in some way. He couldn't explain, however, why the negative electrons aren't attracted into the positive nucleus, causing the atom to collapse. More observations of the atom were needed.

Energy can be transmitted by *electromagnetic radiation,* which travels through space in the form of waves. The various types of electromagnetic radiation differ in their *wavelengths* and amounts of energy. Each color of visible light has a different wavelength. Light also has properties that are more like those of particles rather than waves. A beam of light therefore can be thought of as a stream of tiny packets of energy called *photons.*

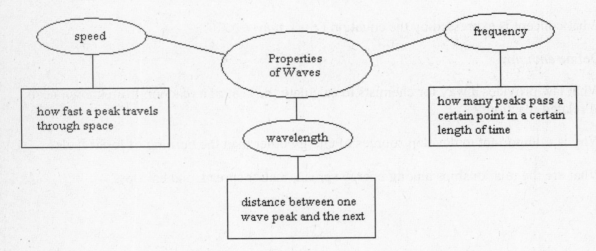

When an atom receives energy from some source, it becomes excited, and it can release this energy by emitting (giving off) light, which is carried away by a photon. The energy of the photon is exactly the same as the energy change of the emitting atom. Short-wavelength light has high-energy photons, and long-wavelength light has low-energy photons.

11.2 The Hydrogen Atom

Key Terms

quantized   wave mechanical model

Summary

When hydrogen atoms are excited, only certain colors of visible light are emitted; that is, only certain types of photons are produced. This tells us that only certain energy changes are occurring. The hydrogen atom must have certain discrete (separate and unique) energy levels. Excited hydrogen atoms always emit photons with the same discrete colors (wavelengths). They never emit photons with energies in between. We can conclude that all hydrogen atoms have the same set of discrete energy levels. The energy levels of atoms are *quantized,* which means that only certain values are allowed.

The Bohr model of the hydrogen atom postulated that an electron moves in circular orbits that match the allowed orbits. The Bohr model worked well for hydrogen but not for other atoms.

According to the *wave mechanical model* of the atom, an electron has the characteristics of both waves and particles. Electron states are described by orbitals. Orbitals are defined as probability maps that are collections of points that indicate how likely it is to find the electron at a given position in space. The wave mechanical model can describe only the probabilities, or likelihoods, of finding the electron in any given point in space around the nucleus. The probability of the electron's presence is highest closest to the positive nucleus.

11.3 Atomic Orbitals

Key Terms

orbital   sublevels   principal energy levels
Pauli exclusion principle

Summary

The probability map for a hydrogen electron is called an *orbital.* The orbital size can be thought of as a surface containing 90% of the total electron probability. The electron can be found inside the sphere 90% of the time.

The discrete energy levels are called *principal energy levels,* and they are labeled with integers (whole numbers) symbolized by n. Level 1 is $n = 1$, level 2 is $n = 2$, and so on. The energy of the level increases as the value of n increases. Each of these levels is divided into *sublevels,* or types of orbitals. The number of sublevels present in a principal energy level equals n.

Orbitals have different shapes. They can be spherical (labeled s) or two-lobed (labeled p). When labeling an orbital, the n value is followed by a letter that indicates the type (shape) of orbital. The designation $3p$ stands for an orbital in level 3 that has two lobes.

All electrons appear to spin as a top spins on its axis. An electron can spin in only one of two directions. An orbital can be empty, or it can contain one or two electrons, but never more than two. According to the *Pauli exclusion principle,* an atomic orbital can hold a maximum of two electrons, and those electrons must have opposite spins.

11.4 Electron Configurations and Atomic Properties

Key Terms

electron configuration	orbital (box) diagram	valence electrons
core electrons	lanthanide series	actinide series
metals	nonmetals	metalloids
ionization energy	atomic size	main-group elements (representative elements)

Summary

For the first 18 elements, the sublevels fill in the following order: $1s$, $2s$, $2p$, $3s$, $3p$. The $1s$ orbital always fills first because in this orbital the negatively charged electron is closer to the positively charged nucleus than in any other orbital. As n increases, the orbital becomes larger. The electron, on average, occupies space farther from the nucleus.

The arrangement of electrons in an atom is called its *electron configuration.* The hydrogen atom, with its lone electron in the $1s$ orbital, has an electron configuration of $1s^1$. This same configuration can be represented by an *orbital (box) diagram.*

Valence electrons are those in the outermost, or highest, principal energy level of an atom. Valence electrons are the electrons involved when atoms form bonds. The inner electrons are called *core electrons.* They are not involved in bonding.

The principles of orbital filling for elements from element 19 (potassium) on are different from those of the first 18 elements. In these elements, a higher principal energy level starts to fill before the previous one is complete. In a principal energy level that has d orbitals, the s orbital from the next level fills before the d orbitals in the current level. The $(n + 1)s$ orbitals fill before the nd orbitals. Figure 11.23 in the text shows the order in which atomic orbitals fill.

Elements with similar properties repeat in a particular pattern on the periodic table because the same types of orbitals repeat as one principal energy level progresses to the next. As a result, particular patterns of valence electrons repeat periodically. Elements with similar valence-electron patterns show very similar chemical behavior.

The basic classification of the chemical elements is into metals and nonmetals. *Metals* tend to lose electrons to form positive ions and are found at the left and center of the periodic table. The most chemically active metals have electrons in orbitals farthest away from the nucleus. *Nonmetals* tend to gain electrons to form negative ions. The most chemically active nonmetals can pull electrons most easily from metals.

The size of an atom is related to the principal energy level and the number of protons in its nucleus. As we go down a group, the principal energy level increases, so the average distance of the electrons from the nucleus also increases. Atoms with their outermost electrons in the same principal energy level get smaller from left to right across a period (horizontal row on the periodic table). This is because their number of protons increases, causing an increase in positive charge, which pulls electrons closer to the nucleus.

Ionization energy, the energy required to remove an electron from a gaseous atom, decreases going down a group and increases going from left to right across a period.

Additional Active Reading Questions

1. What are three basic properties of waves?

2. Which kind of light has higher-energy photons—short-wavelength light or long-wavelength light?

3. What does it mean to say that all atoms are quantized?

4. What is a probability map?

5. Where is the probability of an electron's presence highest?

6. What is the term for the probability map for an electron?

7. What is the relationship between a principal energy level and a sublevel?

8. Describe the Pauli exclusion principle.

9. What is the arrangement of electrons in an atom called?

10. For the first 18 elements, in what order do the individual sublevels fill?

11. Which electrons occupy the outermost, or highest, principal energy level of an atom?

12. Describe the position of the electrons in the most chemically active metals.

Chapter 12   Chemical Bonding

12.1   Characteristics of Chemical Bonds

Key Terms

bonds

ionic compound

electronegativity

bond energy

covalent bond

dipole moment

ionic bond

polar covalent bond

Summary

Chemical *bonds* hold groups of atoms together. They can be classified into several types. An *ionic bond* is formed when a transfer of electrons occurs to form ions. In a purely *covalent bond*, electrons are shared equally between identical atoms. Between these extremes lies the *polar covalent bond*, in which electrons are shared unequally between atoms.

Electronegativity is the relative ability of an atom in a molecule to attract shared electrons to itself. Electronegativity values have been calculated for most of the elements. The higher an element's electronegativity value, the more strongly the atoms of that element attract the electrons in a chemical bond. As a result, the shared electrons tend to be closer to that element's atoms when they form a bond.

A molecule with a center of positive charge and one of negative charge is said to have a *dipole moment*.

12.2   Characteristics of Ions and Ionic Compounds

Summary

In almost all stable chemical compounds, the atoms tend to achieve the valence-electron formation of one of the noble gases. When a nonmetal and a Group 1, 2, or 3 metal react to form a binary ionic compound, the ions form in such a way that the valence-electron configuration of the nonmetal is completed (by gaining one or more electrons) to achieve the electron configuration of the next noble gas on the periodic table. The valence-electron configuration of the metal is emptied (by giving up one or more electrons) to achieve the electron configuration of the previous noble gas on the periodic table. When two nonmetals react to form a covalent bond, they share electrons in a way that completes the valence-electron configurations of both atoms. Both the nonmetals take on the valence-electron configuration of a noble gas by sharing electrons.

When metals and nonmetals form ionic compounds, the attraction between the oppositely charged cations and anions results in very strong bonds and stable molecules. Polyatomic ions (charge units made up of several atoms) with opposite charges attract each other in the same way. However, the individual atoms that make up the polyatomic ions are held together by covalent rather than ionic bonds.

12.3 Lewis Structures

Key Terms

Lewis structures   duet rule   octet rule
bonding pair   lone pairs (unshared pairs)   single bond
double bond   triple bond   resonance

Summary

Lewis structures are simple diagrams that show the arrangement of the valence electrons in a molecule. Because bonding involves only the valence electrons of atoms, when writing Lewis structures, only the valence electrons are included. When forming stable molecules, hydrogen follows the *duet rule,* which means that each hydrogen atom in H_2 has two shared electrons. In the case of many other atoms, a stable molecule is formed only when one *s* and three *p* orbitals are filled. This requires them to follow the *octet rule,* to be surrounded by eight electrons.

Some molecules require double or triple bonds to satisfy the octet rule. In a *double bond,* two atoms share two pairs of electrons. In a *triple bond,* two atoms share three electron pairs. These bonds can be assigned to the atom pairs in more than one way. As a result, some molecules have more than one possible Lewis structure. This property is called *resonance.*

12.4 Structures of Molecules

Key Terms

molecular (geometric) structure   linear structure
trigonal planar structure   trigonal pyramid
valence shell electron pair repulsion tetrahedral structure
(VSEPR) model

Summary

The *molecular (geometric) structure* of a molecule shows how the atoms are arranged in space. There are three types of planar, or flat, structures. In a bent, or V-shaped, structure, the atoms are arranged in the shape of a V with about a 105° bond angle. In a *linear structure,* all atoms are arranged in a line, that is, with a 180° bond angle. A *trigonal planar structure* has three atoms arranged at 120° bond angles around a central atom. A *tetrahedral structure* is a three-dimensional structure with four atoms arranged at 109.5° bond angles around a central atom. Section 12.4 in the text has illustrations of these bond angles.

The molecular structure of a molecule can be predicted by using the *valence shell electron pair repulsion (VSEPR) model.* The main idea of this model is that the structure around a given atom is determined by minimizing repulsions between electron pairs. The electron pairs around a given atom are positioned as far apart as possible. Whenever two pairs of electrons surround an atom, the molecule has a linear structure, three pairs form a trigonal planar structure, and four pairs form a tetrahedral structure.

In using the VSEPR model for molecules with double and triple bonds, each double and triple bond should be treated the same as a single bond. As a result, the rules for modeling molecular structures for molecules with double and triple bonds are exactly the same as those for molecules with single bonds.

Additional Active Reading Questions

1. Describe the three types of chemical bonds.

2. What is the term for the relative ability of an atom in a molecule to attract shared electrons to itself?

3. What types of atoms do the atoms in stable chemical compounds resemble?

4. Why are ionic compounds so stable?

5. What are Lewis structures?

6. List the four molecular structures and their bond angles.

7. How are repulsions between electron pairs minimized in the VSEPR model?

Chapter 13　Gases

13.1　Describing the Properties of Gases

Key Terms

barometer	torr (mm Hg)	standard atmosphere
pascal	Boyle's law	absolute zero
Charles's law	Avogadro's law	

Summary

Gases exert pressure on their surroundings. A *barometer* measures atmospheric pressure. In a barometer, the weight of the atmosphere presses on mercury in a dish, forcing the mercury up a thin tube. At sea level, the height of the column of mercury averages 760 mm. This measurement results in a commonly used unit of measurement for atmospheric pressure, millimeters of mercury (*mm Hg*), or the *torr*. Another unit of measurement is the *standard atmosphere* (atm). The SI unit for pressure is the *pascal* (Pa). The relationship among these units is as follows:

$$1.000 \text{ atm} = 760.0 \text{ mm Hg} = 760.0 \text{ torr} = 101{,}325 \text{ Pa}$$

As the volume of a trapped gas increases, its pressure decreases (at constant temperature and moles of gas). Pressure and volume are inversely proportional. This relationship between pressure and volume can be expressed as an equation, $PV = k$, which means that pressure times volume equals a constant value. This relationship is known as *Boyle's law.*

Charles's law is expressed by the equation $V = bT$, which means that for given sample of gas at constant pressure, volume equals temperature in kelvins times a constant value. Volume and temperature (in kelvins) are directly proportional. Charles's law suggests that every type of gas reaches a volume of zero when it reaches a certain temperature, $-273°C$, which is defined as *absolute zero* on the Kelvin scale.

Avogadro's law states that the volume of a gas is directly proportional to the number of moles if temperature and pressure remain constant. This relationship can be expressed by the following equations: $V = an$ or $V/n = a$.

13.2　Using Gas Laws to Solve Problems

Key Terms

universal gas constant	ideal gas law	ideal gas
combined gas law	partial pressures	molar volume
Dalton's law of partial pressures	standard temperature and pressure (STP)	

Summary

Boyle's law, Charles's law, and Avogadro's law can be combined into the *ideal gas law,* or *PV = nRT,* where *P* stands for pressure, *V* for volume, *n* for number of moles, *T* for temperature, and *R* stands for the *universal gas constant,* which combines the constants of the three individual gas laws. It is equal to 0.08206 L · atm/K · mol, or 8.314 J/K · mol.

Dalton's law of partial pressures states that for a mixture of gases in a container, the total pressure exerted is the sum of the *partial pressures* (the pressures that individual gases would exert if they were alone in a container) of the gases present.

The ideal gas equation makes it possible to calculate the number of moles present in a sample if its pressure, volume, and temperature are known. The *molar volume* of an ideal gas is 22.4 L at 0°C (273 K) and 1 atm. The conditions 0°C and 1 atm are called *standard temperature and pressure* (STP).

13.3 Using a Model to Describe Gases

Key Terms

kinetic molecular theory

Summary

A law is a general statement about behavior that has been observed in many experiments. Laws do not explain why nature behaves the way it does. Theories, or models, attempt to answer this question. Models in chemistry are explanations about how individual atoms or molecules cause the behavior of substances that can be observed.

The *kinetic molecular theory* tries to explain the behavior of an ideal gas. This theory is based on certain postulates, or assumptions. The postulates best explain the behavior of real gases at high temperatures and low pressures.

Postulates Supporting the Kinetic Molecular Theory of Ideal Gas Behavior				
1	2	3	4	5
Gases are made up of tiny particles.	These particles are so small compared with the distances between them that the volume of the individual particles can be treated as zero.	The particles are in constant random motion. Their collisions with the walls of the container cause the pressure of the gas.	The particles neither attract nor repel (drive away) one another.	As the temperature increases, the motion of the particles (and therefore their kinetic energy) increases.

Heating a gas to a higher temperature causes its particles to move faster and hit the walls of its container more often and more forcefully. As a result, pressure increases as temperature increases. If the container is flexible, the gas's volume increases as a result.

Under conditions of high pressure and small volume, real gases behave differently from ideal gases and do not obey the ideal gas law ($PV = nRT$) very well.

Additional Active Reading Questions

1. What is the value in atmospheres of 770. mm Hg?

2. State Boyle's law.

3. What is significant about the temperature –273°C?

4. What is the formula that expresses the ideal gas law? Which three gas laws does it combine?

5. Compute the total pressure for the following mixture of gases: $N_2 = 0.12$ atm, $CO_2 = 0.70$ atm.

6. Describe the postulate of the kinetic molecular theory that relates the average kinetic energy of a gas to its temperature.

7. What change causes the volume and the pressure of gases to increase?

8. What is the volume of 1 mol of an ideal gas at STP?

Chapter 14   Liquids and Solids

14.1   Intermolecular Forces and Phase Changes

Key Terms

intermolecular forces	intramolecular forces	dipole–dipole attraction
hydrogen bonding	London dispersion force	normal boiling point
heating/cooling curve	normal freezing point	molar heat of fusion
molar heat of vaporization		

Summary

Intermolecular forces are forces that occur between molecules. Several types of intermolecular forces exist. Molecules with dipole moments can attract one another by lining up so that the positive and negative ends are close to each other. This is a *dipole–dipole attraction.* *Hydrogen bonding* is a type of particularly strong dipole–dipole force.

Another intermolecular force, the *London dispersion force,* is the only weak force that exists among noble gas atoms and nonpolar molecules. In order for the London dispersion force to hold atoms into a solid, the motions of the atoms must be greatly slowed down.

Pure water is a colorless, tasteless substance that at 1 atm vaporizes to form a gas at 100°C. This temperature is the *normal boiling point* for water. The temperature stays at 100°C until all the water has changed to vapor. At this point, the temperature begins to rise again. When liquid water is cooled, the temperature decreases until it reaches 0°C, at which it begins to freeze. This temperature is the *normal freezing point* of water. The temperature remains at 0°C until all the liquid water has changed to ice and then begins to drop again as cooling continues. This process is the *heating/cooling curve* for water.

Energy is needed to melt ice and vaporize water. The energy needed to melt 1 mol of a substance is the *molar heat of fusion.* The energy needed to change 1 mol of liquid to its vapor is called the *molar heat of vaporization.*

14.2   Vapor Pressure and Boiling Point

Key Terms

vaporization (evaporation)	condensation	vapor pressure

Summary

The escape of molecules from a liquid's surface to form a gas is called *vaporization* or *evaporation.* To escape into the vapor phase, an atom or molecule must have enough kinetic energy to overcome the liquid's intermolecular forces. Thus only the fastest-moving atoms or molecules can escape the surface of the liquid. The average energy of the remaining atoms or molecules then decreases. As this happens, the temperature decreases. Therefore, evaporation is a cooling process. It is endothermic.

The process by which vapor molecules form a liquid is *condensation.* In a closed container, there is a transfer of molecules back and forth between the liquid and the vapor phases. Eventually, the same number of molecules is leaving the liquid as is returned to it: The rate of condensation equals the rate of evaporation. The system is at equilibrium. The pressure of the vapor present at equilibrium with its liquid is the *vapor pressure* of the liquid.

Water boils at 1 atm only when it reaches 100°C because of the relationship between temperature and vapor pressure.

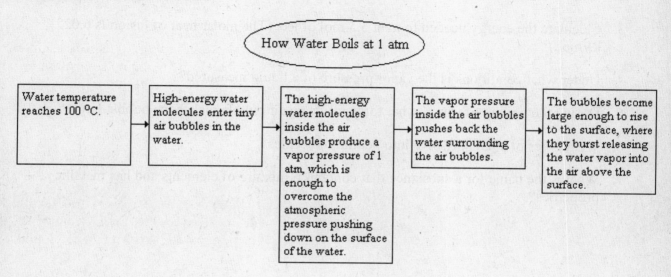

14.3 Properties of Solids

Key Terms

crystalline solids ionic solid molecular solids
atomic solids electron sea model alloy
substitutional alloy interstitial alloy

Summary

Many substances from *crystalline solids,* which have a regular arrangement of their atoms or molecules. An *ionic solid* contains ions. Molecules form *molecular solids. Atomic solids* contain atoms of only one element covalently bonded to one another.

The properties of a solid are determined mainly by the nature of the forces that hold the solid together, that is, differences in bonding. The particles of ionic solids are held together by the strong forces that exist between oppositely charged ions. In a molecular solid, the fundamental particle is a molecule.

According to the *electron sea model,* metal atoms are arranged in a regular pattern in a "sea" of freely moving valence electrons that are shared among the atoms in a nondirectional way. Because of the nature of the metallic crystal, other elements can be introduced relatively easily to produce substances called *alloys.* An alloy is a substance that contains a mixture of elements and has metallic properties.

Additional Active Reading Questions

1. What is a dipole–dipole attraction?

2. What is the normal freezing point of water? the normal boiling point?

3. Calculate the energy needed to melt 3.5 mol of ice. (The molar heat of fusion is 6.02 kJ/mol.)

4. Under what conditions is the vapor pressure of a liquid measured?

5. During the boiling of water, what force inside an air bubble makes the bubble larger?

6. What types of solids dissolve into neutral molecules?

7. What is the name for a substance that contains a mixture of elements and has metallic properties?

Chapter 15   Solutions

15.1   Forming Solutions

Key Terms

solution	solvents	solutes
aqueous solution	saturated	unsaturated
supersaturated	concentrated	dilute

Summary

When ionic substances dissolve in water, they break up into individual anions and cations that are spread evenly throughout the water. The negative end of the water molecule is attracted to the cation, whereas the positive end is attracted to the anion. Polar substances dissolve in water in a similar way. The molecules of substances not soluble in water are not attracted to water molecules.

As a general rule, *solvents* (substances that do the dissolving) usually dissolve *solutes* (substances to be dissolved) with polarities similar to their own.

A *solution* is a mixture in which the individual parts are homogeneously blended. When a solution contains as much solute as it can dissolve at that temperature, it is said to be *saturated*. A solution that has not reached the limit of solute that can be dissolved is *unsaturated*. Sometimes when a saturated solution at a high temperature is cooled quickly, all the solute will remain dissolved. This type of solution is called a *supersaturated* solution and usually is unstable. A *concentrated* solution has a relatively large amount of solute dissolved in it. A *dilute* solution contains a relatively small amount of solute.

The dissolution (dissolving) process may happen quickly or slowly. Three factors affect the speed of the dissolution process.

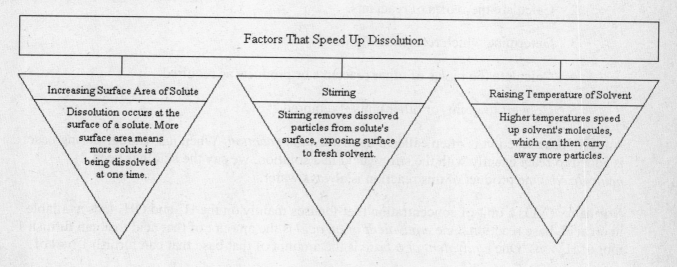

Factors That Speed Up Dissolution

Increasing Surface Area of Solute

Dissolution occurs at the surface of a solute. More surface area means more solute is being dissolved at one time.

Stirring

Stirring removes dissolved particles from solute's surface, exposing surface to fresh solvent.

Raising Temperature of Solvent

Higher temperatures speed up solvent's molecules, which can then carry away more particles.

15.2 Describing Solution Composition

Key Terms

mass percent   molarity (*M*)   standard solution
dilution

Summary

The *mass percent* of a solution's composition is the mass of solute present divided by the total mass of the solution (both solvent and solute) and multiplied by 100%.

Molarity (*M*) expresses the concentration of a solution, or the amount of solute in a given volume of solution. Molarity is the number of moles of solute per volume of solution in liters. A solution in which the concentration is known accurately is called a *standard solution*.

The process of adding more solvent to a solution is called *dilution*.

15.3 Properties of Solutions

Key Terms

neutralization reaction   equivalent of an acid   equivalent of a base
equivalent weight   colligative property

Summary

The following five steps are involved in solving stoichiometric problems involving solutions:

1. Write the balanced equation for the reaction. For reactions involving ions, write the net ionic equation.

2. Calculate the moles of reactants.

3. Determine which reactant is limiting.

4. Calculate the moles of other reactants or products as required.

5. Convert to grams or other units if required.

An acid–base reaction is often called a *neutralization reaction*. When just enough strong base is added to react exactly with the strong acid in a solution, we say the acid has been *neutralized*. One product of this reaction is always water.

Normality (*N*) is a unit of concentration that focuses mainly on the H^+ and OH^- ions available in an acid–base reaction. One *equivalent of an acid* is the amount of that acid that can furnish 1 mol of H^+ ions. One *equivalent of a base* is the amount of that base that can furnish 1 mol of

OH^- ions. The *equivalent weight* of an acid or a base is the mass in grams of 1 equivalent (equiv) of that acid or base.

Normality is defined as the number of equivalents of solute per liter of solution.

The presence of various solutes in solvents affects the boiling points and freezing points of the solvent. Raising of the boiling point of a solvent by a solute is an example of a *colligative property,* which is a property of a solution that depends on the number of solute particles present.

Additional Active Reading Questions

1. Describe the difference between a saturated solution and an unsaturated solution.

2. What are the three factors that speed up dissolution?

3. Calculate the mass percent of a 12,000-g sample of solution containing 846.6 g of solute.

4. What is the molarity of a solution containing 2.7 mol of NaCl in 0.9 L of solution?

5. What is *dilution*?

6. What happens when just enough strong base is added to react exactly with the strong acid in a solution?

7. What is the term for the amount of an acid that can furnish 1 mol of H^+ ions?

8. What is the name for a property of a solution that depends on the number of solute particles present? Give an example.

Chapter 16   Acids and Bases

16.1   Properties of Acids and Bases

Key Terms

acids	bases	Brønsted-Lowry model
Arrhenius concept of acids and bases	conjugate acid	conjugate base
conjugate acid–base pair	hydronium ion	completely ionized (completely dissociated)
strong acid	weak acid	diprotic acid
oxyacids	organic acids	carboxyl group
amphoteric substance	ionization of water	ion-product constant

Summary

The *Arrhenius concept of acids and bases* defines *acids* as substances that produce hydrogen ions in aqueous solutions. *Bases,* on the other hand, produce hydroxide ions. In the *Brønsted-Lowry model,* an *acid* is defined as a proton (H^+) donor, and a *base* is a proton acceptor. A *conjugate acid* is formed when a proton is transferred to the base. A *conjugate base* is everything that remains of the acid molecule after the proton is lost. Two substances related in this way are called a *conjugate acid–base pair.*

Acids are classified as strong or weak depending on a number of characteristics.

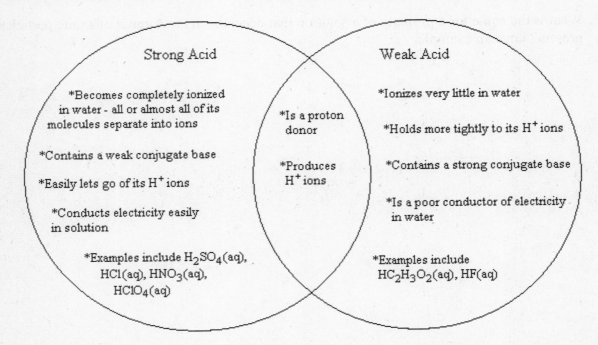

Water can act as either an acid or a base. Such a substance is called an *amphoteric substance.* In pure water, the molecules transfer H^+ ions to produce tiny amounts of H_3O^+ and OH^-. The concentrations for these ions in pure water are always equal and are described by the *ion-product constant* for water K_w. K_w is determined by multiplying the concentrations of H_3O^+ and OH^- at 25°C. The number always equals 1.0×10^{-14} at 25°C.

16.2   Determining the Acidity of a Solution

Key Terms

pH scale   indicators   indicator paper
pH meter

Summary

The *pH scale* represents the acidity of a solution by describing the concentration of H^+ in the solution. Since this number is typically quite small, scientists express it using the pH scale, which is the log of the number multiplied by –1. The equation for calculating pH is $pH = -\log[H^+]$. The lower the pH for a solution, the higher its acidity.

The traditional way of determining the pH of a solution is by using *indicators,* which are substances that turn different colors in acidic and basic solutions. *Indicator paper* is coated with a combination of indicators. It turns a specific color for each pH value. A *pH meter* can measure pH electronically.

If we know a solution contains 1.0 *M* HCl, we can find the pH of the solution by understanding that a 1.0 *M* HCl solution contains H^+ and Cl^- ions rather than HCl molecules. This amount of HCl contains 1.0 *M* H^+, and the pH can be calculated with the following equation:

$$pH = -\log[H^+] = -\log[1.0] = 0$$

16.3   Titrations and Buffers

Key Terms

neutralization reaction   titration   standard solution
buret   stoichiometric (equivalence) point
titration curve (pH curve)   buffered solution

Summary

To analyze the acid or base content of a solution, chemists often perform a titration. A *titration* involves adding a measured volume of a solution of known concentration (the titrant) into the solution being analyzed (the analyte). The titrant contains a substance that reacts in a known way with the analyte. The titrant is added slowly to the analyte until all of the titrant and analyte have reacted. This point is called the *stoichiometric point,* or *equivalence point,* for the titration. For an acid–base titration, the equivalence point can be determined by using a pH meter or indicator. In the titration of a strong acid and a strong base, the equivalence point occurs when an equal amount of H^+ and OH^- have reacted so that the solution is neutral (pH = 7).

A *buffered solution* undergoes only a very slight change in pH when a strong acid or base is added to it. A solution is buffered by the presence of a weak acid and its conjugate base (or vice versa). The buffer resists changes in pH by reacting with any added H^+ or OH^- so that these ions do not form. Any added H^+ reacts with the base. Any added OH^- reacts with the weak acid.

Additional Active Reading Questions

1. Define an acid and a base according to the Brønsted-Lowry model.

2. Name two examples of a weak acid.

3. What is the term for a substance that can act as either an acid or a base?

4. What does a low pH number for a solution indicate?

5. What is a pH indicator?

6. Define *titration*.

7. What is a buffered solution?

Chapter 17   Equilibrium

17.1   Reaction Rates and Equilibrium

Key Terms

collision model   activation energy (E_a)   enzymes
homogeneous reactions   heterogeneous reactions   equilibrium
chemical equilibrium

Summary

The *collision model* assumes that for molecules to react, they must collide. High concentrations of reactants and high temperatures cause more collisions and therefore speed up reactions.

A certain minimum energy, called the *activation energy* (E_a), must be reached for a collision to form products. If a collision has energy less than E_a, the molecules will bounce apart unchanged. A catalyst is a substance that speeds up a reaction without having to change the temperature or the concentrations of reactants and without itself taking part in the reaction.

Reactions involving reactants in only one phase—all gases or all solids, for example—are called *homogeneous reactions*. *Heterogeneous reactions* involve reactants in different phases.

Chemists define *equilibrium* as the exact balance of two opposite processes. When a chemical reaction happens in a closed vessel, the system may achieve *chemical equilibrium*. In this state, the chemical reaction continues in both directions so that the products and reactants are forming in the forward reaction and decomposing in the reverse reaction at exactly the same rate.

As molecules collide, reactants are converted continually into products, and vice versa. The speed of the reaction depends in part on the concentrations of the reactants. As the reaction progresses and products are formed, the concentrations of the reactants decrease. With the presence of products, however, the reaction can begin to occur in the reverse direction as these products begin to act as reactants for the reverse reaction. The concentrations of the original reactants then begin to rise. Eventually, the system reaches equilibrium.

17.2   Characteristics of Equilibrium

Key Terms

equilibrium expression   equilibrium constant (K)   equilibrium position
homogeneous equilibria   heterogeneous equilibria

Summary

The law of chemical equilibrium is represented by an equation called the *equilibrium expression*. The equilibrium expression is a special ratio of the concentrations of the products to the reactants. For each reaction at a given temperature, the ratio defined by the equilibrium expression always will be equal to the same number, which is called the *equilibrium constant* (*K*) for that reaction.

Homogeneous equilibria occur when all reactants and products are in the same state. *Heterogeneous equilibria* occur when reactants and products are in different states.

17.3 Application of Equilibria

Key Terms

Le Châtelier's principle   solubility product constant (K_{sp})

Le Châtelier's principle can predict the effects of changes in concentration, volume, and temperature on a system at equilibrium. This principle states that when a change is made to a system that upsets the equilibrium, the equilibrium shifts in a direction that tends to reduce the effect of that change.

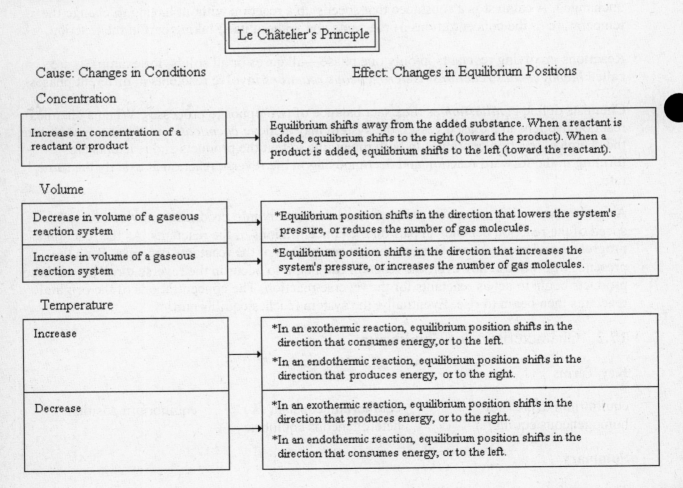

The size of the equilibrium constant (*K*) tells how a reaction is likely to occur. A value of *K* much larger than 1 means that at equilibrium, the reaction system will be made up mostly of products. A small value for K means that the system at equilibrium is made up mostly of reactants.

The principle of equilibrium also can be applied when a large amount of a solid is added to water. At first, the solid dissolves, but as more ions concentrate in the water, they begin to collide and react to re-form a solid. Equilibrium is reached, and the solution becomes saturated. The *solubility product constant* (K_{sp}) is an equilibrium constant defined by the law of chemical equilibrium.

Additional Active Reading Questions

1. Describe the collision model of chemical reactions.

2. What happens if a collision has energy less than E_a?

3. What kind of reaction involves reactants in only one phase? in different phases?

4. Describe a reaction that is in a state of chemical equilibrium.

5. State Le Châtelier's principle.

6. What happens in the process of dissolving when equilibrium is reached?

Chapter 18 Oxidation–Reduction Reactions and Electrochemistry

18.1 Electron Transfer Reactions

Key Terms

oxidation–reduction (redox) reactions
reduction

oxidation
oxidation states

Summary

Oxidation–reduction, or *redox, reactions* involve the transfer of one or more electrons. *Oxidation* is a loss of electrons, and *reduction* is a gain of electrons. Whenever a metal reacts with a nonmetal to form an ionic compound, electrons are transferred from the metal to the nonmetal. Many redox reactions, such as combustion reactions, involve only nonmetals.

Oxidation states are the charges of ions or atoms. Rules for assigning oxidation states are as follows:

1. The oxidation state of an atom in an uncombined element is 0.

2. The oxidation state of a monatomic ion is the same as its charge.

3. Oxygen is assigned an oxidation state of –2 in most of its covalent compounds.

4. In its covalent compounds with nonmetals, hydrogen is assigned an oxidation state of +1.

5. In binary compounds, the element with the greater electronegativity is assigned a negative oxidation state equal to its charge as an anion in its ionic compounds.

6. For an electrically neutral compound, the sum of the oxidation states must be 0.

7. For an ionic species, the sum of the oxidation states must equal the overall charge.

18.2 Balancing Oxidation–Reduction Reactions

Key Terms

oxidizing agent (electron acceptor)
reducing agent (electron donor)

half-reactions

Summary

Oxidation can be defined as an increase in oxidation state (a loss of electrons), and reduction can be defined as a decrease in oxidation state (a gain of electrons). The *electron acceptor* is the *oxidizing agent,* and the *electron donor* is the *reducing agent.*

Oxidation–reduction reactions that occur in aqueous solution are very complicated. As a result, they are difficult to balance using trial and error. Instead, we can balance them by separating them into two *half-reactions,* which are equations that have electrons as reactants or products. The half-reactions are balanced separately. First, the number of electrons gained and lost is equalized. Then the half-reactions are added together, and electrons are canceled to give the overall balanced equation. The key principle here is that the number of electrons lost (from the reactant that is oxidized) must equal the number of electrons gained (from the reactant that is reduced).

18.3 Electrochemistry and Its Applications

Key Terms

electrochemistry

electrochemical battery (galvanic cell)

anode

cathode

electrolysis

potential

lead storage batteries

dry cell batteries

corrosion

cathodic protection

Summary

Electrochemistry is the study of the interchange of chemical and electrical energy. Electrochemistry involves two types of processes: the production of an electric current from an oxidation–reduction reaction and the use of an electric current to produce a chemical change. When an oxidation–reduction reaction occurs with the reactants in the same solution, the electrons are transferred directly, and no usable energy is produced. An *electrochemical battery,* or *galvanic cell,* is a device in which chemical energy is transformed into useful electrical energy. In a galvanic cell, the oxidizing and reducing agents are placed in separate compartments. The electrons flow through a wire that runs between them. This electron flow produces a current that can be used to power devices. Oxidation occurs at the *anode* of a cell. Reduction occurs at the *cathode.*

A battery is a galvanic cell, or group of cells, that serves as a source of electric current.

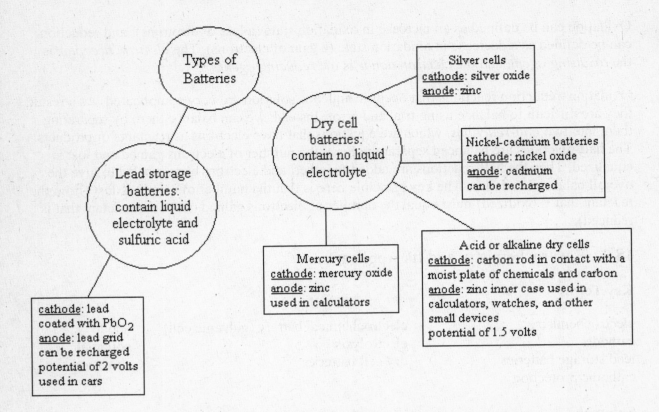

Corrosion involves the oxidation of metals and usually results in a loss of strength and attractiveness. As a result, people have developed various ways to prevent corrosion. Also, most metals develop a thin oxide coating that protects their internal atoms from further oxidation.

The process in which a current is forced through a cell to produce a chemical change that otherwise would not occur is called *electrolysis*. Water can be broken down into oxygen and hydrogen by means of electrolysis. Electrolysis also is used to separate useful metals from their ores.

Additional Active Reading Questions

1. What type of reactions involves the transfer of one or more electrons?

2. What are oxidation states?

3. What two types of processes does electrochemistry involve?

4. How is energy produced in a galvanic cell?

5. List three types of dry cell batteries.

6. Why is it important to prevent corrosion?

7. What is the name for the process in which a current is forced through a cell to produce a chemical change that would not occur otherwise?

Chapter 19   Radioactivity and Nuclear Energy

19.1   Radioactivity

Key Terms

nucleons (protons and neutrons)   atomic number (Z)   mass number (A)
isotopes   nuclide   radioactive
beta particle   nuclear equation   alpha particles
alpha-particle production   beta-particle production   gamma ray
positron   positron production   electron capture
decay series   nuclear transformation   transuranium elements
Gieger-Muller counter   scintillation counter   half-life

Summary

Many nuclei are *radioactive;* that is, they naturally decay (break down), forming a different nucleus and producing one or more particles. There are several types of radioactive decay.

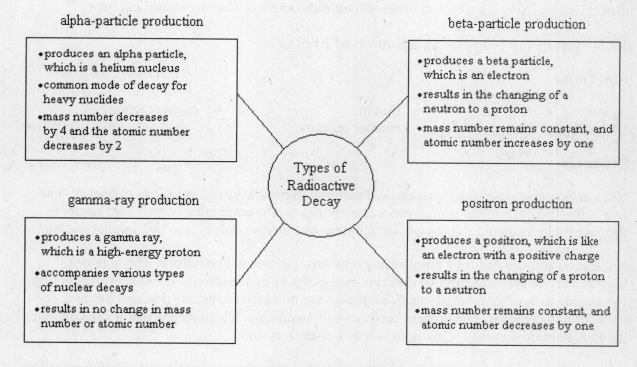

alpha-particle production

- produces an alpha particle, which is a helium nucleus
- common mode of decay for heavy nuclides
- mass number decreases by 4 and the atomic number decreases by 2

beta-particle production

- produces a beta particle, which is an electron
- results in the changing of a neutron to a proton
- mass number remains constant, and atomic number increases by one

gamma-ray production

- produces a gamma ray, which is a high-energy proton
- accompanies various types of nuclear decays
- results in no change in mass number or atomic number

positron production

- produces a positron, which is like an electron with a positive charge
- results in the changing of a proton to a neutron
- mass number remains constant, and atomic number decreases by one

Types of Radioactive Decay

Nuclear transformation is the change of one element into another. This change is achieved by bombarding a *nuclide* (an atom) with nuclei, such as *alpha particles* or neutrons, which penetrate the atom and break it apart. In order to overcome the natural tendency of particles of the same charge to repel each other, the bombarding particle must be traveling at a very high speed.

The most familiar instrument for measuring radioactivity is the *Geiger-Muller counter.*

The *half-life* is the time it takes for half of a radioactive sample of nuclei to decay. Each radioactive nuclide has a specific half-life, which does not change.

19.2   Application of Radioactivity

Key Terms

radiocarbon dating (carbon-14 dating)   radiotracers

Summary

Scientists use the half-lives of radioactive nuclei to determine the dates of rocks and other objects. *Carbon-14 dating,* or *radiocarbon dating,* dates remains of once-living things by using the half-life of radioactive carbon-14. Living things produce a certain amount of carbon-14 in a lifetime. At death, production of carbon-14 stops. Scientists can measure the amount of carbon-14 left in a sample and use carbon-14's half-life of 5730 years to determine the age of the sample.

Radiotracers are radioactive nuclides that can be introduced into drugs or living things and then traced by using a scanner to observe their radioactivity. They have medical uses.

19.3   Using the Nucleus as a Source of Energy

Key Terms

fusion   fission   chain reaction
critical mass   breeder reactors

Summary

Nuclear processes use small quantities of material to produce large quantities of energy. The two main types of nuclear energy processes are *fusion,* the combining of two light nuclei to form a heavier nucleus, and *fission,* the splitting of a heavy nucleus into two smaller nuclei.

Nuclear fission can occur by bombarding uranium nuclides with neutrons. The uranium nuclide may be split to form two different isotopes plus free neutrons. These neutrons, in turn, can collide with other uranium nuclides, producing more fission events that also produce nuclides and neutrons. The process becomes self-sustaining, which means that it can continue without additional energy. This is known as a *chain reaction.*

In a nuclear reactor, controlled fission occurs, and usable energy is produced. Fission reactions heat water that flows through the reactor core. The water turns to steam, which runs turbines that are used to run electrical generators.

Nuclear fusion produces even more energy than does nuclear fission. Stars produce their light and heat by means of nuclear fusion, in which hydrogen protons are fused to form helium.

The high-energy particles produced by radioactive elements are potentially harmful to living things. Energy transferred to cells can break chemical bonds and cause the cell systems to malfunction. Radiation damage can cause sickness or death. Exposure to radiation also can damage the genetic structures in cells, creating problems in the offspring of the organism.

Additional Active Reading Questions

1. What is *nuclear transformation*?

2. Define *half-life*.

3. What is the half-life of carbon-14?

4. Where might radiotracers be used?

5. Name and define the two types of nuclear energy processes.

6. What is another term for a self-sustaining nuclear reaction?

7. How do fission reactions inside a reactor core produce electricity?

8. Place the following three reactions in order from the one that produces the least energy to the one that produces the most: fission, chemical reaction, fusion.

9. How do stars produce energy?

10. How can radiation harm living things?

Chapter 20   Organic Chemistry

20.1   Saturated Hydrocarbons

Key Terms

organic chemistry	biomolecule	hydrocarbons
saturated	unsaturated	alkanes
unbranched hydrocarbons (normal or straight chain)	structural isomerism	petroleum
natural gas	combustion reactions	substitution reactions
dehydrogenation reactions		

Summary

The study of carbon-containing compounds and their properties is called *organic chemistry*. A carbon atom can form bonds to a maximum of four other atoms. When carbon has four atoms bound to it, the atoms will always have a tetrahedral arrangement around the carbon atom. When carbon bonds to fewer than four other atoms, they are joined by double or triple bonds.

Hydrocarbons are compounds made up of carbon and hydrogen. Hydrocarbons in which all the carbon–carbon bonds are single and each carbon is bound to the maximum number of atoms (four) are said to be *saturated*. Saturated hydrocarbons are called *alkanes*. Hydrocarbons containing carbon–carbon multiple bonds are *unsaturated* because the carbon atoms can bond to one or more additional atoms.

Structural isomerism occurs when two molecules have the same atoms but different bonds. The molecules have the same formulas, but their atoms are arranged in different structures. All *alkanes* of three or more carbon atoms have this property.

The names of the alkanes beyond the first four (methane, ethane, propane, and butane) are formed by adding the suffix (word ending) *-ane* to the Greek root for the number of carbon atoms.

The basic rules for naming alkanes are as follows:

1. To determine the base alkane name, find the parent chain, which is the longest continuous chain of carbon atoms.

2. Number the carbons in the parent chain, starting at the end closest to any branching.

3. Using the correct name for each alkyl group, use a number to show its position on the parent chain.

4. When a certain type of alkyl group appears more than once, attach the correct prefix, or word beginning (*di-* for two, *tri-* for three, and so on) to the alkyl name.

5. The alkyl groups are listed in alphabetical order, ignoring any prefix.

Petroleum is a thick, dark liquid made up mostly of hydrocarbons that contain from 5 to more than 25 carbon atoms. *Natural gas,* which is usually found in petroleum deposits, is made up mostly of methane. Petroleum and natural gas probably formed from the remains of marine organisms that lived about 500 million years ago. To be used efficiently, crude petroleum is separated into molecules of various sizes, called fractions. Gasoline, kerosene, heating oil, and asphalt are a few examples of petroleum fractions.

Alkanes can be involved in three main types of reactions. These compounds react strongly with oxygen when the temperature becomes high enough. Such *combustion reactions* are what make alkanes useful as fuels. Alkanes can also undergo *substitution reactions.* In such reactions, one or more hydrogen atoms in the alkane are substituted (replaced) by different atoms. In *dehydrogenation reactions,* hydrogen atoms are removed, and an unsaturated hydrocarbon is produced.

20.2   Unsaturated Hydrocarbons

Key Terms

alkenes	alkynes	addition reactions
hydrogenation reactions	halogenation	polymerization
aromatic hydrocarbons	benzene	phenyl group

Summary

Alkenes are hydrocarbons that contain carbon–carbon double bonds. *Alkynes* are hydrocarbons with carbon–carbon triple bonds. Both are unsaturated. The most important reactions that alkenes and alkynes take part in are *addition reactions,* in which new atoms form single bonds to the carbons formerly involved in the double or triple bonds. In *hydrogenation reactions,* a hydrogen atom is added to each carbon atom formerly involved in the double bond. *Halogenation* of unsaturated hydrocarbons involves the addition of halogen atoms. *Polymerization* is a process in which many small molecules are joined to form a large molecule.

Aromatic hydrocarbons are pleasant-smelling compounds that result when mixtures of natural hydrocarbons are separated. All aromatic hydrocarbons include a ring of six carbon atoms with attached hydrogen atoms, called a benzene ring. *Benzene* has the formula C_6H_6 and a planar (flat) structure in which all of the bond angles are 120°.

Like alkanes, aromatic hydrocarbons can undergo substitution reactions. Substituted benzene molecules are formed by replacing one or more of the hydrogen atoms with other atoms or groups of atoms.

20.3   Introduction to Functional Groups and Alcohols

Key Terms

functional groups   alcohols

Summary

Hydrocarbon derivatives are molecules that are considered to be hydrocarbons but have added atoms or groups of atoms called *functional groups*.

Alcohols are compounds that contain the –OH group. To name an alcohol, we replace the final -e of the parent hydrocarbon name with *-ol* and then use a number, if necessary, to show the position of the –OH group.

Methanol and ethanol are the simplest alcohols and have the most practical uses. Methanol is made by the hydrogenation of carbon monoxide. It is used in the manufacture of acetic acid, adhesives, fibers, and plastics. Ethanol is the alcohol in alcoholic beverages and is an alternative fuel for automobiles. It is made by fermenting the glucose (a type of sugar) in grains and fruits.

Ethylene glycol is one of a group of alcohols that have more than one –OH group. It is an ingredient in antifreeze. Phenol is a type of aromatic alcohol. It is used in the manufacture of adhesives and plastics.

20.4   Additional Organic Compounds

Key Terms

carbonyl group	ketones	aldehydes
carboxylic acids	ester	polymers
addition polymerization	condensation polymerization	copolymer
homopolymer	dimer	polyester

Summary

Aldehydes and ketones contain a carbon–oxygen group called the *carbonyl group*. In *ketones,* this group is bonded to two carbon atoms. In *aldehydes,* the carbonyl group always appears at the end of the hydrocarbon chain. This means at least one hydrogen is always bonded to the carbon atom in the carbonyl group.

To name an aldehyde, we remove the final -e from the parent alkane and add *-al*. For ketones, the final -e is replaced by *-one* and, if necessary, a number that tells the position of the carbonyl group.

Carboxylic acids are compounds that include the carboxyl group, which is –COOH. Carboxylic acids are usually weak acids in aqueous solution. We name carboxylic acids by dropping the final -e from the parent alkane (the longest chain containing the –COOH group) and adding -oic. A carboxylic acid reacts with an alcohol to form an *ester*.

Polymers are large molecules that are usually formed from chains of small molecules called monomers. Many fibers and plastics are made of polymers.

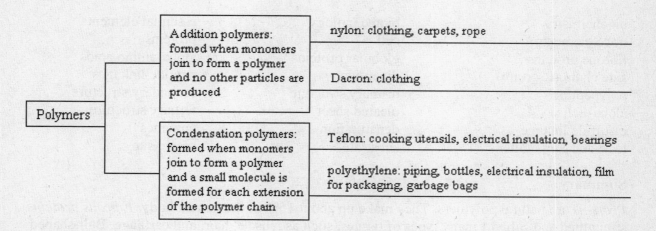

Additional Active Reading Questions

1. What is the study of carbon-containing compounds and their properties?

2. Compare saturated hydrocarbons to unsaturated hydrocarbons.

3. Which property occurs when two molecules have the same formulas but atoms that are arranged in different branched structures?

4. From what materials do scientists believe petroleum and natural gas probably formed?

5. What types of reactions make alkanes useful as fuels?

6. Write the formula for benzene and describe the structure of the molecule.

7. What type of alcohol is made by fermenting the glucose in grains and fruits?

8. Name the carbon–oxygen group that characterizes aldehydes and ketones.

9. Which two compounds react to form esters?

Chapter 21   Biochemistry

21.1   Introduction to Proteins

Key Terms

biochemistry	biotechnology	essential elements
trace elements	cell	proteins
fibrous proteins	globular proteins	alpha-amino acids
side chain (R group)	dipeptide	peptide linkages
polypeptide	primary structure	secondary structure
alpha-helix	pleated sheet	tertiary structure
disulfide linkage	denaturation	enzymes
lock-and-key model	substrate	active site

Summary

Proteins are natural polymers. They make up about 15% of the human body. *Fibrous proteins* strengthen and support many types of tissues, such as muscle, hair, and cartilage. Ball-shaped *globular proteins* are the body's worker molecules.

All proteins are made up of *alpha-amino acids*. They are made up of an amino group ($-NH_2$) attached to the alpha-carbon, which is the one next to the carboxyl group ($-COOH$). Amino acids are classified as polar or nonpolar depending on whether the *side chain,* also known as the *R group,* attached to the alpha-carbon is hydrophilic (attracted to water) or hydrophobic (repellent to water). A protein polymer is built by reactions between amino acids that produce *peptide linkages.* Further reactions create a longer chain called a *polypeptide* and eventually a protein.

There are about 20 different amino acids. They can be put together in any order. The order of amino acids in a protein is called the *primary structure.*

A protein's *secondary structure* is the arrangement of the chain of amino acids in space. The particular job that a protein does in the body determines its shape.

The *tertiary structure* of a protein is its overall shape, for example, whether it is long and narrow, globular, or tube-shaped. Some amino acids get their tertiary structure by bending back on themselves. A particular type of bond called a *disulfide linkage* can fasten together two parts of a protein chain to form and hold a bend in the chain.

Denaturation is the process of breaking down a protein's three-dimensional structure. Any source of energy can cause denaturation of proteins. Ultraviolet radiation, X-ray radiation, nuclear radioactivity, lead, and mercury can damage protein structure.

Enzymes are proteins that catalyze (speed up) specific biologic reactions. Without enzymes, life would be impossible because important biochemical reactions would happen too slowly. Scientists believe that enzymes work according to the *lock-and-key model.* This model states that the shapes of the reacting molecule and the enzyme fit together as a key fits a lock.

21.2 Carbohydrates, Nucleic Acids, and Lipids

Key Terms

carbohydrates	monosaccharides (simple sugars)	disaccharide
sucrose	glycoside linkage	polysaccharides
starch	cellulose	glycogen
DNA (deoxyribonucleic acid)	RNA (ribonucleic acid)	nucleotide
protein synthesis	gene	lipids
mRNA (messenger RNA)	tRNA (transfer RNA)	fats
fatty acids	saponification	micelles
surfactant	phospholipids	waxes
steroids	cholesterol	sex hormones
adrenocorticoid hormones	bile acids	

Summary

Carbohydrates serve as food sources for most living things and as support materials for plants. There are almost countless types of carbohydrates. Many carbohydrates are polymers. They are made up of molecules called *simple sugars,* or *monosaccharides.* Fructose is a monosaccharide. More complex carbohydrates are formed by combining monosaccharides. Two monosaccharides can combine to form a *disaccharide.* Common table sugar, *sucrose,* is a disaccharide. Large polymers containing many monosaccharide units are called *polysaccharides.* Three of the most important polysaccharides are *starch, cellulose,* and *glycogen.*

Deoxyribonucleic acid (DNA) is a huge polymer that stores and transfers genetic information. Together with other similar, but smaller, nucleic acids called *ribonucleic acids (RNA),* DNA carries the information needed for the creation of proteins. The basic unit in DNA and RNA polymers is called a *nucleotide.* Each nucleotide has three parts: a nitrogen-containing organic base, a five-carbon sugar, and a phosphate group. To form DNA and RNA polymers, nucleotides are hooked together into a shape that resembles a twisted ladder. This structure is called the double helix. During cell division the double helix unwinds and new strands of nucleotides are formed on each original strand.

Protein synthesis (creation) is the other major job of DNA. The information for constructing the proteins needed by the body is stored in the organism's DNA. A section of DNA, called a *gene,* contains the code for a particular protein. Various types of RNA molecules help in protein synthesis.

Topic	Protein synthesis
First	Using a gene as the pattern, a messenger RNA (mRNA) molecule is constructed in the cell's nucleus.
Next	mRNA moves from the nucleus to the cytoplasm.
Next	Using mRNA as a pattern and with the help of a cell structure called a *ribosome*, a transfer RNA (tRNA) molecule attaches itself to amino acids.
Last	tRNA puts amino acids into place on the growing protein chain.

Lipids are substances that are found in cells and that do not dissolve in water. There are four types of lipids. *Fats* are esters made up of glycerol and *fatty acids* that are long-chain carboxylic acids. *Phospholipids* are also esters of glycerol. *Waxes* are esters that include alcohols instead of glycerol. *Steroids* are made up of a basic four-ring structure. *Cholesterol*, certain hormones, and *bile acid* are all types of steroids.

Additional Active Reading Questions

1. What is the function of fibrous proteins?

2. What is the name of the units that make up proteins?

3. What is the primary structure of a protein? the secondary structure? the tertiary structure?

4. Define *denaturation*.

5. How do scientists think enzymes work?

6. Name three polysaccharides.

7. What does DNA stand for, and what does it do?

8. What is the basic unit in the DNA and RNA polymer?

9. List the four types of lipids.

Section 5: Challenge Projects

This section offers challenge projects and activities for students who will benefit from the opportunity to stretch their understanding and skills by applying their chemistry knowledge to real-world situations. The projects are appropriate for either group work or individual use.

Contents

Chapter 2 Project: Elements in the News CP–1

Chapter 4 Project: Investigating Polyatomic Ions.. CP–2

Chapter 6 Project: Using Analogies to Explain Molecular and Empirical Formulas CP–3

Chapter 9 Project: Limiting Reactants in a Combustion Reaction CP–4

Chapter 14 Project: Surface Tension and Capillary Action.. CP–5

Chapter 15 Project: Investigating Solubility and Immiscibility CP–6

Chapter 16 Project: Titration Procedure CP–7

Chapter 17 Project: Determining Ksp CP–8

Chapter 19 Project: Medical Treatment by Radioisotopes... CP–9

Chapter 21 Project: Investigating Biological Topics CP–10

Answer Keys..CP–11

Chapter 2 Project: Elements in the News

Metals fail under stress; water, air, and soil are polluted; and the benefits of trace elements in the human body are discovered. Elements are mentioned commonly in the news in the context of their effects on the human body, their effects on the quality of human life, or simply as additions to the body of scientific knowledge.

Search through current newspapers and magazines to find examples of elements in the news. Most newspapers have a section once a week that features science-related articles. Look for headlines that indicate medical breakthroughs or pollution problems. If you are uncertain whether a substance is an element, see whether you can find it on the periodic table on the inside back cover of your text. If it is not on the periodic table, it is a compound, not an element.

Make copies of the articles, their sources, and dates. If you use other resources for additional information about the elements, be sure to include a list of those specific references.

Your final project can be one of the following:

- a news article
- a videotaped news report
- a written report
- an oral report
- a fictional story that uses the facts in the articles as its basis
- a poster or bulletin board
- a mobile that has a different main branch for each element

For each element, you can include the following information in your final product:

- why the element was newsworthy
- why the element was being used in this manner
- implications of the benefit of the element or the harm caused by it
- what other uses exist for this element
- similar or different problems or benefits resulting from these additional uses
- other interesting facts about the element

This list of things to include in your project is not inclusive. You do not need to include everything on the list, and you can add other items that are important regarding your element.

Chapter 4 Project: Investigating Polyatomic Ions

Part 1

You know that halogens, Group 7A, have similar chemical properties because they are all in the same family on the periodic table. You also know from Table 4.4 that chlorine and oxygen form four different polyatomic ions. Do the other halogens form similar ions? For example, does bromine form perbromate, bromate, bromite, and hypobromite ions, or do some of these ions not exist?

Use reference books such as the *CRC Handbook* to investigate what ions are formed from oxygen and fluorine, bromine, and iodine. Use the information you learn to complete the following table with the formulas and names of any existing polyatomic ions that contain a halogen and oxygen. If an ion belonging in a cell in the table does not exist, write *No ion* in the cell.

Polyatomic Ions Containing a Halogen and Oxygen				
Halogen (X)	XO_4^-	XO_3^-	XO_2^-	XO^-
F				
Cl	ClO_4^-, perchlorate	ClO_3^-, chlorate	ClO_2^-, chlorite	Cl^-, hypochlorite
Br				
I				

Part 2

You can use the periodic table to expand your ability to name polyatomic ions and acids. Examine the periodic table as it relates to Table 4.4. Remember that elements in the same family have similar chemical properties. Use these two references to answer the following questions:

1. Consider the ion SeO_4^{2-}.
   a. What is the name of this ion?
   b. What is the formula for the compound formed from this ion and a sodium ion?
   c. What is the name of the compound from part b?
   d. What is the formula of the acid formed from this ion?
   e. What is the name of the acid from part d?

2. Arsenic and phosphorus have similar chemical properties.
   a. What is the name of the AsO_4^{3-} ion?
   b. What is the formula for the compound formed from this ion and a calcium ion?
   c. What is the name of the compound from part b?
   d. If the ion AsO_3^{3-} existed, what would its name be?
   e. What is the formula of the acid formed from this ion?
   f. What is the name of the acid from part e?

Chapter 6 Project: Using Analogies to Explain Molecular and Empirical Formulas

Purpose

To design an everyday situation that is analogous to finding the molecular formula when you know the empirical formula and the molar mass.

Procedure

1. Decide on what common example you will use to form an analogy to determine the molecular formula when the molar mass and the empirical formula are known. The following situation is an example:

    You are asked to bring approximately 3.00 kg of fruit salad to a dinner. The ratio of different types of fruit in the salad is to be 1 banana : 2 apples : 1 orange : 12 grapes. As an average, the edible part of each banana has a mass of 168 g; each apple, 220 g; each orange, 240 g; and each grape, 12 g. How many units of fruit are needed to make the salad?

2. For your situation, work out the problem in a form that would make the solution clear to other students if you explained it to them. Use models to represent different parts of your "formulas." For the preceding example, the following solution could be used:

    Mass of one unit of fruit:

1 banana	=	1 × 168 g	=	168 g
2 apples	=	2 × 220 g	=	440 g
1 orange	=	1 × 240 g	=	240 g
12 grapes	=	12 × 12 g	=	144 g
		Total mass	=	992 g

    Therefore, one unit of fruit has a mass of 992 g. How many units form approximately 3.00 kg, or 3000 g, of fruit salad?

    $$\frac{3000 \text{ g}}{992 \text{ g}} = 3.02, \text{ or approximately 3 units of fruit are needed.}$$

    The fruit salad will consist of three times each number of each type of fruit in one unit.

3 × 1 banana	=	3 bananas
3 × 2 apples	=	6 apples
3 × 1 orange	=	3 oranges
3 × 12 grapes	=	36 grapes

    The ratio for the entire fruit salad is 3 bananas : 6 apples : 3 oranges : 36 grapes. The ratio is no longer in its simplest form (empirical formula), but it accurately represents what is in the entire fruit salad (molecular formula).

3. Present your analogy to the rest of the class. Use whatever models, handouts, or charts you need to make your example clear to other students. Other analogies include different kinds of nuts in a can of mixed nuts, different tools in a toolbox, and different ingredients to make a casserole.

Chapter 9 Project: Limiting Reactants in a Combustion Reaction

Fires provide warmth when they are in a fireplace or campfire. They supply energy for boilers in industrial companies. There are many other positive uses of fires. However, fires sometimes occur when and where they are not supposed to occur. The destruction of an out-of-control fire can be devastating. An unwanted fire needs to be extinguished.

How is a fire extinguished? Fuel, oxygen, and energy are all needed for a fire to start and continue. If the fuel runs out, if oxygen is kept from the fire, or if the fire cools down so that the reaction cannot continue, the fire does not continue to burn. These principles are the basis of extinguishing fires.

Prepare a written report on extinguishing fires. Throughout the report, relate extinguishing fires to limiting at least one of the factors necessary for the fire to continue. Use at least four different sources of information. Your sources may include books, Internet sources approved by your teacher, or materials supplied by your local fire department or department of safety.

Prepare a useful, accurate, and creative report. Include any diagrams you think would add to the reader's understanding of the content. Be sure to list your sources of information and give credit to anyone you interviewed. In other words, cite all your sources.

Your report should include information on the following topics:

- How fire extinguishers work
- Different types of fires based on what the fuel is
- The codes (class A, B, and so on) used to distinguish the types of fires
- Different types of fire extinguishers, based on their contents
- The type of fire extinguisher that works best on each type of fire
- The locations and types of fire extinguishers found in your school and at home
- An evaluation of these fire extinguishers to determine whether they are appropriate to put out the types of fires that might occur where they are located
- The dangers of using the wrong extinguisher on certain fires
- Other methods of extinguishing fires used at airports, by fire departments, and at home and why each is effective

Include any other information that might add interest to your report. You might choose to do one or more of the following:

- Interview a firefighter from your local area.
- Interview a safety manager at an industry where fire is a major concern, such as a paint or chemical manufacturer.
- Collect news reports on fires and note their probable causes.
- Report statistics about the value of sprinkler systems and smoke alarms.
- Investigate how sprinkler systems and smoke alarms work.
- Investigate how forest fires are extinguished.

Chapter 14 Project: Surface Tension and Capillary Action

Purpose

To investigate, define, and examine some of the applications of surface tension and capillary action.

Procedure

Research surface tension and capillary action (both are properties of liquids). When you have answers to the questions below, present the information in a poster, a written report, an oral report, or a demonstration.

Surface Tension

1. What is surface tension? Explain it in terms of intermolecular forces.

2. Make a compass by magnetizing a small sewing needle and placing it on top of the surface of water in a glass. Explain how surface tension keeps the needle from falling to the bottom of the glass.

3. You probably have seen water insects or spiders on the surface of a lake or pond. Explain what features of these insects and spiders enable them to stay on top of the water.

4. How does the surface tension of water compare with the surface tension of other liquids?

5. Find out what a surfactant is. How do surfactants relate to surface tension? What is a common use of a surfactant?

Capillary Action

1. What is capillary action? Explain it in terms of intermolecular forces.

2. What is a meniscus? Compare the shape of a meniscus formed by water to the shape formed by mercury. **Caution:** Do not directly observe mercury unless it is in a sealed container. You can use Figure 14.5 to see the shape of the meniscus that mercury forms. Explain any differences as they relate to surface tension.

3. Explain how capillary action is involved in moving water from the roots of plants to their leaves.

Chapter 15 Project: Investigating Solubility and Immiscibility

Part 1

Relative Solubility

Examine the solubility table in Appendix G and think about why the information is organized the way it is. Reference tables, such as solubility tables, often differ from source to source because different items are chosen to be included. However, it does not mean that one source is more accurate than another source.

Use reference materials, such as other textbooks, reference books, and the Internet, to find samples of alternate ways of organizing a solubility table. You probably will find that there are a number of ways to present solubility information. Basing your decisions on the new examples you find, create a modified version of the table in Appendix G.

After you have completed your revised table, compare it with those of any classmates who did this project. Discuss differences among your tables, and confirm your modifications using reference materials. Submit your final table to your teacher.

Part 2

Immiscibility

Conduct research to find out how scientists and consumers deal with liquids that do not mix with each other. You can use the following ideas or find others of your own.

- When an oil spill occurs, the oil floats on the water and spreads out, destroying ocean life and ruining shorelines. What is done to clean up oil spills and minimize their destructive effects on the environment?

- Oils that are in laundry do not mix with water. What is added to the water when laundering clothes so that water can wash the oils away?

You may wish to test hypotheses and ideas on a smaller scale with common household items.

Part 3

Solubility versus Rate of Dissolution

Perhaps it is because both solubility and rate of dissolution are affected by temperature, but confusion often exists about the difference between these two concepts and the effects that temperature, stirring, and surface area have on them.

Prepare a report or poster to explain the difference between the terms *solubility* and *rate of dissolution*. Include the effects of stirring, temperature, and surface area on each.

Chapter 16 Project: Titration Procedure

Purpose

To outline and display the procedure used for titration.

Procedure

1. Make notes as you read Section 16.3, and do at least one titration in the laboratory. Notes should include anything that might help you to do a titration more effectively.

2. From your notes, outline the procedure you would use to perform a titration, and then do the calculations. Make some type of product from your outline that will help other students to perform a titration correctly. You might want to do one of the following:

   - Make a bulletin board display from the outline so that other students can use it for reference. Illustrate your outline, placing a photo or diagram by the step it illustrates.

   - Make a sequencing game where classmates have to order the steps needed to perform the titration.

   - Make a game of concentration, where classmates match a written titration step to an illustration of that step.

3. Consider the following questions while taking notes and making your outline:

   - How do you set up a buret for use?

   - How do you use a buret?

   - What safety measures should you observe while setting up and performing a titration?

   - If a base is the standard solution, what type of solution should the unknown solution be?

   - At what point do you add an indicator?

   - How do you determine what indicator to use?

   - What might you do to see a color change more clearly in the solution?

   - What do you need to do to be sure that the standard solution is evenly distributed throughout the unknown solution?

   - How do you know when you are at the endpoint of the titration?

   - What type of data do you need to take?

   - How do you plot the data in a titration curve?

   - How do you use these data to calculate the concentration of the unknown solution?

   - What might be possible sources of error in your titration?

Chapter 17 Project: Determining K$_{sp}$

Purpose

To determine the solubility of a slightly soluble salt of your choice.

Materials

slightly soluble salt	distilled water
balance	400-mL beaker
filter paper	thermometer
100-mL graduated cylinder	laboratory burner
funnel	stirring rod
ring and ring stand	

Procedure

1. Obtain a slightly soluble salt from your teacher.

2. Look at the materials available and write a procedure for what you will do to determine the solubility of the salt at 25°C. You might not use all the materials, and you can use additional materials that you might need. Have your teacher approve your procedure before you do the experiment.

3. Use your procedure to carry out the experiment. If you need to adjust the experiment, have your teacher approve your changes.

4. Check a reference book or table of solubilities, and compare the solubility you determined to the accepted value. List any possible sources of error.

5. From the solubility you determined, calculate K_{sp} for your compound.

6. Write a lab report. Include the procedure, calculations, and other items that you want to include.

Chapter 19 Project: Medical Treatment by Radioisotopes

Your textbook examines how certain radioisotopes are used in detecting medical problems. Other radioisotopes are used in treating medical disorders (such as cancer). Do research to determine how ^{198}Au, ^{192}Ir, and ^{60}Co are used in treating cancer. Report your findings. Include answers to the following questions in your report:

1. How are each of these isotopes used in cancer treatment?

2. What is the half-life of ^{192}Ir? Compare this half-life with those of the radioisotopes listed in Table 19.4. Why do you think that the half-lives of these isotopes are so different?

3. Are there any hazards in using these radioisotopes for cancer treatment?

Chapter 21 Project: Investigating Biological Topics

Part 1

Nutrition and Diet

Proteins, carbohydrates, and lipids all release energy when they are metabolized in the human body. Carbohydrates and protein both release 17 kJ, or 4 Cal (kcal), per gram. Lipids release 38 kJ, or 9 Cal (kcal), per gram.

1. Plan a simple, nutritious meal that would release 500 to 600 Cal when the foods in it are metabolized. For foods that involve more than one type of nutrient, such as a meat that contains both protein and lipids, be sure to include all nutrient types in your planning.

2. Create a chart that includes the name of the food, the mass in grams for a serving, and the energy released for the serving size. You can use Calorie charts to calculate the mass of food from the number of Calories, or you can estimate the number of grams in a serving and calculate the appropriate number of Calories. Specify the source of the Calories (carbohydrates, proteins, or lipids), and list the breakdown of Calories by each source.

Part 2

Trace Elements

Table 21.1 in your textbook lists the functions of several different essential elements in the human body. Figure 21.1 shows several other essential trace elements that are not included in the table. Choose two of the trace elements not included in the table, and report on the functions and importance of these elements in the human body.

Part 3

Digestive Enzymes

Do some research on digestive enzymes. Create a concept map that lists several digestive enzymes and explains the role of each. In your concept map, include the following:

- The general roles of amylases, lipases, and proteases
- Some specific enzymes that are included in those three general categories of enzymes
- The location and function in the human body of each specific enzyme

Challenge Projects Answer Key

Chapter 2

Project

Projects will vary depending upon the element or elements chosen.

Chapter 4

Part 1

Polyatomic Ions Containing a Halogen and Oxygen				
Halogen (X)	XO_4^-	XO_3^-	XO_2^-	XO^-
F	No ion	No ion	No ion	No ion
Cl	ClO_4^-, perchlorate	ClO_3^-, chlorate	ClO_2^-, chlorite	Cl^-, hypochlorite
Br	No ion	BrO_3^-, bromate	No ion	No ion
I	IO_4^-, periodate	IO_3^-, iodate	No ion	IO^-, hypoiodite

Part 2

1. a.   selenate ion

    b. Na_2SeO_4

    c.   sodium selenate

    d. H_2SeO_4

    e.   selenic acid

2. a.   arsenate ion

    b. $Ca_3(AsO_4)_2$

    c.   calcium arsenate

    d.   arsenite ion

    e. H_3AsO_3

    f.   arsenous acid

Chapter 6

Project

The key to an effective analogy is determining how many small units make up a larger unit.

Chapter 9

Project

Class A fires involve solid fuel, such as wood, and they are usually extinguished with water. The fuel in Class B fires is a liquid or a gas, which is best extinguished with a CO_2 extinguisher. Class C fires are electrical. They can be extinguished with CO_2. Class D fires involve burning metals and are usually extinguished with powders or other solids, such as salt, graphite, or sand.

Chapter 14

Project

Surface Tension

1. Surface tension is a measurement of the inward pull on surface particles by particles within a liquid. The intermolecular forces in a liquid contribute to the surface tension of that liquid.

2. The mass of a needle is too small to disrupt the surface tension of the water.

3. Their long, thin legs distribute the organisms' weight over a relatively large surface area allowing the surface tension of the water to support the organism.

4. The surface tension of water is greater than that of most other liquids.

5. A surfactant decreases the surface tension of water by disrupting its hydrogen bonds. Soaps and detergents are common surfactants. They are helpful when cleaning objects.

Capillary Action

1. Capillary action is the result of adhesion, cohesion, and surface tension in liquids that are in contact with solids. It occurs when the adhesive intermolecular forces between the liquid and a solid are stronger than the cohesive intermolecular forces inside the liquid.

2. A meniscus is the curved surface of a liquid in a container. Water has a concave meniscus because adhesion is greater than cohesion. Mercury has a convex meniscus because in mercury, cohesion is greater than adhesion.

3. The stem of a plant contains very narrow tubes that allow the water to get from the roots of the plant to the leaves through capillary action. The adhesive intermolecular forces between the water and the plant tube are stronger than the cohesive intermolecular forces inside the water.

Chapter 15

Projects

Part 1: Relative Solubility

Locate a complete and reliable solubility table to use when checking tables for accuracy. Possible revisions include changes in the layout of the table, addition of more examples of soluble and insoluble substances, and expansion of rules found in the existing table.

Part 2: Immiscibility

Information might include that emulsifiers, such as egg, break up the oils into small particles that will remain suspended. Molecules in soaps and detergents have both a polar part that will dissolve in water and a nonpolar part that will dissolve in oils.

Part 3: Solubility Versus Rate of Solution

Solubility refers to how much of a solute will dissolve in a certain amount of solvent. Rate of solution refers to how quickly a solute dissolves.

Chapter 16

Project

Placing the flask on a piece of white paper will enable you to see a color change more clearly.

Chapter 17

Project

A sample procedure might involve placing the salt on a piece of filter paper and finding the mass. Add all of the salt to a measured amount of 25 °C water. Then stir to dissolve as much of the salt as will dissolve. Filter out the undissolved salt on the same filter paper. Dry the paper and salt, and determine how much salt dissolved in the given amount of water.

Chapter 19

Project

1. ^{198}Au and ^{192}Ir are implanted in or near tumors, and ^{60}Co is a source of gamma radiation that can be focused on the tumor.

2. The half-life of ^{192}Ir is 74 days. A short half-life is desired for a tracer, but a radioisotope used for treatment might need to be active for a longer time.

3. Radiation could destroy healthy tissue or cause genetic mutations.

Chapter 21

Projects

Project 1: Nutrition and Diet

Obtain and read nutrition labels to help determine content of foods.

Project 2: Trace Elements

Your classmates might choose other trace elements, and a classroom version of Figure 21.1 could be made that shows the functions in the human body of all the listed elements.

Project 3: Digestive Enzymes

Concept maps should include that amylases break down carbohydrates, fats are broken down by lipases, and proteases break down proteins.